GW00691875

Barcelona

Footprint

The travel guide

Handbook

Mary-Ann Gallagher

'Barcelona! And with your sins, ours, ours!
Our Barcelona, the great enchantress!'

Joan Maragall, Ode to Barcelona

Barcelona Handbook
First edition
© Footprint Handbooks Ltd 2002

Published by Footprint Handbooks
6 Riverside Court
Lower Bristol Road
Bath BA2 3DZ. England
T +44 (0)1225 469141
F +44 (0)1225 469461
Email discover@footprintbooks.com
Web www.footprintbooks.com

ISBN 1 903471 03 6
CIP DATA: A catalogue record for this
book is available from the British Library

Distributed in the USA by
Publishers Group West

Neither the black and white nor
coloured maps are intended to have
any political significance.

The metro map has been printed with
the permission of the Barcelona
transport authority (TMB).

Credits

Series editors
Patrick Dawson and Rachel Fielding

Editorial
Editor: Caroline Lascom
Maps: Sarah Sorensen

Production
Typesetting: Emma Bryers and
Mark Thomas
Maps: Robert Lunn, Claire Benison,
Maxine Foster and Leona Baily
Colour maps: Kevin Feeney
Cover: Camilla Ford

Design
Mytton Williams

Photography
Front cover: Robert Harding Picture
Library
Back cover: Pictor
Inside colour section: Robert Harding
Picture Library, James Davis Worldwide,
Impact, Eye Ubiquitous, Art Directors
and Trip

Print
Manufactured in Italy by LEGOPRINT

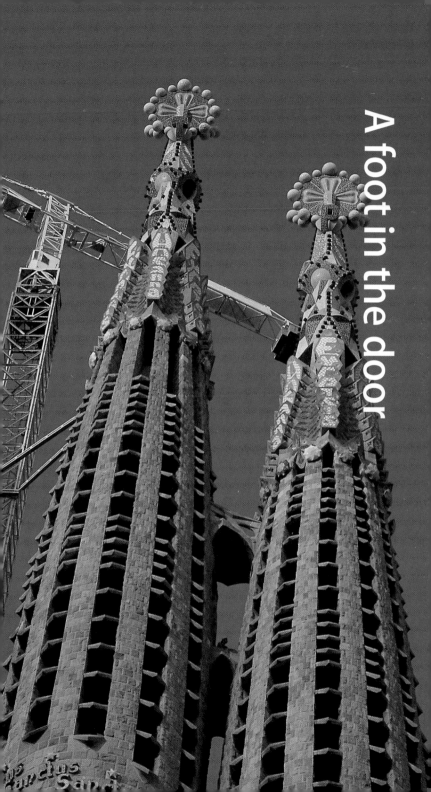

A foot in the door

Previous page *La Sagrada Família is being designed according to Gaudí's 'plans', and is scheduled for completion in 2026.*
Right *Passeig de Gràcia, Barcelona's most chi chi boulevard, has the finest examples of modernista architecture and the best designer shopping in the city.*
Below *The serene Monestir de Montserrat is surrounded by haunting scenery, and is less than one hour from Barcelona by train.*

Right *A chilly, early morning saunter down La Rambla.*
Above *A bit of Bedrock in Barça at Gaudí's surreal wonderland, Park Güell.*

Homage to Barcelona

Barcelona dips its toes in the Mediterranean, lolls back against the Pyrenees, and basks in year-round sunshine. At the heart of Barcelona lie the ancient passages, shadowy alleys, gargoyles and ghostly spires of the old Gothic city, apparently untouched by time. But, Barcelona is at the vanguard of all that is contemporary with cutting edge everything, from architecture to music and from interior design to street fashion.Then there is the skyline: 2002 is the Year of Gaudí, a celebration of one of the world's best known architects, whose delirious buildings, resembling dragons, or cliffs, or ginger-bread houses, seem to have magically erupted across the city. Fashionable bars, res-taurants and shops are springing up daily, and Barcelona is relishing its undisputed role as the style capital of Spain.

Rags to riches

But underneath the flirty, glamorous exterior lies a city that had to work to get atten-tion. A couple of decades ago, the creamy stone of Gaudí's La Pedrera was black with grime and parts of the city were too dangerous to walk through at any time of day; the spectacular legacy of the *modernistas* was slowly disintegrating through lack of interest or money. The 1992 Olympics changed all that; with breathtaking and entirely characteristic energy, the city reinvented itself, demolishing and recon-structing great swathes of land, unfurling itself along the long-ignored Mediterra-nean, and turning the surrounding slopes into parkland. This dynamism is still blazing a trail: the old town *barri* of El Raval, once notorious for sex and drugs, has got a brand new promenade and a gleaming new museum of contemporary art, and, down by the sea, the old worker's neighbourhood of Poble Nou is being entirely revamped to showcase the 2004 Universal Forum of Cultures, Barcelona's next big chance to preen and enjoy the world's attention.

Magical realism

The stock clichés about Spain don't apply to Barcelona – for the very good reason that Barcelona isn't properly part of Spain at all. Ortega y Gasset once wrote that "Spain is a thing made by Castile", an opinion with which the people of Barcelona would vigor-ously agree. Barcelona is the capital of Catalunya, an ancient empire which once strad-dled the Pyrenees and ruled the trading routes of the Mediterranean. It's a proud 'principality' with its own language, customs and traditions and a fiercely democratic history; 1,000 years ago, the Catalans swore loyalty to their king with an oath that began "We, who are as good as you, swear to you, who are no better than we, to accept you as our king and sovereign lord, provided you observe all our liberties and laws; but if not, not." The Catalans haven't lost their reputation for straight-talking – or bloody-mindedness as Castilians would have it. If Castilians think that Catalans are tight-fisted, pedantic and smug, the Catalans despise Castilians for being lazy, effete and, unforgiveably, entirely lacking in common sense. The Catalans are supremely proud of their *seny*, a deep-rooted natural wisdom which is treated with pious rever-ence. But *seny* is only half the Catalan story – the other half is *rauxa*, an outburst of uncontrollable emotion or just plain old craziness. *Rauxa* is what is going on when demons charge down narrow streets spitting flames and surrounded by leaping devils; when ice-cream houses undulate wildly to the sky without a straight line in sight; or when thousands of sweating bodies converge on the beaches for parties which might stop at dawn or maybe next week. The Catalans believe, with characteristic good sense, that a touch of madness will keep them sane.

Barcelona in a nutshell

Barcelona, unlike most big cities, doesn't have a long list of 'must-see' monuments. The city itself is the star attraction and the best way to appreciate it is simply to wander where fancy takes you. Finding your way around Barcelona isn't difficult; and a glance at any map shows the Ciutat Vella (Old City) squeezed into a crooked oval shape at the heart of Barcelona. Spreading inland from the old city is the elegant grid of the Eixample, where the *modernistas* left their fanciful mark on the bourgeois mansions. Beyond the grid lie a ring of traditional towns like Gràcia which were once entirely independent of Barcelona, and beyond them are the Collserola hills. The highest and most famous peak is Tibidabo, with its funfair, from where the whole city is spread out at your feet on a clear day. Hemming in the city on its western end is the hill of Montjüic, the city's favourite playground and site of the 1992 Olympic stadium. Along the seafront are the spanking new developments of the Port Vell and the Port Olímpic, crammed with beaches, restaurants and bars. It's an engagingly walkable city, but if you get footsore, the bus system and the metro are clean, safe and easy to negotiate, and you can swing up to Montjüic in a cable car or take a vintage tram to Tibidabo.

La Rambla   The best introduction to Barcelona is La Rambla, the city's famous tree-lined promenade which meanders down to the port and divides the Ciutat Vella (Old City). Find a café, pull up a chair, and watch the world go by; 'human statues', dancers, Chinese acrobats, and tourists during the day; clubbers and party-goers at night; and families carrying cakes tied up with ribbons for Sundays. Halfway down is **La Boquería**, Barcelona's loveliest market, overflowing with gleaming fruit and local specialities like *bolets* (wild mushrooms) or *calçots* (a kind of spring onion). La Rambla meets the sea at the harbour, elegant and chic after a massive make over for the Olympics.

La Ciutat Vella   The Rambla is one of the main arteries of La Ciutat Vella (Old City). Splintering east off the Rambla are a dozen narrow passages leading into the medieval maze of the Barri Gòtic, (Gothic quarter). At the heart of the ancient city is the flamboyant Gothic **Catedral de la Seu**, surrounded by a web of crooked streets lined with leaning mansions. East again of the Barri Gòtic is **La Ribera**, another medieval district which has become the coolest neighbourhood in a city, famed for its addiction to fashion. It's packed with ultra-chic boutiques, designer stores, and the trendiest restaurants, bars and clubs. In one of Barcelona's delicious contradictions, it rubs shoulders with the dusty old neighbourhood of **Sant Pere**, where the bustling streets are lined with grocers and butchers, and innumerable shops selling sensible underwear, where the old ladies carry baskets and the shop-keepers stand on the street wiping their hands on their aprons. In the middle of all this, the flamboyant **Palau de la Música Catalana** flings out her ceramic blooms and shimmers like a diva. Back on the other side of the Rambla, **El Raval** spreads west to the raffish old theatre district of the **Paral.lel**. Once the most talked-about red light district on the Mediterranean, it's been the focus of a massive clean up and has got its own spanking new Rambla, and a glassy, glossy museum of contemporary art. The hippest young artists have followed, bringing galleries, vintage fashion and record stores, bars, restaurants and clubs in their wake, soaking up what's left of the Raval's seductive bohemianism and putting the neighbourhood at the forefront of the city's alternative culture.

Left The wild exhuberance of Casa Batlló, which shimmers like a mermaid on the 'Block of Discord'.
Below The bars and tabernas, like the Taberna de Santa Maria, make Barcelona one of the best 24-hour cities in the world.

Above Go out on a high and make the heart-stopping views from the Montjüic cable car your last impression of the city.
Left Antigua Casa Figueres, the home of the renowned pâtisserie Escribà, has a modernista façade that is good enough to eat.

Eixample When the city burst out of its medieval walls in the 19th century, the rich commissioned brand new mansions in the airy new grid of the Eixample (extension). Gaudí and his *modernista* colleagues had a ball; houses turned into dragons, or Gothic castles, or witches hats, bristled with spires, or plump towers made apparently from ice-cream, leaving a spectacular legacy which now comprises one of the greatest concentrations of Art Nouveau architecture in the world. Gaudí's most celebrated achievement is the enormous cathedral which he neither began nor completed, the **Sagrada Família**, an epic work which seems to have erupted from the earth and which has caused controversy since the first stone was laid in 1882.

Gràcia, Tibidabo & outer districts Gràcia, on the outskirts of the city, was once independent and still feels that way. It's a relaxed neighbourhood with a reputation for liberalism and feistiness which has mellowed over the years. On the outskirts is the **Park Güell**, Gaudí's fairytale park with its toadstool-topped pavilions, forests of stone trees, and its huge, sinuous tile-covered bench which delivers magical views over the city below. The best views in all the city can be had from **Tibidabo**, Barcelona's funfair mountain and highest peak, reached by a rickety tram and a funicular.

El Litoral The most dramatic change to Barcelona's skyline in the last few years has been down by the seaside. The long-neglected coastline was cleared for the construction of the glistening **Olympic Village**, a futuristic city of steel trees and glassy towers. The new development of the **Port Olímpic** is hugely popular, crammed with restaurants and bars and some excellent seafood restaurants, and sandy beaches stretch for miles in both directions. The traditional dock-workers' neighbourhood of **Barceloneta** is close by and more atmospheric, with tiny tapas bars tucked away in its depths. The former warehouses of **Port Vell** have been handsomely restored to hold smart restaurants, museums, and elegant shops, and across the harbour is a gleaming entertainment complex with bars, clubs, an Imax cinema and an aquarium.

Montjüic Cable-cars swing across the bay and up to the mountain of Montjüic, which overlooks the sea. The Olympics left their mark here too with a string of excellent sports facilities, including a great outdoor pool. Close by is the **Fundació Miró**, a lovely light-filled museum dedicated to the Catalan artist, and at the bottom of the hill is the **MNAC**, with a mesmerising collection of Romanesque art taken from the tiny Pyrenean churches. There's plenty of enjoyable kitsch on Montjüic, from the mini-Spain on show at the **Poble Espanyol**, to the glorious **Font Màgica**, where the fountains leap colourfully to the sounds of ABBA.

Trips from Barcelona There's so much to see and do in Barcelona that you may not want to leave it – ever. If you do, you can head towards the beaches of the **Costa Brava** to the north or the **Costa Daurada** to the south. There are marinas with facilities for sailing and snorkelling in most of the towns, but if you are into diving, head for the coves around **Cadaqués** or the **Illes Medes** marine reserve. Inland, there are several natural parks offering walking, biking, horse-riding and ballooning – across the otherworldly moonscape of the volcanic region of **La Garrotxa**. The Pyrenees are only a few hours away from Barcelona – here you'll find the stunning **National Park of Aigüestortes**, remote valleys for trekking, a string of ski resorts and whitewater rafting and canyoning down the **Noguera Palleresa** valley.

Right A symbol of Barcelona's Olympic ideals, the Torre de Calatrava.

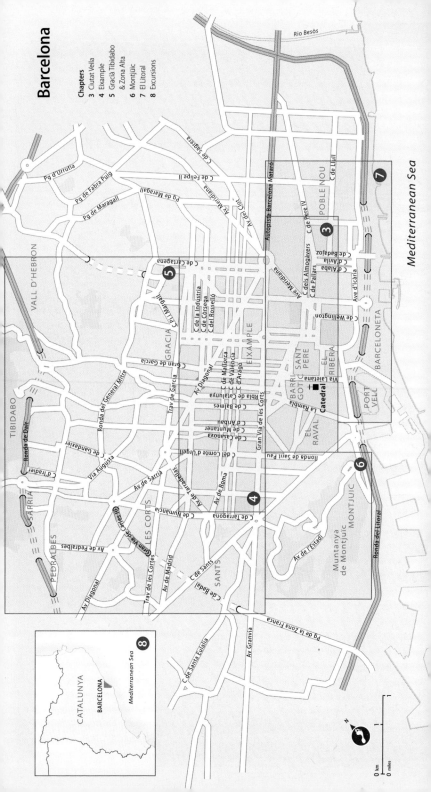

Contents

1

1 **A foot in the door**

2

11 **Essentials**
13 **Planning your trip**
13 Essential Barcelona
14 When to go
16 Tours and tour operators
17 Finding out more
17 Disabled travellers
18 Gay and lesbian travellers
18 Travelling with children
20 **Before you travel**
20 Entry requirements
20 Visas
20 Customs, regulations and tax
21 What to take
21 **Money**
23 **Getting there**
23 By air
25 Land and sea travel
29 **Touching down**
29 Barcelona Airport
30 Tourist information
31 Safety
32 **Where to stay**
35 **Getting around**
35 By bus
36 By metro
36 By tram and funicular
36 Telefèric/Cable cars
37 By taxi
37 By car
39 By bicycle
39 By foot
39 **Entertainment and nightlife**
40 **Holidays and festivals**
41 Calendar of events
45 **Food and drink**
47 **Shopping**
48 **Sports**
48 Spectator sports
49 Participation sports
51 **Keeping in touch**
51 Communications

52 Media
52 **Health**
53 **Further reading**
55 Useful websites

3

57 **Ciutat Vella: The Old City**
60 **La Rambla**
60 History
61 **Sights**
61 Plaça de Catalunya
63 La Boquería
64 Gran Teatre de Liceu
66 Eating and drinking
67 Shopping
68 Transport
69 **Barri Gòtic**
69 History
70 Sights
70 Muses d'Història de la Ciutat
74 Catedral de la Seu
78 Santa Ana
79 Plaça Sant Jaume
82 Eating and drinking
85 Shopping
87 Transport
87 **La Ribera**
87 History
89 Sights
90 Carrer Montcada
92 Museu Picasso
94 Sant Pere
96 Parc de la Ciutadella
98 Eating and drinking
101 Shopping
102 Transport
103 **El Raval**
103 History
103 Sights
104 Palau Güell
109 Museu d'Art Contemporani de Barcelona
111 Eating and drinking
114 Shopping
114 Transport

4

115 **Eixample**
118 History
118 Dreta de l'Eixample
119 **Sights**
119 Passeig de Gràcia and around
119 Museo Egipci
121 Fundació Francisco Godia
122 Fundació Antoni Tàpies
124 Mansana de la Discòrdia
126 Casa Milà (La Pedrera)
127 Around La Pedrera
128 Rambla de Catalunya
128 Diagonal and around
131 **Sagrada Família**
132 Around Sagrada Família
118 Dreta de l'Eixample
134 Esquerra de l'Eixample
134 Sights
135 Eating and drinking
138 Shopping
140 Transport

5

141 **Gràcia, Tibidabo and the outer districts**
144 **Gràcia**
144 History
144 Sights
147 Casa Vicens
148 Park Güell
151 Eating and drinking
153 Shopping
153 Transport
154 **Tibidabo & outer districts**
154 **Sants**
154 **Les Corts**
155 **Pedralbes**
155 Palau Reial
158 Monestir de Santa Maria de Pedralbes
160 **Sarrià**
161 **Parc de Collserola**
162 **Tibidabo**
165 Horta and the Vall d'Hebron

9

165 Jardins de Laberint d'Horta
166 **Glòries**
166 Eating and drinking
168 Shopping
169 Transport

6

171 **Montjüic**
174 History
174 Sights
178 Palau Nacional
184 Poble Espanyol
184 Anella Olímpica
186 Fundacío Miró
188 Castell Montjüic
189 Around Passeig Santa Madrona
190 **Poble Sec**
191 Eating and drinking
192 Transport

7

193 **El Litoral**
196 **Port Vell**
196 Plaça Portal de la Pau
198 La Rambla de Mar
200 Palau del Mar
201 Eating and drinking
202 Shopping
202 Transport
203 **Barceloneta**
203 History
203 Sights
204 Eating and drinking
205 Transport
206 **Vila Olímpica**
206 History
207 Sights
208 Eating and drinking
208 Transport
209 **Poble Nou and Diagonal Mar**
209 History
210 Eating and drinking
210 Transport

8

211 **Trips from Barcelona**
214 **North of Barcelona**
214 **The Costa Brava**

215 Cap de Creus
216 Ins and outs
217 **Girona**
219 La Garrotxa
220 **Figueres**
221 Ins and outs
221 **Noguera Palleresa Valley**
222 Ins and outs
223 **West of Barcelona**
223 Montserrat
224 Wine routes
225 Monestir de Santa María de Poblet
226 Ins and outs
227 **South of Barcelona**
227 Sitges
228 Tarragona
230 Ins and outs

9

231 **Entertainment**
233 **Theatre**
234 **The Barcelona music scene**
234 Classical and opera
236 World music
237 Contemporary music
238 **Clubs**
242 **Bars**
248 **Cinema**
249 Cinemas
249 **Dance**

10

251 **Sleeping**
253 **Hotels**
253 **Ciutat Vella**
253 La Rambla and Plaça de Catalunya
254 Barri Gòtic
255 La Ribera
256 El Raval
258 **Eixample**
260 **Gràcia**
260 **Tibidabo and outer districts**
261 **El Litoral**
261 Campsites
262 Apartment hotels
262 Youth hostels

11

263 **Background**
265 History
275 Art
279 Architecture

12

285 **Footnotes**
287 Spanish and Catalan words and phrases
290 Index
293 Map index
293 Shorts
293 Five of the best index
294 Barcelona by cuisine
297 Colour maps

Inside front cover
Hotel and restaurant price guide
Exchange rates
Dialling codes
Useful numbers

Inside back cover
Map symbols
Abbreviations

Essentials

Essentials

13 **Planning your trip**

13 Essential Barcelona

14 When to go

16 Tours and tour operators

17 Finding out more

17 Disabled travellers

18 Gay and lesbian travellers

18 Travelling with children

20 **Before you travel**

20 Getting in

21 What to take

21 **Money**

23 **Getting there**

23 Air

25 Land and sea travel

29 **Touching down**

29 Barcelona Airport

30 Tourist information

31 Safety

32 **Where to stay**

35 **Getting around**

39 **Entertainment and nightlife**

40 **Holidays and festivals**

41 Calendar of events

45 **Food and drink**

47 **Shopping**

48 **Sports**

48 Spectator sports

49 Participation sports

51 **Keeping in touch**

51 Communications

52 Media

52 **Health**

53 **Further reading**

55 Useful websites

Planning your trip

Essential Barcelona

Barcelona is bursting at the seams with sights and monuments, beaches, gardens and mountain parks. On top of that, there are enough bars, restaurants and shops to keep you going even if you never step inside a museum or a *modernista* landmark. To make choosing a bit easier, we've made a few suggestions.

There are some things no one will want to miss in Barcelona.

First-time visitors should stroll along **La Rambla**, Barcelona's most famous street and considered its best free show with dancers, acrobats and human statues. Wander into the crooked maze of **Barri Gòtic** (Gothic Quarter), crammed with restaurants, shops and bars. This part of the medieval city is huddled around the vast **Catedral de la Seu**, worth a visit for the rooftop views and the white geese in the lovely cloister.

The most famous Catalan architect is undoubtedly Gaudí, whose swirling, ice-creamy buildings draw huge numbers of visitors: Stroll up the Passeig de Gràcia, past the shimmering **Casa Batlló** and up to **La Pedrera**, the apartment block with the playful, undulating roof terrace. Visit the massive unfinished spires of **Sagrada Família** and take a bus to the magical gardens of **Park Güell**.

Another famous Catalan is remembered in the beautiful **Fundació Miró**, a cool, white, light-filled building on top of **Montjüic** which holds the most extensive collection of Miró's work in the world. Fans of contemporary art should also visit **MACBA**, the glistening new museum in the funky **Raval** area, where there are also plenty of great galleries, bars and clubs.

If it's sunny (and it almost always is) you won't want to miss out on the beaches and the glossy, buzzy new developments of **Port Vell** and the **Port Olímpic**. The best place for a birds-eye-view of Barcelona is up on top of **Tibidabo**, where the old fashioned funfair has a great ferris wheel for panoramic views.

For those who've been to Barcelona before, there is plenty more to discover. In **La Ribera**, you'll find the sublimely beautiful church of **Santa Maria del Mar**, as well as some of the best shopping and nightlife in the city. Explore the old fishermen's neighbourhood, seaside **Barceloneta** – try some fresh fish tapas at an old fashioned *tasca*, or go for a swim at one of the six city beaches.

There are several museums which don't get the crowds but are well worth a visit: among them are the **Museu Marítim** which has a great 'virtual' adventure; **MNAC** which has an utterly spellbinding collection of Romanesque art gathered from the tiny chapels of the Pyrenees, and the serene **Monestir de Pedralbes** which holds part of the Thyssen collection, up in the hills surrounding Barcelona. Football fans (and even those who aren't) should trek out to the **Camp Nou** stadium for the museum of FC Barça – as their slogan says 'More than a club'.

If you get a kick out of eccentricity, Barcelona is good at that too – among its kookiest attractions are the ultra-kitsch **Font Màgica**, with its dancing fountains and sound and light show, or the museums of the sewer or funeral carriages. And for a surprising breath of fresh-air, you could even go horse-riding in the beautiful, secluded **Parc de Collserola** which sprawls along the Collserola hills, or get lost in the **Horta Laberint**, a treacherous 18th-century maze.

If the bright lights pall, there are some great day trips. **Montserrat**, Catalunya's sacred mountain, is one of the most popular – avoid the bus-loads at the monastery – there's some great walking in the hills and a giddy cable car ride to get there. **Sitges** is

Average minimum /maximum daily temperatures

January: 10ºC/50ºF   *July: 25ºC/77ºF*
February: 13ºC/55.4ºF   *August: 25ºC/77ºF*
March: 13ºC/55.4ºF   *September: 22ºC/71.6ºF*
April: 14ºC/57.2ºF   *October: 18ºC/64.4ºF*
May: 18ºC/64.4ºF   *November: 16ºC/60.8ºF*
June: 21ºC/69.8ºF   *December: 12ºC/53.6ºF*

the prettiest town (30 minutes by train) on the Catalan coast; it's become a gay mecca and has a big reputation for partying. The wild windswept headland of **Cap de Creus**, with the whitewashed arty town of **Cadaqués** right at its tip, is a good 2-3 hours drive but stunningly beautiful. There are dozens of historic towns and villages – **Girona** is particularly lovely. Besides the winter sports on offer at the dozen or so ski resorts, there's hiking, fishing, mountain-climbing, adventure sports from whitewater rafting to bunjee-jumping, and the hauntingly beautiful **National Park of Aigüestortes**.

When to go

Climate   There's never really a bad time to go to Barcelona: when it gets too hot and sticky in the summer months you can head for the beaches or up into the breezy hills. It can get chilly in winter and surprisingly damp in spring but the sun is never far away. October, November, March and April are the rainiest months. May, June and September are the nicest months to visit, when the weather is warm but it's still not too humid and some of the best festivals take place in these months too (see page 42). July and August are

Learning Spanish or Catalan in Barcelona

American-British College, C/Guillem Tell 27, T93 415 57 57, www.ambricol.es Offers reasonably priced Spanish classes and can organize accommodation with families or in student residences.

Amerispan, PO Box 40007, Philadelphia, PA 19106, T215-751 1100 (worldwide), T1-800-879 6640 (USA, Canada), F215-751 1986, www.amerispan.com Offers Spanish immersion programs, educational tours and volunteer and internship programmes throughout Spain and Latin America.

Bla Bla and Company, C/Muntaner 82, T93 454 68 77, www.blabla.es Multimedia based language school offering Spanish language courses and can tailor tuition schedules to suit individual needs.

Consorci per la Normalització Lingüística, C/Mallorca 272, 8th Floor, T93 272 31 00, www.cpnl.org This is the official Generalitat organization for the support of the Catalan language. There are centres dotted around the city, offering very well-priced Catalan language classes for all levels.

Escola Oficial d'Idiomes, Avda Drassanes, T93 324 93 30, www.eoibd.es This is one of the most popular institutions in the city, with well-priced three-month courses in Catalan, Spanish and other languages. It's got a good reputation and is worth booking well in advance.

International House, C/Trafalgar 14, T93 268 45 11, www.ihes.com/bcn This is the main Barcelona centre for TEFL training, but it also offers year-round intensive Spanish courses.

The following will organize **classes** and **accommodation**: Don Quijote UK, 2-4 Stoneleigh Park Road, Stoneleigh, Epsom, Surrey KT19 OQR, T020-8786-8081, F8786-8086; **Languages Abroad (CESA)**, Western House, Malpas, Truro, Cornwall TR1 1SQ, T01872-225300, F01872-225400; **Spanish Study Holidays**, 35 Woodbrook Road, Loughborough, Leics LE11 3QB, T01509-211612, F260037.

Essentials

Sports and activity tours

Bike and Sun Tours, 42 Whitby Avenue, Guiseborough, Cleveland TS14 7AN, T01287-639739, F638217. Bike and motorbike tours throughout Spain.

Alternative Travel Group Ltd, 69-71 Banbury Road, Oxford OX2 6PE, T01865-315679, F315697/8/9, www.atg-oxford.co.uk Offer walking tours in Catalunya.

Exodus Worldwide Adventures, 9 Weir Road, London SW12 OLT, T020-8675-5550, F673-0779, www.exodus.co.uk Offer walking and trekking tours to suit all ages and pockets.

Gourmet Birds, Windrush, Coles Lane, Brasted Westerham, Kent TN16 1NN, T01959-563627, F562906, gourmetbirds@aol.com Bird-watching tours with accommodation in paradores all over Spain, and occasionally in Catalunya.

Spirit Of Adventure, Powder Mills, Princetown-Yelverton, Devon PL20 6SP, T01822-880277, F880277, www.spirit-of-adventure.com Offer an amazing tour which travels from the Pyrenees to the Mediterranean taking in some canyoning, cycling, horse-riding, hiking and sea-canoeing on the way.

Tall Stories, 67a High Street, Walton on Thames, Surrey KT12 1DJ, T01932-252002, F225145, www.tallstories.co.uk Multi-sport holidays from their base in Estartit – sports include snorkelling, mountain-biking, sailing, sea-kayaking and diving (they also run the PADI diving course).

Winetrails, Greenways, Vann Lake, Ockley, Dorking RH5 5NT, T01306-712111, F713504, www.winetrails.co.uk Tailor-made tours to all the wine areas of Catalunya, with prices to suit most pockets.

Arblaster & Clarke Wine Tours, Clarke House, The Green, West Liss, Hants GU33 6JQ, T01730-893344. Visits to Barcelona with excursions to the Tarragona vineyards.

sweltering, but the streets are buzzing and there's a great party atmosphere. A surprising number of shops and restaurants still close down for the whole of August, so it's well worth calling ahead.

Tours and tour operators

General tours
There are all kinds of special interest tours in Barcelona and Catalunya

There are hundreds of tour operators offering flight and accommodation packages: **Exodus Travels**, 9 Weir Rd, London SW12 OLT, T020-8772 3822, www.exodus.co.uk **Abercrombie and Kent**, Sloane Square House, Holbein Place, London, SW1W 8NS, T020-7730 9600, F7730 9376 and **Magic of Spain**, 227 Shepherd's Bush Road, London, W6 7AS, T020-7533 8888, F7533 8830 are both pretty upmarket, reliable agencies. **Mundi Color**, 276 Vauxhall Bridge Road, London, SW1 1BE, T020-7828 6021, is part of the Spanish airline *Iberia* and offers some moderately priced packages. **Solo's Holidays**, 54-8 High Street, Edgware, Middlesex, HA8 7ED, T020-8951 2800, F8951 2848, do just what they say, and organise holidays for people travelling alone. **Trailfinders**, 194 Kensington High Street, London, W8 4QY, T020-7937 1234, www.trailfinders.com **Council Travel** in the USA, T1-888-COUNCIL, www.counciltravel.com and **STA Travel** in Australia and New Zealand, T1300-360960, www.statravelaus.com.au 72 Harris St, Ultimo, Sydney, and 256 Flinders St, Melbourne or 10 High St, Auckland, T09-3090 458, are all great for budget and student travellers. In the USA, **Marketing Ahead Inc**, 433 Fifth Avenue, New York, NY 10016, T212-686 9213, F686 0271, are the leading Spanish hotel and parador agents (see below for more information on paradores).

Tourist offices abroad

The city council and the Catalan government both have excellent and very informative websites in English (see page 31), and provide a dizzying array of brochures and leaflets. You can get information from the **Spanish tourist offices** *listed below, or at the helpful tourist offices in Barcelona (see page 31).*
Australia *203 Castlereagh Street, Suite 21A, PO Box A-685, Sydney South NSW 2000, T2-264-7966, F2-267-5111.*
Canada *102 Bloor Street West, Toronto, Ontario M5S 1M8, T416- 961-3131,*

F416- 961-1992.
UK *22-3 Manchester Square, London W1M 5AP, T020-7486 8077, F7486-8034. Brochure information line, T09063640630.*
Catalan Tourist Board, *17 Fleet Street, EC4Y, T020-7583-8855, catalonia@ catalantouristboard.co.uk*
USA *8383 Wiltshire Boulevard, Suite 960, Beverly Hills, California 90211, T213-658-7188, F213-658-061. 665 Fifth Avenue, New York, NY 10022, T212-759-8822, F212-980- 1053.*

Essentials

Finding out more

Barcelona has got its tourist industry all wrapped up, with helpful, well-informed tourist information offices in the city itself, excellent websites, and a host of useful leaflets, maps, events calendars and other information. Get in touch with the Spanish tourist information offices in your home country before leaving (for addresses, see above and browse through the useful websites. The city also runs an online information service for its residents which is also a good resource for visitors (www.bcn.es), and there's a telephone information line (T010, most operators will speak at least a little bit of English).

For a list of useful websites, see page 55

Barcelona is a bilingual city: the official languages are Castilian (Spanish) and Catalan. Franco was the latest in a long line of rulers who have tried to stamp out Catalan nationalism by depriving the country of its language, but, like others before him, he failed. Since the establishment of democracy in the late 1970s, the Generalitat has put Catalan language right at the top of the political agenda: civil service officials are required to speak it; university classes are held in it; road signs and street names have been Catalanised; and most opening hours at museums, shops and banks are usually signposted exclusively in Catalan. You will need to know a few basic phrases (see page 287) to get by as few Barcelonans speak English; they will speak Spanish to you, but any effort, however small, to speak in Catalan will be greeted with a big smile of thanks.

Language
Some tour operators will organize lessons and accommodation from your home country (see page 15). There are also plenty of Barcelona-based agencies who can offer the same service

Disabled travellers

Barcelona is getting better at catering for disabled travellers, but it's still not great. Most of the newer and bigger museums have wheelchair access (for a list, see below), as do many of the more expensive hotels.

The sightseeing *Bus Turístic* and *Aerobúses* from the airport are equipped for wheelchairs, as are about a third of public buses. **Taxis** are required by law to transport wheelchairs and guidedogs free of charge, although in practice the cars are too small and the drivers usually unhelpful. The *Taxi Amic* service, T93 420 80 88, can provide mini-vans but there is high demand so book as early as possible. Few metro and FGC train stations have lifts.

Wheelchair-friendly museums Fundació Joan Miró; Col.leció Thyssen Bornemisza; Monastir de Pedralbes (wheelchair access to art collection only); MACBA; MNAC; Museu d'Art Modern; Museu de les Arts Decoratives; Museu D'Arqueologia de

Catalunya; Museu d'Historia de Catalunya; Museu de la Ciencia; Museu de la Zoologia; La Capella; CCCB; Col.legi d'Arquitectes; Fundació Antoni Tàpies; Palau de la Virreina

For more information before you leave, contact *RADAR* (The Royal Association for Disability and Rehabilitation), 12 City Forum, 250 City Road, London EC1V 8 AF, T020-7250 3222, F020-7250 0212, www.radar.org.uk who publish an annual guide called *Holidays and Travel Abroad: A Guide for Disabled People*, with a section on Spain covering contact addresses, transport, services and accommodation (£11). Contact the city's bureau for the disabled, the *Institut Municipal de Persones amb Disminució*, C/Llacuna 161, T93 291 84 00, F93 291 84 09 (metro Glòries, bus nos 56, 60 or 92), for detailed information on building access to museums, restaurants, monuments, theatres and other establishments.

Gay and lesbian travellers

The gay scene in Barcelona is growing all the time and it's generally an easy place for gay and lesbian travellers to feel safe and comfortable

Just half an hour by train out of the city is the seaside town of Sitges (see page 227), one of the most popular gay holiday spots in Europe. In Barcelona itself, most of the gay bars, restaurants and clubs are located in the Left Eixample (see page 134), which has become known as the *Gaixample* or *Eixample Rosa*. Spring and summer are the best times to come, but the *Carnaval* in mid-February is a blast. If you are just looking to party, head straight for *Zeus*, C/Riera Alta 20, T93 442 97 95, or *Sestienda*, C/Rauric 11, T93 318 86 76, two gay sex shops which produce a free gay map to Barcelona and Sitges with everything you ever wanted to know clearly marked up. The local magazine *Nois* has details on gay-owned or gay-friendly places throughout Catalunya, and also has a related website, www.revistanois.com *Mensual* is a gay listings and entertainment magazine which covers the whole of Spain; you can find an online version at www.mensual.com

There are several helpful information centres which deal with cultural, health and other issues. *Casal Lambda*, C/Ample 5, T93 412 72 72, www.lambdaweb.org This is a friendly, gay cultural organization which produces its own magazine, *LAMBDA*, and hosts all kinds of different activities. *Coordinadora Gai-Lesbiana*, C/Buenaventura Munoz 4, T90 060 16 01. A gay umbrella organization which works with the city council on all kinds of gay issues, and produces a free magazine. *Front d'Alliberament Gai de Catalunya*, C/Verdi 88, T93 217 26 69. A high-profile organization which promotes gay issues and publishes a free bulletin, *Barcelona Gai*.

Some gay and gay-friendly hotels are: *Hotel California*, C/Rauric 14, T93 317 77 66, F93 317 54 74. Affordable, central and friendly. Double rooms are about €57. *Pensión La Nau*, Rda/de Sant Pere 53, T/F 93 245 10 13. Basic rooms on the edge of the Eixample. Double rooms are about €39. *Hostal Que Tal*, C/Mallorca 290, T93 459 23 66. Spotless, friendly and cheerful, this is a very popular spot in the Eixample, so book well in advance. Double rooms are between €43-57. *Hostal Centro*, C/Balmes 38, T64-955 02 38 (mobile), F93 272 08 75. Well located for the Gaixample, with friendly helpful owners.

Travelling with children

In Barcelona, most museums offer reduced admission for children and free admission to children under four

Barcelona is a great place to visit with children, with fairy-tale buildings, beaches, and plenty of child-friendly activities from the Chocolate Museum to sailing ships and mountain-top funfairs. Spaniards love children, and you'll find yours are treated indulgently wherever you go – and however badly they behave. Before you go, inform the airline in advance that you're travelling with a baby or a toddler and check out the facilities when booking as these vary with each aircraft. *British Airways* now has a special seat for the children under two; check which aircraft has been fitted when booking. Pushchairs can be taken on as hand luggage or stored in the hold.

Child-friendly museums and attractions

Museu de la Xocolata (see page 89). Chocolate museum with tastings and interactive exhibits.

Globo Turístic, Pg/de Circumval.lacio (see page 32).

Magic BCN, 10-12 Pg/Lluis Companys. Hot air balloon, operates: Mon-Fri at 1415 and 1915; Sat at 1315, 1615, 1745 and 1915; Sun and holidays at 1215, 1315, 1415, 1615, 1745 and 1915 Admission: Adults 875 ptas, children under 12, 700 ptas. Virtual reality train ride with special effects takes visitors on a journey along the railways of the world.

Las Golondrinas (see page 32). Old-fashioned double-decker sightseeing boats which do tours around the port.

La Rambla (see page 60). Puppet shows, mime artists and buskers on the city's most famous street.

L' Aquàrium (see page 199). Sharks, penguins and jellyfish with a new interactive centre.

Museu de la Ciència (see page 164). Has a special section for the under-fives.

Museu del Futbol Club Barcelona (see page 155). A mecca for football fans of all ages.

Zoo, (page 98). Pony rides and the world's only albino gorilla, Snowflake.

Tibidabo Parc d'Attraciones (see page 163). Fun fair on top of the mountain. Get there by the old-fashioned **Tramvia Blau** (see page 36) and the **Tibidabo funicular** (see page 36).

Parks and Beaches

Barcelona has six beaches stretching from Barceloneta out past the Port Olímpic with snack bars, ice cream vendors and cafés close by. There are outdoor showers but no changing facilities, unless you use a restaurant bathroom. The beaches get jam-packed at weekends. The city council organizes children's sports and activities on the beaches between March and May, culminating in the **Festa de la Platja** in May. The tourist office can supply all the details (see page 31).

Park Güell (see page 148). Gaudí's dreamy park is always a favourite with kids.

Parc de la Creuta del Coll. The park has a small boating lake and picnic areas.

Parc del Castell de l'Oreneta (see page 160). Pony rides and miniature train rides.

Parc de Collserola (see page 161). Wonderful natural park with hiking trails, horse-riding (see page 49) and picnic spots.

Adventure parks and theme parks out of town

Isla Fantasia, Vilassar del Dalt, 24 km from Barcelona, T93 751 45 53, www.islafantasia34w.com One of Europe's largest waterparks, which becomes a water disco in the evenings.

Aqualéon Safari, Finca les Basses, 65 km from Barcelona, T97 768 57 76, www.asprohocia.es A combined water and safari park with tigers, eagles and parrots as well as wave machines, water slides and dolphins.

Catalunya en Miniatura, Torrelles de Llobregat, T93 689 09 60, www.catalunyaenminiatura.com One of the largest model village in Europe, with 170 best monuments of Catalunya; a mini-train does the rounds and there are clown shows on Sundays.

Universal Studios Port Aventura, near Salou, T97 777 90 00. Huge theme park, which even has its own railway station, with very scary rides, a virtual underwater 'Sea Odyssey', and plenty for little kids too.

Essentials

Public transport is free for children under four. However, reduced ticket prices are offered for the Barcelona Bus Turístic and the various cable cars for children under 12. You'll find everything you need (nappies, etc) in the local supermarkets and pharmacies, but bear in mind that almost everything is closed on Sundays. Festivals usually offer fireworks, flamethrowers and parades that kids love – check the festival listings on page 40.

Eating out with children is no problem in Barcelona. Children are treated like small adults and it's not unusual to see them out in restaurants with their parents late at night, or playing outside a café while their families chat away. Perversely, this also means that few restaurants have child-specific facilities – high chairs are rare, and you'll probably have to ask for a small portion rather than being given a child's menu. Some restaurants cater for kids and tapas bars are a good place to give them a taste of local food and still get them to bed before 2200.

There are several **babysitting services**, if you want to take the night off. The tourist information office on Plaça de Catalunya has a full list, or you could call one of the agencies listed below. *Baby Home*, C/de la Diputacio 188, T93 453 85 29. *Cangur Serveis*, C/Arago 50, T93 488 26 01. *Happy Parc*, 74-78 C/dels Comptes de Bell Lloc 74-78, T93 490 08 35. This is a drop-off daycare with indoor play facilities. *Servinens*, Travessera de Gracia 117, T93 218 23 87

Before you travel

Getting in

Visas Visitors from the UK or other EU countries must present a valid passport or identity card. Holders of US, Canadian or New Zealand passports can enter Spain for up to 90 days without a visa. Other foreign nationals will need a visa, available from any Spanish consulate.

If you intend to stay for more than three months, you must apply for a *permiso de residencia* (community resident's card) at the **Oficina de Extranjeros** (Foreign Nationals Office) at the Delegación de Gobierno, Avinguda Marques de l'Argentera, T93 483 05 44, for appointments call T93 482 05 60. The bureaucracy can be mind-boggling, and you should consider getting a *gestor*, a cross between a lawyer, book-keeper and general advisor, to deal with the paperwork: try *LEC*, Travessera de Gràcia 96, second floor, Gràcia, T93 415 02 50, or *Tutzo Assessors*, C/Aribau 226, Eixample, T93 209 67 88, tutzoass@fonocom.es Both these companies have some English-speakers.

Customs regulations & tax
Non EU-residents can claim back VAT (IVA) on purchases of more than 90 euros

EU residents don't have to declare goods imported into Spain for personal use if they have paid duty on them in the country of origin. You are allowed to bring in, duty paid, up to 800 cigarettes or 400 cigarillos, 200 cigars or 1kg of loose tobacco; plus 10 litres of spirits, 90 litres of wine and 110 litres of beer. Non-EU residents are allowed to bring in duty-free 200 cigarettes or 100 cigarillos, 50 cigars or 250g of loose tobacco; plus one litre of spirits (or two litres of fortified wine or other spirits under 22% alcohol); plus two litres of wine and 50 grammes of perfume.

Insurance
Check out www.travel insurance.co.uk for a good round-up of what's on offer. For health information, see page 52

EU residents are entitled to make use of Spanish state healthcare if they are in possession of a E111 form (available from major post offices, health centres and Social Security offices in the UK). But this is a complicated process and it is probably worthwhile taking out private holiday insurance, which is usually fairly inexpensive. Your travel agent will probably be able to advise you on the best deals available. *STA Travel* and other reputable student travel organizations often offer good-value travel policies. Travellers from North America can try the *International Student Insurance Service* (ISIS) which is available through *STA Travel*, T1-800-777 0112, www.sta-travel.com Some other recommended travel insurance companies in North America include *Travel Guard*, T1-800-826 1300, www.noelgroup.com; *Access America*, T1-800-284 8300; *Travel Insurance Services*, T1-800-937 1387; *Travel Assistance International*, T1-800-821 2828 and *Council Travel*, T1-888-COUNCIL, www.counciltravel.com In the UK, another company worth calling for a quote is *Columbus Direct*, T020-7375 0011. **Older travellers** should note that some companies won't cover people over 65 years old, or may charge higher premiums. Policies for older travellers are offered by *Age Concern*, T01883 346964, though these can be expensive.

Overseas embassies/consulates

There's a full list of embassies and consulates in the phone book under Consolats/Consulados. You'll also find a selective list in the small magazine See Barcelona, issued by tourist information offices. Recorded messages will give you an emergency phone number outside of office hours.

Australia Gran Via Carles III 98, metro Maria Cristina, T93 330 94 96, F93 4110904, www.embaustralia.es Open Mon-Fri 1000-1200, closed Aug.
Canada C/Elisanda de Pinós 10, FCG Reina Elisanda, T93 215 07 04, F93 204 27 01, www.canada-es.org Open Mon-Fri 1000-1200.

Ireland Gran Via Carles III 94, metro Maria Cristina or Les Corts, T93 491 50 21, F93 411 29 21. Open Mon-Fri 1000-1300.
New Zealand Travessera de Gràcia 64, FCG Gràcia, T93 209 03 99, F93 202 08 90. Open Sep-Jun 0900-1400 and 1600-1900. Call to check reduced hours in Jul and Aug.
UK Avinguda Diagonal 477, metro Hospital Clinic, T93 419 90 44, F93 366 62 21, bcon@cyberbcn.com Open end-Sep to mid-Jun Mon-Fri 0930-1330 and 1600-1700; mid-Jun to mid-Sep Mon-Fri 0900-1400.
USA Passeig Reina Elisenda 23, FCG Reina Elisenda, T93 280 22 27, F93 205 52 06, www.embusa.es Open 0900-1230 and 1500-1700.

Essentials

Check the small print on any insurance policy you take out – some do not offer ambulance, helicopter rescue or emergency flights home. Find out if your policy pays medical expenses direct to the hospital or doctor, or if you have to pay them and claim the money back later. If the latter applies, make sure you keep all records. If you are unfortunate enough to have something stolen, make sure you get a copy of the police report. These are printed in four languages (English, French, German and Italian) and you should be given a copy with an order number to help you with insurance claims.

What to take

Pack warm clothes for winter and something rainproof for spring – it gets colder and wetter than you might expect. The evenings are cool until June, when the city starts to swelter and doesn't cool down again until September. As in most of western Europe, the **voltage** in Barcelona is 220V 50hz, so visitors from North America should bring a transformer – easily and cheaply bought in the city if you forget. Spanish plugs have two pins, so UK devices will need an adaptor. If you are planning on hiking in the mountains, visit a good map shop in your home country before coming to be sure of getting maps in English (see page 53 for further reading). A sleeping bag is useful in hostels and a sleeping sheet with a pillow cover will save you the cost of hiring one if you are on a tight budget.

Be aware that the current in some of the cheaper hostels may still be 125V and so your electrical equipment won't work

Money

On 1 January 1999, the euro became the official currency of Spain (at the rate of 166.386 pts to the euro). Euro notes and coins have been in circulation since 1 January 2002. ATM machines and banks now only issue euros. The short transition period, as pesetas are phased out, will last until 28 February 2002. You can exchange your pesetas for euros until this date. If you are still familiar with working in pesetas, a useful rule of thumb is to remember that 500 pts is almost exactly €3, so 1,000 pts is €6, and so on. See inside cover for exchange rates.

For more information on the euro in Spain, call T90 111 20 02

Travellers' cheques Most banks in Barcelona will exchange money or travellers' cheques from a major company for a hefty commission. Look for the *cambio/canvi* change signs, and bring your passport if you have traveller's cheques. Commission rates vary considerably, so shop around for the best deal. Banking hours are usually Monday-Friday 0830-1400, and most also open on Saturday mornings 0830-1400 from October-April. Savings banks (*caixas*) open later on Thursdays (usually 1630-1945) from October to April. All banks and savings banks are closed on public holidays.

Bureaux de change Outside banking hours, there are dozens of private bureaux de change (*cambios*) in the Barri Gòtic, along La Rambla and around the Sants train station. These often open as late as 0300; their rates are usually less favourable than the banks and savings banks, but they don't always charge a commission. If you have pristine notes, you can use the automatic machines at the airport and Sants train station. For visitors travelling from the UK, it's worth noting that **Marks and Spencer** have a currency exchange service which offers good rates and charges no commission. There's also a secure online foreign currency service, www.onlinefx.co.uk, which also has good rates for cash and travellers' cheques and doesn't charge commission.

American Express, C/Rosselló 259, T93 217 00 70. Open Monday-Friday 0930-1800, Saturday 1000-1200. **American Express**, La Rambla 74, T93-3011166. Open April-September daily 0900-2400; October-March Monday-Friday 0900-2030, Saturday 1000–1400 and 1500-1900. For traveller's cheque emergencies, call free on T90-0994426. **Western Union Money Transfer**, Loterías Manual Martin, La Rambla 41, T93-4127041. Open 0930-2400, Sunday 1000-2400.

Credit cards & ATMs The cheapest and easiest option for getting money in Spain is by using your credit card in an ATM (Telebanco). The fee (usually about 1.5%) is not normally as high as the commission charged by the banks and rates are not too bad. But don't forget that you will have to pay interest. ATMs are everywhere, and instructions for use are in English. Most hotels, shops and restaurants take credit cards as do the ticket machines in the train stations and metro stops.

Emergency numbers If your card gets swallowed up or stolen, call the numbers below as soon as possible: **American Express**: T91-5720303/for travellers' cheques call free T90-0994426. **Diner's Club**: T90-1101011. **MasterCard**: T90-0971231. **Visa**: T90-0974445.

Cost of travelling Spain in general is no longer the cheap holiday destination it once was and Barcelona is one of the most expensive cities in Spain. Not for nothing was the local phrase coined: 'it doesn't stink if the purse clinks'. Nonetheless, it is still considerably cheaper than many other countries in Europe. There's plenty of cheap accommodation: you can get a very basic double room for about €15, and eating can be very cheap. Look out for the excellent value *menú del dia*, a fixed-price menu which most establishments will offer at lunchtime (a few places also offer them in the evenings) which will give you several filling courses often including wine for less than €6. Bars and clubs are usually much cheaper than their equivalents in the UK and North America, and drinks are much cheaper than at home, too. Note also that cinemas are traditionally cheaper on Monday nights, and theatre tickets are usually cheaper on Tuesday nights. Travel is cheap, too, but most sights are within easy walking distance and it's a great city to explore on foot anyway. Outside of the city, prices drop still further. If you want to take to the road under your own steam, be aware that petrol, motorway tolls and car hire are surprisingly expensive. Otherwise, trains and buses are very well-priced. In hotels, single travellers will be stung by the practice of charging per room rather than per person, although several of the cheaper places offer single rooms at reduced rates. In general, a single traveller should budget on spending around 60% of what a couple would spend.

There are various official youth/student ID cards available. The most useful is the **International Student ID card** (ISIC) which costs a mere £6, and gives you a series of discounts including discounts on international air fares, reduced entrance prices to museums and major sights. Under-26s are elegible for a discount on bus and train travel regardless of whether or not they are students. Not all youth hostels in Barcelona require a **International Youth Hostel card** (IYH card) , but the official ones do. If you don't have one, you can get one from the **Viatgeteca** student travel agency, C/Rocafort 116-122, 08015 Barcelona, T93 483 83 78, www.bcu.cesca.es which is part of the Catalan government's well-equipped 'youth information point'.

    If you're aged under 26 but not a student, you can apply for a **Federation of International Youth Travel Organizations (FIYTO)** card, or a **Euro-26** card which give you the same discounts. If you're 25 or younger you can qualify for a **Go-25** card which gives yo the same benefits as an ISIC card. These discount cards are issued by discount travel agencies (see pages 25-27) and hostelling organizations (see page 35).

Youth & student discounts

Tipping is at the customer's discretion in Barcelona and there are no hard-and-fast rules. In restaurants, locals leave a few coins from the change, rarely more than €3. In bars, they might drop a few pesetas on the bar. Tourists generally leave a bit more, around 5-10% in restaurants, and about the same for taxis – count on 10% if the driver helped with luggage or drove long distances. It's usual to tip hotel porters and toilet attendants with a few coins.

Tipping

Getting there

Air

Barcelona's international airport is in *El Prat de Llobregat*, 12 km (7 miles) to the south of the city. There are a mind-boggling number of outlets and finding the best deal can be a confusing business. **Fares** will depend on the season, and the kind of ticket you buy. Ticket prices are at their highest from June to September, but it's usually possible to find a reasonably priced ticket at all times of the year thanks to the tight competition.

For airport information, see page 29

Cheap flight tickets fall into two categories: official and unofficial. Official tickets are called budget fares, Apex, super-Apex, advance-purchase tickets, or whatever a particular airline chooses to call them. Unofficial tickets are discounted tickets which are released by airlines through selected travel agents. They are not sold directly by airlines. Discounted tickets are usually as low or lower than the official budget-price tickets. Return tickets are usually a lot cheaper than two one-way tickets (unless you are buying them with one of the so-called 'no-frills' airlines, like *easyJet* and *Go* who both fly from London and regional airports). **Round-the-World** (RTW) tickets for travellers flying from outside Europe can be a real bargain and may even work out cheaper than a return fare, but it's probably cheaper and easiest to pick up a cheap flight to Barcelona from London than to include it on your itinerary. One of the best ways of finding the cheapest deals is to look on the Internet: some of the most useful websites are: **www.expedia.co.uk   e-bookers.com   cheapflights.co.uk   deckchair.com flynow.com and dialaflight.co.uk**

    When trying to find the best deal, make sure you check the route, the duration of the journey, stopovers allowed, any travel restrictions such as minimum and maximum periods away, and cancellation penalties. Many of the cheapest flights are sold

Buying a ticket

Essentials

Arriving late

Arriving in Barcelona without arranging accommodation in advance is always a bad idea. Arriving in the middle of the night without arranging accommodation in advance is 'loco'.

Transport *If you arrive at the airport too late to get the bus or train into the city centre, you will have to get a taxi. These thin out considerably late at night, but if all else fails you could order a taxi by phone:*
Fono-Taxi *T93 300 11 00;* ***Ràdio Taxi*** *T93 225 00 00;* ***Taxi Ràdio Móbil*** *T93 358 11 11. Very few drivers will speak English.*

Accommodation *There is only one hotel close to the airport and it is very expensive:* ***Alfa Aeropuerto****, Zona Franca, Carrer K s/n, T93 336 25 64. It's a large* ***Best Western*** *hotel and they can organise for a taxi to collect you. There are a few hotels close to Sants station (see page 261) but if*

you can't find anywhere with a room, head for the Plaça de Catalunya in the centre of the city. Most of the ***budget hotels*** *and hostels are in Barri Gòtic. If you have a reservation find out in advance if you can check in late.*

If all else fails and you can't get anywhere to stay, you may as well find a ***bar*** *or a* ***club*** *and hang out there until the morning. Again, most bars and clubs are concentrated in the Barri Gòtic in the centre of the old city. You can get some breakfast at* ***La Boquería*** *market which opens around 5am and is just off the Rambla. There has been an increasing number of crimes against tourists reported in Barcelona and it is not advisable to sleep outdoors, even in summer when the temperature allows it.*

---

by small agencies, most of whom are honest and reliable, but there may be some risks involved with buying tickets at rock-bottom prices. You should avoid paying too much in advance and you could check with the airline directly to make sure you have a reservation. You may be safer choosing a better-known travel agent such as *STA*, which has offices worldwide, or *Trailfinders* in the UK, or *Council Travel* in the USA. For other reputable discount companies and agents see pages 25-27.

Flights from the UK There are regular direct flights to Barcelona from Heathrow, Gatwick, Manchester and Birmingham, Luton and Stansted. The cheapest flights usually leave from Luton or Stansted, with the so-called 'no-frills' airlines, **easyJet** and **Go**, which offer good deals because they don't allocate seats or provide free meals. **Buzz** is another 'no-frills' airline which offers very good deals to Girona, about an hour and a half away from Barcelona. It might be worth checking out **Ryanair**, which offers very low fares to Perpignan, on the French side of the Pyrenees, and then taking a train from there. In the low season, Ryanair has offered special fares of £19 each way. All these tickets are often subject to rigid restrictions but the savings can make the extra effort worthwhile. There is usually a very small extra discount if you book your ticket on the internet. Ticket prices rise the later you book before you travel, but they can usually only be booked up to two months in advance. Cheaper tickets from all airlines usually have to be bought at least a week in advance, apply to only a few mid-week flights and must include a Saturday night stayover. They are also non-refundable, or only partly refundable, and non-transferable. A standard flexible and refundable fare from London to Barcelona will cost at least £200 return, and often considerably more.

Charter flights can be incredibly cheap, and many also depart from local airports. Companies such as *Thomson*, *Airtours* and *Unijet* can offer return flights from as little £80. Check out your local travel agency, the weekend papers, especially the *Guardian* travel section, which locates the cheapest deals every Saturday and TV *Teletext*. The London listings magazine *Time Out* is another good source of cheap deals.

Airlines flying from Britain and Ireland

British Airways, T0845 779 9977, www.britishairways.com Flies direct to Barcelona from Heathrow, Gatwick, Manchester and Birmingham.
Iberia, T08705 341 341, www.iberia.com Also offers a direct service from Heathrow, Gatwick, Manchester and Birmingham.
Air France, T0845 0845 111, www.airfrance.co.uk Flies to Barcelona from Heathrow via Paris.
KLM, T08705 074 074, www.klmuk.com Flies to Barcelona from Heathrow via Amsterdam.
Virgin Express, T020 7744 0004, www.virgin-express.com Flies to Barcelona from Heathrow and Gatwick with prices starting from £90.
British Midland, T08706 070 555,

www.flybmi.com Flies to Barcelona from Heathrow and Manchester
No-frills airlines
Note that the cheapest prices are only available if booked well in advance. Last-minute fares are rarely cheaper than those of the major carriers.
Go, T0345 605 4321, www.go-fly.com Offers return flights from Stansted to Barcelona from £80.
easyJet, T0870 600 0000, www.easyjet.com Flies from Luton to Barcelona with prices starting at around £90.
Buzz, T0870 240 7070, www.buzzaway.com Has flights to Girona for about £90 return.
Ryanair, T0870 333 1231. Offers very cheap flights to Perpignan in France.

Discount travel agents in Britain and Ireland

Council Travel, 28a Poland Street, London W1V3DB, T020-7437-7767, www.destinations-group.com
STA Travel, 86 Old Brompton Road, London SW7 3LH, T020-7361 6161, www.statravel.co.uk They have other branches in London, as well as in Brighton, Cambridge, Leeds, Manchester, Newcastle-upon-Tyne and Oxford and on many university campuses. Specialists in low-cost student and youth flights and tours,

also good for student IDs and insurance.
Trailfinders, 195 Kensington High Street, London W8 6FT, T020-79383939.
Usit Campus, 52 Grosvenor Gardens, London SW1 OAG, T020-77303402, www.campustravel.co.uk Student/youth travel specialists with branches in Belfast, Brighton, Bristol, Cambridge, Manchester and Oxford. The main Ireland branch is at 19 Aston Quay, Dublin 2, T01-6021777 or 677 8117.

There are dozens of regular flights to Barcelona from North America, but it might be worth checking out cheap deals to London and then getting an inexpensive onward flight from there (see box page 26). Other major European airlines offer competitive fares to Barcelona via other European capitals. For low-season **Apex fares**, expect to pay around US$400-600 from New York and other East Coast cities and around US$600-800 from the West Coast. Prices soar to up to US$1000 during the summer months (mid-June to mid-September). Low season Apex fares with **Iberia** from Toronto and Montreal directly to Barcelona cost around CAN$700-900, rising to CAN$850-1000 during the summer. **Flights from North America**

There are no direct flights to Spain from Australia and New Zealand; the cheapest option is usually to fly to London and get an inexpensive flight from there (see page 27). Some Asian airlines offer good deals, flying via their major cities. **Flights from Australia & New Zealand**

Land and sea travel

The journey to Barcelona by coach is long and uncomfortable, but can be a cheap alternative in the summer months when flight prices soar. The main European **Coach**

Essentials

Airlines flying from North America

Iberia offices in the USA include: New York: 655 Madison Avenue, New York, NY 10022, T212-644 8797. Los Angeles: 4227 Wilshire Bd, 3209, Los Angeles, CA, T323-692 2965.

Airlines with direct routes to Spain include:
American Airlines: *toll-free T1-800 433 7300 (flights to Madrid only), www.americanairlines.com*
Continental Airlines: *toll-free T1-800 231 0856 (flights to Madrid only), www.contintentalairlines.com*
Delta: *toll free T1-800 241 4141 (flies direct*

to Barcelona), www.delta-air.com
United Airlines: *toll-free T1-800 538 2929 (flights to Madrid only)*
Air Canada: *toll-free T1-888 247 2262, www.aircanada.ca*

Airlines with routes to Spain via Europe include:
British Airways: *toll-free T800-247 9297*
KLM: *toll-free T800-777 5553*
Lufthansa: *toll-free T800-645 3880*
TAP Air Portugal: *toll-free T800-221 7370*
Virgin Atlantic: *toll-free T800-862 8621*

Discount travel agents in North America

Air Brokers International, *323 Geary Street, Suite 411, San Francisco, CA 94102, T1-800-8833272, www.airbrokers.com Consolidator and specialist on RTW fares and Circle Pacific tickets.*
Council Travel, *205 E 42nd Street, New York, NY 10017, T1-8888-COUNCIL, www.counciltravel.com Student/budget agency with branches in many other US cities.*
Discount Airfares Worldwide On-line, *www.etn.nl/discount.htm A hub of consolidator and discount agent links.*
International Travel Network/Airlines of the Web, *www.itn.net/airlines On-line air*

travel information and reservations.
STA travel, *5900 Wiltshire Boulevard, Suite 2110, Los Angeles, CA 90036, T1-800-7770112, www.sta-travel.com Discount student/youth travel company with branches in New York, San Francisco, Boston, Miami, Chicago, Seattle and Washington DC.*
Travel Cuts, *187 College Street, Toronto, ON M5T 1P7, T1-800 6672887, www.travelcuts.com Specialist in student discount fares, IDs and other travel services. Other Canadian city branches:*
Travelocity, *www.travelocity.com On-line consolidator.*

long-distance coach company, **Eurolines**, 52 Grosvenor Gardens, London SW1, T020-77308235, offers several departures several times a week in the summer (once a week out of season) from London to Spain; the journey to Barcelona takes 24 hours. Single fares are about £80; return fares around £110. Peak-season fares between the end of July and the beginning of September are slightly higher. There are discounts for anyone under 26, senior citizens and children under 12. The main bus and coach station in Barcelona is the Estació d'Autobuses Barcelona-Nord, C/Ali Bei 80, metro Arc de Triomf. This has services departing for destinations all over Spain; general information T93 265 65 08. The bus station next to Barcelona-Sants station is a stop on many routes, but it is the final destination for most Eurolines coaches.

Train London to Barcelona by train takes at least one day, and you'll have to change trains in Paris and perhaps again closer to the Spanish border. The **Eurostar**, T08705 186 186, www.eurostar.com takes just three hours from London Waterloo to Paris Gare du Nord and offers some very good deals if you book early enough (at least 14 days in advance).

From Paris, there are several options to Barcelona. The most comfortable is the Train-Hotel *TALGO*, which leaves Paris-Austerlitz every evening at 2047, arriving in Barcelona-Sants station the next morning at 0900. The cabins are divided into three

Flying from Australia and New Zealand

Air France, T02-9231 1030 (Sydney), www.airfrance.com

Air New Zealand, T09-357 3000 (Auckland), T02-9937 5111 (Sydney), T03-9670 3499 (Melbourne, www.airnz.nz)

British Airways, T02-9258 3200 (Sydney); T09-3568960 (Auckland), www.british-airways.com

Cathay Pacific, T02-9931 5500 (Sydney), www.cathaypacific.com

Gulf Air, T02-9244 2199 (Sydney)

Japan Airlines (JAL), Y02-9272 1111 (Sydney); T09-9262 6000 (Sydney); T09-307 3687 (Auckland)

Qantas, T09-357 8900 (Auckland), www.qantas.com.au

Singapore Airlines, T02-9350 0100 (Sydney), T131011 (reservations); T09-3793209 (Auckland)

South African Airways, T02-9223 4448 (Sydney), www.szz.co.za

Thai Airways, T02-9251 1922 (Sydney); T09-3773886 (Auckland), www.thaiair.com

United Airlines, T02-9292 4111 (Sydney); T131777 (reservations); T09-3793800 (Auckland), www.ual.com

Virgin Atlantic, T02-9352 6199, www.flyvirgin.com/atlantic

Discount travel agents in Australia and New Zealand

Flight Centres, 82 Elizabeth Street, Sydney, T13-1600; 205 Queen Street, Auckland, T09-3096171. Also branches in other cities.

STA Travel, T1300-360960, www.statravelaus.com.au 72 Harris Street, Ultimo, Sydney, and 256 Flinders Street, Melbourne. In new Zealand: 10 High Street, Auckland, T09-3090458. Also in major

towns and cities and university campuses.

Travel.com.au, 80 Clarence Street, Sydney, T02-929011500, www.travel.com.au

UK Flight Shop, 7 Macquarie Place, Sydney, T02-92474833

www.ukflightshop.com.au They also have branches in Melbourne, T03-9600 3022, and Perth, T08-9226 1222.

---

classes (first, business, and tourist) and start at 568 French Francs one-way, offering surprisingly good value for money. Travellers are also given a free **Art Ticket** (see page 30) which gives discounts on some of the main museums, and saves another €15. The *TGV* service from Paris to Barcelona via Montpellier takes around nine and half hours, or it's possible to take a night train and change at Port Bou or Narbonne (about 15 hours). Prices vary considerably depending on the season and the time of day. Under-26s are automatically entitled to a reduction. For more information, log on to www.sncf.fr which is also in English.

Rail deals There are plenty of rail deals available but they are only worthwhile if you intend to travel extensively throughout Europe. EU citizens over 60 and under the age of 26 and non-EU citizens who've been resident in Europe for six months are all eligible for the three-zone **InterRail** pass (currently £275 if you're over 26 or £199 if you're under 26). A one-zone pass costs £129 for under-26s and £185 for over-26s. Passes entitle holders to a month's unlimited travel across Europe, plus 30-50% discounts on trains to cross-Channel ferry terminals. The **Euro Domino Pass** offers unlimited travel for three days for £69 within Spain. For more information, contact Rail Europe, 179 Piccadilly, London W1V 0BA, T08705 848 848, www.raileurope.co.uk The **North American EuroRail** pass can be bought in the USA, for 15, 21, 30, 60 or 90 days and is valid in 17 countries; note that it excludes some European countries (such as the UK) and countries outside the EU. Two weeks' travel is $388 for those under 26; those over 26 can get a 15-day pass for $554, a 21-day pass for $718, or a month for $890. The **Youth Pass** offers unlimited travel for 10 or 15 days within a 2-month period for $458 and $599 respectively, and the **Spain FlexiPass** offers 3-10 days travel within Spain

Essentials

Ferries between the UK and France

Condor Ferries, The Quay, Weymouth, Dorset DT4 8DX, T0845-345 2000, www.condorferries.co.uk Crossings between the Channel Islands and Poole to St Malo.

Hoverspeed Fast Ferries, International Hoverport, Dover CT17 9TG, T08705-240241, F01304-240088, www.hoverspeed.co.uk, info@hoverspeed.co.uk Crossings between Dover-Calais, Folkstone-Boulogne, Newhaven-Dieppe.

P&O Portsmouth, Peninsular House, Wharf Road, Portsmouth PO2 8TA, T0870-2424999, F02392-864211, www.poportsmouth.com Crossings from Portsmouth to Le Havre and Cherbourg.

SeaFrance, Whitfield Court, Honeywood Road, Whitfield, Kent CT16 3PX, T08705-711711, www.seafrance.com Dover-Calais crossings.

P&O Stena Line, Channel House, Channel View Road, Dover CT17 9TJ, T0870-600 0600, F01304-863464, www.posl.com

during a two-month period for $155-$365. For more information contact **Rail Europe US**, T1-800-438 7245, www.raileurope.com

Car

Barcelona is 1,555 km (966 miles) from London, and going by car will take you a good day and a half of steady driving

Be aware that motorways in France and Spain charge expensive **tolls** and ferry fares (see below) can be extremely expensive in high season. Petrol is considerably more expensive than in North America but roughly the same price in France, Spain and the UK. The main access road into Barcelona is the A-7 autopista, which crosses the eastern Pyrenees and runs down past Girona and Figueres. The tolls are high, which means that the other main access road, the N-II, is clogged with traffic most of the time. For information on driving through France, check the following websites: www.iti.fr (route planner), www.autoroute.fr (for information on motorways), www.equipment.gouv.fr (roads and traffic info).

All vehicles must be roadworthy, registered and insured, at least for third party. The **Green Card**, an internationally recognized proof of insurance, is no longer compulsory, but it is advisable to carry it all the same as it offers fully comprehensive insurance. EU driving licences are accepted throughout the European Union. For more information, contact the AA (T08705 50 0600) or the RAC (T08705 722722) or log onto their excellent websites, www.theaa.co.uk and www.rac.co.uk which provide everything from suggested routes, to roadside hotels and restaurants so that you don't go to sleep at the wheel.

In general, standard European **road rules** apply. The legal alcohol limit is a mere 0.05%, and foreigners can get fined up to €300 on the spot. The speed limit in built-up areas is usually 50 km (31 miles) per hour, on major roads it goes up to 100 km (62 miles) per hour, and is 120 km (74 miles) per hour on motorways.

Ferry

There is one ferry linking the UK directly with Spain: **Brittany Ferries**, The Brittany Centre, Wharf Rd, Portsmouth, PO2 8RU, T08705 360360, www.brittany-ferries.com, operate the Plymouth to Santander service. Prices range dramatically according to the season, but you should count on paying between £350-750 for a car and four people. Travel with all companies in July and August is extremely expensive, and it's always worth checking out mid-week crossings and crossing at unsociable hours. **SeaFrance** always seem to come through with the best deals.

Eurotunnel

For more information, T08705-353153, www.eurotunnel.com

The fastest way of crossing the Channel by car is with **Eurotunnel,** which runs trains through the Channel Tunnel. Prices begin at £130 for a flexible return ticket if you depart before 0700 and the journey time is a mere 40 minutes including boarding and disembarking. It's worth looking into the prices of day return tickets and getting one each way – this isn't strictly legal, but it can cut costs dramatically.

Touching down

Electricity The current in Spain is 220V 50hz. North American appliances will require an adaptor, and UK plugs will need a two-pin adaptor, easily available in Barcelona. Some of the older hotels and hostals still have 125V circuits which means your machines just won't work, so check before bringing them.

Emergencies (see under safety, page 31)

Laundry There are only a few coin-operated laundries around, mostly in the old city. The **Lavanderia Tigre**, C/Rauric 20, (Barri Gòtic) will do service washes or there are coin-operated machines.

Time Local time is one hour ahead of GMT/UTC. Clocks go forward one hour on the last Sunday in March and back one hour on the last Sunday in October (as in the UK).

Telephone codes All telephone numbers listed in this book must be dialled in full. The access code to Spain from abroad is +34.

Toilets Public toilets are not common, although you'll find them in train stations. It's usually ok to use the ones in bars and cafés. You might have to use the bin next to the loo for your toilet paper if the system can't cope, particularly in out-of-the-way places. There are usually toilets in the big department stores, too.

Weights and measures Spaniards use the metric system. Decimal places are indicated with commas, and thousands with points.

Water The water in Barcelona is perfectly safe to drink, although it tastes odd. Locals drink bottled water in preference, and you will be given bottles in restaurants if you ask for water.

Touching down

Barcelona airport

Barcelona's international airport is in **El Prat de Llobregat**, 12 km (7 miles) to the south of the city. Each airline is allocated to one of the two main terminals – A and B – for its arrivals and departures. The airport authority produces a small fold-out map of the airport which can be useful for orientating yourself and is available from the helpful information desks in all terminals. There are tourist information offices in both Terminals A and B, as well as car hire agencies, plenty of ATMs, bureaux de change (open 0700-2300), **left luggage** offices, cafés and small shops. The left luggage lockers are located at the far end of Terminal B and cost €3.60 for 24 hours. The train station is clearly visible, joined to both terminals by a long passageway across the top of the car park and the airport buses stop at the main entrances of both terminals.

For flight information, the general number is T93 298 38 28, or check the website www.aena.es/ae/bcn/ homepage.htm which also gives details of flight delays or changes

Several transport options are available for the 12- km (12-mile) journey from Barcelona airport to the city centre

Getting there

By train Trains link the airport with Barcelona's Plaça de Catalunya and Estació de Sants every 30 minutes from 0608 to 2238. Tickets cost €2.20, and the journey time is about 25 minutes.

By bus The **A1 Aerobús** departs from both terminals A and B, and ends up at the Plaça de Catalunya, with stops at the Estació de Sants and Plaça d'Espanya. Buses depart Monday-Friday 0530-2315 every 15 minutes; Saturday and Sunday 0600-2320 every 30 minutes. Journey times depend on the traffic, but usually take about 30-mins off-peak. Tickets cost €3.

Essentials

Essentials

Airline contact numbers in Barcelona

You can also find airlines listed under Línias Aèrias/Líneas Aéreas in the phone book.
Air France: *T93 379 7463,*
www.airfrance.com
British Airways: *T902111333,*
www.british-airways.com
Delta: *T901116946, www.delta-air.com*

EasyJet: *T902299992, www.easyjet.com*
Go: *T901333500, www.go-fly.com*
Iberia: *T902400500, www.iberia.com*
KLM: *T93 379 54 58,*
http://en.nederland.klm.com
Virgin Express: *T90-046 7612,*
www.virgin-express.com

By taxi Taxis wait outside both terminals; it costs about €18 (including the €1.80 airport surcharge but not including a tip) depending on traffic and where you are going in the city. Fares rise after 2200 and at weekends and there are supplements for luggage and pets. Use the taxi ranks outside the terminals, there are usually plenty of taxis waiting, rather than the touts who will approach you in the arrival halls.

Tourist information

The Ajuntament (city council) and the Generalitat (Catalan government) both offer tourist information services, and the Generalitat also has a cultural information centre which will tell you everything you need to know about theatre, festivals, opera and art exhibitions. The main **tourist office** offers a package containing a good city map, a booklet detailing all the museums, including temporary exhibitions, with full details of times and prices, and three leaflets covering suggested walking tours (Roman Barcelona, *modernista* Barcelona, and Romanesque and Gothic Barcelona) for a mere €3. The city-run tourist offices also offer an array of bus and walking tours, and sell the Barcelona Card, and Art Ticket (see below).

Discount passes The **Barcelona Card** offers unlimited travel on public transport (metro, buses, FGC, airport bus, the shopping *Tombbus*, the *Tibibus* up to Tibidabo) plus discounts at dozens of shops, restaurants and museums. It costs €15.70 for one day, €18.70 for two days and €21.70 for three days. Children under six go free and there are discounts for children between 6 and 15. **Ruta del Modernisme**: this ticket is available from the Centre del Modernisme in the Casa Amatller, Passeig de Gràcia 41, T93 488 01 39, www.bcn.es It offers discounts of up to 50% at many of the main *modernista* attractions (and some restaurants) which lie along the route, and you'll get a helpful booklet with the ticket. The attractions included in the ticket include: the Palau Güell, the Palau de la Música, la Pedrera, Fundació Antoni Tàpies, Museu d'Art Modern, Sagrada Família, and the Museu de Zoologia. Tickets cost €3.61.

The **Art Ticket** offers free entrance to six of Barcelona's best art museums: the Museu Nacional d'Art de Catalunya (MNAC); Fundació Joan Miró; Fundació Antoni Tàpies; Centre de Cultura Contemporània de Barcelona (CCCB); Centre Cultural Caixa Catalunya (La Pedrera); Museu d'Art Contemporani de Barcelona (MACBA). It costs €15 and is available from tourist offices, all the six museums listed above, and through the Caixa Catalunya (savings bank), who run the www.telentrada.com website.

Tourist information offices

Ajuntament (City Council), www.barcelonaturisme.com: Plaça de Catalunya, T90-630 12 82, calling from outside Spain T93 368 97 30. For hotel information T93 304 32 32. Open daily 0900-2100. This is the main information centre, set in underground offices just opposite the El Corte Inglés department store. It offers an information service, a bookshop and gift shop, a hotel booking service (reservations for the same day only) and a bureau de change. There's also coin-operated Internet access. There are other **branches** across the city:
Plaça Sant Jaume (in the corner of the Ajuntament building), Barri Gòtic. Open Mon-Sat 1000-2000, Sun and public holidays 1000-1400.
Estació Barcelona-Sants Open winter Mon-Fri 0800-2000, Sat, Sun and public holidays 0800-1400, open daily in summer 0800-2000.
Palau de Congressos (Trade Fair office), Avinguda Reina Maria Cristina, Montjüic. Open 1000-1400 and 1600-2000.
Airport (Terminals A and B). Open daily 0900-1700.
In summer, there's a **mobile information booth** next to the Sagrada Família and you'll also see pairs of red-coated tourist information officers wandering around the old city and the main sights.

Generalitat (Catalan Government), www.gencat.es: Palau Robert, 107 Passeig de Gràcia, T93 238 40 00, www.gencat.es/probert Open Mon-Fri 1000-1900, Sat 1000-1430. Here you will find information about Catalunya, including plenty about Barcelona. It's a great resource if you want to spend time outside the city, with leaflets covering all kinds of activities, natural parks, rural accommodation and festivals in the remotest corners of the region. There are also interesting exhibitions on various aspects of Catalunya, and a good bookshop which also stocks some maps.
Centre d'Informació de la Virreina, Palau de la Virreina, La Rambla 99, T93 301 77 75. Open Mon-Fri 1000-1400 and 1600-2000, ticket sales Tue-Sat 1100-2000, Sun 1100-1430. This is the information service for the Generalitat's culture department, with details of concerts, exhibitions and festivals, including the prestigious **Grec festival** (see page 44). There's a good bookshop here, with a range of titles in English. The main Generalitat bookshop is across the street under the arcades of the Palau Moja and offers a complete range of their titles, including the useful guides to hotels and casas rurales (rural accommodation).

Safety

In general, Barcelona is pretty safe; violent crime is less common than in many other major European cities, but street crime – bag-snatching and pick-pocketing – is rife, and tourists are the major target. Take some simple precautions and be especially wary anywhere in the old city, particularly along La Rambla, or in El Raval.

If you have the bad luck to be robbed, go immediately to the **Turisme Atenció** station on La Rambla 43, (T93 301 90 60 or T93 344 13 00, open daily 24 hours), a special police service for assisting tourists, with multilingual staff. You'll have to make a statement and fill in a special form (denuncia). These are printed in four languages (English, French, German and Italian) and you should be given a copy with an order number. Sadly, it's highly unlikely that your goods will be recovered, but you'll need the police report for your insurance claims. If you are robbed outside the city, look up the nearest Policía Nacional station (Comisaria) in the phone book and report the crime to them.

The other thing to watch out for in Barcelona is the **traffic**: no one ever stops at pedestrian crossings, so don't stride out until you know you are safe. Cars and

It's not hard to get into the habit of keeping a relaxed eye out for possible thieves, and you'll find friendly shopkeepers and waiters will remind you if you forget

Sightseeing tours and discount tickets

Bus The special sightseeing **Bus Turístic** has two loops, a red/north one and a blue/south one, taking in the best-known sights of the city. Most are adapted for wheelchairs and all have multilingual guides. The buses run every 20 to 30 minutes, allowing you to get off and on at will, on either route. A one-day ticket (buy it on the bus) is €12, two days (consecutive) €15, and children cost €10.24 a day (under-fours go free). You get a number of discount vouchers with the ticket which need not be used the same day.

The **Rodamolls** (quay-wander) is a special bus service which runs from the statue of Columbus to the Port Olímpic and back. The service runs from April-October 1100-2130, daily from mid-June to mid-September and weekends only for the rest of the time. Tickets cost €1.80. For more information, contact the tourist information office.

The **Tibibus** is run by the funfair on top of Tibidabo (see page 163). The service begins at Plaça Catalunya and runs past the Park Güell on its way up to the Plaça Tibidabo on top of the mountain; hours are the same as those of the funfair (see page 163).

Balloon The sightseeing balloon, between the Port Olímpic and the Zoo, doesn't really count as a tour as it is static, but it's a great way to get a feel for the lay-out of the city, with fabulous views. **Globo Turístic**, Passeig de Circumval.lacio, T93 342 97 90, www.globusbcn.es Open Monday-Thursday 1030-1800, Friday, Saturday and holidays 1030-2000; adults €12, children €10.24, free for children under 6.

Boat The pretty, old-fashioned **Golondrines** (swallow boats) sail elegantly around the harbour, or you can take more modern boats out for slightly longer trips. They leave from the Moll de la Fusta (just in front of the Columbus monument) and run from October to March. For more information, call T93 442 31 06, or visit the website www.lasgolondrines.com Tickets for the shorter ride cost €3.16, and include

motorbikes will zoom away from traffic lights, and accelerate just as the lights change from amber to red, so watch out.

There are several **police forces** in Spain. The *Guárdia Urbana* wear pale blue and navy uniforms and mainly deal with traffic and general law and order. The *Policía Nacional* deal with more serious crimes and wear dark blue and white outfits. The Catalan government's police, *Mossos d'Esquadra*, are in charge of traffic control in Catalunya although not in the city itself. They can be identified by their navy and blue uniforms with red trim. Finally, there's the *Guardia Civil*, who wear military green uniforms and can often be seen at customs points (such as those at the borders with Andorra and France) but are rarely spotted in Barcelona.

The Basque separatist group *ETA* have been responsible for a bombing campaign on mainland Spain. There have been few incidents and few casualties, but, as *ETA* have specifically targeted tourist areas in the past it's worth being vigilant. For up to date information, contact the foreign office or visit the web site www.fco.gov.uk/travel

Where to stay

Don't leave it until the last minute and don't go blithely expecting to find somewhere to stay when you get there

Barcelona is now one of the most popular weekend destinations in Europe, with the result that finding accommodation can be a truly nerve-shattering experience. It won't just happen. Book as early as possible. It's worth bearing in mind that many of the cheaper establishments will only take reservations on the day you want to arrive, but they are often full by midday so call early. There are several accommodation-finding stops out on the breakwater where there are snack bars in high summer. The longer tour costs €7.98.

A number of smaller, motorized launches do impromptu tours of the harbour for as little as €1.80 – just walk along the Moll de la Fusta and check out the handwritten signs.

Walking tours The tourist office organizes walking tours of the Barri Gòtic; they are very popular and you would be well advised to book early. Tours in English begin at 1000 on Saturday and Sunday; in Catalan and Castilian, they start at noon, and cost €6. The tourist office also publishes three booklets with suggested walking tours covering Roman Barcelona, modernista Barcelona, and Romanesque and Gothic Barcelona, which costs €0.90, or can be bought as part of a package (along with a map and museum guide, see above) for €3. For more information, check the website www.barcelonaturisme.com

The **Museu d'Història de la Ciutat** (see page 70) organizes a series of tours through the Barri Gòtic, including the wonderful night time tour (Nit al Museu) of the buildings around the Plaça del Rei. Times change, so call ahead for information call T93 315 11 11, www.bcn.es/icub

Bike tours For bicycle hire, see page 39. **Un Cotxe Menys**, C/Esparteria 3, T93 268 21 05 (metro Barceloneta) offer excellent 22-hour day tours and 33-hour night tours with snacks and bike hire included. Booking is essential. **Mike's Bike Tours**, mobile tel 669281476, haynesworld@hotmail.com Engaging English-speaking bike tours around the city, including a break for lunch on the beach (bring a picnic or money for lunch); cost is €21 for the 3½ to 4-hour tours.

Train The **Montjüic Tourist Train** is actually a rickety trolley dragged uphill from the Plaça d'Espanya to Miramar. It runs every 30 minutes from June to September between 1100-2030, and costs €1.80 for a ticket, or €3 for an all-day ticket that lets you jump on and off at will.

---

agencies who will, usually for a fee, take the sting out of finding a place to stay and do it for you. The other effect of Barcelona's soaring popularity is that demand for accommodation has pushed prices up, and there are very few bargains left in the city. The business hotels used to offer discount weekend rates, but those have virtually disappeared. Some online accommodation agencies offer good discounts, particularly for the grander hotels, so it is worth checking them out for good deals (see page 55 for websites).

Most of the cheaper places can be found in the old city. The hip, youthful Raval area can offer some good deals because the neighbourhood, although on the up, is still a bit seedy. The Barri Gòtic is the noisiest and perhaps the most characterful district with most of the budget back-packer hostels, as well as a couple of swanky gems. The Eixample and the business district around Diagonal offer the grandest hotels – both modernista palaces and gleaming towers of steel and glass. There are relatively few places near the seaside, although that will probably change, and just a sprinkling of hotels around the edge of the city, which offer a breath of fresh air from the city crowds, but are often geared towards business travellers. Transport links to the centre are excellent, so you need never feel stranded. **Areas**

The old classification system which had several different categories of establishment has been thankfully simplified by the Catalan government to include just two: hotels and pensions, the difference being that all rooms in hotels have to have certain amenities including en suite bathrooms. The word 'hostal' is still used, and usually means a budget hotel with fewer amenities than a regular hotel. Hotels are given a ranking of **Categories**
For accommodation listings see page 253

Essentials

Safety precautions

Lock your cash and valuables up in the hostal or hotel if they have a safe, and only carry as much money as you think you are going to need with you, particularly if you are going out drinking. Drunk tourists are an even bigger target than sober ones. Make a photocopy of your passport and insurance documents and store them separately.

Don't put your purse or wallet in your back pocket, or in the outside pocket of a backpack.

If possible, carry a bag that straps over you and carry it in front of you.

If you sit down at a café, keep your valuables in sight – or on your lap if need be – and don't put them under the table. Try not to pull out bulging wallets or notes of big denominations in full view.

There are some common scams to watch out for (so common, that you will almost certainly see them happening right in front of you at some point during your stay). If a stranger tells you that a bird has crapped on you, or drops their keys right in front of you, you can be sure that there will be a partner right behind you who is about to snatch your bag. Watch out for people offering you flowers on the street your wallet will be emptied without you feeling a thing. Don't listen to hard luck stories about losing money and needing the fare home. Be wary on metros and buses and keep a hand on your bag.

If you hire a car, always park it in a supervised car park. Foreign and hired car plates are common targets for thieves.

Emergency numbers:

Ambulance/Ambulància T061 or T93-300 20 20

Fire service/Bombers/Bomberos T080

National Police/Policia Nacional T091 or T93 290 33 26

Municipal Police/Policia Municipal T092 or T93 291 50 92

Catalan Government Police/ Mossos d'Esquadra T088 or T93 300 91 91

Emergency repairs (24 hours): Electricity (all companies) freephone 900 77 00 77; Gas/Gas Natural freephone 900 75 07 50; Water/Aigües de Barcelona T93 265 1111

one to five stars depending on the quality of the services and amenities and pensions are ranked from one to three stars. The star-system will give you a very rough idea of what to expect, but don't rely on it.

Cases de pagès If you plan on travelling into Catalunya, it's worth visiting the Palau Robert (see page 127), which provides information on *cases de pagès* (B&B type accommodation, often in old farmhouses). The Catalan government publishes guides (available from their bookshop on La Rambla, opposite the Palau de la Virreina) which cover hotels, *cases de pagès*, and camping sites throughout Catalunya. They provide basic details of amenities and addresses but don't comment on the kind of accommodation.

Paradores If you are interested in staying in one of the five state-owned paradores in Catalunya, contact one of their representatives in your own country (addresses below) or check out the website: www.parador.es info@parador.es

UK *Keytel International*, 402 Edgware Road, London W2 1ED, T020-7616 0300, F7616 0317, paradors@keytel.co.uk **USA** *Marketing Ahead*, 433 Fifth Avenue, New York 10016, T1-212-6869213, F6860271, tollfree 1-800-22311356, mahrep@aol.com *PTB Hotels*, 19710 Ventura Boulevard, Suite 210, Woodland Hills, California 91364, T1-818-8841984, F8844075, tollfree T1-800-6341188, info@paradors.com *PTB Miami*, 100 N.Biscaye Boulevard, Suite 604, Miami, Florida 33132, T1-305-3718057, F3587003, outptbxmania@aol.com **Australia** *Ibertours Travel*, Level 1, 84 William Street, Melbourne, Victoria 3000, T03-96708388, F96708588, ibertours@bigpond.com

Youth hostels

There are several youth hostels, some run
by the official Youth Hostel Association,
and other private ones. For a list, see page
262. An excellent resource is the website
www.hostellinginternational.com

Youth Hostel Associations abroad:
Australia: Australia Youth Hostels
Association, 422 Kent Street, Sydney,
T02-92611111.
Canada: Hostelling International
Canada, Room 400, 205 Catherine Street,
Ottowa, ON K2P 1C3, T800-66357777.
England and Wales: Youth Hostel
Association (YHA), Trevalyan House,
8 St Stephen's Hill, St Albans, Herts AL1 2DY,
T0870-8708808,
www.yha/england/wales.org.uk
France: FUAJ, 7 Rue Pajol, 75018 Paris,
T1-4498727.

Germany: Deutsches
Jungendherbergswerk, hauptverband,
Postfach 1455, 32704 Detmold, T5231-74010.
Ireland: An Oige, 61 Mountjoy Street,
Dublin 7, T01-8304555, ww.irelandyha.org
New Zealand: Youth Hostels
Association, PO Box 436, Christchurch 1,
T03-379970.
Northern Ireland: Youth Hostel
Association of Northern Ireland,
22 Donegal Road, Belfast BT12 5JN,
T01232-324733.
Scotland: Scottish Youth Hostel
Association (SYHA), 7 Glebe Crescent,
Stirling FK8 2JA, T01786-451181,
www.syha.org.uk
USA: Hostelling International-American
Youth Hostels (HI-AYH), 733 15th Street
NW, Suite 840, PO Box 37613, Washington
DC 20005, T202-7836161, www.hostel.com

Essentials

Getting around

The old town is easy to get around without public transport, but some of the sights – like the Park Güell or Tibidabo – are further afield. The tourist information office can provide you with a metro or bus map, but in general, the public transport service is cheap, efficient and user-friendly. Local buses and the metro are run by the city transport authority (*TMB*) which runs a useful website, www.tmb.net and has an information office in the metro station at Plaça Universitat. There are two underground train lines – from Plaça de Catalunya to Reina Elisanda, Les Planes or Avinguda del Tibidabo; and from Plaça d'Espanya to Cornelià – which connect with the metro. These are run by the Catalan government railways, the **Ferrocarrils de la Generalitat de Catalunya** (FGC, often known simply as 'els Ferrocarrils'). They have an information office at Plaça Catalunya FGC station, T93 205 15 15, and a website, www.fgc.catalunya.net Local trains run by the national Spanish network, *RENFE*, are called *cercanías* (in Castilian) or *rodalies* (in Catalan), but these are unlikely to be of any interest to visitors, unless you are planning a trip out of town (see page 55). The T010 information line (see above) will also give out transport information.

For further information call the city transport authority on T93 318 70 74

The main hub for buses is the Plaça de Catalunya. The bus stops display clear, user-friendly bus maps listing the stops made on each route. A single ticket currently costs €0.96, and you can't buy any of the *targetas* (discount passes) on board. Use the machine behind the driver to stamp your pass if you have one, or your ticket. You board buses at the front and get off in the middle or rear doors. If you have a *targeta*, you can make a free transfer within 75 minutes. Buses on most routes usually run from Monday-Saturday 0600-2230, with a less frequent service on Sundays.

Bus

Nitbus: the **night bus** service runs from 2230-0400 daily and covers 16 routes. Most pass through Plaça Catalunya, and arrive roughly every half hour. The discount passes (*targetes*) mentioned above are not valid; you must buy a single ticket, €1, or

Essentials

Useful bus routes

The buses are not an especially useful way of getting about town - most of the sights are within walking distance of each other, and those further out are generally more accessible by metro. There are some exceptions, though, notably the Park Güell and along the seafront from Barceloneta to Vila Olímpica.

Park Güell

No *24* from Carmel to Paral.lel, via Park Güell, Gràcia, Placa Catalunya, Placa Universitat.

No *28* from Carmel to Plaça Catalunya, via Parc Creuta del Coll, Park Güell, Gràcia and Pg de Gràcia

No *17* from Pg Joan de Borbó to Avda Jordà, via Via Laietana, Pg de Gràcia, Gràcia and Avda Tibidabo.

No *19* from Sant Genís to Port Vell, via Hospital Santa Pau, Sagrada Família, Avda Paral.lel and Drassanes.

No *45* from Horta to Pg Marítim, via Hospital Santa Pau, Catedral, and Port Vell.

No *59* from Plaça Maria Cristina to Pg Marítim, via Sarrià, Gran Via, Rambla, Port Vell, and Parc de Ciutadella.

Vila Olímpica:

No *14* from Bonanova to the Vila Olímpica, via the Gran Via, the Rambla, Monument a Colom, and Parc Ciutadella.

No *45* from Horta to Pg Marítim, via Hospital Santa Pau, Catedral, and Port Vell.

No *59* from Plaça Maria Cristina to Pg Marítim, via Sarrià, Gran Via, Rambla, Port Vell, and Parc de Ciutadella.

invest in the 10-trip night bus *targetes* which costs €6.32. These are only available on board the bus.

TombBus: this has nothing to do with cemeteries; it's just a special shopping service bus which runs between Plaça de Catalunya and the smart boutiques and the L'Illa shopping mall (see page 68) on Diagonal. Again, normal *targetes* are not valid and you will need to buy a single ticket, €1.08.

Metro There are five metro lines in Barcelona, which are identified by number and colour. A single ticket currently costs €0.96. Push your ticket through the machine and wait for it to reappear. You won't need it at the exit, but you should hang on to it in case of an inspection. At interchanges, the direction of the train is indicated by the destination at the end of the line. For example, if you wanted to go to the Sagrada Família, you would take Line 5, direction Horta. The metro is open Monday-Thursday 0500-2300, Friday-Saturday 0500-0200, Sunday 0600-2400.

Tram & funicular The city transport authority also operates the funiculars up to Tibidabo and Montjüic and the lovely little *Tramvia Blau*, a refurbished old tram which trundles up to Plaça Dr Andreu to meet the Tibidabo funicular. For more information, call the *TMB* on T93 443 08 59, or check the website, www.tmb.net The Tramvia Blau runs from Plaça Kennedy (just by the FGC train stop, Avinguda del Tibidabo) up Plaça Andreu. It costs €1.65 one way and €2.40 for a return ticket. It runs about every 15-30 minutes between 0900-2130, weekends only in winter (mid-September to mid-May) and daily in summer.

The *Tibidabo funicular* runs from Plaça Andreu to the top of the hill at Plaça Tibidabo. A single ticket costs €1.80 and a return is €2.40. It runs end-September to early June, Saturday, Sunday and public holidays 1030-1930; in May also Thursday and Friday 1000-1800; June-August Monday-Friday 1030-2230, Saturday and Sunday 1030-1330. Montjüic funicular leaves from the Paral.lel metro station and heads up to Avinguda Miramar. Single tickets cost €1.50 and return tickets are €2.40. Open November-April Saturday and Sunday 1045-2000, April-June daily 1045-2000, June-October daily 1100-2300.

Telefèric/ Cable cars There are two cable cars in Barcelona: one meets the Montjüic funicular (see above) and then sways up to the top of the mountain. The other swings across the harbour

Discount passes

The following are available in all metro stations and valid for metro, buses and FGC and local trains

T-10: *ten single rides for €5.33. It can be shared.*

T-50/30: *fifty single rides within thirty days of buying the pass; it costs €22.28, and can also be shared.*

T-Mes: *monthly ticket which allows unlimited trips, and costs €35.09. You'll also need to get an identity card with photograph from the* **TMB** *or* **FGC** *offices, €1.20.*

T-Dia: *unlimited travel for one person for one day; it costs €4.03. Passes for three, and five days are available,costing €9.63 and €14.45 respectively.*

from Montjuïc to Barceloneta. The cable car ride (Telefèric de Monjüic) begins at the funicular station on Avinguda Miramar and heads up toward the castle right at the top. Open June to mid-September, Monday-Friday 1115-2000, Saturday-Sunday 1115-2100; mid-September to October daily 1130-1945 and 1600-1930; November-May weekends only 1115-2100. Tickets cost €2.85 single and €4.06 return.

The cable car ride (**Telefèric de Barceloneta**), across the bay is one of the most thrilling activities in Barcelona, and definitely not for people suffering from vertigo. To add some spice to the excitement, the cable car has been out of service for years and was only recently refurbished. It's already had some problems though, so don't count on it running while you are there. It runs from the Miramar station at the end of Avinguda Miramar down to Passeig de Joan de Borbo in Barceloneta, with a pause at the tower near the new World Trade Center. Open daily mid-October to February 1030-1730, March to mid-June and mid-September to mid-October 1030-1900, mid-June to mid-September 1030-2000. Ticket prices are hefty: €8.43 for a return or €4.21 for a single. If you don't want to get into the cable car, you can just climb the tower at the Barceloneta end,€3.61, for stunning views.

Taxi City taxis are yellow and black, and there are usually plenty of them. There's a taxi stand on Plaça de Catalunya, just across the street from the main tourist information office. They can be hailed if the green light is showing on the top, and the sign saying *lliure/libre* (free) is illuminated. Prices are reasonable, but bear in mind that there are supplements for luggage, pets, and after 2200 and at weekends. The current minimum fare is €1.80. Taxi drivers won't necessarily have change for big notes. It's likely that you'll manage to flag down a cab, but if you prefer to book one, here are a few numbers. Note that cab meters begin as soon as you order the cab, and few cab drivers speak English.

Taxi numbers: **Barnataxi**, T93 357 77 55; **Fono-Taxi** T93 300 11 00; **Ràdio Taxi**, T93 225 00 00; **Taxi Ràdio Mòbil**, T93 358 11 11. Receipts and complaints: To ask for a receipt, say '*un rebut, si us plau*' or '*un recibo, por favor*'. It should include the fare, the taxi number, the driver's tax number, the registration number of the car and the date. If you want to make a complaint, insist on getting as many of these details as possible as well as the driver's signature if you can. Call the T010 information line, which also deals with transport issues, for help on how to deal with complaints.

Car Driving in Barcelona is not to be recommended: the streets are tiny or clogged or both, the drivers crazy and the parking appalling. Cars are very handy if you decide to explore the Catalan countryside, though (for more information, see page 211). Remember that all vehicles must be roadworthy, registered and insured, at least for third party. Most valid driving licences from other countries are accepted in Spain, and you should keep your licence and your Green Card insurance with you at all times. Drivers are required by law to wear seatbelts, and to carry warning triangles, spares (tyres, bulbs, fanbelt)

The Green Card, an internationally recognized proof of insurance, is highly recommended

Essentials

Car hire

Companies abroad (with offices in Barcelona):
Britain:
Avis, T0870 6060100; **Budget**, T0800 181181; **Europcar**, T0345 222525; **Hertz**, T08705-996699; **National Car Rental**, T020-7278 2273.
North America:
Avis, T1-800-3311084; **Budget**, T1-800-5270700; **Hertz**, T1-800-6543001; **Holiday Autos**, T1-800-4227737; **National**, T1-800-CAR-RENT; **Thrifty**, T1-800-3672277.
Australia:
Avis, T1800-225533; **Budget**, T1-300-362848; **Hertz**, T1800-550067.
New Zealand:
Avis, T09-5262847; **Budget**, T09-3752222; **Hertz**, T09-3676350.

Car hire companies (in Barcelona):
Avis, T902 135 531, www.avis.com   Several offices in Barcelona, including the airport and Estació de Sants station.
National (which is a partner of the Spanish car hire firm, Atesa), T902 100 101, www.national.com, www.atesa.es   Several offices in Barcelona, including the airport and Estació de Sants.
Vanguard, T93 439 38 80, C/Villadomat 297, www.vanguardrent.com   Local car hire firm, which also rents out motorbikes and scooters.
Europcar, T93 491 4822, www.europcar.com   Several offices in Barcelona, including the airport and Sants station (this tel no is for the Estació de Sants office).

and the tools to fit them. You may also need to fit special prisms to your headlights for driving on the right if you are bringing your car from the UK or Ireland (so that they dip to the right). Watch out for the sudden surge at traffic lights about to turn red – you might get hit from behind, so don't brake suddenly. If you have foreign number plates, or have hired a car in Spain (which will also have easily identifiable plates), you should park your car in a secure car park to avoid getting your car broken into. Don't ever leave anything valuable in it.

For information, take a look at the AA and RAC websites, www.theaa.co.uk and www.rac.co.uk

Car and motorbike hire Car hire is surprisingly expensive. The best deals can usually be found on the web and some companies do deals with the airlines, so it's worth checking out prices before you arrive. Other useful websites offering cheap car hire deals include www.dialaflight.com, who offer good deals even if you don't buy your airline ticket with them. In Barcelona, you'll find car hire offices at the airport, and at Barcelona-Sants train station, as well as several local firms dotted around the city. You will need to have held a valid driving licence for at least a year, and be over 21 (25 for some firms). Check out what is included in the price: unlimited mileage, 16% VAT (IVA), and full insurance cover rather than the third-party minimum (seguro obligatorio). You will probably have to give an imprint of your credit card as security, and you will need to show your passport. **Petrol** costs roughly the same as in France and the UK – which will come as a shock to North Americans. Unleaded is sense plomb/sin plomo, regular is super and diesel is gas-oil. Petrol stations are marked on the city map given out by the tourist office.

Parking **Parking** can be a nightmare in this overcrowded city. Don't park in front of a sign reading 'Gual Permanent', which means that the entry has the right to 24-hour access and be careful that you are not parking in a residents-only zone (much of the old city). You'll get a ticket if you park illegally (although it's also true that hardly anyone pays them). If you are parking your car overnight in the city, consider using a supervised car park, especially if you are driving a foreign or hired car. There are two big car park companies: SABA and the city-run firm SMASSA. SABA car parks: Plaça de Catalunya, Plaça Urquinaona, Arc de Triomf, Avenguda Catedral, Passeig de Gràcia, C/Diputació/C/Pau Claris. SMASSA car parks: Plaça dels Angels-MACBA, Moll de la Fusta, Avenguda

Francesc Cambó, Avenguda Paral.lel. If you are driving into the city for the day, the **Metro-Park**, a park-and-ride facility in Gloriés, is easily the most convenient option. For €4.22, you'll get a ticket which will also give you unlimited travel on the metro and city buses. The car park is located at Plaça de les Gloriés in the Eixample, at the junction with three of the big city access roads (the Diagonal, Meridiano and Gran Via). For more information, call T93 265 10 47.

If you return to your car to find that it has disappeared and a triangle sticker has been left in its place, then it's been towed away by the municipal police. You'll have to get a Spanish or Catalan speaker to call T93 428 45 95 to find out which pound it has gone to. You'll probably be charged a parking fine, and will have to pay a charge of €95 if you collect the car within four hours, plus €1.70 for every hour after that.

There are very few cycle lanes in Barcelona, and cycling through the maze of narrow streets in the old city isn't very practical. However, if you're happy to brave the kami-kaze drivers on the roads in the Eixample, bikes can be a practical way of seeing the sights which are more spread-out (see page 119). Bikes are great if you want to do some off-road cycling in the wonderful Parc de Collserola (see page 161) behind Tibidabo. The tourist information centre on Plaça de Catalunya has a free cycling map of the city. Bike hire: **Al Punt de Trobada**, C/Badajóz 24, T93 225 05 85, www.lasguias.com   Bike (including tandems) and roller-blade rental. They also offer guided tours by arrangement.

Bicycle
Cycling along the seafront, from Barceloneta, along the Port Olímpic and out to the beaches of Mar Bella is a great way to spend an afternoon

Decathlon Ciutat Vella, Plaça Villa de Madrid 1-3, T93 342 61 61. Scenic, C/Marina 22, T93 221 16 66, www.gdesigners.com/scenic   Bike and roller-blades for sale or rental. They can also organize day or night-time excursions. **Un Cotxe Menys**, C/Esparteria 3, T93 268 21 05. 'One car less' (in Catalan) do bike rentals, and offer guided tours (see above, bike tours). **Bicitram**, C/Marques de l'Argentera 15 and 27. Bike and roller-blade rentals, **Biciclot-Marítim**, Passeig Marítim, Platja de Barceloneta, www.biciclot.net   Bikes and tandems for rent – great location on the beach front if you want to cycle along the boardwalk.

Barcelona is a delightful city to walk around, and seeing it on foot is definitely the best way to appreciate its myriad charms. It's a relatively small city and all the sights of the old town are within easy walking distance, although it's easy to get lost in the maze of tiny streets of the old neighbourhoods. The enormous grid of the Eixample can some-times be a bit disorientating, but you'll come across creamy *modernista* mansions, and down-to-earth neighbourhood cafés which are well off the tourist trail. There are free maps provided by the tourist information offices, and the big department store *El Corte Inglés*, but it's worth investing in the slightly better tourist office map (€1.20). There's also a great interactive Barcelona street map at www.bcn.es/guia   For walking tours, see page 16.

Foot

Entertainment and nightlife

Barcelona is one of the best cities on the Mediterranean for showing you a good time, with hundreds of bars, live music venues, and clubs, ranging from old-fashioned *bodegas* with massive oak barrels, to ultra-trendy nightclubs. For lovers of electronica, the *Sonar festival* (see page 44) is an unmissable three-day party celebrating the latest in multimedia music and art. (For details of bars and clubs, see pages 238-242)

Theatre, opera, classical music and dance are all extremely popular, and music lov-ers should try to get in a performance at Domènech i Montaner's stunning *modernista* masterpiece, the **Palau de la Mùsica Catalana** or at the much-loved **Liceu** opera house. The local theatre and dance groups are some of the most innovative in Spain,

For the most comprehensive and up-to-date information, look at the cultural agenda section of the city's website, www.bcn.es

with a year-round programme of challenging work, often incorporating mime and multimedia which cross language divides. The *Grec festival* (see page 44) is an annual event, showcasing new and established talents in all areas of the arts, and the *Festival de Música Antiga* (see page 42) in May gives you the chance to hear early music from world-famous performers in atmospheric spots like the Plaça del Rei.

Listings magazines
(see also media page 52)

The weekly listings guide *La Guia del Ocio*, €1, is on sale at most news kiosks. You'll also find entertainment supplements in the local daily newspapers (see below), usually in the Friday or Saturday editions. The quarterly bilingual style magazine *b-Guided* (which includes a map) is on sale at some kiosks and distributed free in some bars and restaurants. There are dozens of free, usually very glossy and stylish, magazines distributed in bars and music shops: among them are *AB*, *Go Mag*, *Punto H*, *Venus* and *Mondo Sonoro*.

For information on theatre, classical music and opera, visit the Palau de la Virreina (see page 63), or the cultural information office underneath the Centro d'Art de Santa Monica and pick up the free leaflets. There's a monthly leaflet entitled *Informatiu Musical*, which gives details of concerts in all genres, and another monthly booklet called *butxaca*, which gives comprehensive music, theatre, exhibition and cinema listings.

Booking tickets

Theatre, opera and concert tickets can be often be bought through one of the two savings banks, or through their websites or over the phone. Some concert tickets can be bought through music shops (look out for the details on posters) or at FNAC. The Palau de la Virreina (see page 63) also has a ticket sales counter. **FNAC**, El Triangle, Plaça de Catalunya 4, T93 344 18 00. FNAC offers an efficient ticket service and is mainly good for pop and rock concerts.

Servi-Caixa, T90 233 22 11, www.serviticket.com This service is run by the biggest savings bank. You'll see the Servi-Caixa machines next to the ordinary ATMs at the banks; using your credit card, you cam buy some metro tickets (T2 and T50/30, see above) and get information and tickets for a number of big attractions, including the Port Aventura theme park, the Teatre Nacional and the Liceu. You can also order tickets by phone (some of their staff speak English) or over the Internet.

Tel-entrada, T902 10 12 12, http://cec.caixacet.es This ticket service is offered by another savings bank, the Caixa Catalunya (main branch is on Plaça de Catalunya). Buy tickets over the counter at any of its branches, or use the phone line (again, there are some English-speakers) or buy them on the Internet. You can also buy half-price tickets at the Plaça de Catalunya office (cash only) three hours before performances begin. They also have a phoneline for those calling from outside Spain, T+34 93 479 99 20.

Holidays and festivals

Barcelona loves to party, and the calendar is packed with excellent festivals showcasing music, art and dance; popular neighbourhood festivals animated by the pandemonium of giants, dragons, fatheads, human castles, fire-running (see box, page 42); and city-wide festivals which get everyone out onto the streets and squares. It's always worth checking dates and details in advance, as changes are made annually. For more information, check out the cultural agenda section of the city website, www.bcn.es, or visit the tourist information office (see page 31), or call the T010 information line. For a list of local festivals elsewhere in Catalunya, see below.

Public holidays

On public holidays, many bars and restaurants close down, as do most shops. The transport system runs restricted services. Some of these public holidays are celebrated with some of the city's best festivals .

1 January	**Cap d'Any** *(New Year's Day)*
6 January	**Día des Reis** *(Three Kings)*
March/April	**Divendres Sant** *(Good Friday)*
March/April	**Pasqua Florida** *(Easter Monday)*
1 May	**Festa del Treball** *(Labour Day)*
May/June	**Dillluns de Pasqua Granada** *(Whit Monday)*
24 June	**Sant Joan** *(St John's Day)*
15 August	**L'Assumpció** *(Assumption)*
11 September	**Diada Nacional de Catalunya** *(Catalan National Day)*
24 September	**La Mercè** *(Our Lady of Mercy)*
12 October	**Dia de la Hispanitat** *(Columbus Day)*
1 November	**Tots Sants** *(All Saints' Day)*
6 December	**Dia de la Constitució** *(Constitution Day)*
8 December	**La Imaculada** *(Immaculate Conception)*
25 December	**Nadal** *(Christmas Day)*
26 December	**Sant Esteve** *(St Stephen's Day)*

Essentials

Calendar of events

1 January: *Cap d'Any/Noche Vieja* Street parties and much public carousing accompany the arrival of the New Year, when Spaniards customarily eat a grape with each stroke of the clock at midnight. Big parties in the clubs – although prices can be high. **5 January**: *Cavalcada des Reis* The Three Kings arrive in Barcelona along the Moll de la Fusta by the harbour, and a parade winds up through the streets, tossing out sweets to the children. Spanish kids get their Christmas presents the following day. **17 January**: *Festes dels Tres Tombs* A parade on horseback through the streets. Part of the district festival of Sant Antoni, it was once massive but has become increasingly muted.

January

February/March: *Festes de Santa Eulàlia and Carnestoltes/Carnaval* The festival in honour of Barcelona's patron saint coincides with the beginning of Carnival. The city council organizes parades and events throughout the city. Carnival is not such a big event as in other parts of Spain, but there's a great party atmosphere all the same. Lots of parades and parties, and the festival culminates with the *Enterrament de la Sardina*, (burial of the sardine) usually up in Montjüic to mark the end of winter.

February/ March

23 April: *Sant Jordi* Big celebration for the festival of the patron saint of Catalunya. Lovers traditionally exchange gifts on this day - books for men and roses for women, although nowadays the gifts are quite often given the other way around. Thousands queue in front of the Generalitat (see page 80) to see the rose display and there are hundreds of book and flower stalls. **Holy Week**: *Setmana Santa* Easter celebrations don't compare with those in the south of Spain, but there's plenty of interest. Holy Week begins on Palm Sunday with the blessing of the palms, and there's a series of processions at the cathedral on Good Friday. There's a taste of the south in the Good Friday parade which leaves from the Església de Sant Agustí in the Raval, with a teary Virgin as the centrepiece, and surrounded by cloaked and hooded members of the various confraternities. **Late April/Early May**: *Feria de Abril* A taste of Seville in Barcelona, with ten days of Andalucian flamenco and carousing.

April

Essentials

Giants, dragons and castles in the air

Catalans might congratulate themselves on their seny (common sense or wisdom) most of the time, but when the festivals hit, they lose themselves to the madness of their other great national characteristic, rauxa or uncontrollable emotion. After years of repression during the Franco era, Catalunya is celebrating its festivals with ever-greater verve and exuberance, resuscitating centuries-old customs and traditions in an outpouring of national pride and optimism.

Correfoc

'Fire-running' is an ancient, paganistic custom. Pandemonium rules as drummers beat a pulse-quickening march through the streets, heralding the arrival of fleets of dragons (dracs), weaving their way through the crowds, hissing and spitting fire. Packs of sprightly demons (demonis) cavort around them, taunting them and the crowd with fireworks fizzing at the end of long poles. Youths step out from the crowd to prevent the dragons passing, standing or kneeling in their path and getting showered with sparks as they shout '¡No pasaran¡' (You will not pass). Kids throw fire crackers and send up fireworks, adding to the general mayhem. Dragons have been a integral part of Catalan mythology for centuries: Sant Jordi, who famously slew the dragon and saved the princess, is the patron saint of the city ever since he came to the rescue at the battle of Mallorca in 1229, and the Moors are credited with bringing over a baby dragon in the ninth century. It was captured and killed by Guifré the Hairy's father, who skinned and displayed it in the earliest version of the correfoc.

Fire-running can be dangerous, and the tightly packed mass of the crowd means escape isn't easy – if you want to join in, you should wear old cotton clothes and put something protective over your head and mouth. The old custom of lighting bonfires has more or less died out – it was just too dangerous – but occasionally you'll see a small one with devils leaping around it.

Gegants and Capsgrossos

Back in the Middle Ages when the Corpus Christ festival was the biggest event on the Catalan calendar, gegants or giants made their first appearance - perhaps as a means of grafting on pagan and folkloric characters to the stories of the Christian tradition, although no one really knows. They are enormous figures made of wood and papier-mâché who lumber along in the main parades – see them at the Festa of La Mercé and other big city festivals. The

May **1 May**: *Dia del Treball* Labour Day brings parades from the different trade unions out onto the streets. **Early May**: *Saló International del Còmic* One of the biggest and best comics fairs in the world. More information from www.ficomic.com **11 May**: *Festa de Sant Ponç* A delightful, old-fashioned market is held along Carrer Hospital in the Raval to celebrate the patron saint of beekeepers and herbalists. **Mid-May**: *Festa de la Diversitat* Under the auspices of the anti-racism organization, SOS Racisme, this is a three-day festival celebrating the city's ethnic diversity. It's held along the harbour front and attracts huge crowds. **Mid-May**: *Barcelona Poesia* The International Poetry Fair has been combined with the Jocs Florals to create a week-long celebration of poetry. Much of it is in Catalan, but the final day features poets in many other languages. **May**: *Festa de la Bicicleta* There's a lot of work to be done before cycling is as safe and easy in the city as it should be, but this festival brings bikes out onto the streets. Held one Sunday in May, it's a popular event for families who come together for a 10-km (6-mile) bike ride around the city. Special bike hire available. **May**: *Festival de Flamenco* and *Festival de Música Antigua* The *Flamenco festival* is held at the Centre de Cultura Contemporani (see page 110), and different locations around the Raval, including outdoor concerts on the Rambla de Raval. The excellent *Festival of Early Music* takes place in different locations around the city, and brings together official city ones (sometimes on display in the Palau de la Virreina, see above) represent King Jaume I and his queen, Vilant of Hungary, but the oldest are the Gegants del Pi, which are kept in the church of Santa Maria del Pi.

The capsgrossos or 'fatheads' are squat leering versions, who accompany the giants on the parades. Mischievous little figures, some of the modern ones bear the faces of famous celebrities and politicians. If you want to see some of the most spectacular modern example being made today, visit El Ingenio (see page 86).

Castellers

The art of building human towers unites seny and rauxa; the sheer bizarreness is rauxa, but the careful co-operation which it involves is pure seny. The custom dates back to the 1700s, and has undergone a major revival in recent years. It's a perfect example of the civic pride which marks the Catalans, each person having an important part to play, and the whole depending on the co-operation and steadiness of each individual. The bottom layer with its central sturdy knot of people known as the pine cone or pinya looks like a rugby scrum, upon which, gradually, carefully, the layers are built up. A child (the aixedor) provides the support for an even

smaller child (the anxenata) who nimbly scampers to the top and grins like a gargoyle, waving to the crowd below. Details of forthcoming 'trobadas' (casteller meetings) are listed in newspapers, or you can call the T010 information line.

Sardana

The grave, stately dance of the Catalans is a world away from the flamboyant headiness of Andalusian flamenco. It's an ancient folkloric tradition which was revived during the 19th-century Renaixança, when the Catalans were rediscovering their cultural identity, and now it can be seen most weekends in towns and villages. You can watch it – or join in – on Saturdays at 1830 or on Sundays at noon in the cathedral square, or on Plaça Sant Jaume on Sunday evenings. But beware – you have to take it seriously, and it's not as easy as it looks. You should always join the circle on the man's left, so as not to break up a couple. The cobla (the band) strike up, and a knot of people, sometimes as few as four, will link hands and circle with slow sedate steps, interspersed with longer, rising ones. The circles get bigger and bigger as more and more people join in. True aficionados will wear espadrilles tied with coloured ribbons.

Essentials

internationally celebrated performers; try and hear a concert in the Saló de Tinell (see page 71), or on the steps of the old Palau de Rei.

May/June: *Corpus Christi* Little remains of what was once the city's biggest festival; the old tradition of 'l'ou com balla' was rescucitated in the 1980s, and now you can see the dancing of the hollow egg on the fountain in the cloister of the Cathedral of La Seu, and at the Museu Frederic, the Ateneu Barcelonès, and in the Casa de l'Ardiaca (see page 75).
June: *Trobada Castellera* A great chance to see the Catalan folk tradition of building human castles when some of the most accomplished casteller groups show their stuff in the Plaça Sant Jaume. **Early June**: *Marató de l'Espectacle* Two nights of non-stop alternative performances at the Mercat de les Flors. For more information, call the **Associació Marató de l'Espactacle**, T93 268 18 68. **21 June**: *Festa de la Música* Imported from France, this musical festival is celebrated with city-wide free concerts on the streets. **23 and 24 June**: *Festa de Sant Joan* The craziest and most exuberant festival in the Catalan calendar, this marks the beginning of the summer and the feast of St John the Baptist explosively - literally. Bonfires and non-stop fireworks have given it the popular name of *la nit del foc* (the night of fire), and everyone goes mad. Swig back some cava, eat the sweet cakes known as the *cocas de Sant Joan*, and party till dawn when you should traditionally be at

May/ June

the beach to watch the sunrise. The next day is, thankfully, a public holiday. **28 June**: *Dia per l'Alliberament Lesbià i Gia* Gay pride parade though the city.

June/July **June/July**: *Sonar* An unmissable three-day festival of multimedia and music, culminating in the all-night rave, *Sonarnit*. For more information, call T93 442 29 72, www.sonar.es, advance@sonar.es **June/July**: *Classics als Parcs* A series of classical concerts are held throughout the early summer in the city's parks and gardens. For more information, call T93 413 24 00, www.bcn.es/parcsijardins **June/July**: *Festival del Grec* This is the city's biggest performing arts festival, which gets its name from the Greek-style amphitheatre built on Montjüic for the 1929 International Exhibition. There's an excellent selection of drama, music and dance from at home and abroad. For more information, contact the Palau de la Virreina.

August **Mid-late August**: *Festa Major de Gràcia and Festa Major de Sants* Gràcia's neighbourhood festival has grown massively. The streets are beautifully decorated (there's a prize for the best), music nightly out on the squares, and all the Catalan favourites *gegants*, *castells* on the opening day in Plaça Rius i Taulet and culminates with a *correfoc* and fireworks. The **Festa Major de Sants** is smaller, but still lively.

September **11 September**: *Diada National de Catalunya* The anniversary of the heroic defeat of the besieged city by the Bourbons in 1714 has become the Catalan National Day. Flags are hung from balconies and there are parades, speeches and rallies. **Mid-September**: *Dies de Dansa* Three-day festival of dance with locations around the city; some of the outdoor performances are spectacular. **24 September**: *Festes de la Mercè* Perhaps the biggest and best festival in Barcelona's calendar, dedicated to Our Lady of La Mercè, a massive week-long celebration, with dragons, fatheads, human castles, fire-running and fireworks. There are all kinds of free events, a swimming race across the harbour, as well as concerts and the BAM alternative music festival. **End-September**: *Festa Major de la Barceloneta* Big, popular neighbourhood festival with all the folkloric trimmings. **End-September**: *Mostra de Vins i Caves* Wine and cava festival which coincides with the celebrations of La Mercé (see above). Plenty of stalls with traditional Catalan produce like *embutits* (cured sausage), cheeses and anchovies.

October **October**: *Festival de Jazz de Ciutat Vella* Popular local festival with lots of jazz and blues events in the bars and clubs of the old city. **October to December**: *International Jazz Festival* Big names and local bands play at the Palau de la Música, and Luz de Gaz, and lots of other bars and cafés around town.

November **1 November**: *Tots Sants (Castanyada)* All Saints Day is traditionally the day to remember the dead, when families visit the graves of their loved ones. It's traditional to eat *castanyas* (roast chestnuts), *moniatoes* (sweet potatoes) and *panellets* (little sweet cakes). **Early November**: *Fira del Disc de Col.lectionista* Barcelona hosts one of the biggest second-hand record fairs in Europe. For more information, call T93 233 20 00, firadisc@catradio.com

December **1-22 December**: *Fira de Santa Llúcia* The feast day of Santa Llúcia marks the beginning of the Christmas season; get all your Christmas goodies from the Christmas market which huddles around the cathedral, including figurines for Nativity scenes – among which is the infamous Catalan *cagoner* (see page 76). **25-26 December**: *Nadal and Sant Esteve* Christmas and the Catalan equivalent of Boxing Day are low-key family affairs, with big family lunches; kids beat the Christmas Log, shouting '¡Caga Tio¡ ¡Caga¡' (Shit, log! Shit!) and the log bursts open to reveal a small gift. The main present giving doesn't happen until 6 January – (see box page 41).

Food and drink

Catalan cuisine is justly renowned throughout Spain. Catalans don't have to go far to get all the produce they could want: the mountains are filled with game, the lush plains bring in vegetables and rice, and there's a lively fishing industry along the coast. There are more than 30 fresh produce markets in Barcelona alone, the most famous is la Boquería (see page 63) where you can marvel at the range and freshness of the goods. The result of all this abundance is a remarkably varied cuisine which makes the most of fresh ingredients, and combines the produce of the mountain, plains and sea in unusual but delicious ways.

Underpinning all the dishes are the hallowed four sauces, used at various points in the preparation of the food: *sofregit*, *samfaina*, *picada* and *allioli*. *Sofregit* was mentioned in the first serious Catalan cookery book, the *Llibre de Sent Soví* written in 1324; it's made by slowly cooking onions until they are almost caramelized, then adding fresh tomatoes, sometimes some herbs, and letting the whole lot reduce. *Samfaina* is similar but adds aubergines, courgettes, and roasted peppers in a kind of ratatouille and is often used to accompany meat and fish dishes. *Picada* (meaning 'peck' or 'sting'), which is made with all kinds of ingredients, the most common being fried bread, garlic, garlic, almonds, saffron, pine nuts and chopped chicken livers. They are ground down to a paste and added to the cooking process, imparting a delicious sweet and sour flavour. *Allioli* is a kind of garlicky mayonnaise made of olive oil, garlic and salt (no eggs), used as a condiment with grilled meats and poultry.

The staple dish is *pa amb tomàquet*, country bread rubbed with fresh tomatoes and sometimes a little garlic, drizzled with olive oil and sprinkled with salt. The bread is sometimes toasted and topped with anchovies, cured meat and slabs of cheese – these are *torrades*, the heartiest and most authentic Catalan tapas. Sturdy, country dishes using pork, lamb, and rabbit are very popular, or you could try one of the tasty stews simmered slowly in an earthenware pot, called *cassoles*. Meat and fish are quite often served simply grilled, with just a dash of parsley or other herbs, and perhaps some *allioli* on the side, or cooked slowly in the oven (*al horno*) in a tomato-based sauce. The region around Figueres, known as the Alt Empordà, is famous for its *mar i muntanya* dishes, combining seafood and game, such as *mandonguilles amb sèpia* (meatballs with cuttlefish), or *gambas con pollastre* (prawns with chicken). There are several delicious local vegetable dishes – like the refreshing *escalivada*, a simple salad made from roasted aubergine, peppers and onions, or *espinacas a la catalana*, spinach cooked with pine nuts and raisins.

The seasons bring traditional dishes too: *calçots*, which look like large spring onions, appear in spring and are roasted whole. Peel off the blackened outer spring and dip the white bulb into some romesco sauce – they're heavenly. Spring is also the time to try *faves a la catalana*, sweet new broad beans stewed with cured sausage. In October, the markets are filled with wild mushrooms (*bolets*), not popular elsewhere in Spain, but a passion for many Catalans; there's a stall at the back of the Boquería market (*Petras, Fruits del Bosc*) with an astonishing array. Fresh roasted chestnuts are eaten around All Saints, and Christmas is the time to try the hearty soup *escudella*, followed the next day by *carn d'olla*, the meat and vegetables used to make the soup. Rice dishes are also popular, with such variations on the famous Valencian dish *paella* as *arros nègre*, rice cooked slowly with squid ink and shellfish, or *fideuà*, which is made with tiny noodles cooked in a large flat dish with meat and fish. The most popular Catalan dessert is *crema Catalana*, a kind of local version of crème brûlée, a creamy, vanilla or lemon-flavoured custard with a topping of burnt caramel. *Mel i mató*, curd cheese with honey, is another delicious dessert, or you might also be offered a *postre de músic*, just a handful of dried nuts and fruits served with a glass of sweet wine like moscatel.

When to eat

Dinner is rarely eaten before about 2130, but, thankfully, you can fall back on tapas if you can't hold out that long

Catalunya is the power house of Spain and take their role very seriously; people work hard and don't party or eat as late as elsewhere in Spain. Dining times are still likely to be later than you are used to, but it's worth acclimatizing yourself or you'll end up facing a plastic menu with pictures like all the other starving tourists who can't wait any longer. Busy Catalans rarely have time for the old-fashioned *esmorzar de forquilla* ('fork breakfast', usually pig's trotters with stewed beans) any more; they tend to make do with a *café amb llet*, a large milky coffee and a pastry, perhaps the Majorcan import, *ensaïmada*, a doughy whirl of pastry dusted with icing sugar. *Chocolate y churros* isn't quite as popular in Barcelona as in other parts of Spain, but you can indulge your sweet tooth with a very thick hot chocolate and the doughnut-like twist of pastry at one of the delightful *xocolaterías* along Carrer Petritxol. A slice of *truita* (tortilla, thick omelette made with potatoes or other fillings) might fill a gap at about 1000. Lunch is eaten late – usually around 1430 – and this is a good time to eat if you are on a budget as many restaurants offer a very well-priced *menú del dia*, a fixed-price menu of several courses.

Tapas & snacks

Tapas are not really a Catalan tradition, but they have become increasingly popular nonetheless, with hundreds of bars offering anything from a few tidbits to a full menu. One of the nicest things to do in Barcelona is visit the harbour-side *tascas* (see page 81) which offer fresh seafood tapas – freshly caught grilled sardines, octopus (*calamares*) or whitebait (*pescaditos fritos*). The most common Catalan tapas are *truita*, thick omelettes made with potatoes, or other fillings (try a *truita* with artichokes), or slabs of cheese (pungent *manchego*, a cheese made from ewe's milk; *cabrales*, a creamy strong Asturian blue cheese; or *cabra*, goat's cheese) or a plate of local *embutits* (charcuterie).

There are dozens of different hams, but the *pernil salada/jamon serrano* is generally considered one of the best. *Torrades*, the traditional Catalan tomato bread (see above), topped with anything from cheese to anchovies, is an important part of the local tapas tradition, and some bars (called *llesquerias*) specialize in them. Other Catalan favourites include *escalivada*, a salad made from roasted aubergine, peppers and onions, or *esqueixada*, a similar salad with salted cod. Imports from the rest of Spain include *boquerones*, pickled fresh anchovies; *croquetas*, croquettes with tuna, chicken, ham or cheese; *empanadas*, pies filled with anything from tuna to spinach (*empanadillas* are the mini-version); *aceitunas*, olives; *mejillones*, mussels; *pulpo a la gallega*, octopus in paprika and olive oil; *anchoas*, salted anchovies; *chiperones en su tinta*, squid cooked in its own ink; *patatas bravas*, fried potatoes served with a spicy, creamy sauce.

The biggest import must be the sudden proliferation of Basque-style tapas bars, which offer their own brand of delicious tapas called *pintxos*; these are slices of crusty bread topped with all manner of toppings, and are best accompanied with the sharp, young Basque white wine called *txacoli* (pronounced 'chacoli'). Each *pintxo* has a cocktail stick in it, and your bill will be calculated by the number of cocktail sticks left on your plate. Sandwiches (*bocadillos*) are standard lunchtime snacks, usually made with crusty bread and served in most bars; your waiter will almost certainly ask you if you want the bread spread with tomato in the Catalan style (*amb tomàquet?* with tomato?).

Coffee & tea

Locals generally drink the large milky *café amb llet/café con leche* for breakfast. If you want a short strong espresso with a dash of milk, order a *tallat/cortado*. A simple espresso is a *café sol/café solo* and if you want a shot of brandy or rum in it ask for a *carajillo de cognac/de ron*. Decaffeinated (*descafeinado*) coffee is widely available, but you'll have to ask for it to be *de máquina* if you don't want to end up with coffee made with instant granules. It's virtually impossible to get a decent cup of tea in the city, unless you prefer herbal teas (*infusiones*), which come in a variety of flavours, including *manta* (mint) and *manzanilla* (camomile).

The *Damm* company has sewn up the local beer market, and you'll find their refreshing lager, Estrella, in almost every bar. They also produce a stronger, heavier version called Voll-Damm, and a darker, less common beer called Bock-Damm. Damm beers are served in bottles and on draught; a *caña* is a small draught beer, and a *jarra* is a about half a litre (almost 1 pint). If you want a shandy, ask for a *clara*. The most common spirits are whiskey, rum and vodka; *cuba-libre* (rum and coke), *gin-tonic* and *vodka-límon* are all popular choices. There are plenty of very classy cocktail bars (see page 242) if you want something sophisticated and international.

Beer, spirits & cocktails
▶▶ *For clubs and bars, go to entertainment page 238*

Catalunya has several wine-producing regions and most bars will have a basic red (*tinto*), white (*blanco*) and rosé (*rosado*). Some bars offer an exceptional range of wines. For a refreshing summer drink, order a *gaseosa*, which is red wine mixed with lemonade – much nicer than it sounds.

Wine
(see Trips from Barcelona page 224)

Bitter-kas, a dark red herby brew which tastes a bit like Campari, is the ubiquitous Spanish favourite. A simple glass of tonic water (*una tónica*) with ice and lemon is also refreshing. Many bars offer fresh orange juice, although they might think it's an odd thing to order after breakfast time. Mineral water is *aigua/agua*; you can get it with bubbles (*amb gas/con gas*) or still (*sense gas/sin gas*). *Orxata* is a delicious creamy drink made with ground tiger nuts, and served in dozens of old-fashioned *orxaterías* around the city.

Non-alcoholic drinks

Shopping

The designer shop *Vinçon* on the Passeig de Gràcia used to have the slogan 'I shop therefore I am' blazoned across its packaging. Shops range from tiny old-fashioned establishments which haven't changed in decades, perhaps even centuries, to grand glitzy shopping malls where you can get everything you want under one roof. Best buys are leather goods, designer fashions and unusual household designer goods. Local wines and deli items – such as jars of anchovies, dried salted cod or stuffed olives – are also good buys. As a general guide, the Barri Gòtic has most of the unusual one-off shops as well as branches of most of the fashion chains (see page 86) along Carrer Portaferrissa. The Eixample has all the big international fashion names as well as smart boutiques offering exclusive fashions and designer household goods, and the Raval has the fashionable vintage clothes stores and hip music outlets. The Ribera has lots of unusual fashion and interior design shops.

No other city makes shopping so easy, with more shops per capita than anywhere else in Europe

Look for signs saying *rebaixes* (in Catalan) or *rebajas* (in Castilian). The January sales begin after 8 January when all the Spanish kids get their Christmas presents. They last for about six weeks. There are also summer sales in July and August when prices are slashed by up to 50%.

Sales

Smaller shops tend to open from 0900 or 1000 to about 1330 and then reopen from around 1600 until 2000 or 2100. Large chain stores, department stores and shopping malls often stay open all day. Most shops, including supermarkets, close on Sundays.

Opening hours

Non EU residents can claim the tax back (16% on most items) on purchases of more than €90. Ask for a Tax Free Cheque (there are signs in the windows of most of the

Tax refunds & discounts

Essentials

bigger shops, including the big Spanish department store El Corte Inglés, which provide the service) when you buy your goods and then get it signed at the customs desk in the airport when you leave. You can cash it or get a credit-card refund at the Banco Exterio de España, just outside the departure gate in Terminal A. See page 30 for information about the Barcelona Card (available at the tourist office) which offers free public transport as well as discounts at some museums, theatres, and shops.

Sport

Since Barcelona hosted the Olympic Games in 1992 the city's sports facilities have been improving all the time. There's a helpful information centre next to the Piscina Bernat Martorell, (see below). The city's website, www.bnc.es is a valuable resource for information on sporting activities and locations within the city. The information centre, *Servei d'Informació Esportiva*, T93 402 30 00 has leaflets and information on local sports centres.

Spectator sports

Football   Football is the city's biggest obsession. *FC Barça's* slogan *Barça, mes que un club* (Barça, more than a club), shows the extent to which the club has been identified with Catalan nationalism over the years. The city has two first-division clubs: *FC Barcelona* and *RCD Espanyol*. Getting hold of tickets for the Camp Nou stadium is next to impossible, but you stand a good chance of seeing *Espanyol* play. The season runs from late August to May. FC Barcelona, Camp Nou, Avenguda d'Arisitides Maillol, Les Corts, metro Collblanc, T93 496 36 00, ticket hotline: T93 49 63 702, tickets from €18.07 to €90.36, www.fcbarcelona.com An online ticket sales service is on the way, but for now you'll have to buy tickets directly from the stadium ticket office. There are more season-ticket-holders than there are seats in the stadium, so getting your hands on a ticket could prove difficult. A week before each match, about 4,000 tickets go on sale. Call in advance to find out exactly when they will be on sale and then queue at least an hour in advance. Getting to see the B team who play in the adjoining mini-stadium is easier and if both teams are playing at home, tickets are usually valid for both matches. *RCD Espanyol Estadi Olimpic*, Passeig Olimpic, 17-19, Montjüic, metro Paral.lel then funicular, or metro to Plaça Espanya then shuttle bus (match days only), www.rcdespanyol.com Tickets can be purchased near the stadium entrance, but the atmosphere just doesn't compare to Camp Nou.

Bullfighting   Bullfighting just hasn't caught on in Catalunya. One of the bullrings has closed and the other is only used sporadically. The *corrida* season runs from April to September and bullfights are usually held on Sunday afternoons at 1700. Children under 14 are not admitted. *Plaza de Toros Monumental*, 749 Gran Via de les Catalanes 749, T93 215 95 70, metro Monumental. Tickets from €15 to €84.33.

Motor sports   The Circuit de Catalunya, about 20 km (12 miles) north of the city near Granollers, hosts the Formula 1 Grand Prix in the spring and other motoring events throughout the year, including the motorcycle Grand Prix. *Circuit de Catalunya Carretera de Parets del Vallés a Granollers*, Montmeló, T93 571 97 08, www.circuitcat.com Tickets can be ordered on line or purchased at the circuit.

Basketball   Basketball is popular throughout Spain. FC Barça's basketball team has a huge following, and their rival team, Club Joventut Badalona, have won the European Basketball Cup. The season runs from September to May. *FC Barcelona*, Palau Blau Grana (next to Camp Nou stadium), Avenguda d'Arisitides Maillol, Les Corts, metro Collblanc,

T934963675, tickets from €3 to €22.28, www.fcbarcelona.com *Club Joventut Badalona*, C/Ponent 143-161, Badalona (on the outskirts of the city), T93 460 20 40, metro Gorg, tickets from €14.45 to €19.87, www.penya.com

The Barcelona Open, a prestigious ten-day international tournament, takes place at Barcelona's smartest tennis club during the last week of April. Tickets are available through Servi-Caixa (see above) and through the club. *Reial Club de Tennis Barcelona-1899*, C/Bosch i Gimpera 5-13, Les Corts, T93 203 78 52, bus 63, 78, tickets €18 to €59.83, *bono*-tickets give you admission to all 10 days and cost €141.56-271.08, www.rctb1899.es **Tennis**

FC Barcelona also have an ice-hockey team and a roller-hockey team. For information on matches, call T93 496 30 00 or check out the website, www.fcbarcelona.com For address details, see above. **Hockey**

Essentials

Participation sports

The sea is great for splashing about, but if you want to put in some serious lengths, Barcelona has 27 municipal swimming pools. Call the sports information service (details above) to find out which of the municipal pools are closest to you. *Club de Natació Barceloneta*/Banys de Sant Sebastià, Plaça del Mar, T93 221 00 10, metro Barceloneta. Open June to mid-September Monday-Saturday 0700-2300, Sunday 0800-200, mid-September to June Monday-Saturday 0700-2300, Sunday 0800-1700. Admission for one day €6.17 for non-members. Very close to Barceloneta beach. Indoor and outdoor pools, gym, sauna, restaurant and café. **Swimming**

  Piscina Bernat Picornell, Avenguda de l'Estadi 30-40, T93 423 40 41, metro Paral.lel then funicular, or metro to Plaça Espanya then bus no 61. Open Monday-Friday 0700-2400, Saturday 0700-2100, Sunday 0730-1600 (until 2000 June-September). Admission to outdoor pool €4.21, all facilities €7.83. Magnificent pools used in 1992 Olympics. Indoor and outdoor pools, gym/weights room. There is a naturist session on Saturday mornings and films are shown during swimming sessions from 2230 during the *Festival del Grec* in June-July. *Piscina Municipal Folch i Torres*, C/Reina Amalia 31, T93 441 01 22, metro Paral.lel. Open Monday-Friday 0730-2230, Saturday 0800-1930, Sunday 0830-1330, admission €5.43. Three covered pools, sauna and weights room on the edge of the Raval.

There are plenty of fine golf courses in Catalunya. The website, www.golfonline.com, has links (excuse the pun) to a golf course directory. Call in advance from October-May if you want to play at weekends – sometimes they admit only members on Saturdays and Sundays. The closest courses to Barcelona are: *Club de Golf Sant Cugat*, C/de la Villa s/n, Sant Cugat del Vallès, T93 674 39 58, FGC from Plaça de Catalunya to Sant Cugat. Open daily 0800-2200. Rates: Monday €42, Tuesday-Friday €54, Saturday-Sunday €120. This attractive 18-hole course also has a bar, restaurant and pool. *Club de Golf El Prat*, El Prat de Llobregat, T93 379 02 78. Open daily 0800-2200. Rates: €74 non-members, €149 Saturday, Sunday. This club is out near the airport. It's probably easiest to get a taxi. In past years, this club which has two 18-hole courses has been used for the Spanish Open. You must be a member of a federated club to play. **Golf**

Rides through the countryside around Sant Cugat and the Serra de Collserola with *Hípica Severino de Sant Cugat*, Passeig Calado, Sant Cugat de Vallès, T93 674 11 40. All day-rides include lunch. Book in advance, particularly at weekends. *Hípica Sant Jordi*, Carretera de Sant Llorenç Savall, Km 42, Cànoves I Samalús, T93 843 40 17. Varied programme of rides and excursions suitable for all levels and ages. One of the owners is English, so language isn't a problem. **Horse-riding**

Yoga Getting bigger all the time in Barcelona. Classes are usually held in Spanish or Catalan, but non-beginners shouldn't find it difficult to cotton on. Call ahead for class times and details of the kind of yoga on offer. *Happy Yoga Centre*, Rambla de Catalunya 7, T93 318 11 07, metro Catalunya. *Equilibrium*, Ronda Universitat 33, T93 301 68 80, metro Universitat. Centre de *loga Iyengar de Barcelona*, C/Pelai 52-3, T 93 318 35 33.

Tennis The snooty *Reial Club de Tennis Barcelona-1899*, C/Bosch i Gimpera 5-13, Les Corts, T93 203 78 52, bus 63, 78 (see above), only lets in members. If you get in, you'll be playing with Spain's top professionals. But there are lots of other places to practise your serve. *Centre Municipal de Tennis Vall d'Hebron*, Passeig de la Vall d'Hebron 178-196, T93 427 65 00, bto@fctennis.org, metro Montbau. Open Monday-Saturday 0800-2300, Sunday 0800-1900. Rates: non-members €13.60 per hour, floodlights €3.91. Built for the 1992 Olympics, this centre has 17 clay courts, seven asphalt courts and two open-air pools. Raquets can be hired and balls are for sale. *Club Vall Parc*, C/de l'Arrabassada 97, T93 212 67 89, bus A6. Open 0800-2400 daily. Rates: €13 per hour, floodlights €3.61. Located on Tibidabo, this tennis club has 14 outdoor asphalt courts and two open air swimming pools. You can rent rackets but bring your own tennis balls.

Sailing & The Catalan coast has dozens of marinas and sailing schools – for more information
watersports (see page 227). For information on ports throughout Catalunya, contact the Dirreció General de Ports i Transports (Ports Esportius), Avda Josep Tarradellas, Barcelona 08029, T93 495 80 00, F93 495 84 70. If you want to do some sailing or windsurfing in the city itself, there are a couple of options. *Base Nàutica de la Mar Bella*, Avda de Litoral (between the beaches of Bogatell and Mar Bella), T93 221 04 32, www.basenautica.net Open daily winter 0930-1730, summer 0930-2100. Call or check the website for rates. Windsurf rentals, boat rentals, snorkelling equipment rentals and a wide range of courses. There's also the added bonus of DJ sessions in summer (see page 248). *Centre Municipal de Vela*, Moll de Gregal, Port Olímpic, T93 225 79 40, www.vela-barcelona.com Open Monday-Friday 0900-2100, Saturday and Sunday 0900-2000, office open daily 1000-2000. Sailing courses for all levels. *Reial Club Marítim de Barcelona*, Moll d'espanya s/n, T93 221 88 05, F221 62 53. Private club offering sailing courses and watersports.

Ice skating Part of the FC Barça complex, the rink is open to skaters whenever it is not in use for ice hockey games. *Skating Pista de Gel*, C/Roger de Flor 168, T93 245 2800, www.skatingbcn.com Open Monday 1700-2200, Tuesday-Thursday 1030-1330 and 1700-2200, Friday-Saturday 1030-1330 and 1700-2400. Rates: €6, plus €3 to rent skates.

Walking Barcelona is a very walkable city, with narrow atmospheric streets in the old city and
& parks fabulous architecture up in the Eixample, but there are also several parks if you want a leisurely stroll or a picnic. Walking along the seafront or around Montjüic is always a pleasure. **Parc de la Ciutadella** (see page 96), metro Arc de Triomf. The city's favourite park, with a boating lake, snack bars, the delightful Hivernacle café-bar, museums and zoo. Graceful esplanades and gardens. **Parc Joan Miró** (see page 134), metro Tarragona or Espanya. Concrete expanse studded with stubby palms and surmounted by Miró's enormous *Woman and Bird* sculpture. **Parc del Laberint d'Horta** (see page 165), metro Montbau. Utterly delightful, leafy park with a surprisingly difficult maze. It's quite far out, but well worth the trip. **Parc del Collserola** (see page 161), FGC Baixador de Vallvidrera. Large, beautiful natural park which seems a world away from the city. Hiking trails, mountain-biking trails, horse-riding (see page 49), natural springs and abandoned farmhouses. **Parc de l'Estacio de Nord**, metro Arc de Triomf. Modern grassy park with ceramic undulating sculptures by Beverly Pepper. **Park del Creuta**

del Coll, metro Penitents. Small park with a lake and artificial beach overhung by Eduardo Chillida's massive sculpture, *In Praise of Water*. **Park Güell** (see page 148), metro Vallcarca. Gaudí's famous, fabulous fairytale park in the hills above the city. **Parc de l'Espanya Industrial** (see page 154), metro Sants-Estaci. Modern, popular park with ten neon watchtowers overlooking a boating lake, and a massive dragon with a slide for kids.

Keeping in touch

Communications

There are hundreds of Internet cafés springing up, and you'll find coin-operated Internet access in some hostals, and in the main tourist information centre in Plaça Catalunya (see box).

Internet

Spain goes in for grand post offices. The one in Madrid is perhaps the most florid, but the main Barcelona office looks like a very imposing court. Sadly, despite all the grandeur, the postal service is not particularly reliable – don't count on your postcards getting home. Postboxes, marked *Correos y Telégrafos*, are yellow. Most *estancos* (tobacconists), marked with a brown and yellow symbol, sell stamps. You can send or receive faxes from any post office. If you want to receive your post here using the post *restante* system, use the address Lista de Correos, 08070 Barcelona, Spain, and bring your passport when you come to collect it. The *Postal Exprés* system is available at all post offices and guarantees next-day delivery to provincial capitals and 48-hour delivery elsewhere in Spain. It's the most reliable method of sending small packages within Spain. If you want to send something express, say it is *urgente*. Main post office: Plaça d'Anton López (at the port end of Vía Laietana), T93 318 3507. Open Monday-Saturday 0830-2130, Sunday 0900-1400.

Post (Correos)

The main telephone operator is the formerly state-owned company *Téléfonica*, who still retain the monopoly on local calls. Most public payphones (which you'll find on almost every street corner) will accept coins and pre-paid telephone cards: most newsagents, post offices and tobacconists sell pre-paid Téléfonica cards in denominations of €6 and €12 and €30. These are more economical for long distance or international calls, but cheaper still are the pre-paid cards from a variety of companies which provide a pin number and are much cheaper for international calls. Calls are cheaper after 2000 during the week and all day at weekends. Phones in bars and cafés usually have more expensive rates than public payphones.

Telephones
The code for Barcelona is 93, which has now been incorporated into the telephone number and must be dialled in full, even within the city

Locutarios (phone centres) are the cheapest method for calling abroad; there's one in the Plaça de Catalunya RENFE station, one in the Estació del Autobuses del Nord, and another in the Estació Sants and a sprinkling in the narrow alleys of the Raval. To make an **international call** from Barcelona, dial 00, wait until the tone changes to a higher pitch, and then add the country code from the list below and the rest of the telephone number minus the first zero if there is one. **UK 44**; **USA 1**; **Australia 61**; **Canada 1**; **Irish Republic 353**; **New Zealand 64**. To call **Spain from abroad**, the country code is **+34**.

Mobile phones can be used in Spain with a 'Roaming system'. You may need to contact your operator at home to set this up. Don't forget that you pay to receive mobile phone calls as well as make them when you are not in your home country. It's possible to buy and rent mobile phones in Barcelona, which may be a cheaper option if you think you will use your phone a lot. **Rent a Phone**, C/Numància 212, T93 280 21 31, www.rphone.es Rents mobile phones and accessories for use in Spain and other countries. Daytime rates are a hefty €0.90-1.20 per minute.

Media

The kiosks along the Rambla and some of the larger bookshops carry an enormous selection of international newspapers and magazines.

Newspapers & magazines
As in most of Spain, regional papers are much more popular than the national press, and Spanish taste runs more to tabloids than broadsheets

Avui, Catalan-language newspaper, with strong pro-Generalitat bias. *El País* (Catalonia edition), Spain's only real national daily, with socialist leanings. The entertainment and arts supplements appear on Fridays and Saturdays respectively. It is mainly in Castilian, but has Catalan-language pullouts on some days. *El Periódico*, a tabloid-style populist newspaper which appears in Spanish and Catalan. *La Vanguardia*, traditionally conservative newspaper which has got livelier over the years, and has an excellent local listings section on Fridays. English-language newspapers: *Barcelona Business*, business news in Catalunya. *Barcelona Metropolitan*, freebie newspaper directed at ex-pats, distributed in some hotels and bars. For listings look out for the weekly supplements in *La Vanguardia* and *El País* newspapers.

Television & radio

Spanish television can sometimes seem to consist almost entirely of game shows and ads. Most films are dubbed – look out for the VO (original version) sign in TV listings for undubbed films, and *Dual* symbol in the top corner. Not all TVs can receive dual-band movies. There are eight main channels: *TVE1* (la Primera) and *TVE2* (la Dos) are the state-run channels. *La Dos* is less commercial and has some good late night films. *TV3* is the Catalan regional channel, with the output entirely in Catalan. *Canal 33* is another Catalan-language regional channel, which offers more documentaries and sports programmes. *Antena 3* is a private channel which offers bland family-orientated programming and some spicy late night shows. *Tele 5* is another private channel, which got huge ratings for its equivalent of the *Big Brother* show. *Canal +* (Canal Plus) is a subscriber channel which shows mainly films, US TV re-runs, and sports. Its news and other programmes are shown unscrambled. *BTV* is the local city-run TV station in Barcelona which shows an interesting variety of programmes, often produced by students. Unfortunately, it can be quite hard to pick up.

There are hundreds of stations, mainly in Catalan, and particularly on the FM band. *Catalunya Mùsica* (101.5FM) is mainly classical; *Rádio 3* has a mixed bag of rock, pop and ethnic music. The *BBC World Service* can be found on shortwave at 15485, 12095, 9410 and 6195 KHz, depending on the time of day.

Health

EU residents are entitled to health care in the state hospitals, but it is still a complicated process and you will need to get the E111 form before you leave your home country. If you plan to visit Andorra, you will not be covered by the E11. Private insurance smoothes the path miraculously and is usually well worth investing in (see above) if you are a short-term visitor. This is also true for visitors from countries outside Europe, although it is possible to use the state facilities if you pay. If you don't have insurance, it's best to go to a private clinic. There are no reciprocal agreements for dentists, and dentistry can be pricey. Spain doesn't require any **vaccinations**, unless you are coming from an area infected with yellow fever, in which case you may be asked for proof of vaccination.

For minor ailments, a pharmacy should be able to sort you out. There are plenty which are open 24 hours a day (see below) or you can call the T010 information line, or

Internet cafés

EasyEverything, Ronda Universitat 35, T93 244 80 80, and La Rambla 41, www.inetcorner.net Both branches open 24 hours. The monster of the Internet cafés, there are 300 terminals in the Eixample branch and 450 at the branch on La Rambla. Prices depend on demand, but €0.90 will get you about 30 minutes at peak times (lunchtimes and early evening) and up to three hours early in the morning. It's worth getting a ticket for €3 or more to avoid queueing.

Inetcorner, C/Sardenya 306, T93 244 80 80, inetcorner@sagrada, familia and Plaça Ramon Berenguer 2, Entr, T93 268 73 55, www.inetcorner.net Open Mon-Sat 1000-2200, Sun 1200-2000. Friendly, English-speaking staff. Prices from €1.80 for the first 20 minutes then €0.10 per minute after that. The website is a good source of info on Barcelona.

Interlight C@fé, C/ Pau Claris 106 bajos, T93 301 11 80. Open Mon-Fri 0900-1000, Sat 1100-2200 and Sun 1200-2200. Relaxed spacious café with plenty of terminals. Prices

from €1.50 per hour or you can get a bono which will give you 10 hours for €12.

Cybermundo, C/Bergara 3 and C/Balmes 8. Open Mon-Fri 0900-0100, Sat 1000-0100 and Sun 1100-0100. Prices from €1.14 per hour. In an effort to draw in the crowds heading to

Idea, Plaça Comercial 2, T93 268 87 87, www.ideaborn.com Open Mon-Thu 0830-2400, Fri 0830-0300, Sat 1000-0300, Sun 1000-2300. Delightful bookshop, café and Internet centre, with comfy chairs, reading areas, books for sale or loan, magazines to flick through with your coffee. Prices start at €1.05 for 30 minutes.

Bcnet-Internet gallery Café, C/ Barra de Ferro 3, T93 268 15 07, www.bcnetcafe.com Open daily 1000-0100. Relaxed little Internet café in a cool brick vaulted space, just down a side street close to the Picasso museum. It's very friendly and has its own decks playing soothing music, as well as regularly changing art exhibitions on the walls. Rates are from €2.40 for 30 minutes.

T098, to find out details of which one is the closest to you. Pharmacies are identifiable by a large green cross on a white background. **24-hour pharmacies:** *Farmàcia Alvarez*, Passeig de Gràcia 26, metro Passeig de Gràcia. *Farmàcia Clapés*, La Rambla 98, metro Liceu.

Further reading

Burns, Jimmy, *Barça: A People's Passion* (Trafalgar Square, 2000). Fascinating history of the most football popular club in the world.

History & society

Carr, Raymond, *Modern Spain 1875-1980* and *The Spanish Tragedy; the Civil War in Perspective*. Excellent, well-written accounts of recent Spanish history.

Elliott, JH, *The Revolt of the Catalans* (Cambridge University Press, 1963). Vigorous, detailed account of the *Guerra dels Segadors* (the Reapers' War) and the Catalan rising of the 1640s.

Fernández Armesto, Felipe, *Barcelona: A Thousand Years of the City's Past* (London, 1991, out of print). An engrossing history, presented thematically rather than chronologically, which is sadly hard to get hold of now.

Hooper, John, *The New Spaniards* (Penguin, 1995). An updated version of his excellent portrait of Spain post-Franco, *Spaniards; A Portrait of the New Spain*.

Hughes, Robert, *Barcelona* (Harvill Press, 1992). A highly personal, immensely entertaining history of the city by the outspoken art critic who veers between boisterous enthusiasm and loving exasperation. One of the very best books on Barcelona.

Montalbán Vázquez, Manuel, *Barcelonas* (Verso, London, 1992). Beautifully written history of the city, covering culture, design, history and some of the city's personalities by one of Spain's foremost writers.

Tóibín, Colm, *Homage to Barcelona* (Simon & Schuster, London, 1991). Affectionate, wry account of life in the city in the 1970s and 80s by a well-known Irish journalist. His entertaining novel, *The South* (London 1990), is also set in the city.

Balcells, Albert, *Catalan Nationalism Past and Present* (Macmillan, 1996). Spirited, engrossing history, by one of Spain's foremost historians.

Conversi, Daniele, *The Basques, the Catalans and Spain* (Hurst and Company, 1997). Scholarly account of the development of Basque and Catalan nationalism.

Fiction & autobiography

Catalá, Victor, *Solitude* (Readers International, 1992). Celebrated novel by the woman writer Caterina Albert, which shocked the public when it first appeared with its candid account of a woman in love.

Dalí, Salvador, *Diary of a Genius* (Hutchinson, 1990). Entertaining diaries of a megalomaniac.

Genet, Jean, *The Thief's Journal* (Faber, 1973). Famous autobiographical account of life during the heyday of the Barri Xinés in the early part of the 20th century.

Marsé, Juan, *The Fallen* (Quartet, 1994). Grim tale of the struggles for survival in Barcelona after the Civil War.

Martrell, Joanot, *Tirant lo Blanc*, trans David H. Rosenthal (Johns Hopkins University Press, 1996). Rabelaisian, satirical tale of adventure, bawdy excess, and courtly love from the 1400s.

Mendoza, Eduardo, *City of Marvels* (Collins, 1999). One of the Catalunya's most highly acclaimed novelists and writers. This is a wonderful, richly detailed novel set around the time of the 1888 Universal Exhibition; he has also written several highly acclaimed novels, including *The Year of the Flood* (Harvill, 1995).

Nuñez, Raul, *Lonely Hearts Club* (Serpent's Tail, 1988). Amusing, quirky novel about a strange love affair in Barcelona.

Orwell, George, *Homage to Catalonia* (Penguin, 2000). The classic account of the Civil War; perceptive and personal.

Rodera, Mercé, *The Time of the Doves*. The most widely read Catalan novel, a bittersweet romantic tale.

Vázquez Montalbán, Manuel. A series of amusing adventures about the gourmet detective, Pepe Carvalho, set in Barcelona. Three of his best are *Offside*, *An Olympic Death* and *South Seas* – absolutely brilliant.

Essentials

Güell, Xavier, *Antoni Gaudí: Works and Projects* (Gustavo Gili, 1997). Bilingual (Spanish/English) and packed with illustrations and plans; interesting, clear descriptions of all Gaudí's major projects.

Art & architecture

Homage to Barcelona: The City and its Art 1888-1936, (Hayward Gallery, 1986). Beautifully illustrated exhibition catalogue with several thoughtful, interesting essays on the period.

Mendoza, Eduardo, *Barcelona modernista*. This was co-written with his sister Christina, and is one of the best guides to the subject, but is hard to get hold of.

Ocana, Maria Teresa, *Picasso and Els 4 Gats* (Bullfinch, 1996). Glossy, beautifully illustrated account of the famous bohemian tavern which hosted Picasso's first one-man exhibition.

Pomés Leiz, Juliet and Feriche, Ricardo, *Barcelona Design Guide* (Gustavo Gili). Everything you ever wanted to know about design in Barcelona, including a list of designer bars and shops.

Solà-Morales, Ignasi, *Fin-de-Siècle Architecture in Barcelona* (Gustavo Gili). Absorbing description of Barcelona's *modernista* heritage.

Van Hensbergen, Gijs, *Catalonia's Son* (Harper Collins, 2001). One of the most recent and most illuminating biographies to appear on the city's most famous architect, Gaudí.

Andrews, Colman, *Catalan Cuisine* (Grub Street, 1998). An excellent, thorough account of Catalan food, with plenty of interesting details and delicious recipes. **Casas, Penelope**, *Food and Wines of Spain* (Penguin, 1985). This is a good general guide, with a chapter on Catalunya.

Food & wine

Useful websites

Useful for finding accommodation are www.barcelonahotels.com; www.room-service.co.uk www.hotelselect.com www.barcelona-on-line.com

Accommodation

www.tmb.es The official site for the Barcelona city transport network – covering metros, buses and local trains.
www.renfe.es The official site for the Spanish national railways, **RENFE**.
www.sncf.fr French railways, including ticket-booking facility.
www.raileurope.com For information on railpasses within Europe for North Americans.
www.raileurope.co.uk UK-based version of above.
www.aena.es/ae/bcn/ homepage.htm Barcelona airport information; you can also check for flight delays.

Transport

www.barcelonaturisme.com The official city tourist information site.
www.bcn.esis A city-run site for residents which also has useful information for visitors.
www.tourspain.es Spanish tourist office website.

Tourist information

www.barcelonareview.com Online literary review.
www.diaridebarcelona.com Local newspaper site, with comprehensive listings.
www.barnanetro.com Barcelona entertainment listings – in Spanish only.
www.bcn.es/english/ihome.htm A cultural overview of the area around and including Barcelona.

Culture & entertainment listings

www.tourism.catalonia.net/ckw/sports.html General information on adventure sports in the Province of Girona includes air, sea and land.
www.gencat.es/turistex/4marques.htm Has information on accommodation, sports, events of interest etc in the eight major areas of Catalunya. Gencat.es has an inbuilt search facility for all different sports/parks/etc.

Adventure sports & outdoor activities

Essentials

www.stagnites.co.uk/extreme/pom/unmissable_catalan.htm For the more adventurous, this site will allow you to book a pre arranged/organized adventure sports holiday (much as the name suggests!).

www.stone-spirit.com/stone/english/e-imagecatalogne.html For the serious rock climber, it also includes areas other than Catalunya.

www.cataloniaadventure.com/index2.html An organization run by two Spaniards who have a very 'hands on' approach to getting close to nature. Well worth a look.

General information **www.es.weather.yahoo.com** A weather site.

www.fco.gov.uk/travel/default.asp The first website for the British tourist to go for the latest information on foreign travel. It includes information as to what reponsibilities and obligations the traveller should remember. It also has advice on little-known travel tips such as visa requirements, medical documents, etc.

www.vilaweb.com/english.html Allows more experienced surfers the opportunities to track down specific and esoteric points of interest. This Catalonian website holds a database on most relevent websites to do with the area. It also has a search engine incorporated.

www.publintur.es/ A more general tourist interest site for the area of Catalunya. It includes details of parks, beaches, areas of interest and accommodation.

www.bcu.cesca.es A city-run online 'youth information point'.

www.footprintbooks.com
A new place to visit

La Ciutat Vella: The Old City

La Ciutat Vella: The Old City

60	**La Rambla**
60	History
61	**Sights**
61	Plaça de Catalunya
63	La Boqueria
64	Gran Teatre de Liceu
66	Eating and drinking
67	Shopping
68	Transport
69	**Barri Gòtic**
69	History
70	Sights
70	Muses d'Història de la Ciutat
74	Catedral de la Seu
78	Santa Ana
79	Plaça Sant Jaume
82	Eating and drinking
85	Shopping
87	Transport

87	**La Ribera**
87	History
89	Sights
90	Carrer Montcada
92	Museu Picasso
94	Sant Pere
96	Parc de la Ciutadella
98	Eating and drinking
101	Shopping
102	Transport
103	**El Raval**
103	History
103	Sights
104	Palau Güell
109	Museu d'Art Contemporani de Barcelona
111	Eating and drinking
114	Shopping
114	Transport

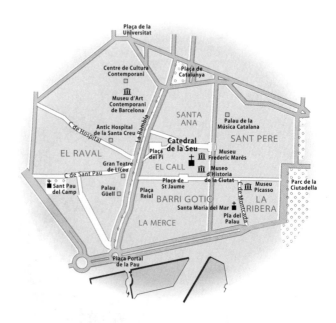

The old city is the real heart of Barcelona. It is one of the best preserved Gothic quarters in Europe and yet has all the colour and chaos of an ancient Mediterranean town. But this is no picture-perfect tourist-museum – it's a noisy, chaotic maze packed with shops, bars and clubs, and where the streets are just as crowded at midnight as they are at midday.

The old city is divided into neighbourhoods, each with their own distinct character. On the eastern side of La Rambla is **Barri Gòtic** (Gothic Quarter) with the biggest concentration of sights, shops and bars. Just beyond, **La Ribera**, once the ancient merchants' quarter, is now arty and slick. On the other side of La Rambla is **El Raval**, the former red-light district, still edgy but now bulging with artists, bars, vintage clothes shops and hip music stores.

Tucked away in the old city are some of Barcelona's most enjoyable sights, from the lacy spires of the Gothic **Catedral de la Seu** to Muntaner's greatest creation, the fulsome **Palau de la Música Catalana** which glistens like an exotic flower in a corner of El Raval. On La Rambla, Barcelona's most famous promenade, there's the celebrated **Boquería** market, and beneath the tiny **Plaça del Rei** lie the remarkable ruins of the ancient Roman settlement.

La Rambla

"La Rambla isn't an urban artery, La Rambla is a public vein where you end up going to inject the city into the most venial part of your body, that is the eyes."
Quim Soler

La Rambla is pure theatre; all of human life seems to drift down it at some time or another, and it bustles chaotically, day and night. La Rambla is the city's most famous promenade, a mile-long ribbon, made up of five streets placed end to end in a seamless progress to the seafront. It has even inspired its own specific verb: ramblejant, *meaning simply 'to go down La Rambla'. The mouth of the promenade, and the inevitable starting point for a stroll, is* **Plaça de Catalunya***, a huge square which links the old city with the new, dotted with fountains and benches.*

In some ways La Rambla has lost much of the magic of a century ago. The kiosks are lost between countless 'human statues', many of the fine old buildings have been appropriated by generic fast food chains, pickpockets preying on unwary tourists do a brisk trade, and pavement cafés charge outrageously for a front row seat. But, on a fine, slow Sunday, when the old men gather in clumps around the **Font de las Canaletes***, families dawdle between the bird kiosks, and couples saunter hand in hand down to the port, it can still feel like "the most beautiful street in the world." (Lorca)*

History

Bus nos 14, 38, 59 and 51 run the whole length of La Rambla

When the Romans arrived, La Rambla was a river, although silted up and sluggish even then. The name itself comes from the Arabic *raml,* meaning sand, so the Arabs can't have thought much of it either. In the late 14th century it was officially converted into a covered sewer, having been an unofficial one for centuries previously.

At the end of the late 15th century, the first of a series of large religious buildings was constructed here, facing the medieval walls which encircled the straining city. When the walls finally came down, palaces and gardens sprang up in their place, and a long line of plane trees were planted for shade. In the early 15th century, anti-religious sentiment was running high. Murderous monks tore down the old religious buildings and their land was auctioned off for squares, markets, and a glittering new opera house.

The river couldn't be counted on to stay underground: Hans Christian Andersen watched, astonished, from his hotel room on the Rambla as, one winter night in 1862, the waters rose to waist-height, sweeping through the shops and cafés and swallowing people down the holes of the sewers. Despite this, the fashionable promenade was moving up in the world; no longer merely a boundary, it had become the heart of the city. It also acquired its most enduring symbols, the wrought-iron stalls and kiosks which still spill over with flowers, or resound with the twitter of songbirds. La Rambla had become one of the most famous boulevards in Europe, mimicked in a dozen capitals and adored by travellers, writers and artists.

Things to do on La Rambla

- Drink from the Font de las Canaletes to be sure you return to Barcelona (see below)
- Have a counter-top breakfast in the Boquería market (see page 63)
- Go to the opera at the opulent Liceu theatre (see page 64)
- Sit out on the buzzy Plaça Reial and watch the (weird) world go by (see page 65)

Sights

Plaça de Catalunya

When Franco's troops took Barcelona in 1939, they held a massive military parade in the vast Plaça de Catalunya; but this cocky show of strength was nothing in comparison with the celebrations which took place here on the first official Catalan National Day to be celebrated after El Caudillo's death nearly four decades later. A quarter of a million people danced through the streets in one of the city's largest popular celebrations ever. It's a shame that the Plaça de Catalunya couldn't have provided a more glamorous back-drop; in this self-consciously beautiful city, the square forms a surprisingly dull connection between the old city and the honeycomb grid of its 19th-century extension, the Eixample.

This corner is the mouth of La Rambla, and a favourite meeting point before heading out to explore the old city

Today the square's greatest charm is the people who fill it: it's always packed with commuters and party-goers pouring out of the city's trains, metros and buses which converge here, and gamblers, ice-cream sellers, and musicians jostle for the attention of the tourists and idlers.

La Rambla de las Canaletes and dels Estudis

The first of the five adjoining *ramblas,* the one nearest Plaça de Catalunya, is **La Rambla de las Canaletes**, named for the celebrated **Font de las Canaletes**. For years, the expression 'to drink from the waters of the Canaletes' was a popular way of describing a Barcelonan. Nowadays, the legend goes that anyone who drinks from the waters of the fountain will return to Barcelona, which explains the eager queues of tourists lining up to have their pictures taken. When *FC Barça* win a game, their fans come here to swing off the fountain and celebrate wildly. They are generally ignored by the knots of older folk who gather nearby to enjoy a good gossip or a game of cards.

 Catalunya

The next *rambla*, **La Rambla dels Estudis**, got its name from the university buildings which once stood here. The university was abolished by Philip V in reprisal for the anti-Castillian uprisings which marked the end of the 17th century. Today, the air is filled with the clamour of songbirds which have given rise to the street's popular name, **La Rambla dels Ocells** (Rambla of the Birds). The kiosks are hung with countless cages, stuffed with everything from parrots and canaries to blackbirds and a few scraggy chickens. This is also the place to pick up a rabbit or gerbil, with several kiosks devoted to pets.

During the Civil War, soldiers from all factions would take pot shots at each other from either side of the Rambla: George Orwell describes one such shoot out that took place in the **Café Moka** (No 26) in *Homage to Catalonia*. The lumpish former Jesuit **Església de Betlem** (Church of Bethlehem) which squats at the corner of the *rambla* and the Carrer del Carme was another of the victims of this war; once one of the most richly gilded and decorated churches in the city, it was stripped of its precious marble and sumptuous fittings, and burned out.

La Rambla

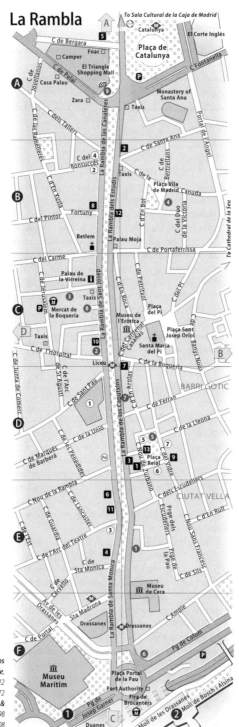

To Sala Cultural de la Caja de Madrid

Catalunya

El Corte Inglés

Plaça de Catalunya

C de Bergara

Fnac

Camper

El Triangle Shopping Mall

C de Pelai

C de Fontanella

Casa Palau

C de Jovellanos

Zara

Monastery of Santa Ana

Taxis

Portal de l'Àngel

C de las Sitjes

C dels Tallers

C de Santa Ana

C de la

C del Bonsuccés

C de Berrrellans

Taxis

Plaça Vila de Madrid

C d'En Xuclà

Canuda

Fortuny

C del Duc de la Victòria

C del Pintor

Betlem

Palau Moja

C de Portaferrissa

To Cathedral de la Seu

C del Carme

Palau de la Vitreina

C de Ferlandina

C d'En Roca

C de Petritxol

C del Pi

Mercat de la Boqueria

Taxis

Plaça del Pi

Banys Nous

Museu de l'Eròtica

Plaça Sant Josep Oriol

Taxis

C de l'Hospital

Santa Maria del Pi

C de la Boqueria

Liceu

C de Sant Pau

C d'En Arolas

BARRI GÒTIC

C de Ferran

C de Junta de Comerç

C de l'Arc de St Agustí

C de la Unió

C de la Leona

C de Marquès de Barberá

C dels Escudellers

CIUTAT VELLA

Plaça Reial

Pge dels Escudellers

C de les Penedides

C Nou de la Rambla

C de Lancaster

C d'En Rull

C de Guàrdia

Pge de la Pau

C de l'Est

C de l'Arc del Teatre

C de Sta Mònica

C de Sils

Museu de Cera

C de Cervelló

Av de les Drassanes

Sta Madrona

Drassanes

C Ample

Drassanes

Pg de Colom

C de Portal

Plaça Portal de la Pau

Museu Marítim

Port Authority

Fira de Brocanters

Moll de les Drassanes

Moll de Bosch i Alsina

Pg de Josep Garner

Duanes

Related maps

A Eixample, page 122
B Barri Gòtic, page 72
C Port Vell & Barceloneta, page 198
D El Raval, page 108

Ciutat Vella: The Old City

N

0 metres   100
0 yards   100

Sleeping ■

1 Albergue Kabul *D2*
2 Continental *B2*
3 Cuatro Naciones *D2*
4 de l'Arc *E1*
5 Ducs de Bergara *A1*
6 Hostal Benidorm *E1*
7 Internacional *D2*
8 Le Meridien Barcelona *B1*
9 Pension Ambos Mundos *D2*
10 Pension Las Flores *C1*
11 Ramblas *E1*
12 Rivoli Ramblas *B1*
13 Roma Reial *D2*

Eating ●

1 Amaya *E2*
2 Egipte *C1*
3 Gèminis *C1*
4 Govinda *B2*
5 Les Quinze Nits *D2*

Cafés & tapas bars ●

6 Cava Universal *F2*
7 de l'Opéra *D2*
8 Pinotxo *C1*
9 Zurich *A1*

Entertainment ○

1 Gran Teatre del Liceu *D1*
2 Teatre Poliorama *B1*
3 Teatre Principal *E1*

Clubs & bars ○

4 Boadas *B1*
5 Glaciar *D2*
6 Jamboree *D2*
7 Karma *D2*

La Rambla de Sant Josep

No one calls this strip of La Rambla by its original name 'de Sant Josep'. It's one of the prettiest sections of the street, filled with kiosks bursting with flowers, and is much better known as **La Rambla de las Flores**. At the turn of the 19th century, poets and painters sighed after the flower girls, who were as famous for their beauty as for their wares. The sentimental painter Ramón Casas couldn't live without one of them, and married her.

One of the most graceful palaces in the city is set back from the Rambla at No 105. The Palau de la Virreina was built for Manuel Amat i Junyet, who acquired a great fortune and a terrible reputation while Viceroy of Peru. His affair with the Peruvian actress called Perricholi caused a scandal, but the old man must have had a twinkle in his eye: when he returned to Barcelona, he managed to charm the young woman who was betrothed to his nephew by gallantly telling her that he would have married her himself if he hadn't been so old. She apparently replied that the walls of the convent where she had been staying were much older and yet very much to her taste. The poor nephew was cast aside and the pair were soon married and took up residence in this grand palace, one of the finest on La Rambla. Sadly, the ex-Viceroy died soon after and the Palau de la Virreina was named after his young widow. *(margin: Palau de la Virreina)*

The palace now houses one of the city's **information offices** where plenty of leaflets on cultural events and festivals, including the main performing arts festival, the *Festival del Grec* (see page 44) are available. There's also a decent bookshop, the *Botiga de la Virreina*, which has a good selection of books, some in English, and souvenirs. You can also see some of the lofty *Gegants* (see page 42) which are carried at festivals, and for dedicated numismatists there's a collection of old Catalan coins upstairs in the **Gabinet Numismatic de Catalunya**. ■ *Information office, Tue-Sat 1000-2030; Sun 1000-1430. To see the Catalan coin collection, call for an appointment, T93 622 03 60 www.mnac.es*

When the city walls were still standing, this colourful section of the old town provided the meeting point between town and country. Farmers brought their produce to the city gate to sell to the townsfolk, and many of the city's festivals and markets – as well as its hangings – took place here. When the old convent of St Josep was demolished in the 19th century, it became the Mercat de Sant Josep, affectionately known as La Boquería; one of the largest and most famous covered markets in Europe, capped with a lacy wrought-iron roof and a stained-glass 1914 *modernista* sign in bright jewel colours. Inside, the tidy grid is jam-packed with stalls heaped high with the freshest fruit, vegetables, meat, fish and cheeses, as well as stalls with more exotic produce from wild mushrooms to strange imports from South America. There's a liberal sprinkling of tiny bars and kiosks, where you can sip a beer, linger over a coffee or try some oysters. *(margin: La Boquería — Dive straight to the back of the market to avoid tourist prices and to enjoy the atmosphere)*

Outside in the Plaça de Boquería, also known as the **Pla de l'Os**, a large colourful pavement mosaic by Miró marks the spot where the old city gates of Santa Eulàlia once stood. It's overlooked by the delightful **Casa Bruno Quadros**, now occupied by a bank, but formerly a *modernista* umbrella shop; it's still marked by a giant scaly Chinese dragon supporting a huge furled umbrella and a lantern, and the façade is covered with pirouetting parasols. *(margin: La Plaça de Boquería)*

Just up, on the opposite side of the street, there's another pretty *modernista* monument, the **Antigua Casa Figueres**, a confectionery shop with a graceful

(margin, rotated: Ciutat Vella: The Old City)

green and gold façade; there are a couple of tables outside for sampling its delicious pastries and chocolates, made by the city's most famous *patissiers*, *Escribá* – great people watching without the customary surcharges of La Rambla

Museu de
L'Eròtica

There are pleasures of a different kind to be had at the Museu de l'Eròtica at No 96, rather unprepossessingly set up a dank staircase in a shabby old building. It offers some rare Japanese engravings and *Kama Sutra* illustrations, along with a glimpse of the tawdry pleasures offered by the music halls and brothels of the Barrio Chino a century or more ago. There's also a collection of early erotic films of the 1920s, and a mind-boggling selection of 'toys', including a curious 'pleasure chair'. ■ *1000-2400. €5.95.*

La Rambla de los Caputxins

◀Ⓜ Liceu

The Capuchin monastery, which gave this stretch of La Rambla its name, has the dubious distinction of being the first to be demolished in the vicious anti-religious uprisings which erupted in 1835. When the dust finally settled, the parcels of land were auctioned off and all kinds of plans were submitted for new public buildings, among them the arcaded Plaça Reial (see page 65) and a glamorous new opera house.

This section of the Rambla begins in a blaze of glory with the revamped Liceu Opera House, but the grandeur fizzles out into shabby gentility pretty quickly. Once-grand theatres and hotels struggle gamely to keep up appearances despite their ageing façades, while life on the street below carries on cheerfully oblivious, the crowds' eyes fixed on the *Dracula* in his coffin or the droopy *Pierrot* who'll twirl for a few pesetas.

Gran Teatre del Liceu

The Art Nouveau Café de l'Opéra is one of the nicest places to enjoy a coffee and watch the world go by

The Gran Teatre del Liceu has become one of Barcelona's best-loved institutions, and is almost hidden behind the plane trees at the corner of the Rambla and Carrer de Sant Pau. The original sumptuous designs by Miquel Garriga i Roca were loosely based on *La Scala* in Milan, although it couldn't quite match the Italian opera house for size and had to make do with becoming the second-largest in Europe. When the plans were first touted, some shook their heads at the sacrilegious notion of opening a house of idle entertainment and prophesied disaster. It's certainly true that the opera house has been plagued by fire and misfortune since it first opened in 1847; it has been burned to the ground twice and bombed once.

In October 1893, a fervent young revolutionary, Santiago Salvador, threw a bomb into the 13th stall, killing 20 people and wounding dozens of others. A month later Salvador was the first to be put to death in a specifically designed execution chair, invented by the city executioner Nicomedes Méndez, which slowly garroted its victims. He was executed, still singing an anarchist anthem, in front of a large jeering audience, an event commemorated in **Ramón Casas'** frightening painting *Garrote vil* (1894), which is held in Olot (see page 219).

In 1999, its latest reincarnation was opened, a more or less faithful reproduction of the original design but with some state-of-the-art technical improvements, not least of which was a spanking new heavy fire curtain. The interior is a dizzy whirl of gilt and marble, with an opulent staircase heading up to the **Salon of Mirrors**, awash with nymphs, muses and musical quotations.

The main **auditorium** is vast, with tiered waves of neo-Baroque balconies overlooking an opulent sea of deep red velvet seating, designed by Pere

Falqués in 1884, and carefully copied after being destroyed by fire. The plush, gilded chairs have become such an icon of the theatre that the artist Pere Jaume used them in his contemporary fresco which now adorns the ceiling, where they have been transformed into a series of gentle mountain peaks, fading softly into the distance.

■ *Daily 1000-1100; last admission 1015. Information and box office open Mon-Fri 1400-1830. T93 485 99 00, www.liceu.com*

Almost opposite the Liceu, a pair of tall arches lead into Plaça Reial, a grand illustration of 19th-century urban design, and the successor of the original Capuchin monastery destroyed by the mob in 1835. Inspired by the broad public squares of Napoleanic France, it retains a singularly French air with its generous neo-classical arcades and lofty palm trees. The Three Graces frolic around the central fountain which is flanked by twin – unmistakably Catalan – lamp posts designed by Gaudí for his first municipal commission. Dripping with coiled red and gold ornamentation and drapped with open-mouthed snakes coiling up to meet winged helmets they are decidedly at odds with the austere arcades which surround them.

Plaça Reial
A lively place to enjoy a drink in the evenings, but it's wise to keep an eye on your bag

The Plaça languished for a long time; the grand houses filled up with budget hotels and squalid apartments, and squatters took possession of it. The city council's latest zealous attempt at a clean-up seem to have had an effect but sadly, the refurbishment has taken its toll on some of the square's instituitions, like the old taxidermist's shop in the corner, which is now a restaurant and bar. Dalí, one of their most faithful customers, once had a rhinoceros stuffed and then dragged outside so that he could have his picture taken astride it.

Now the Plaça Reial is unashamedly touristy and just a little bit tacky, with cafés brandishing multi-lingual menus, mediocre street musicians hoping for the best, and beggars with London accents trying out their hard luck stories on anyone who'll listen. The city's dispossessed still come here despite the crack down on drugs and prostitution and gather in uneasy clumps; hordes of stag and hen parties over for a cheap weekend rarely get any further than the square's buzzy bars; and yet this is still the starting point for a good night out for most of Barcelona's youth. It's also one of the very best places in the city for nursing a drink and watching the ebb and flow of people. Surprisingly few visitors make it into the streets and passages running off the square, and yet they are tightly crammed with bars and clubs including some of the very best in the city (see page 238). It may be brash and neon-lit, but it still knows how to show anyone a good time.

La Rambla de Santa Monica

It is hard to believe that this was once the most aristocratic section of La Rambla and the first to be given the title *paseo* (promenade); until recently, La Rambla de Santa Monica was coloured by the seedy spillover from the poverty-stricken red light districts which flanked the lower end of the street. But all the prostitutes and sex shops, bar one which blares out with a defiant neon sign, have been chased out by the city's energetic regeneration campaign. Now cafés sprawl across the broad pavements, and painters and artisans sell their wares at a virtually unbroken stream of stalls.

◆ *Drassanes*

The Rambla widens at Plaça del Teatre, with a monumental statue of **Frederic Soler**, the father of Catalan theatre, coasting along on the crest of a huge marble

Around Plaça del Teatre

Ciutat Vella: The Old City

wave. Better known as Serafí Pitarro (1839-95), Soler is the author of dozens of popular Catalan comedies. Here, his mild gaze is fixed on the dowdy **Teatre Principal**; Barcelona's first theatre, a wooden construction erected in 1579.

Another remnant of a glorious past almost faces the theatre at No 40: the **Hotel Cuatro Naciones**. Built in 1770, it struggles nowadays to maintain its haughty air of grandeur, but in its heyday was the smartest hotel on La Rambla. At No 45 the **Hotel Oriente**, built in 1842, is another of the city's oldest hotels and it has managed to cling on to its reputation. You can twirl around the ballroom and admire the ancient cloister at the same time.

Around Palau March The patchy thread of 18th-century palaces at the bottom of a Rambla were the first to be built when the city walls were tumbled, and this became one of the city's most exclusive addresses. One of the smartest was the severe Palau March at No 8, which now belongs to the Generalitat. In time, these smart homes lost their glamour and local government offices and banks took them over. Watch out that you don't stumble over a pretty drinking fountain supported by four winsome caryatids. It is one of the few survivors of a dozen fountains donated to the city by the English philanthropist Richard Wallace to mark the occasion of the Universal Exhibition in 1888.

Museu de Cera A particularly grand bank built its headquarters just off La Rambla in the Passatge de la Banca, but now C3PO and Superman swing among the neo-classical statues on the roof, as it has become the Museu de Cera (Waxwork Museum). Towards the end of the 19th century, Nicomedes Méndez, the city executioner, couldn't help but notice the enthusiastic crowds drawn to public executions and suggested an exhibition of waxworks depicting the city's executed criminals. The city didn't want to draw attention to its own felons (bad for the tourist business) but were perfectly happy to make dummies of foreign criminals. There are now more than 300 figures: Spanish and Catalan personalities rub shoulders with Hollywood stars, the cast of *Star Wars*, a scattering of Royals and the 1992 Olympic mascot, Cobi.

The museum's popular café-bar, the 'Bosc de les Fades' is decked out like a fairytale forest

■ *1000-1330 and 1430-1930; summer 1000-2000. €6.60.*

Centre d'Art Santa Mònica By the 1980s, convent-burning had gone out of fashion and the architects of the new Centre d'Art Santa Mònica at No 7 incorporated the cloister and tower of the 17th-century Augustinian convent of Santa Mònica in their glistening white building. The art on offer is generally a mixed bag of temporary shows, but there is a very pleasant air of buzzy enthusiasm not found at some of the better-known museums which means it's always worth a look.

■ *Mon-Fri 0930-1400 and 1530-1930; Sat 1000-1400. Free.*

Eating and drinking

Mid-range *Amaya*, La Rambla 20, T93 302 10 37, daily 1300-1700 and 2030-2400, metro Drassanes. Despite its unprepossessing exterior, this is an excellent Basque restaurant, specializing in seafood dishes accompanied by wines from the Basque lands and Navarra. It's popular with everyone from local businessmen to opera stars from the Liceu, and there's a terrace out on La Rambla in summer.

Price codes: see inside front cover ● on map, page 62

Cheap *Egipte*, La Rambla 79, T93 317 95 45, daily 1300-1600 and 2000-2400, metro Liceu. A great budget choice with a wide choice of popular Catalan dishes including stuffed aubergines and pigs' trotters stuffed with prawns. *Les Quinze Nits*, Plaça Reial 6, T93 317 30 75, daily 1300-1545 and 2030-2330, metro Liceu. The long queues snaking across Plaça Reial are for this good-value restaurant, which serves up simple, fresh Catalan dishes in modern surroundings. They don't take bookings, so be prepared to wait. *Govinda*, Plaça Vila de Madrid 4-5, T93 318 77 29, open Mon-Thu 1300-1600, Fri and Sat 1300-1600 and 2030-2330, metro Catalunya. A great little veggie Indian restaurant in a small square just off La Rambla – cheap, cheerful and tasty, with an excellent salad bar and home-made bread, but no alcohol or coffee. *Menú del dia* €7.65.

El Café de l'Opéra, La Rambla 74, T93 317 75 86, Mon-Thu and Sun 0800-0215, Fri-Sat 0800-0300, metro Liceu. Sitting right on the Rambla opposite the Liceu Opera house, this is the perfect café for people-watching. Original *modernista*-style fittings and an Old World ambience add to its charm, it's popular with locals and with foreigners. *Café Zurich*, Plaça de Catalunya, T93 317 91 53, daily Jun-Oct 0800-0200, until 2300 on Sun; Nov-May Mon-Thu, Sun 0800-2300, Fri-Sat 0800-2400, metro Catalunya. Perfect location at the top of the Rambla.

Café-bars with food/tapas
▶▶ *Go to page 238 for clubs and bars*

    Cava Universal, Plaça Portal de la Pau 4, T93 302 61 84, daily 0900-2200, metro Drassanes. Simple, unassuming little bar just at the foot of the monument to Columbus; good, reasonably priced *bocadillos* and great views. *Bar Pinotxo*, Mercat de la Boquería 66-67, T93 317 731 Mon-Sat 0600-1700, metro Liceu. The best-known and best-loved counter bar in the market, serving surprisingly excellent, freshly prepared food. Order the best *tallat* (coffee with a dash of milk) in the city, and don't miss the tortilla with artichokes. For the indecisive, the dashing, charmingly eccentric bar tender will make suggestions for you.

Shopping

Fira de Brocanters, Moll de Drassanes, metro Drassanes, Sat and Sun 1000-2000. So-called antiques laid out on a few tables just in front of the Columbus monument. Don't expect any bargains, but you might get a few laughs from some of the bizarre items that pop up. *Mercat de Numismàtica*, Plaça Reial, metro Liceu, 0900-1400. Stamp and coins from around the world.

Antiques & Bric-a-Brac

FNAC, EL Triangle, Plaça de Catalunya 4, metro Catalunya. Part of the French-owned chain, this is an enormous store with books, music, a concert ticket service, and an international newsstand and café on the ground floor. There's a good selection of books in English, including a selection of guides to Barcelona. *Palau de la Virreina*, La Rambla 99, metro Liceu. The information office of the city's culture department also has a small bookshop with a good selection of titles covering all aspects of Barcelona, many in English.

Books
The stalls along La Rambla have a good selection of foreign newspapers and magazines and some even have a few novels in English

There are three outstanding Spanish chains which have gained worldwide acclaim for their reasonable prices and innovative designs: *Camper*, *Zara* and *Mango*, which are even cheaper in Barcelona than they are at home. You'll find branches all over the city. *Camper*, El Triangle, C/Pelai 13, metro Catalunya. Trendy well-priced Camper shoes can be found on the most fashionably shod feet around the world. *Zara*, C/Pelai 58, metro Catalunya. Great fashion – clothes and accessories – for men, women, teenagers and kids at very affordable prices. There's a good range of clothes from the latest, hippest designs to simpler lines in linen and cotton. *Mango*, C/Canuda, metro Catalunya. The latest styles at reasonable prices; cater mainly for sleek, hip professional women. The biggest branch is at Pg de Gràcia No 65.

Fashion

Herboristeria del Rei, C/del Vidre 1, metro Liceu. This tiny shop just off the Placa Reial was founded in 1818 and has retained many of its opulent old fittings. There are hundreds of exquisitely painted miniature drawers stuffed with all kinds of herbs.

Food & drink

Malls & department stores *El Triangle*, C/Pelai 39, metro Catalunya. This gleaming mall overlooks Plaça de Catalunya, and contains an enormous *FNAC* (good for books, music and concert tickets), a *Habitat*, a vast *Sephora* perfume store (reputedly the largest in the world), a *Camper* shoe store and several other smaller fashion shops. *El Corte Inglés* Plaça de Catalunya 14, metro Catalunya. This huge department store is part of a vast Spanish chain. You'll find everything from a basement supermarket and delicatessen to fashion for men, women and children, toys, electrical goods and souvenirs. There's a café on the top floor with fabulous views, and look out for the *oportunidads* (bargains) on the 8th floor. There's another branch just down the road at Avda Portal de l'Àngel which has books, music and DVDs.

Markets *La Boquería* La Rambla 91, metro Liceu. Barcelona's most central and best-known food market with hundreds of speciality stalls – try some of the wonderful mushrooms at stall 869-870. Stalls at the front have tourist prices – be prepared to browse and price- check.

Music For mainstream music, try *FNAC* (see page 67), *El Corte Inglés* (see page 68) and *Discos Castelló*, C/Tallers 3, metro Catalunya. There are several branches of this music shop , including three more along C/Tallers, which each specialize in a different kind of music. This is the one to go to if you are looking for classical music.

Transport

For the most important bus routes, see Essentials page 36

Bus Plaça de Catalunya is the city's main transport hub and most parts of the city can be reached from here. There are several bus shelters with timetables just outside the massive *El Corte Inglés* department store on the eastern side of the square. As well as local buses, you can catch the blue *Airbus* out to the airport, and the *TombBus* for the *l'Illa* shopping centre (see page 168) along the Diagonal from outside *El Corte Inglés*. Plaça de Catalunya is also the starting point for all but one of the 16 *Nitbus* lines (night bus). They are easy to spot because the number is prefixed with an 'N'.
Bus nos **14**, **38**, **59** and **51** run the whole length of La Rambla.
Bus no **22** heads up Passeig de Gràcia and on to Gràcia.
Bus no **24** goes to Park Güell.
Bus no **41** goes to Parc de la Ciutadella and Vila Olímpica.

Ferrocarrils Regional and suburban trains run by the Catalan government (FGV: *Ferrocarrils de la Generalitat de Catalunya* , www.fgc.catalunya.net) leave from the station which is marked by two interlocking white symbols on a dark blue background. There are five lines operating from this station: U6 for **Reina Elisanda** (via **Gràcia**, **Muntaner** and **Sarrià**); S1 for **Terrassa** (via **Baixador de Vallvidrera** for the **Parc de Collserola**, and **Sant Cugat**); S5 for **Sarrià** and **Sant Cugat**; S2 for **Sarrià**, **Sant Cugat** and **Sabadell**; and the U7 which goes to **Avinguda Tibidabo** (for connections with the *Tramvia Blau* and the funicular for Tibidabo).

Metro Lines 1 (red) and 3 (green) stop at Catalunya; Line 3 also stops at Liceu (for the Opera house) and Drassanes (for the Museu Marítim see page 197).
Taxis There's a taxi stand opposite the tourist information office on Plaça de Catalunya.
Trains There are two train stations under the Plaça de Catalunya. This can cause enormous confusion for visitors: make sure that you use the entrance marked with the symbol for the line you want to take. The regional trains (*cercanías/rodalies*), run by the Spanish rail company *RENFE*, leave from the station which is marked by a curved white symbol on a circular red background. Trains depart from here for stations outside the city, including **Blanes** (for the Costa Brava), **Figueres**, **Girona** and the **Pyrenees**. Note that the airport train also departs from here (it also stops at the main *RENFE* station at Sants).

Barri Gòtic

This cramped nub of narrow streets is one of the best-preserved Gothic quar-
ters in Europe, a dizzy maze of palaces, squares and churches piled on top of
the remnants of the original Roman settlement – still visible today in the city's
history museum. Perched on top of Roman Barcino is the medieval palace of
the Catalan count-kings, with its extraordinary throne room spanned with
vast stone arches.

*On the old forum at **Plaça Sant Jaume** stand the palaces of the **Generalitat***
*(Catalan parliament) and the **Ajuntament** (city council), facing each other in a*
stand-off which has lasted for years centuries. Behind them wind the narrow streets
*of the ancient Jewish quarter and the old artisan neighbourhoods of **La Mercé** and*
***Santa Ana**, now packed with throngs of shoppers and sightseers lingering among*
*the museums, restaurants and bars. Picasso drank at **Els 4 Gats**, a modernista tav-*
*ern which has been carefully restored, and haunted the bordellos on **Carrer***
***d'Avinyó**, which is now lined with ultra-fashionable shops and bars.*

The Barri Gòtic, with its bewildering twists and turns, lends itself to surprises –
an old bar propped up with a Roman tower, or a sudden stone square which the
city's babble can't reach. There's an eccentric collection of museums hidden away
*here too; the strangest is the **Museu Marès**, a monument to obsession created by*
*the crackpot sculptor Frederic Marès, but the **Museu de Calçat**, devoted to odd*
shoes, is nearly as bizarre. And, soaring above them all, are the theatrical spikes of
*the enormous Gothic **Catedral de la Seu**.*

History

This is where Barcelona began: the city known as 'Barcino' was founded here
by the Romans between 10 and 15 BC, establishing an urban plan which was
stuck to ever after. The hub of the Roman town was the forum, which in turn
became the administrative centre of the medieval city, now the Plaça Sant
Jaume where the Generalitat (Catalan government) and the Ajuntament,
(City Hall) still squabble about what's best for Barcelona.

Almost all the major streets in the Barri Gòtic follow Roman roads, or the
line of the old city walls; the Gothic cathedral was built on top of the ruins of
at least three former churches, and, even now, local DIYers are constantly
discovering a Roman pillar supporting the basement ceiling, or a stretch of
the old city walls underneath the floorboards. The medieval city
was hemmed in behind the ring of old walls for centuries, growing increasingly
crowded and miserable; finally the walls were toppled in the 19th century,
and everyone who could afford to fled to the wide open spaces of the city's
shiny new extension (Eixample). Abandoned by all but the very poor, the
old city was initially forgotten.

Finally in the 1920s it became apparent that the citizens had turned their
backs on a miraculously intact medieval city, which was immediately chris-
tened Barri Gòtic (Gothic Quarter). For some, it was a symbol of the glory
years of the Catalan empire, and, for others, a nice little money-spinner with a
huge appeal for tourists.

Sights

Plaça de l'Àngel
Jaume I;
bus nos 16, 17,
19, 22 and 45

Plaça de l'Àngel, marking the spot where the Romans placed their northern gate, is the best place to enter the Gothic quarter. The gate has long disappeared and the square itself is now just a blip on the noisy Via Laietana, which emphatically split the old city when it was constructed in 1908. Two lengthy stretches of Roman wall survive on either side. The most imposing section overlooks a little sandy square punctuated with Josep Llimona's statue of **Ramon Berenguer III el Gran**, whose bold expansionist exploits inspired the troubadours of the Middle Ages to sing about his boldness. The square was previously known as *Plaça del Blat* (Wheat Square) after the city's main grain market which during the Middle Ages gathered here at the city gates. The square is now just a thoroughfare; the metro station emerges here, and the traffic whizzing down Via Laietana makes it too noisy to linger.

Carrer de la
Llibretaria

The Carrer de la Llibretaria, a narrow passage running parallel with broader, newer Carrer de Jaume I, is an ancient little street, lined with animated shops and cafés, including *La Colmena*, one of Barcelona's oldest and most delicious pastry shops, and *Méson del Café*, not much bigger than a hole in the wall but credited with making the best cup of coffee in town. Just off the Carrer de la Llibretaria to the right is short **Carrer del Veguer** which leads into the small but imposing **Plaça del Rei** where the counts and kings of Barcelona held court for centuries.

The ancient palace, the Palau Reial Major, faces the entrance to the square, while to the right is the dainty belltower surmounting the Royal Chapel, and to the left is the **Palau del Lloctinet**, built in the mid-16th century as a residence for the despised Viceroy of Catalunya. At the corner of the square is a boxy iron sculpture by the prolific Basque artist **Eduardo Chillida**, entitled *Topo* from the Greek word for space – which is exactly what it is used for by musicians during the day and itinerants at night. The Plaça del Rei is often used for concerts during the summer, with the graceful flight of steps up to the Royal Palace making a natural and very attractive stage.

Museu d' Història de la Ciutat

Buses don't enter
the narrow streets of
the Barri Gòtic. Take
a bus to La Rambla
or Via Laietana

Standing in the middle of the lovely Plaça del Rei, it's hard to believe that the most extensive Roman ruins in Europe are spread out beneath your feet. And yet it's true: this corner of medieval Barcelona is built on top of the astonishingly intact remains of Roman Barcino.

At the entrance to the Plaça del Rei (at the top of the Carrer del Veguer) is the entrance to one of Barcelona's most fascinating museums, the Museu d'Història de la Ciutat, which reveals the history of the city layer by layer. The deepest layer contains the Roman city, established here more than 2,000 years ago. Tacked on to it are Visigothic ruins which were built during the fifth and sixth centuries and built on top of the whole lot are the palaces and churches of the Middle Ages, including those which now flank the Plaça del Rei.

Visits to the museum begin with a multi-media show, 'A Virtual History of Barcelona', which gives the potted version in a 3-D film with lots of spangly special effects, and then everyone piles in a glass lift which glides down a couple of millennia to drop you off in Roman Barcelona. And it really does feel like Roman Barcelona – the roads are rutted with cart tracks, the vats in the laundry quarter are still stained with plant dyes, and those in the wine-producing neighbourhood are still flecked with grape skins and pips. Somehow these signs of ordinary human life are much more affecting than the mosaics and paintings which once adorned the grandest Roman villas. Glass walkways lead across the excavated areas and are well marked with multi-lingual descriptions of life in Roman Barcino.

Still underground but heading steadily towards the cathedral, the Roman ruins become interspersed with Visigothic ones. The Visigoths left fewer reminders of their passage

Five of the best: sights in Barri Gòtic

- *Museu d'Història de la Ciutat* (see below)
- *Catedral de la Seu* (see page 74)
- *El Call* (see page 79)
- *Plaça del Pi* (see page 79)
- *Generalitat* (see page 80)

through the city; unlike the stirring ruins of Barcino only a few hundred metres away, it's almost impossible to get a sense of how this area of ancient Barcelona might have looked.

Stairs lead up to the next layer of the city's history, the Golden Age of the medieval period. You are now in the heart of the Palau Reial Major, palace of the counts and kings of Barcelona from at least the end of the 10th century. The Romanesque vaulted room which formed part of the Count's Palace in the 11th century is currently being restored in order to hold a permanent exhibition showing the evolution of Barcelona from the eighth to the 15th centuries. In the hallway, two remarkable frescoes, painted late in the Romanesque era but only discovered in 1998, depict a handsome parade of knights on prancing chargers. Sadly, much of the most engaging section has been lost – still, you can just make out the delightfully mischievous mythical beasts in the patchy border, squabbling among themselves and attacking unwary clerics. — **Palau Reial Major**

The echoing throne room, the Saló de Tinell, now used mainly as a temporary exhibition hall, was fittingly commissioned by Pere III the Ceremonious in 1359. Seven solemn arches succeed each other in great broad arcs, creating an overwhelming impression of enormous space and grandeur. Another faded Romanesque fresco relates the conquest of Mallorca in 1229, with Jaume I at the head of a procession formed by members of the kingdom's most illustrious families. When Barcelona ceased to be the capital of the Kingdom of Aragon, the palace was handed over to the Inquisition, who claimed that the very stones of the great hall would shudder if a suspect insisted on telling them lies. From the 18th century, the hall's austere Gothic lines were hidden behind a raffish Baroque makeover. For once, the looting soldiers of the Civil War did the city a favour when they stripped the church of its Baroque splendour, and the austere, graceful lines of the Saló de Tinell appeared once more. In May, the Saló de Tinell is one of the loveliest venues for the city's annual Festival de Música Antiga — **Saló de Tinell**

Near the Saló de Tinell, a door leads into the Royal Chapel of Saint Agatha, a slim, elegant construction with a single graceful nave and a dazzling polychrome ceiling supported by diaphragm arches. It was built at the beginning of the 14th century, and topped with a whimsical octagonal belltower in the form of a crown. The magnificent, glittering 15th-century retablo of the Epiphany is by **Jaume Huguet**, and is considered one of the finest works of Catalan Gothic painting. A small chapel set off the nave contains the stone tablet said to have held the severed breasts of the saint, and a painting by the Master of Burgo de Osuma, a Castilian, who has given sweet-faced Agatha a couple of musical angels for company, and a platter for her snipped-off breasts to hold in one hand, while the other wields the nasty-looking snipping instrument. — **Capella de Saint Agatha**

Ciutat Vella: The Old City

Mirador
del Rei Martí
*There is a glorious
view from the
look-out point*

Back at the chapel entrance, a stairway leads to the Mirador del Rei Martí, a much-loved monarch whose name was appended posthumously to the tower, perhaps to hide the fact that it was used by the spies of the hated Viceroys appointed by Ferdinand. At the top, a huge wooden model of Barcelona during the Gothic era marks the three ever-widening circles formed by the city walls as Barcelona burst out of their successive confines.

Barri Gòtic

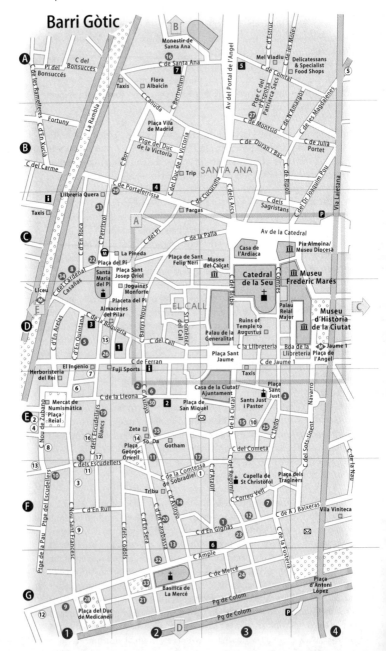

■ *Oct-May Tue-Sat 1000-1400 and 1600-2000, Sun and holidays 1000-1400; Jun-Sep Tue-Sat 1000-2000, Sun and holidays 1000-2000. €4.80 including the multimedia show 'A Virtual History of Barcelona', www.museuhistoria.bcn.es Free the first Sat of month from 1600-2000. Guided tours and special night visits available, T93 315 11 11. For information on the Festival de Música Antigua, see page 42.*

0 metres 100
0 yards 100

■ Sleeping
1 Adagio *D2*
2 Hostal Levante *E2*
3 Hostal Palermo *D1*
4 Hostal Rembrandt *B2*
5 Lausanne *A3*
6 Metropol *F3*
7 Nouvel *A2*

● Eating
1 Agut *F3*
2 Agut d'Avignon *E2*
3 Café de l'Acàdemia *E3*
4 Cometacinc *E3*
5 Can Culleretes *D1*
6 El Gran Café *E2*
7 El Salón *F3*
8 Juicy Jones *C1*
9 La Dentellière *G1*
10 La Fonda *F1*
11 La Veronica *E2*
12 Oolong *F3*
13 Pakistani *F2*
14 Pitarra *F2*
15 Plà *E3*
16 Self-Naturista *A2*
17 Slokai *E2*
18 Zoo *E1*

● Cafés & tapas bars
19 Al Limón Negro *E1*
20 Arc Café *F2*
21 Bar Celta *G2*
22 Bar del Pi *C1*
23 Bar El Tropezón *F3*
24 Bar La Plata *G3*
25 Bodega La Palmera *E3*
26 Café Schilling *D1*
27 Els Quatre Gats *B3*
28 Gotto Zero *G1*
29 Granja Dulcinea *B2*
30 La Cereria Café *E2*
31 La Pallaresa *C1*
32 La Soccarena *G2*
33 Taberna del Prior *G2*
34 Taverna Irati *C1*
35 Venus *E2*

○ Entertainment
1 Harlem Jazz Club *F3*
2 Jamboree *E1*
3 La Macarena *F1*
4 Los Tarantos *E1*
5 Palau de la Música Catalana *A4*
6 Sidecar Factory Club *E1*

○ Clubs & bars
7 Bar Malpaso *E1*
8 Café Royale *E1*
9 Dot *F1*
10 El Ascensor *E3*
11 Fonefone *F1*
12 Margarita Blue *G1*
13 New York *F1*
14 Ovisos *E2*
15 Padam Padam *D1*
16 Pilé 43 *E1*
17 Shanghai *E1*

Museu Frederic Marès

Next to the city's history museum, and visible from the Mirador del Rei Martì, is the former Bishop's Palace, which was annexed to the Royal Palace by Jaume II in the late 13th century. The entrance, with a pretty glade of orange trees (at their most fragrant in early spring), is in Plaça de Sant Iu, just off Carrer dels Comtes. Once the headquarters of the Inquisition, it now contains the Frederic Marès Museum, devoted to the obsessive, patchwork collection of the eccentric sculptor and painter Frederic Marès i Deulovol (1893-1991), who had obviously never heard the phrase 'less is more'.

A passionate collector, traveller and prolific artist, Marès managed to accumulate one of the largest collections of Spanish sculpture in the country, ferreting through junk stalls and markets, and disappearing off into the Catalan countryside on treasure hunts. Among the earliest pieces are the ranks of tiny Iberian ex-votos which have survived millennia and stand shoulder-to-shoulder in their glass cases. The extraordinary medieval sculpture collection begins with a seemingly endless series of elaborately stylized 13th-century crucifixes, all unnervingly gory. The bloodiness is briefly offset by a fleet of radiant, polychrome Madonnas, but begins again on the next floor with legions of saints and martyrs perpetually dying horrible deaths – shot with arrows, stoned or flayed alive. The sentimental depictions of 19th-century saints, sitting in their gilded arbours and surrounded by clouds of chubby *putti*, are gloriously kitsch.

Ciutat Vella: The Old City

Sculpture collection
A whole room is devoted to santons (nativity scene figures) dating from the 17th-19th centuries

Detailed map
A *Around La Seu*, *page 77*
Related maps
B *Eixample*, *page 122*
C *La Ribera and Sant Pere*, *page 88*
D *Port Vell & Barceloneta*, *page 198*
E *El Raval*, *page 108*

Thing to do in Barri Gòtic

- Join in the Sardana dancing on Sundays (see page 42)
- Visit Roman Barcino underneath Plaça del Rei (see page 70)
- Take the lift up to the spires of Catedral de la Seu (see below)
- Shop till you drop at the hip boutiques along Carrer d'Avinyó (see page 81)

Museu Sentimental
This is a veritable temple to Marès obsession

The floors above contain the Museu Sentimental, more than a dozen rooms devoted to a mind-boggling collection of 18th- and 19th-century ephemera, a veritable temple to obsession. Marès compiled precise inventories of his collection – the 108 snuffboxes, 1,295 books of cigarette papers, 158 pairs of opera glasses, and 73 floral bouquets made from seashells and set under glass domes he painstakingly itemized barely scratch the surface. There are hundred of pieces of Catalan ironwork – 1,478, in fact – from door handles, locks, and keys, to candle-snuffers, scissors and hinges.

The **Sala Femenina** is perhaps the most atmospheric, and contains a dizzying array of fans, jewellery, hatpins, gloves, sewing implements, card-cases and umbrellas which eloquently convey the hothouse atmosphere of a 19th-century bourgeois home. Marè's study-cum-studio is at the top of the building, and contains the battered old suitcase that he would take with him on foraging expeditions, and a handful of his sculptures. Back downstairs in the courtyard, there's a pretty outdoor café, the *Café d'Estiu* which is one of the most peaceful in the city (only open Apr-Sep, see page 85).

■ *Tue-Sat 1000-1700, Sun and holidays 1000-1400.* €*3, www.museumares.bcn.es*

Catedral de la Seu

On Carrer des Comtes stands the unobtrusive side entrance to the towering cathedral, the Romanesque Catedral de la Seu. The first Christian church on the site, the fourth-century basilica, was flattened by the Moorish armies in 985. Work began on a Romanesque replacement in the mid-11th century, but the present construction dates from 1298 as the plaques around the **Portal de Sant Iu** (St Ives gate) attest. It was, unusually, the first part of the cathedral to be erected. The final part, the western façade which overlooks Plaça Nova, didn't go up until the 19th century – which should give the builders working on Gaudí's Sagrada Família some hope.

The cathedral's grand main entrance is at the end of the Carrer de Santa Llúcia, overlooking Plaça Nova. The monumental **façade** was only finally added at the end of the 19th century, when Josep Oriol Mestres was given a dollop of cash by the wealthy (and famously stingy) banker Manuel Girona to complete the cathedral to the 14th-century plans. Mestres took liberties with the original designs, but the final outcome, which owes more to the flamboyant detailing of northern European Gothic than to the austere restraint of the Catalan strain, gives the old city a thrillingly theatrical skyline.

The Cathedral **interior** is overpowering in its magnificence with three soaring naves supported by heavily decorated Gothic cross vaults, all saved from the sackings of the Civil War by the vigilance of the Generalitat. At the centre of the cathedral is the richly decorated **choir**, enclosed with a delirious, pointy Renaissance screen; the entrance, for a small fee, is at the other end of the cathedral near the main doorway. Continue around the ambulatory and you'll find the cathedral **lift**, which, for a few pesetas, will whip you up to the roof for some extraordinary views. The massive 16th-century **organ** is clamped above the doorway of the Portal de Sant Iu; a wooden Moor's head tucked beneath it once spouted out sweets for children on *El Dia de los Inocentes* (Feast of the Innocents), the Spanish equivalent of April Fool's Day.

At the back of the elaborate crypt beneath the altar lie the remains of **Santa Eulàlia** in an exquisite 14th-century alabaster sarcophagus adorned with grisly depictions of the trials she suffered before her martyrdom at the hands of the Romans. It's an operatic setting; to get the full effect, put a coin in the slot and watch the whole thing light up.

To the right of the crypt, Ramon Berenguer I and his wife Almodis, who commissioned the construction of the cathedral, lie peacefully in oddly small wooden sarcophagi fixed to the wall near the sacristy, and, in one of the chapels leading off the elegantly columned ambulatory, there's a dazzling, gilded retablo of the *Transfiguration* (1450) by **Bernat Martorell**.

The cloister is the most popular spot in the cathedral with its fanciful arcades surrounding a lush palm-filled garden. This oasis is home to the cathedral's geese, who squawk among the fountains and pools, and poke their bills through the iron trellis hoping for a snack. The old tradition of dancing an egg

(margin: Crypt)

(margin: Cloister)

(vertical margin text: Ciutat Vella: The Old City)

Catedral de la Seu

Plaça de la Seu

C del Bisbe

C de la Pietat

C des Comtes

1 Portal de St Iu
2 Main entrance
3 Choir
4 Ambulatory
5 Lift to roof

6 Remains of Santa Eulàlia (Crypt)
7 Sarcophagi of Ramón Berenguer & Almodis
8 Sacristy

9 Cloister
10 Sala Capitular/ Museum
11 Shop
12 Porta de Santa Eulàlia

Not to scale

(known as *l'ou com balla*) on the delicate 15th-century fountain of St George was recently revived, and takes place on the feast of Corpus Christi in early June (see page 43). This custom was just a part of the extravagant festivities which used to take place on this day: the cloister was strewn with rose petals (now just the fountains are wreathed with flowers) and swathed in canopies. There was a grand ecclesiastical procession, and the guilds staged spectacular parades, attended by lumbering gegants and gegantessas (see page 42). These parades cemented the ties between the powerful Church and the wealthy guilds: the cloister is their old burial ground, the worn slabs commemorating dead guild masters.

Sala Capitular Just off the cloister, set in the Sala Capitular (Chapter House), is the **Cathedral Museum**, with a small collection of paintings from the 14th to the 18th centuries. The star of the show is undoubtedly **Bartolomé Bermejo's** stunning retablo of *La Pietat* (1490), one of the earliest Spanish oil paintings, with an aching portrayal of the anguished Mary.
■ *Museum open daily 1000-1300 and 1600-1830. €0.60.*

Capella de Santa Llúcia Next to the Sala Capitular is the plain Romanesque chapel of Santa Llúcia, dedicated to the patron saint of seamstresses, who queue up here for her blessing on the saint's day, 13 December. This date also officially marks the opening of the *Feria de Santa Llúcia*, a Christmas fair, which has usually been underway since the beginning of the month, (see page 44), when artisans display their collection of Nativity scene figures in the streets around the cathedral. As well as the usual figures – the crib, the Holy Family, the Three Kings, animals – the Catalans wouldn't consider a manger scene complete without the bizarre, squatting figure of the *Cagoner* (Crapper), usually wearing a cheerful red Catalan cap and an entranced expression, with his little pile of poo beneath him. The faded words 'A 2 Canas la Pou' are just visible at about waist height near the simple entrance to the Capella Santa Llúcia. A *pou* (well), stood nearby and a *cana* was a unit of measurement – roughly 1.5 m – and if anyone suspected they had been diddled by a tailor they could come here to check. ■ *Cathedral; daily 0800-1330 and 1600-1930.*

Around the cathedral

Plaça de Sant Felip Neri Leaving the cathedral cloister by the Porta de Santa Eulàlia, you'll emerge on Carrer del Bisbe. In the square opposite, besides the portrait painters and musicians, there's a monument to the Martyrs of 1809 by Josep Llimona. A short detour down Carrer de Montjüic des Bisbe will bring you to the enchanting Plaça de Sant Felip Neri, a leafy, peaceful little square with shady trees, an old church pock-marked with the scars of bombing during the Civil War, and a tinkling stone fountain.

One of the enormous shoes made for Columbus' wedding to the Statue of Liberty in 1992 (see page 196) stands at the entrance to the **Museu de Calçat**, a shoe museum at No 5 run by the shoemaker's guild, with an assortment of shoes from Roman sandals and red pointy devil shoes with flames erupting from the heel, to embroidered Baroque slippers and a pair of neatly buttoned two-toned boots belonging to the cellist Pau Casals. ■ *Tue-Sun 1100-1400; €1.20.*

Casa de l'Ardiaca From Plaça Felipe Neri retrace your steps back to Carrer de la Bisbe and turn into Carrer de Santa Llúcia. There's another pretty cloister at the Casa de l'Ardiaca, (Archbishop's Palace). This is now home to the city's newspaper and magazine archive (not open for visits). It was given a modest facelift in 1902 by Domènech i Montaner, who decorated his *modernista* letter box at the entrance with a swallow to symbolize the speed at which the postal service should run, and then gave it a tortoise as a reminder of the true state of affairs. On the feast of Corpus Christi, you can watch eggs dance on the flower- decked Gothic fountain here too.

The Plaça Nova is as blank as its name, a bland expanse of concrete with little to redeem itself. In 1994, the poet Joan Brossa did his best to add some sparkle with his sculptural poem *Barcino* which spills out in a narrow string beneath the Roman towers to the right of the cathedral (at the beginning of Carrer del Bisbe), which form an arch across to the 18th-century Palau Episcopal (Bishop's Palace). In the evenings, there are always plenty of bands, flame-throwers, tango dancers and the inevitable human statues. The frolicking frieze of *sardana* dancers and parades which sweeps across the modern **Col.legi d'Arquitectes** (College of Architects) on the opposite side of the square was designed by Picasso, but executed by the Norwegian Carl Nesjar in 1961 because Picasso refused to set foot in his homeland while it remained under a dictatorship. There are two more murals inside the building as well as a fine restaurant and an excellent architectural bookshop.

Plaça Nova
On Sunday between 1200-1400 you can join in with a Sardana, the stately Catalan circle dance (see page 42)

To the left of the cathedral entrance is the Pia Almoina, a Gothic almshouse which incorporates part of the Roman walls and tower and which once provided food and shelter for hundreds of the city's suffering. It has been thoroughly and beautifully renovated to hold the **Museu Diocesà** (Diocesan

Pia Almoina

Ciutat Vella: The Old City

Around La Seu

C del Boters
C del Arcs
Plaça Nova
Av de la Catedral
Plaça Antoni Maura
Mercat d'Antiquitats
Artur Ramon
Cañas
C de la Palla
C de Pí
Drap
C de la Palla
Casa de l'Ardiaca
Plaça de la Seu
Pia Almoina/ Museu Diocesà
Plaça de Sant Felip Neri
C de Santa Llúcia
Banys Nous
Sta Eulàlia
Museu de Calçat
C de Sant Sever
C del Bisbe
Catedral de la Seu
Museu Frederic Marés
C de la Tapineria
L'Arca de l'Àvia
EL CALL
C de la Pietat
Palau Reial Major
Plaça del Rei
Via Laietana
Arc de Sant Ramón de Call
C de Sant Honorat
Palau de la Generalitat
C de la Fruita
Joguines Foyé
C de Marlet
Grafiques El Tinell
Paradís
Ruins of Temple to Augustus
Cereria Subirà
Museu d'Història de la Ciutat
C del Veguer
Vins I Caves La Catedral
C d'Avinyó
C el Call
Sombrería Obach
C de la Llibreteria
Plaça de l'Àngel
C de Ferran
C d'en Eixalada
Plaça St Jaume
C de Jaume I Carrer
Tribu
Casa de la Ciutat/ Ajuntament
Taxis

0 metres 50
0 yards 50

3 Gótico
4 Grand Hotel Barcino
5 Hostal Galerías Maldà
6 Hostal Jardí
7 Hostal Layetana
8 Hostal Rey Don Jaime
9 Pensión Vitoria
10 Suizo

● **Eating**
1 Ateneu Gastronòmic
2 Hostal El Pintor
3 La Bona Cuina
4 La Vinateria del Call

● **Cafés & tapas bars**
5 Bliss
6 Café d'Estiu

7 El Portalón
8 Méson del Café

○ **Entertainment**
1 Maldá Cinema

○ **Clubs & bars**
2 El Paraigua

■ **Sleeping**
1 Call
2 Colón

Museum), whose entrance is on Plaça Nova. The museum is a gold mine of religious treasures from the Middle Ages onwards, encompassing paintings, sculpture, gold and silver work, vestments and coins.

■ *Museu Diocesà de Barcelona*, www.arquebisbatbcn.es Tue-Sat 1000-1400 and 1700-2000, Sun 1000-1400. €1.80.

Santa Ana

North of Plaça Nova is the small, unassuming district of Santa Ana, with few eye-catching monuments or museums, but plenty of opportunities to shop. The two main shopping streets of the Barri Gòtic meet here: the **Carrer Portaferrissa**, with lots of trendy fashion stores, and the **Avinguda del Portal de l'Àngel**, with several of the major chains and a branch of *El Corte Inglés*. Tucked away in dim passages are tiny shops which haven't changed in decades selling everything from shawls and fans to honey and chocolates.

The Avinguda del Portal de l'Àngel, the main artery of this neighbourhood, links Plaça Nova with Plaça de Catalunya. It's pedestrianized but always busy, and packed with street entertainers who are usually several notches better than their counterparts on La Rambla. One of the most flamboyant *modernista* buildings is at No 20, a gaudy palace to gas with flickering blue flames erupting from torches at the entrance.

Els Quatre Gats & around Just past the gas palace, on the right, is narrow Carrer de Montsió, where the famous Els Quatre Gats tavern has been faithfully recreated at No 3 in the splendid *modernista* **Casa Martí**, Puig i Cadafalch's first commission in the city, which features sumptuous carvings by Eusebi Arnau, including a triumphant St George bearing the standard of Catalunya.

Els Quatre Gats began life here in 1897, when the painters Ramon Casas and Santiago Rusiñol, along with Miquel Utrillo and Pere Romeu, nostalgic for their old stomping ground of Montmartre, rented the ground floor of the newly built mansion in order to provide a meeting place for all their friends. It was partly inspired by the celebrated Parisian café *Le Chat Noir*, alluded to in the name, which also happily means a 'handful of friends' in Catalan slang.

The tavern survived just six years, but was a roaring success among its varied clientele of artists, intellectuals, bohemian hangers-on and tourist gawpers. It produced its own review – a custom it has recently taken up again, although the new version is really just an advertising sheet – held concerts, puppet shows, poetry concerts and art exhibitions and encouraged protegés, including Picasso who designed the menus.

The famous painting depicting Casas and Romeu on a tandem is now at the *Museu d'Art Modern* in the *Parc de la Ciutadella* (see page 96), but a copy hangs here. Romeu spoilt the party by leaving to devote himself to cycling and his sports car, one of the first in the city, and ended his days as a garage owner. Ironically, the building became the headquarters of the reactionary *Cercle de Sant Luc*, of which Gaudí was a member, and which was dedicated to the glory of God – and stamping out the hedonism of the Catalan bohemians.

Monestir de Santa Ana Off to the left of Avinguida del Portal de l'Àngel runs bustling **Carrer de Santa Ana**, named for the simple and often overlooked, Romanesque Monestir de Santa Ana, set back in its own quiet square. Founded by the Knights Templar in the early 12th century, it was dramatically revamped during the Gothic period and gained a graceful, two-tiered cloister and a pretty fountain, although little of note remains inside.

Ciutat Vella: The Old City

Almost opposite the monastery's gates, narrow Carrer Bertrellans heads down to join Carrer Canuda. At the bottom is a massive, ugly building site: this is the sorry Plaça Vila de Madrid, a wide square which has been mostly dug up in archaeological excavations and building works. In a grassy corner, excavators turned up a Roman sepulchural way, a series of simple funerary monuments lined up beside one of the smaller Roman access roads into the city. This necropolis, now sunk several feet beneath ground level, was placed outside the city walls in accordance with ancient Roman law. These are very simple graves: the finest funerary decorations, including a very sexy dancing Maenad, are exhibited at the Museu de l'Història de la Ciutat (see page 70).

Plaça Vila de Madrid

Plaça del Pi and around

Heading back towards the hub of the old city down Carrer Bot, a quick right onto **Carrer Portaferrissa**, which is full of trendy young fashion shops, and then left will take you down **Carrer Petritxol**. Once the *chocolate* street, many of the confectioners have now been replaced by designer boutiques and art stores. You can still try some of the city's best *chocolate y churros* at the **Granja Dulcinea**, at No 2, or be tempted by the chocolate display at *Xocoa*. The newly renovated art gallery **Sala Paré**, at No 5, was established in 1840 and gave Picasso his break by commissioning his first solo show.

Carrer Petritxol opens up at **Plaça del Pi**, a lovely square named for a glade of pine trees which once stood here, their memory recalled now by a single pine. The hulking 15th-century Gothic church of **Santa Maria del Pi** brandishes its tall octagonal bell tower and glowers over the square. It is now solely remarkable for its enormous rose window, the biggest in Europe, as looters burnt the interior to a crisp during the Civil War. Opposite the church is the old retailers' guild at No 3, covered in elegant, swirling *esgrafido* from 1685.

Plaça del Pi, adjoining **Plaça Sant Josep Oriol** and miniature **Plaçeta del Pi** are now lively spots for an evening *copa* out on the terrace, with plenty of wandering musicians, fire-throwers and jugglers for entertainment. On the first Friday and Saturday of the month, a market selling local cheeses, honey and *embutits* (cured meats) sets up its stalls, and on Thursdays there's an antiques market. Plaça Sant Josep Oriol has artists of dubious quality most weekends, and an art market on the first weekend of each month.

Around Plaça Sant Jaume

Carrer Banys Nous, off Plaça Sant Josep Oriol, follows the line of the old Roman walls. A tiny section has been incorporated into the friendly *Granja* at No 4, one of the city's many old milk bars that have become cafés. The New Baths of the street name refer to the Jewish baths, as this street also marks the boundary of the old Jewish Quarter, known as El Call from the Hebrew word quahal, meaning 'meeting place'. The area is a shadowy maze of twisting passages and overhanging buildings with few reminders of what was once the most important Jewish population in medieval Spain. The only vestige of the medieval Jewish presence in the city is a faded stone with a Hebrew inscription from 1314 which was erected at the corner of Carrer Arc de Sant Ramon de Call and Carrer Marlet in the 19th century. It is thought to have come from the main synagogue on nearby Carrer Sant Domènec del Call. The main street of the old ghetto was Carrer el Call, which carries a plaque at No 14 to mark the site of the printer and bookseller Cormellas, who pops up in Cervantes' *Don*

El Call
🚇 *Jaume I;*
buses 16, 17,
19, 22 and 45

Quixote. The quarter is now mainly known for its antique shops, and is a delightful place for a wander or a good rummage.

Palau de la Generalitat

Presidents of the Generalitat are put up comfortably in the 16th-century former canon's house

The Palau de la Generalitat has housed the Catalan parliament since the early 15th century. A string of houses belonging to wealthy Jews were peremptorily appropriated to form the nucleus of the assembly's first permanent home. The architect in charge was Marc Safont, who designed the graceful Gothic inner **Courtyard** with a slender colonnaded staircase airily balanced on a wide arch, with an upper arcade covered with swarms of leering gargoyles. Safont also designed the richly decorated **chapel** (1432) on the first floor, entered by an exuberant, finely detailed and flamboyant Gothic doorway. The chapel is dedicated to St George – who was adopted by the Catalans after making a posthumous appearance at the battle of Mallorca in 1229 and saving the day – and he and his dragon fight it out in paintings, sculpture and an embroidered altarpiece encrusted with gold and silver. The **Pati dels Tarrongers** (Courtyard of Orange Trees) was begun a century later, the soft pink of the marble columns echoed in the blossom in early spring. The **Golden Room**, named for its overpowering 16th-century gilded ceiling, is purely ceremonial, and the assembly prefer the modern **Sala Antoni Tàpies** to conduct business – blazoned with the eponymous artist's four-part series of medieval chronicles of Catalunya.

The main **façade** on Plaça Sant Jaume is mainly 16th-century, with a couple of 19th-century flourishes: another statue of St George, and a balcony from which the Catalan Republic was proclaimed by Francesc Macià in 1931 – it lasted a single day. In 1977, Josep Tarradellas returned from a four-decade exile to lead the Generalitat once more, greeting the cheering crowds from this balcony with the words 'Ja sóc acqui!' – 'I am here!'

■ *Guided visits only on the second and fourth Sundays of the month 1000-1400. Arrive early to sign up for the English tour and bring ID, entrance around the side on Carrer del Bisbe.*

Casa de la Ciutat

Facing the Palau de la Generalitat on the Plaça Sant Jaume, the late 14th-century Casa de la Ciutat contains the offices of the **Ajuntament** (city council) – the successors of the medieval Consell de Cent (see page 269). It was given a banal neo-classical facelift when the square was being laid out in the early 19th century.

The old Gothic entrance still sits quietly on Carrer de la Ciutat, the delicate tracery of the doorway overlooked by the Archangel Raphael. The shady arches of the courtyard through the main entrance are dotted with sculptures, including an amorphous figure by Joan Miró, and others by Francesc Marés and Josep Clarà. The sumptuous **Escala d'Honor** (Staircase of Honour) leads up to the 16th-century Gothic gallery, a series of slim arches with a menagerie of cavorting creatures around the capitals.

A magnificently carved wooden door leads into the **Saló de Cent**, the core of the old Gothic palace. Designed by Pere Llobet, the hall was inaugurated in 1373, and echoes the Saló de Tinell of the Royal Palace in its monumental simplicity. It was heavily restored after bombing in 1842, and again in the early 20th century. It blazes with light from chandeliers emblazoned with the city's coats of arms and the walls are hung with red and gold striped tapestries representing the coats of arms of the towns which were annexed to Barcelona at the end of the 19th century.

Just off the hall to the right is the circular, domed **Sala Reina Regente**, designed in 1860 by Francesc Daniel Molina, and now used for plenary meetings; it makes up for its small dimensions with plenty of pompous statuary and frilly fittings. On the other side of the Saló de Cent is the **Saló de les**

Cróniques, awash with enormous sepia murals, painted by Josep Maria Sert for the Exhibition of 1929, with dramatic depictions of Catalan exploits in Greece and Asia Minor during the 14th century. A black marble staircase overlooked by a sugary mural of skipping Catalan peasants heads back down to the courtyard, where you'll also find the city hall's municipal **information office**. It's currently displaying models of the city's next big transformation project – the projected seaside development in Poble Nou, at Diagonal Mar for the 2004 Forum of Cultures (see page 210). ■ *Daily Sun 1000-1400. Free.*

Plaça Sant Just and around

Close to the Ajuntament, down narrow Carrer Dagueria, is little **Plaça Sant Just**, edged with some of the city's most elegant palaces, including the richly sgraffitoed **Palau Moixó**, swarming with putti and garlands. The square is named for the Església de Sants Just i Pastor which overlooks it and is reputedly the burial place of the city's first martyrs. Said to date from the fourth century, this was perhaps the first church constructed in Barcelona, but no one really knows. Inside, there's a beautiful 16th-century *retablo* in the **Capella de Sant Feliu**, and some curious Visigothic capitals which have been turned into fonts. The High Altar is a florid 19th-century affair, which features the Black Madonna of Montserrat, who is supposed to have made a miraculous appearance here before heading back to her mountain refuge.

Església de Sants Just i Pastor

Heading in the direction of La Rambla, bustling Carrer Ferran leads off from Plaça Sant Jaume. You are now in the entertainment heart of the city. Carrer d'Avinyó was once a notorious red-light district and a favourite haunt of Picasso, whose studio was close by on Carrer de la Plata. His black-eyed models were the women who worked along it. His famous painting *Les Demoiselles d'Avignon* ('How that name irritates me!' he later wrote) was originally titled the *Avignon Brothel*. Nothing remains of Carrer d Avinyó's scandalous past besides the odd stone face leering above the door lintels – these marked brothels in the days before mass literacy. It's now a very trendy street packed with designer shops and hip bars – some places even double up as both. The boutiques here show the very latest stuff by Barcelona's newest designers, some of whom studied at the art school half way down the street where the graffitied neo-classical statues have been given fluorescent bikinis.

Carrer d'Avinyó

Carrer de n'Arai leads off to the right and onto Plaça George Orwell, studded with a large metal sculpture that looks like a giant eyeball. This has been thoroughly taken over by the city's youth – who call it the '*Plaça del Trippy*' and has several cafés and bars spilling out onto the square. From here, the grungy **Carrer Escudellers** is lined with dozens more bars, and is packed in the evenings. At No 8, the *Grill Room* bar and restaurant has managed to hang on to its swirling *modernista* façade and fittings from 1902.

Plaça George Orwell

La Mercé

Carrer Nou de Sant Francesc heads seawards into the old barrio of La Mercé; a formerly grand district of palaces and merchants' town houses from the 18th century. By the 19th century, this neighbourhood was too close to the grit and grime of the port to retain any illusions of grandeur and the grandees were all heading out to the new Eixample (see page 115). The smart houses were chopped into flats and warehouses, and *tascas* – old-fashioned bars serving

◆ Drassanes; buses 14, 59 and 91

Ciutat Vella: The Old City

seafood tapas which sprang up everywhere – still survive, and it's a great place to begin an evening.

Carrer Ample & around

Carrer Ample (Wide Street) was the city's smartest address in the days when streets wide enough for two carriages to pass were exceptional. The grandest remaining residence is at No 28, the **Palau Sessa Larrard**, built for the Viceroy of Catalunya, but soon taken over by a rich banker. Nearby is **Plaça del Duc de Medicaneli**, a small palm-filled square used as a set by Almodovar in his Oscar-winning film *Todo Sobre mi Madre* (All About My Mother).

Plaça de Mercé

This is where FC Barça come to celebrate their victories

The heart of La Mercé is the vast, domed Basilica de La Mercé, which stands on the quiet Plaça of the same name and is where the whole city erupts for the *Festival de la Mercé* (see page 44) in early September. The **façade**, the only characteristically Baroque frontispiece left in the city, was pinched from the dismantled Església de Sant Miquel, which also provided it with the delightful Gothic doorway topped with a carving of the archangel Michael wrestling with a scaly devil which is tucked away on Carrer Ample.

The basilica was built in the late 18th century on the site of an old convent founded in 1267 after the Virgin appeared to King Jaume I and asked that he found an order dedicated to the deliverance of Christians held by pirates. The enormous statue of the Virgin which seems to float high above the roof was only made in 1953, a replacement for an earlier statue destroyed during the Civil War; this one was cast in bronze from the melted-down statues of Catalan heroes which lined the Passeig de Lluis Companys (see page 97).

Inside, somewhere in the shadowy gloom, the remains of Barcelona's Santa Maria de Cervelló are venerated, but not as much as the Gothic statue of the *Virgin of Mercy* (1361) by **Pere Moragues** which stands in a side chapel. The Virgin was credited with saving the city from a plague of locusts in 1687 and was even appointed commander of the army during the city's clash with the Bourbons in 1714 – although Bourbons proved hardier than locusts and refused to be crushed.

Eating and drinking

Expensive

• on maps, pages 72 and 77

Agut d'Avignon, C/Trinitat 3, just off C/de Avinyó, T93 302 60 34, daily 1300-1530 and 2100-2330, metro Jaume I. Set down an unprepossessing narrow side street, this is an unexpected gem. A very fine, traditional restaurant with comfortably old-fashioned décor reminisce from the market. Try the *farcellets de col* (stuffed cabbage leaves) or the succulent roast meats. *La Bona Cuina*, C/Pietat 12, T93 268 23 94, metro Jaume I. Housed in an elegantly converted antiques shop with views overlooking the apse of the Gothic cathedral, offers imaginative variations of Catalan favourites.

Mid-range

For information on Catalan cuisine see page 45

Agut, C/Gignàs 16, T93 315 17 09, Tue-Sat 1330-1600 and 2100-2400, Sun 1330-600, metro Jaume I. A comfortable, family-run restaurant serving excellent Catalan fare using the freshest produce: try the *fideuá* (a Catalan rice dish served with fish and prawns) and finish up with the home made profiteroles. *Ateneu Gastronòmic*, Plaça de Sant Miquel 2, T93 302 11 98, Mon-Fri 1330-1530 and 2030-2330, Sat 2030-2330, metro Jaume I. A lovely place which offers very imaginative Mediterranean and Catalan cuisine. Intriguing contemporary art and it has an adjoining cigar bar.

Café de l'Acadèmia, C/Lledó 1, T93 319 82 53, Mon-Fri 0900-1200 and 1330-1600 and 2045-1130, metro Jaume I. An elegant and romantic restaurant just off the lovely little Plaça Sant Just, with shaded tables out on the square in summer, lit by flickering torches in the evenings serving excellent, classic Catalan cuisine along with a few international touches – try the *rossejat* (rice cooked in fish broth).

Can Culleretes, C/d'en Quintana 5, T93 317 31 22, open Tue-Sat 1330-1600 and 2100-2300, Sun 1330-1600, metro Liceu. This is the city's oldest restaurant, founded in 1786, with a series of interconnected, wooden panelled and beamed rooms papered with pictures of celebrity visitors. There is an extensive selection of both heavy, meaty dishes – goose with apples or *botifarra amb mongetes* (sausage with beans) – and lighter seafood dishes, including grilled lobster. The home made desserts are especially good, and the wine list is surprisingly inexpensive. It's a very popular and friendly place, and worth booking in advance.

Cometacinc, C/Cometa 5, T93 310 15 58, open Tue-Thu 2000-0100, metro Jaume I. A charmingly set in an old 19th-century mansion. Relaxed jazz and fresh, Mediterranean dishes with some exotic influences and a very decent wine list. *El Gran Café*, C/de Avinyó 9, T93 318 79 86, daily 1300-1630 and 2000-0030, metro Liceu. A sumptuous, old *modernista* establishment, this has been recently refurbished to gleam with pre-war splendour. The food is classic Catalan and the prices are very good value. *El Salón*, C/Hostal d'en Sol 6-8, T93 315 21 59, Mon-Sat 1400-1700 and 2030-2400, metro Jaume I. There's a pleasingly louche feel to El Salón, with its burnished mirrors, and antique couches. An excellent cocktail list and a good selection of light dishes and more serious fare.

Hostal El Pintor, C/Sant Honorat 7, T93 301 40 65, open daily 1300-1645 and 2000-0130, metro Jaume I. Just off Plaça Sant Jaume I, this is an elegant restaurant set in an old mansion. Fresh, modern seasonal Catalan dishes; try the salmon tartare with armagnac or the excellent duck with strawberry sauce, or the *bacalao* (cod) with honey. Delicious homemade desserts.

Pitarra, C/de Avinyó 56, T93 301 16 47, Mon-Sat 1330-1600 and 2030-2300, metro Drassanes. Another classic old restaurant founded in 1890 and named after Serafí Pitarro (1839-95), the popular Catalan dramatist and writer. The cuisine – inventive Catalan – is excellent. *La Dentellière*, 26 C/Ample, T93 319 68 21, open 1330-1600, 2030-2330, closed Mon and Sun, metro Drassanes. A pretty, Parisian-style restaurant serving intricate and imaginative French and Catalan dishes; good choices include the small pastries stuffed with wild mushrooms and asparagus, or the deliciously light pear bavaroise.

Slokai, C/del Palau 5, T93 317 90 94, open Mon-Fri 1300-1600 and 2100-2400, Sat 2100-2400, metro Jaume I. A very fashionable, minimalist white restaurant with extraordinary sculptures and art; on Fri and Sat evenings audiovisuals will accompany your dinner. *Plà*, C/de Bellafila 5, T93 412 65 52, open dusk-0230, dinner served Sun-Thu 2100-2400, Fri and Sat 2100-0100, metro Jaume I. An attractive, brick-walled vaulted restaurant, with a galleried upper floor. The emphasis is on modern Mediterranean cuisine , but there are international flourishes. Desserts are extraordinary – try the apple and pear cake served with a sweet and sour sauce.

Juicy Jones, C/Cardenal Casañas 7, T93 302 43 30, open daily 1300-2400, metro Liceu. A **Cheap** long, brightly lit juice counter with a little restaurant downstairs. The set menu is very good value (€10.20), although it leans towards earnest vegetarian cooking. There are organic beers and wines on offer, as well as the delicious, freshly made juices and smoothies. *La Fonda*, C/Escudellers 10, T93 301 75 15, open 1300-1545 and 2030-2330, metro Liceu. Wooden floors, lots of plants and modern lighting are a perfect setting for the simple Catalan cuisine at good prices. No bookings are taken, so you'll have to queue. *La Veronica*, C/de Avinyó 30, T93 412 11 22, open Tue 2000-1330, Wed-Sun 1200-0130, metro Jaume I. A bright, contemporary space with a terrace out on the Plaça George Orwell in summer. Great, imaginative pizzas and an interesting range of starters. *La Vinateria del Call*, C/de Sant Domènec del Call 9, T93 302 60 92, open Mon-Sat 2030-0100, metro Liceu. A dark, wooden-panelled bar with very friendly and knowledgeable staff. Excellent, very fresh tapas (choose from the menu) and an excellent wine list featuring local wines.

● on maps, pages
72 and 77

Oolong, C/Gignás 25, T93 315 12 59, open Mon-Sat 0830-0230, Sun 1800-0200, metro Jaume I. Two-leveled, arty, low-lit. Offers fusion cuisine from Thailand, Japan and Spain ; though not exclusively vegetarian, it offers just a few meaty dishes. The music is jazzy or world music, and there are changing art exhibitions on the walls. *Menú del dia* €6. *Restaurante Pakistani*, C/d'En Carabassa 3, T93 302 60 25, metro Drassanes, open daily 1300-0100. A budget favourite, this cheap and cheerful restaurant dishes up plenty of excellent curries and vegetarian dishes. *Self-Naturista*, C/Santa Ana 11-17, T93 318 23 88, open Mon-Sat 1130-2200, metro Catalunya. A large, very popular vegetarian canteen. Functional décor, wide range of dishes and very good value. *Zoo*, C/Escudellers 33, T93 302 77 28, open daily 1800-0200, until 0230 Fri and Sat, metro Liceu. Funky, kitsch decor. The dishes are mostly simple variations on very substantial toasted sandwiches, named after animals – the Penguin, a veggie option with spinach and pine nuts, is delicious. Salads are also good, and there's a couscous of the day and a few daily specials.

Café-bars
with food/
tapas

Arc Café, C/Carabassa 19, T93 302 52 04, open 1000-0200, metro Drassanes. A charming café just off the C/Ample with small marble-topped tables, creamy walls, a special's blackboard (good Thai curries) and lots of newspapers. *Al Limón Negro*, C/Escudellers Blancs 3, T93 318 9770, open Tue-Sun 1100-0300, metro Liceu. A friendly, dimly lit, slightly hippyish, split-level bar just behind Plaça Reial with live music on Sunday nights and a resident DJ spinning mainly mellow tunes. *Bar Celta*, C/Mercé 16, T93 315 00 06, open Mon-Sat 1000-0100 and Sun 1000-2400, metro Drassanes. A friendly Galician bar specializing in octopus and squid washed down with fresh, sharp Galician white wine – there are plenty of other great traditional tapas too, from *patatas bravas* (sautéed potatoes), to *pescaditos fritos* (whitebait).

Bar del Pi, Plaça Sant Josep Oriol, T93 302 21 23, open Mon-Sat 0930-2300, Sun 1000-1500 and 1700-2200, metro Liceu. A narrow, old-fashioned split-level bar with a terrace offering views of the art market and the non-stop buskers. *Bar El Tropezón*, C/del Regomir 26, open daily 1300-0100, until 0300 Fri and Sat, metro Drassanes or Jaume I. Tiny, cheerful bar with wooden tables, jugs and hams hanging from the ceilings and a resolutely down-to-earth atmosphere. The tapas are fresh and great. It can get a bit smoky. *Bar La Plata*, C/Mercé 28, T93 315 10 09, open daily, metro Drassanes or Jaume I. A tiny, beautifully tiled, atmospheric bar with great barrels heaped up behind the counter serving wine and a few kinds of fresh and delicious tapas.

Bodega La Palmera, C/Palma de St Just 7, T93 315 06 56, open 0800-1530, 1900-1000. Metro Jaume I. Old-fashioned neighbourhood bar with a rippled roof, old wooden tables and benches, hanging hams, oil paintings, wine by the jar and simple tapas. *Café Schilling*, C/Ferran 23, T93 317 67 98, open 1000-0200 , until 0230 on Fri and Sat. A large, elegant and gay-friendly café with scattered wooden tables and red velvet banquettes. In the evenings, it's much livelier with a slightly older clientele. *Bliss*, Plaça Sants Just i Pastor, T93 268 10 22, open Mon-Sat 1000-0030, metro Jaume I. A cosy teashop and café, with lots of newspapers and magazines and a couple of leopard print sofas to sink into.

El Portalón, C/Banys Nous 20, T93 302 11 87, open Mon-Sat 0900-2400, metro Liceu. A delightful, traditional *bodega* set in an old stable with stone walls and vaults. There's a good range of tapas available and full menu of sturdy Catalan classics. *Els Quatre Gats*, C/Montsió 3-bis, T93 302 41 40, open Mon-Sat 0900-0200, Sun 1700-0200. The bohemian, tavern which put on Picasso's first show (see page 55) may have been beautifully recreated, but it hasn't managed to retain its old atmosphere. *La Cereria Café*, C/Baixada Sant Miquel 3-5, no phone, metro Liceu open Mon-Sat 0930-2200. Set in a lovely *modernista* wax-shop, this friendly café is run as a co-op. *La Soccarena*, C/de la Mercé 21 (no phone), open 1330-1500 and 1800-0300, metro Drassanes or Jaume I. A traditional Asturian bar serving sturdy tapas like pungent Asturian goat's cheese, or spicy cured meats washed down with cider.

Méson del Café, C/Libreteria 16, T93 315 07 54, open Mon-Sat 0700-2300, metro Jaume I. This tiny coffee shop is always bursting with crowds enjoying what is widely acknowledged to be the best cup of java in the city.

Taberna del Prior, C/Ample 18, T93 268 74 27, open Mon-Sat 1000-0100 and Sun 1000-2400, metro Drassanes. An old-fashioned bar and restaurant with all kinds of tapas. *Taverna Irati*, C/Cardenal Casañas 17, T93 302 20 84, open Tue-Sun 1200-midnight, *pintxos* served 1200-1500 and 1900-2300, metro Liceu. The hours are erratic at this long, narrow, unassuming bar. Although firmly on the tourist trail, plenty of locals go there too and the *pintxos* are acknowledged to be among the best in the city. Get there early. *Venus*, C/Avinyó 25, T93 301 15 85, open 1200-2400, metro Liceu. A deli-style café on a very fashionable street, cool without being pretentious. Wooden tables, mellow music and plenty of reading matter make it a very welcoming spot. There are light meals – salads, quiches – as well as homemade cakes.

> ## Five of the best: cheap eats
>
>
> - *Zoo* (see page 84)
> - *Bar-Restaurante Rodrigo* (see page 100)
> - *Pla dels Angels* (see page 112)
> - *Restaurante Romesco* (see page 112)
> - *La Singular* (see page 152)

Café d'Estiu, Plaça Sant Iu 5, T93 310 30 14, open Easter-Sep. Tue-Sun 1000-2200, metro Jaume I. One of the nicest cafés in the city set in the courtyard by the Museu Frederic Marès. A peaceful, romantic urban oasis with creamy umbrellas, cooling orange trees and candles. Simple snacks, pastries and cakes are on offer. *Gotto Zero*, Plaça Duc de Medicanelli, T60 783 97 27, open daily Sep-May 1000-0200, Jun-Aug 1200-0400, metro Drassanes. Set on one of the prettiest and leafiest squares, this relaxed juice bar also offers refreshing *horchatas*, *granitas*, and beer as well as ice-creams and sorbets. *Granja Dulcinea*, C/Petritxol 2, T93 302 68 24, open daily 0900-1300 and 1630-2100. This is perhaps the best-known *granja* in the city; you'll be served by white-jacketed, bow-tied waiters, and this pretty little café has an awesome reputation for its *chocolate con churros*. *La Pallaresa* C/Petritxol 11, T93 302 20 36, www.lapallaresa.com open Sat, Sun 0900-2200, Mon-Fri 0900-2100, metro Liceu. This is where to get your *chocolate con churros* in the morning – locals swear it's the best *xocolatería* and an unwitting temple to kitsch.

Cafés
For local specialities see page 45

Shopping

The old Jewish quarter known as El Call has dozens of tiny antiquarians in its narrow streets, particularly around Carrer Banys Nous and Carrer de la Palla. *Gothsland Galeria d'Art*, C/Consell de Cent 331, metro Passeig de Gràcia. This gallery and exhibition space has an incredible collection of *modernista* art, from beautiful furniture to sculptures and paintings. *Artur Ramon*, C/de la Palla, T93 302 59 70, metro Jaume I. Long established antiquarian with two adjacent shops displaying antique paintings and sculpture. *Cañas*, C/de la Palla, T93 302 69 93, metro Jaume I. Specializes in old maps, mainly of rural areas.

Antiques

Mercat d'Antiguitats de la Catedral, Plaça Nova, metro Jaume I, open Thu 1000-2200. Stalls with everything from antique lace to porcelain dolls, old stamps, and furniture. *Mercat de Numismàtica*, Plaça Reial, metro Liceu, open 0900-1400. Stamp and coins from around the world.

Antiques & Bric-a-Brac

Libreria Quera, C/Petritxol 2, metro Liceu. Maps and guides to the Catalan countryside and staff provide information on adventure sports. An excellent resource.

Books

Ciutat Vella: The Old City

Fashion

There are hundreds of boutiques in Barri Gòtic offering the unusual work of local designers

Barcelona has an excellent reputation for cutting-edge design; Carrer Portaferrissa is lined with young fashion shops. *Zsu Zsa*, C/de Avinyó 50, metro Jaume I. The work of several young Barcelonan designers can be found here – from floaty retro dresses, to cool t-shirts and a range of shoes and accessories. **Second-hand and vintage fashion** at *L'Arca de l'Àvia*, C/Banys Nous 20, metro Liceu. Antique embroidered dresses and bags, as well as bedding and household linens. **Streetwear** at *So_Da*, C/de Avinyó 24, metro Jaume I. A slick, minimalist shop with clubwear and street fashion for men and women. There's a bar tucked away at the back. *Tribu*, C/de Avinyó 12, metro Jaume I. Trendy outlet for designers like *D&G*, *E-Play* and *Diesel Style* as well as their own label. Look out for guest DJ nights. *Trip*, C/del Duc de la Victòria 9-11, metro Catalunya. Hip-hop fashion and clubwear for skateboarders.

Food & drink

See page 224 for a description of Catalan wines

Fargas, C/del Pi 1, metro Liceu. A lovely *modernista* chocolate shop, with spellbinding window displays which can feature chocolate rockets and steam trains, whole galleons with sails made of slivers of chocolate, and chocolate trophies blazoned with FC Barça's logo. *Casa del Bacalao*, C/Comtal 8, metro Urquinaona. This wonderful little shop sells nothing but dried and salted cod. *Herboristeria del Rei*, C/del Vidre 1, metro Liceu. Just off Plaça Reial, founded in 1818, has hundreds of exquisitely painted miniature drawers stuffed with all kinds of herbs. *La Pineda*, C/del Pi 16, metro Liceu. A charming old-fashioned grocery store and *bodega* specializing in cured meats, cheeses and wines with a few tables and chairs where you can taste the delicacies on offer.

Mel Viadiu, C/Comtal 20, metro Catalunya. A honey specialist founded in 1898, you'll find more than a dozen different kinds from all over Spain, as well as honey drop sweets and *turrón* (soft sweet nougat). *Vila Viniteca,* C/Agullers 7-9, metro Jaume I. This is a family-run wine store, with a dizzying selection of wines and cavas from all over Catalunya and Spain. *Vins i Caves La Catedral*, Plaça Ramon Berenguer el Gran I, metro Jaume I. A good, central wine store with an excellent selection of local and Spanish wine and helpful staff.

Interiors

Design is unquestionably what Barcelona does best

As well as the famous big names, there are a clutch of innovative young designers along Carrer Avinyó in the Barri Gòtic, who are always worth checking out. *Gotham*, C/Cervantes 7, metro Jaume I or Liceu. Very hip, slightly off-the-wall, run by interior designers, with all kinds of retro items from the 1940s and 50s, as well as sleek contemporary designs. *Zeta*, C/Avinyó 22, metro Jaume I. Quirky but very hip furniture, lamps and decorative objects.

Markets

Plaça del Pi, metro Liceu. The Plaça del Pi hosts several markets. On the first Friday and Saturday of the month, there's a charming honey market, when you'll also find other things like cured hams and farmhouse cheeses for sale. There's an antiques market on Thursday, and art is for sale on weekends in the adjoining Plaça Josep Oriol.

Specialist shops

Almacenes del Pilar, C/Boquería 43, metro Liceu. A stunning selection of traditional fringed Spanish silk shawls and elaborate fans. *Cereria Subirà*, Baixada de Llibreteria 7, metro Jaume I. Founded in 1761, this delightful old shop retains its original gallery and staircase, and is painted in a delicate eau-de-nil. *Flora Albaicin*, C/Canuda 3, metro Liceu. A small old-fashioned shop with a beautiful range of flamenco dresses, shawls and hair combs. *Grafiques El Tinell*, C/Freneria 1, metro Jaume I. A tiny little shop devoted to handmade paper items, from exquisite stationery to notebooks. *Sombrería Obach*, C/Call 2, metro Jaume. An extraordinary hat shop with dozens of different styles, from traditional Catalan felt berets to straw panamas. Specialist shops

El Ingenio, C/Rauric 6, metro Liceu. This magical old shop was founded in 1838. Inside you'll find everything you need for a fiesta – puppets, masks, carnival and fancy dress outfits. *Joguines Foyé*, C/Banys Nous 13, metro Liceu. A variety of new and old-fashioned toys, including furniture for dolls houses, music boxes and tin toys.

Joguines Monforte, Plaça Sant Josep Oriol 3, metro Liceu. Another delightfully old-fashioned toy shop with traditional toys like train sets and puppets as well as a selection of modern toys. *Drap*, C/del Pi 14, metro Liceu. The window displays are fabulous at this small shop devoted to exquisite dolls' houses. The furniture and accoutrements are made with extraordinary attention to detail: you can even buy a miniature goldfish bowl complete with a cat angling his paw inside.

Fuji Sports, C/Ferran 44, metro Jaume I. Everything you need for martial arts.

Sports

Transport

Bus Buses don't enter the narrow streets of Barri Gòtic. Take a bus to La Rambla or to Via Laietana.
Buses which run along La Rambla: Nos **14, 38, 59** and **91**.
Buses which run along Via Laietana: Nos **17,19, 40** and **45**.

Metro Line 3 (green) to Catalunya, Liceu or Drassanes; Line 4 (yellow) to Jaume I or Plaça Urquinaona; Line 1 (red) for Catalunya or Plaça Urquinaona.
Taxi There is a taxi rank on Plaça Nova in front of Cathedral de la Seu.
Train The nearest train station is at Plaça de Catalunya (see page 68).

Ciutat Vella: The Old City

La Ribera

In 1908, the city's planners decided to open up the old city by running a broad avenue through it and down to the port. The result was Via Laietana, now a traffic-filled boulevard with little to recommend it. Stranded to the north is the old artisan's district of La Ribera, which has got its own back by becoming a funky, fashionable neighbourhood with some of the city's trendiest bars, restaurants and shopping, as well as its most popular museum: the **Museu Picasso**; *its most beautiful church:* **Església Santa Maria del Mar**; *a string of elegant palaces along* **Carrer de Montcada**; *and the* **Parc de la Ciutadella**.

Nudging up to the fashionable Ribera is the resolutely unfashionable barri of **Sant Pere**. *There's nothing cutting edge about the grocers, bakers and pharmacies with their patient queues, or the shabby streets and run-down squares. This was historically a workers' neighbourhood and not much has changed; as families moved out, immigrants moved in, many from Latin America, and the sounds of salsa occasionally float through the streets. The 19th-century workers left their mark with the flamboyant* **Palau de la Música Catalana**, *the* modernista *concert hall built to house the celebrated workers choir, the* Orfeo Català.

History

During the middle ages, La Ribera was the hub of all the maritime activity that was making Barcelona rich. The sea encroached much further inland at that time, and the beautiful church of Santa Maria del Mar, dedicated to Mary, Star of the Sea and Patroness of Sailors, was at the heart of the harbour activity. Medieval tradesmen and maritime superstitions are still recalled in the street names of this ancient neighbourhood – like 'hat-makers street', or 'rope-makers street'. If a violent storm whipped up at sea, the captain would often swear to marry the first women he saw on dry land if he and his ship were saved – as a consequence, 'Ladies Street' (Carrer de les

Dames) got its name from the hopeful spinsters and widows who strolled there on stormy days hoping to catch themselves a ship's captain.

Neighbouring Sant Pere grew up around the gloomy monastery of the same name and has long been devoted to textile manufacture. It really took off from the late 17th century when the surrounding fields were filled with cotton ready to be made into cloth and exported to the American colonies. By the 19th-century, this was a slum district, crammed with factories and workers living in

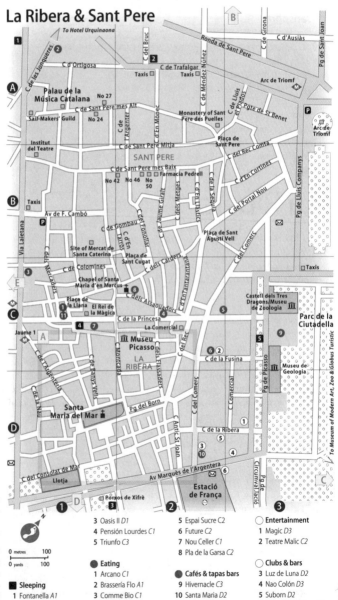

La Ribera & Sant Pere

Detailed map
A *Carrer Montcada &*
around, page 91
Related maps
B *Eixample,*
page 122
C *Vila Olímpica &*
Poble Nou, page 206
D *Port Vell &*
Barceloneta, page 198
E *Barri Gòtic, page 72*

0 metres 100
0 yards 100

3 Oasis II *D1*
4 Pensión Lourdes *C1*
5 Triunfo *C3*

● **Sleeping**
1 Fontanella *A1*
2 Hostal de Ribagorza *A2*

● **Eating**
1 Arcano *C1*
2 Brassería Flo *A1*
3 Comme Bio *C1*
4 El Foro *C2*

5 Espai Sucre *C2*
6 Future *C2*
7 Nou Celler *C1*
8 Pla de la Garsa *C2*

● **Cafés & tapas bars**
9 Hivernacle *C3*
10 Santa Maria *D2*
11 Txirimiri *C1*

○ **Entertainment**
1 Magic *D3*
2 Teatre Malic *C2*

○ **Clubs & bars**
3 Luz de Luna *D2*
4 Nao Colón *D3*
5 Suborn *D2*
6 Woman Caballero *D2*

Five of the best: sights in La Ribera

- *Església Santa Maria del Mar (see below)*
- *Passeig del Borne* (see below)
- *Carrer Montcada* and *Museu Picasso* (see page 90 and 92)
- *Palau de la Música Catalana* (see page 95)
- *Parc de la Ciutadella* (see page 96)

squalor and misery. Redevelopment of this district has been slow, but is gradually underway; the bulldozers may have moved in but nothing seems to faze the gossiping shopkeepers or their elderly customers.

Sights

From Via Laietana, head down Carrer Argenteria to the loveliest church in all Catalunya and one of the finest and purest examples of Catalan Gothic: Santa Maria del Mar. The main entrance overlooks the pretty **Plaça de Santa Maria del Mar** which has a couple of elegant tapas bars (see page 101) with tables out on the square, perfect for admiring its restrained façade with a vast rose window, flanked by twin octagonal towers.

Església Santa Maria del Mar
The city cultural office at the Palau de la Virreina (see page 63) can provide details of the concerts which are regularly held at the church

The church was begun in 1329, on the site of an ancient chapel dedicated to Santa Eulàlia, the patron saint of Barcelona. It took just 54 years to build, with most of the population of Barcelona giving a hand at some point or another. The speed of its construction meant that other styles and forms couldn't creep in as successive architects took over the job. The hulking exterior, built to withstand wind and storms, gives no hint of its spellbinding interior; a soaring central nave flanked with supporting columns of almost ethereal slimness. The awe-inspiring spaciousness is intensified by the lofty aisles, half as broad as the central nave and studded with shallow chapels between the buttresses. The ornate fittings accumulated over centuries were lost when the church was gutted during the Civil War; only the stained-glass windows, some dating back to the 15th century, were spared, but the bare brickwork only adds to its sublime beauty. ■ *Daily 0900-1330 and 1630-2000.*

Plaça de Santa María del Mar leads into the **Passeig del Born**, once a theatre for medieval jousting tournaments and 18th-century carnivals. At the opening of the *passeig*, facing the eastern wall of Santa María del Mar, is the **Fossar de les Morares** (Mulberry Cemetery), once the church cemetery and now a small square. This was the burial place of the martyrs of 1714, who defended the besieged city against the Bourbon armies (see page 271), and are remembered here annually on 11 September, *Catalan National Day.*

El Born
The fiesta spirit of El Born continues at the string of bars and cafés which line the broad street

At the end of Passeig del Born, you'll see the handsome, silent wrought-iron **Antic Mercat del Born** which has given the whole area its common name – El Born. Built in the 1870s, as the city's main produce market, it was abandoned in the 1970s. Plans are now afoot to convert it into a library and arts centre. There are more fashionable cafés and bars with terraces overlooking the **Plaça Comercial** in front of the market (see page 101).

Just around the corner on Carrer Comerç is one of the city's newest museums, the Museu de Xocolata (Chocolate Museum), housed in the old Monestir de San Agustín. The museum is run by the guild of pastry chefs which has an excellent school and restaurant next door. It has interesting displays on the fashionable custom of making chocolate, which came from the newly discovered Americas, and explores the stories behind its aphrodisiac and medicinal properties. Best of all is the chocolate tasting, and the shop sells particularly good chocolate in all its guises. ■ *Daily except Tue, Mon-Sat 1000-1900, Sun and holidays 1000-1500. €3.*

Museu de Xocolata

Ciutat Vella: The Old City

★ Things to do in La Ribera

- Tour the neighbourhood bars with a 'tapas crawl' around El Born (see page 89)
- Take in a concert at the beautiful Església de Santa Maria del Mar (see page 89)
- Go for a picnic and hire a boat in Parc de la Ciutadella (see page 96)
- Rummage around in the unusual fashion and art shops (see page 101)

The tiny streets which lead down to the port from Passeig del Born still bear the names of the trades once practised here; **Carrer Vidrieria** (Glassmakers' Street) leads into delightful, leafy **Plaça de les Olles**, (Pots and Pans Square), where there are more outdoor cafés and tapas bars.

Pla del Palau

Llotja — A narrow street leads out from the Plaça de les Olles onto noisy, traffic-filled Pla del Palau, a spacious 19th-century square flanked with grand edifices. The grandest is the Llotja (Exchange); this was the oldest continually functioning stock exchange in Europe, until the wheeler-dealers moved to their spanking new offices in the Passeig de Gràcia in 1994. Behind the 18th-century façade sits the the original Gothic construction: the magnificent **Sala de Contractaciones** (circa 1380), designed by Pere Llobet who was also responsible for the Saló de Cent (see page 80). The top floor once housed the **Academia Provincial de Belles Artes de la Llotja**, the art academy where Picasso's father taught when the family arrived in Barcelona in 1895. Picasso, Miró and plenty of lesser known artists studied here – although Miró got thrown out for poor draughtsmanship. The whole building is currently under wraps for renovation and plans for its future remain undecided.

Porxos de Xifre — Opposite the Llotja is the Porxos de Xifrè, a block of five houses built in the
Picasso's family ate at — 1830s and ringed with arcades or porches (hence the name). It was built by
the famous restaurant — Josep de Xifrè, who had gone to the Americas to make his fortune as a penni-
Les Set Portes in the — less young man, and returned a few decades later with a vast fortune. The
Porxos de Xifrè — building was deliberately constructed as a kind of paen to the New World and the fortunes that could be made. Portraits of famous explorers and conquistadors line the central pilasters, and beneath the arches are carved trophies depicting the richness of the New World.

Facing the Porxos de Xifrè is the 18th-century **Duana Vella** (Customs House), another graceful neo-classical building which was transformed in 1902 into the seat of the Civil government. Behind it, continuing along the Avinguda Marquès de l'Argentera, is the graceful **Estació de França**, a lovely old train station with a rippling glass roof which was built in preparation for the 1929 International Exhibition (see page 174).

Carrer Montcada

◉ *Jaume I;* — Back on Passeig del Born, turn right just before the Església Santa Maria del Mar
bus nos 17, 19, — and head down Carrer Montcada. In the 12th century this street was undoubt-
40 and 45 — edly the swankiest address. Squeezed up against each other, these monuments to Barcelona's medieval mercantile wealth are largely constructed around wide, airy courtyards, closed off from the prying eyes of the curious or the hostile behind thick wooden doors. Anyone can have a look around now as many of them have been elegantly converted to house galleries, bars and museums. The Carrer Montcada has become one of the most popular streets in Barcelona,

Ciutat Vella: The Old City

mainly thanks to the pulling power of its biggest attraction, the Museu Picasso.

Despite the crowds, Carrer Montcada is refreshingly free of tourist tat, and the smart galleries and shops live up to their aristocratic surroundings. The **Gallery Maeght**, at No 25, has a sweeping courtyard with a staircase of ethereally light columns. It exhibits the work of new and established artists and also has an excellent bookshop. At No 20 the 17th-century **Palau Dalmases**, complete with overblown staircase and spacious inner court, now promotes itself as an *Espai Barroc* (Baroque Space), where you can sip an expensive cocktail amid red velvet and dripping candles (see page 244).

At Carrer Montcada No 12, the Museu Textil is a fashionista's dream. Housed in the Palau dels Marquesos de Lló, the collection includes 16th to 20th-century fashion – from richly embroidered Baroque frocks and silver-soled shoes to **Cristóbal Balenciaga's** tailored suits and fluffy 'Baby Doll' dress, and **Paco Rabanne's** funky 1960s chainmail hotpants. There is a collection of rare fabrics and exquisite tapestries dating back to the third century, an exhibit of lace and

Museu Tèxtil
A combined ticket is available with adjoining Museu Barbier-Mueller d'Art Precolumbi and costs 4.20 euros

Ciutat Vella: The Old City

Carrer Montcada & around

■ Sleeping
1 Park *C3*

● Eating
1 Hofmann *A1*
2 L'Ou Com Balla *A2*
3 La Flauta Magica *A2*
4 Little Italy *A3*

5 Passadís d'en Pep *C1*
6 Rodrigo *B1*
7 Salero *C3*
8 Sandwich & Friends *B3*
9 Senyor Parellada *A1*
10 Sikkim *B3*
11 Vascelum *C1*

● Cafés & tapas bars
12 Bodega La Tinaja *B2*
13 Cal Pep *C2*
14 Del Born Nou *B3*
15 El Xampanyet *A2*

16 Estrella de Plata *C2*
17 Euskal Etxea *B2*
18 La Vinyor del Senyor *B1*
19 Sagardi *B1*
20 Tèxtil *A2*
21 Va de Vi *B2*
22 Xador Granja *B1*

○ Entertainment
1 Abaixadors Deu *B1*
2 Astín *B1*
3 Ribborn *B3*

○ Clubs & bars
4 Barroc *B3*
5 Bier Art *B2*
6 Borneo *B3*
7 Gimlet *A3*
8 Lola *C2*
9 Palau Dalmases *A2*
10 Pas del Born *B3*
11 Pitin *B3*
12 Plàstic Café *B2*

another of dolls. The basement features the designs of Barcelona's up-and-coming fashion and textile designers in temporary exhibitions. Up in the attic, old looms and sewing machines illustrate the mechanisation of the textile trade which made the city's fortune in the 17th and 18th centuries, and the views out across the rooftops are delightful. ■ *Tue-Sat 1000-1800, Sun and holidays 1000-1500. €3.60. Free first Sat of the month from 1500, www.museutextil.bcn.es*

Museu Barbier-Mueller d'Art Precolumbí
The city spent millions expensively converting another of Carrer Montcada's palaces, the Palau Nadal, to exhibit 170 pieces loaned on a rotating basis from the Swiss museum of the same name – now three millennia of art treasures encompassing powerful sculpture, jewellery and ceramic ware from the ancient civilizations of Central and South America are theatrically arranged on spotlit plinths. A gallery is devoted to the lesser-known treasures of the Caviana and Marajó islands which sit at the gaping mouth of the Amazon river, including a selection of beautiful ancient funerary urns featuring designs which still reappear in the contemporary works of Brazil's indigenous peoples.

Next door is the **Sala Montcada**, a cultural space run by Spain's largest savings bank, a *Caixa*, which offers a changing programme of innovative, contemporary art. ■ *Tue-Sat 1000-1800, Sun and holidays 1000-1500. €3. Free first Sat of the month 1000-150,* www.bcn.es/icub Sala Montcada. *Tue-Sat 1100-2000, Sun 1100-1500, T93 310 06 99, www.fundacio.lacaixa.es*

Museu Picasso

The museum vies with Museu FC Barcelona at Camp Nou (see page 155) for the title of Barcelona's most visited museum
Further down on the right is the Museu Picasso spectacularly housed in a string of adjoining palaces at Nos 15-23. The museum contains few of Picasso's most famous paintings, apart from the series based on **Velázquez's** *Las Meninas*, and focuses instead on the artist's early work in Barcelona. The nucleus of the collection is formed by a gift of early paintings and sketches from Picasso's lifelong friend and secretary, Jaume Sabartés i Gural. The holdings were substantially enlarged when Picasso donated a large collection of works that his sister had squirrelled away in her house on Passeig de Gràcia, and once again when Picasso died, bequeathing to the museum a substantial body of graphic work. Finally, in 1980, Picasso's widow, Jacqueline, donated a large collection – almost 150 pieces – of ceramic work.

Sabartés donated his collection of Picasso's works to the city on the condition that a new museum be built to house them. The Museu Picasso finally opened in the beautifully restored Palau Berenguer d'Aguilar in 1963, while Picasso worked in self-imposed exile in southern France; he had outspokenly refused to set foot in Spain while it suffered under the dictatorship of Franco.

Early period
It's worth visiting the temporary exhibitions, often linked to Picasso's time in Barcelona, held in two adjoining palaces
The collection begins with Picasso's assured drawings and sketches of his family and friends created during his childhood in Málaga. Some critics suspect he destroyed everything he had done before the age of nine, in order to substantiate his boast that he never drew like a child. *Ciència i Caritat* (Science and Charity, 1897), an early rigorously realistic piece, was painted at his father's insistence and won a prestigious prize in Madrid. Unfortunately, the work didn't attract the wealthy sponsor Picasso's father had hoped for. There are also portraits of his fellow artists – including one of Jaume Sabartés, and another of the darkly devilish Carles Casegamas, Picasso's companion on his first jaunt to Paris, who was eventually to commit suicide.

A walk in Picasso's footsteps

In 1895, Picasso's family arrived in Barcelona where, his father, Don José Ruiz I Blasco, was to take up a post as professor of fine arts at the Academia Provincial de Bellas Artes, located on the top floor of the Llotja (stock exchange building) near the harbour. The family took a small apartment nearby at **No 3 Carrer Reina Cristina***, and then moved again to rooms just around the corner at No.4 Carrer Llauder. In 1896, the family moved yet again, this time to* **No 3 Carrer de la Mercé***, and José Ruiz rented a small studio for his gifted son at* **No 4 Carrer de la Plata***. This is where he sat as a model for the figure of a doctor sitting by the bedside in Picasso's first important painting,* **Ciencia i Caritat** *(Science and Charity), painted in 1897 when Picasso was just 17.*

This was also the year when Rusiñol and Casas inaugurated their famous tavern, Els 4 Gats at **No 3 Carrer de Montsió***, for which the young Picasso designed the menus and where he held impromptu exhibitions. In 1899, Picasso, who had very little money, was sharing a studio at* **No 1 Carrer Escudellers** *Blancs with two sculptors, which quickly became a sociable hang-out for all their friends. Not far away is* **Carrer d'Avinyo***, which was lined with brothels and which is said to have given Picasso the inspiration for his celebrated painting Les Demoiselles d'Avignon (it was also here that he contracted gonorrhea). He later shared a studio with his haunted, handsome friend, Carlos Casegamas, on the* **Carrer Riera de Sant Joan** *(the house and street are long demolished) in the seedy red-light district of the Barri Xinès.*

In 1900, the young friends took a third-class ticket to Paris, where one of Picasso's paintings was on show at the Universal Exhibition there. They quickly sought out the Catalan community in the French capital, eagerly soaking up the new ideas and techniques which were being discussed in what was then the mecca of the art world. Casegamas, troubled and addicted to drink and drugs, killed himself the following year, and Picasso returned to Barcelona. He was able to afford a studio by himself at **No 28 Carrer del Comerç***, where he created many of the haunting works of his Blue Period, using as his models the beggars, prostitutes and gipsies who filled the poor streets.*

In 1904, he moved permanently to Paris, although he regularly returned to Barcelona for visits. His last extended stay in the city was in 1917, when he came to oversee a production of Parade, an avant-garde ballet by Serge Diaghilev and his Ballets Russes for which he had designed the costumes and sets. He fell headlong in love with a beautiful ballerina called Olga Kokhlova, whom he married the following year. He was adamant that he would not set foot on Spanish soil under the dictatorship of General Franco, but in 1961 he sent sketches for the friezes which adorn the **Col.legi d'Arquitectes** *on the Plaça Nova.*

The early selection includes some of the chilly paintings of his Blue Period, like the stricken mother and child of *Desamperados (*The Despairing, 1904) or the capering ragamuffin *El Loco* (The Madman, 1904). These studies of figures on the fringes of society – beggars, street musicians, whores – are infused with a haunting light reminiscent of the mystical paintings of El Greco, who was much admired by early *modernistas*. Picasso was also influenced by the grim studies of gypsies and beggars painted by Isidro Nonell. Both young men were poor, and knew the grim lives of their impoverished subjects at first hand. In 1904, Picasso left permanently for Paris, returning for just a few brief visits.

Blue period

Rose period The works of Picasso's Rose Period are well represented but there is almost
& beyond nothing, just a small *Head* (1913), from the **Cubist** years, and a single *Harlequin* (1917), from the **celebrated series**. From 1917, there's another leap in time to the extraordinary series of 44 paintings and drawings based on **Velázquez**'s *Las Meninas*, which Picasso painted in a concentrated six-month burst at the end of 1956. Every detail of Velázquez's masterpiece has been picked out, pored over and reinterpreted. Picasso donated the series to the museum in 1968, as a gesture to his old friend Jaume Sabartés who died after a long illness. The *Las Meninas* series forms part of a wider project of interpretations of three major paintings which also included **Delacroix**'s *Les Femmes d'Alger* and **Manet**'s *Le Déjeuner sur l'Herbe*. ■ *Tue-Sat 1000-1930. €4.40. www.museupicasso.bcn.es Free first Sun of the month.*

Sant Pere

Dusty Sant Pere sits quietly across the Carrer Princessa, a wide road which divided Sant Pere from La Ribera a century ago. These two *barris* may be neighbours but they have nothing in common: fashionable La Ribera, with its museums, shops, and nightlife, is a world away from humble Sant Pere where life continues much as it has done for decades. Sant Pere grew up around the **Monestir Sant Pere de les Puelles**, which also gave its name to the three main streets of the barri, but was destroyed by looters during the Civil War. Sant Pere's lack of obvious charms is perversely its greatest attraction; Barcelona's watchwords – 'fashion', 'design' and 'urban development' – have no place here, making it refreshingly down-to-earth. Nonetheless, Sant Pere does boast one important monument, the opulent **Palau de la Música Catalana**, one of the loveliest *modernista* structures in the city.

Around Carrer Carrer Montcada meets Carrer Princesa, which was built in 1853 as the final
Princesa stage of the sweeping 19th-century plan to connect La Rambla with a Ciutadella. A plaque at **No 37** highlights the street's brief moment of glory as one of the city's most exclusive addresses, and the birthplace of the painter Santiago Rusiñol (see page 281).

Carrer Montcada leads to the tiny Romanesque **Capella de Santa Maria d'en Marcus**, once part of the long-demolished Hostal de la Bona Sort, a traveller's hostel and hospital for the poor. Carrer Montcada then meets Carrer Corders (rope-makers street), which follows the old Roman access road into the city. Turn left onto it to find shabby little **Plaça de la Llana**, named for the wool market which once took place here, and which in turn leads into Carrer Bòria, where criminals were punished by being given a sound whipping as they scampered down the street.

Carrer If you retrace your footsteps back along up Carrer Corders, the street becomes
Carders Carrer Carders. A spider's web of narrow streets to the left leads to the 19th-century **Mercat de Santa Caterina** which is now just a building site; market activity has been temporarily moved to a giant, unabashedly ugly tent cluttering up Passeig de Lluis Companys (see page 97) until the new market is finished. Carrer Carders culminates in **Plaça de Sant Agustí Vell**, a pretty, small square which still preserves some Gothic townhouses, a medieval horse-trough, and a couple of nice little bars with tables out on the square.

From Plaça de Sant Agustí Vell, head up Carrer Sant Pere les Basses to the triangular Plaça de Sant Pere which is flanked by the former monastery of Sant Pere de les Puelles. It looks more like a prison or a fortress and has in fact been both. Church burnings in the 1830s incinerated many of its fittings and then looters finished the job off during the Civil War: just a few Gothic columns and capitals remain, but parts of the old Romanesque cloister can be seen at the Museu Nacional d'Arte de Catalunya (see page 178).

Monestir de Sant Pere de les Puelles
A cross-shaped modernista iron fountain by Pere Falqués sprouts surreally out in the square

Retrace your steps and turn right onto Carrer Sant Pere més Baix, one of the three parallel streets which form the hub of the medieval neighbourhood. This is now a lively shopping street dotted with mouldering remnants of the medieval and 18th-century palaces. At **No 52** is one of the oldest pharmacies in the city – **Farmacia Pedrell** (now Farmacia Fonoll), founded in 1561 and given a peppy *modernista* makeover in 1890, including some delicious stained glass by Joan Espinagosa. The painter Isidre Nonell was born next door at **No 50**, and lemon-painted **No 46** has some lovely *sgraffito*. A much-restored factory down a passage at **No 42** is a reminder of the neighbourhood's industrial might in the 19th century. The grand, gloomy building at **No 9**, now the **Institut del Teatre**, was once the *Biblioteca Popular de la Dona*, the first public library in Spain to be devoted exclusively to women.

Carrer Sant Pere més Baix

Ciutat Vella: The Old City

Heading up Carrer de la Mare de Déu del Pilar, a narrow passage leads into Carrer Sant Pere més Alt, the most important of the three medieval streets, and home to Lluis Domènech i Muntaner's Palau de la Música Catalana, sprouting flowers, garlanded columns and stained glass.

The Palau de la Música Catalana was built for the **Orfeó Català**, a celebrated choral society founded in 1891 by two young musicians Lluís Millet and Amadeu Vives, who hoped to continue the work begun by Josep Anselm Clavé. Popular music had become an important strand of the Renaixença (see page 279), a patriotic movement which celebrated a rather rosy-hued vision of Catalanism. The newly formed Orfeó Català gave its first recital in 1892 to great acclaim; by 1905 it had 185 singers and more than a thousand contributors.

Palau de la Música Catalana
Buying concert tickets is the best way to appreciate this sublime construction

It was time that the Orfeó Català had a new home and **Domènech i Montaner** (see page 279) – one of the most important exponents of *modernista* architecture – was chosen to build it. Several of Catalunya's most celebrated craftsmen and artists, including the mosaic artist Lluis Bru and the sculptors Miquel Blay and Pau Gargallo, collaborated with Domènech i Montaner on the decoration. Work began in 1905, and was completed three years later, despite being periodically held up by financial hiccups. The site was not ideal, too small for Domènech's grand ideas, but it was close to the workers whom the choir, notionally at any rate, claimed to represent.

The grandiloquent **façade** is a hymn to music and Catalanism: at the top the Orfeó Català warbles in front of the sacred peaks of Montserrat and busts of famous composers – Wagner, Beethoven, Palestrina, Bach – look out over the street from the balconies below. But perhaps most extraordinary is **Miquel Blay**'s fulsome *Allegory of Catalan Folksong*, which billows out from the corner of the building. The large painting just inside the vestibule is by **Miquel Massot**, who was told by Domènech that all his daring and inventive *modernista* architecture was insulted by the staid classicism of this painting.

The whole building is encrusted with ceramic floral motifs transforming it into an exuberant sculptural bouquet

Domènech overcame the problems represented by the tiny site by situating the vast **auditorium** on the upper floor, and keeping the administration offices and practice rooms on the ground floor. A double flight of stairs edged with wrought-iron balusters encased in amber-coloured glass leads up to the magnificent auditorium, Domènech's astonishingly beautiful 'glass box'. Light streams in through the vast stained-glass ceiling covered with rainbow-coloured flowers and musical angels, and through lofty arched windows of pale pink glass, garlanded with flowers. The acres of glass are supported by a spindly iron skeleton, a new method of construction which Gaudí was also trying out on the Sagrada Família (see page 131), and which was behind the rash of skyscrapers sprouting up in the cities of North America.

The **stage** is overwhelming, thickly encrusted with massive sculptural groups by **Didac Masana** and **Pau Gargallo**; galloping winged horses bearing Valkyries leap over Beethoven's unfazed bust on one side and on the other Anselm Clavé sits beneath a gnarled tree. Behind them, 18 garlanded maidens, part painting and part sculpture flutter across the back wall of the stage. These 'spirits of music' are the work of **Eusebi Arnau**, who might not have approved of the musicians' habit of using the projecting figures as coat racks.

The charming museum shop 'Les Muses de Palau', on the corner of the square, has a range of beautiful modernista-inspired gifts

The Palau de la Música Catalana won the 1908 Building of the Year award, but only two decades later it was sneeringly referred to as the 'Palace of Catalan Junk'. Whatever the punters thought of the decor, no one argued about the appalling **acoustics**. The glass walls may have allowed the sunlight to flood in – but with it came all the street noise. Concerts were regularly punctuated with church bells, the crowing of cocks, and the honking of cars. It barely escaped demolition. After decades on the sidelines, interest in the building was revived: In the early 1980s Oscar Tusquets, the local celebrity architect and designer, was responsible for the extension of the building and made a largely unsuccessful attempt to improve the terrible acoustics.

■ *Daily 1000-1530, visits by guided tour only. Tours in English, Castilian and Catalan depart every 30 mins and last 50 mins, including a 20-min video. Admission €4.20. Note, the long and rather overblown video takes up almost half of the 50-min tour, and so visiting the rest of the Palau can be a breathless whirl.*

Parc de la Ciutadella

'*Gardens are to the city what lungs are to a man*'.

Josep Fontseréi Mestres (1829-97)

Barceloneta, Ciutadella-Vila Olímpica, Arc de Triomf. Bus nos: 14, 39, 41, 42, 51 and 141

The Parc de la Ciutadella is no great beauty, but it has a place in every Barcelonan's heart. Families come for picnics, schoolkids hang out on benches and smoke furtively, romantics stroll through the gardens, and office-workers sprawl on the grass for a siesta. The **1888 Universal Exhibition** has left an extraordinary legacy of *modernista* architecture, including the exhibition restaurant housed in a cartoon castle complete with turrets, and the peaceful **Museu d'Art Modern**, in the middle of the park, has a fascinating collecton of modernista art and furnishings.

History   When Barcelona was forced to surrender to the Bourbons on 11 September 1714 (now celebrated as Catalan National Day), the victor's pay-back was vicious and immediate. A swathe of buildings in the Ribera district were razed to the ground, and the enormous citadel began to rise in their place. It was only finally destroyed in 1869, when the townspeople tore it down with their bare hands. In its place rose one of the city's first public spaces, an elegant horseshoe-shaped park filled with gardens, fountains, a botanical museum and a Museum of Modern Art set in the remodelled arsenal.

In 1888, the park was chosen as the site of the Universal Exhibition by Barcelona's self-aggrandizing mayor, Rius i Taulet. He was determined to put the city (and himself) on the European map in a big way. Pavilions, hotels, cafés, restaurants, new roads and even triumphal arches were constructed, and, on the appointed day, the World Fair was opened with much pomp and ceremony. It changed the face of the city dramatically; after this, Barcelona would always pin her redevelopment projects around one showcase event – she did it again for the International Exhibition of 1929 (see page 174), and, perhaps most spectacularly, for the 1992 Olympics.

The Passeig de Lluis Companys was designed as a ceremonial entrance to the park, and is lined with delicate wrought-iron lamp posts designed by Pere Falqués. The statues of Catalan heroes which were once ranked along the *Passeig* were melted down under Franco to make the huge Virgin which floats above the Basilica de la Mercé (see page 82). Nowadays, a great tent squats in the middle – this is the temporary home of the *Mercat Santa Caterina*. The whole boulevard is overwhelmed by the pompous, neo-Moorish red-brick **Arc de Triomf** which was conceived as the gateway to the 1888 Exhibition; it wasn't quite finished in time.

Passeig de Lluis Companys

Just inside the park's red brick entrance at the end of Passeig de Lluis Companys is Domènech i Montaner's **Castell dels Tres Dragons**, one of the earliest *modernista* edifices, showcasing the use of Catalan red brick hung on an iron skeleton. The castle is now home to the dusty old-fashioned Museu de Zoologia with a vast whale skeleton suspended over the central hall and the bones of one of the first residents of the nearby Zoo, an elephant called l'Avi (the ancestor), peering out over the park at the back. Upstairs, there's case after case of stuffed creatures including bears and wolves, and flocks of beady-eyed raptors flying in for the kill. ■ *Daily except Mon 1000-1400, until 1800 on Thu. €3, free first Sun of the month.*

Museu de Zoologia

The Museu de Geologia was opened in 1882 and is the oldest museum in the city. One wing contains meticulously classified minerals and explanations of the geological phenomena of Catalunya, while the other is devoted to fossils, including some containing the imprints of dinosaurs, dating back millennia. ■ *Daily except Mon 1000-1400, until 1800 on Thu. €3.*

Museu de Geologia

Next to the Geology Museum is the delightful **Hivernacle** (winter greenhouse), a glassy pavilion which contains a very charming café (see page 100). In the opposite corner of the park is the extravagant **Cascade**, a flamboyant fountain with twin flights of steps, a triumphal arch and a host of Classical gods and goddesses from Neptune to Aphrodite surrounding a grotto said to have been designed by Gaudí. It overlooks a small boating pond, a popular Sunday picnic spot for Barcelonan families.

At the centre of the park is the small **Plaça des Armes**, named after the old arsenal which is home to both the Catalan parliament and the small Museu d'Art Modern. It's not much of a crowd-pleaser, concentrating almost exclusively on Catalan art from the mid-19th to the early 20th centuries, but this means it is usually enjoyably quiet.

Museu d'Art Modern

The art is arranged chronologically, beginning with the paintings of **Marià Fortuny**, a very popular painter whose minutely detailed works found immense favour with bourgeois society. In 1860 he was sent off to North Africa to paint battle scenes by the Catalan government: his enormous *Battle* *of Tetuan* (1863) fills almost an entire gallery. In the latter part of the 19th century, the Renaixança was inspiring painters to celebrate *La Terra Catalana* (The Catalan landscape): **Joaquim Vayreda** (1843-94), one of the early leaders of the Olot School (see page 219), painted enchanting landscapes using delicate brushwork and a misty light conferred by the application of a very thin layer of green or brown paint.

The Sitges Luminists are represented here by **Joan Roig i Solé** and **Arcadi Mas i Fontdevila**; both artists were admirers of Marià Fortuny, and were impressed by the use of colour and rapid recording techniques of the Italian *Macchiaioli*. **Santiago Rusiñol** and **Ramón Casas** were at the forefront of the *modernista* art movement, using new techniques and unusual subject matter. They managed to squeeze in some painting between the hedonistic pursuit of the good life in Sitges (see page 227), and the establishment of their bohemian tavern, Els Quatre Gats (see page 281); the famous painting of the two friends on a tandem which became a symbol of the tavern is held here.

The next series of galleries contain an extraordinary selection of furniture, including several fine pieces by **Gaudí**, **Puig i Cadafalch** and **Gasper Homer**, and a stunning chapel studded with elaborate stained glass. *Modernista* sculpture is also well represented; **Josep Llimona** struggles with his Catholic conscience but fails to strip his pale goddesses of sexiness, and there are also works by **Miquel Blay**, **Eusebi Arnau** and **Josep Clarà**.

This is followed by paintings from the 'Second Generation' of *modernista* artists: **Isidro Nonell** was part of the new generation influenced by Rusiñol and Casas, particularly by their choice of subjects. He began to paint gypsies and beggars, living for long periods in gypsy communities, his work in turn influencing Picasso's Blue Period. There are also several beautiful landscapes by **Joaquim Mir**, **Francesc Gimeno** and **Nicolau Raurich** and a sumptuous early landscape from **Dalí**. The small selection of works by **Pau Gargallo** and **Juan Gris** point the way towards abstract sculpture: on display are Gargallo's stone head of Picasso from 1913, an expressive metalwork *Great Dancer* from 1929 and **Gris**' unsettling welded head, *The Tunnel* (1932-33).

Zoo   The Zoo is cramped, even though it takes up almost half of the park. It is set to move to a new site at Diagonal del Mar in 2004 when it is hoped that the animals will be given larger enclosures than the miserable concrete boxes they now endure. The highlight is *Copito de Nieve* (Snowflake), the only albino gorilla in captivity, now old and bored with all the cameras. There's a petting zoo with farm animals and pony rides, a new penguin enclosure, and a **Dolphinarium** with regular shows. ■ *Oct-May Mon-Thu 1030-1930, Sat 1030-2130, Sun 1030-2030; Jun-Sep Mon-Fri 1000-2100, Sat and Sun 1000-2300. €9.33.*

Eating and drinking

Expensive   *Hofmann*, C/de l'Argenteria 74-78, T93 319 58 89, closed Sat and Sun, metro Jaume I
● *on maps, pages*   Just next door to the famous cookery school run by Mey Hofmann, this restaurant
88 and 91   offers outstanding cordon bleu cuisine impeccably served in a series of utterly charming, plant-filled dining rooms. *Passadís d'en Pep*, Pla del Palau 2, T93 310 10 21, open Mon-Sat 1330-1530 and 2100-2330, metro Barceloneta. A wonderfully eccentric seafood restaurant, hidden down a narrow internal passage next to a *caixa* (bank) on the Pla del Palau. Simple but very elegant. There are no menus; just sit back as plate after plate of the freshest seafood offerings are brought to you. It's a real gourmet treat.

Espai Sucre, C/Princesa 53, T93 268 16 30. Elegant, contemporary building – huge frosted glass windows, minimalist interior. New cooking school, with the emphasis on desserts – *menú de degustación* is €42, average meal is €18. You can book a special room with a glass window and tilted mirror into the kitchen if you want to see how it's done.

Brassería Flo, C/Junqueres 10, T93 319 31 02, open daily 1330-1600 and 2030-2430, metro Urquinaona. A lavish Parisian-style restaurant in a stunning *modernista* building, conveniently close to the *Palau de la Música Catalana*. It's a copy of the *Brasserie Flo* in Paris and offers a varied menu of French and Catalan cuisine; try the shellfish platters, or foie gras or the sole stuffed with spinach, but don't forget to leave room for the wonderful desserts. There are three good-value fixed-price menus, including one at €19.74.

Mid-range

    El Foro, C/de la Princesa 53, T93 310 1020, open Sun, Wed, Thu 1330-1630 and 2100-2400 Fri-Sat 1330-1630 and 2100-0400, metro Jaume I. A big, airy warehouse-style restaurant on two levels which dishes up good pizza and pasta, as well as Argentinian grilled meats, to a stylish crowd. *Little Italy*, C/Rec 30, T93 319 79 73, open 1300-1600 and 2100-2400, closed Sun, metro Arc de Triomf. Live jazz and Meditterean cuisine in the Born. Mixed crowd of older people and young jazz fans, good mellow atmosphere.

    La Flauta Magica, C/Banys Vells 18, T93 268 46 94, open daily 1330-2400, metro Jaume I. Another of the stylish Born restaurants catering to a laid-back fashionable crowd. It serves mainly vegetarian cuisine – like the delicious crêpes with a mushroom and spinach filling – and a couple of dishes using organic meat. Daily specials are on offer at lunchtimes. *L'Ou Com Balla*, C/Banys Vells 20, T93 310 53 78, open Mon-Sat 2100-2400, metro Jaume I. This is a relaxed, low-lit stylish restaurant with an eclectic menu which draws together dishes from Greece, Morocco, France and dozens of other countries. Try the goat's cheese salad with red fruits or the coq au vin – and finish up with one of their amazing desserts. It's related to the equally delightful *El Pebre Blau* close by at C/Banys Vells 21, T93 319 13 08.

    Salero, C/del Rec 60, T93 319 80 22, open Mon-Thu 0845-1730 and 2000-0100, Fri 0845-1730 and 2000-0300, Sat 2000-0300, metro Jaume I. An ultra-stylish cool white New York-style restaurant in the heart of the Born. Serves creative Mediterranean-Japanese cuisine at surprisingly low prices. Try the tuna tartare or the sardine tempura. Popular with a young hip crowd and a good starting point for the excellent bars in the area. Great breakfasts too – like the brie waffle with apricot jam or homemade muesli.

    Senyor Parellada, C/de l'Argenteria 37, T93 310 50 94, open daily except Sun 1300-1530 and 2100-2330, metro Jaume I. Call in advance as this very popular restaurant is currently closed for renovation. Set in a magnificent 18th-century building, this is a comfortable, buzzy and stylish restaurant. The menu concentrates on modern Catalan dishes using the freshest market produce; try the *papillotte* of French beans with mushrooms or the delicious sole cooked with almonds and pine nuts.

    Sikkim, Plaça Comercial 1, T93 268 43 13, open Mon-Sat 2100-0100, metro Barceloneta or Jaume I. A welcoming, intimate, low lit restaurant with ochre walls and lots of Indian and Eastern hangings and carpets, serving very inventive Mediterranean and International cuisine; try the risotto with cuttlefish and aubergine, which melts in the mouth. *Vascelum*, Plaça de Santa Maria 4, T93 319 0167, Tue-Sun 1230-1600 and 2000-2400, metro Barceloneta. A relaxed, modern restaurant painted in cool greens, with wooden floors and racks of bottles. Offers a good range of seafood and modern Catalan dishes, an extensive wine list and some very well-priced fixed menus.

Arcano, C/Mercaders 10, T93 310 2179, open Mon-Sat 1920-0130, metro Barceloneta. Tucked down a narrow little side street, Arcano is warm and welcoming with attractively rustic décor and changing art exhibitions. There's a good range of simple tapas and a choice of several excellent full meals including a rich aubergine moussaka and delicious *escalivada*; finish up with some pastries. After you have eaten, get your fortune read by Luis, a Tarot expert. *Comme Bio*, Via Laitana 28, T93 319 89 68, restaurant

Cheap
For Catalan specialities see Essentials, page 45

Ciutat Vella: The Old City

Five of the best: cafés with terraces

- *Cafè d'Estiu* (see page 85)
- *Bar Kasparo* (see page 113)
- *Glaciar* (see page 242)
- *Pitin Bar* (see page 244)
- *Bar del Sol* (see page 246)

open daily Mon-Fri 1300-1545 and 2000-2300, shop and bar open Mon-Sat 0900-2300, Sun 1200-2300, metro Jaume I. This is a large, stylish vegetarian restaurant, café and health food shop in one; the food is simple but tasty, with lots of tofu, rice and lentils spiced up with Oriental flavours. The café serves good juices and snacks, and downstairs there's a clothes shop devoted to natural fabrics.

Future, C/Fusina 5, T93 319 92 99, open Mon-Thu 0830-2330, bar open until 0230, Fri 0830-2330 and 2330-2330, Sat 1100-2400, bar open until 0300, metro Jaume I or Arc de Triomf. With its minimalist décor and stylishly retro light fittings, Future attracts a lively, fashionable crowd. Catalan dishes are given a creative, fresh twist. There's a resident DJ on Saturday nights until 0300. *Nou Celler*, C/Princesa 16. T93 310 47 73, open Mon-Fri 0800-2330, Sun 1100-1500, closed Sat, Metro Jaume I. This small down-to-earth, bustling restaurant is always packed and serves traditional Catalan dishes to locals in an old-world setting.

Pla de la Garsa, C/dels Assaonadors 13, T93 315 24 13, open Mon-Sat 1330-1545 and 2000-0100, Sun 2000-0100, metro Jaume I. This attractive old stone building was once a stables but has been very charmingly converted with marble-topped tables, tiled walls and a spindly spiral staircase. There are good tapas and the upstairs dining room (not quite as atmospheric as the downstairs) has good Catalan dishes on offer at lunchtimes and evenings. There's a good value *menú del dia* at lunchtimes.

Bar-Restaurante Rodrigo, C/Argenteria 67, T93 310 78 14, open 1300-1600 and 2030-2400, closed Wed night and Thu, metro Jaume I. A very popular budget favourite near the cathedral of Santa Maria del Mar, this is an old-fashioned restaurant serving big portions of Catalan fare at lunchtimes and good sandwiches and light snacks in the evenings. *Sandwich & Friends*, Passeig del Born 27, T93 310 07 86, open 1000-0100 daily, metro Jaume I. A bright, buzzy, white café with a huge Pop Art mural across one wall, serving dozens of different kinds of sandwiches, both hot and cold, all named after friends. The food is served on the outdoor terrace in summer.

Café-bars serving tapas/food *Bodega La Tinaja*, C/Espartería 9, T93 310 22 50, (parallel to Passeig del Born), T93 310 22 50, open daily 1800-0200, metro Barceloneta/Jaume I. This brick-vaulted *bodega* dripping with old furnishings and antique clay wine pots has tables tucked into dim corners and a fashionable candlelit, romantic atmosphere. Good tapas, some hot dishes – like *habitas* (baby broad beans cooked with cured meat), and an excellent selection of wines, but all this comes at a price. *Txirimiri*, C/Princesa 11, T93 310 18 05, open daily 1130-0100, metro Jaume I. Cheerful, rowdy bar with lots of wooden tables. *Pintxos* are laid out on the bar between 1130-1530 and 1900-2300. Wash them down with cider and crisp Basque wine.

Santa Maria, C/Comerç 17, T 93-315 1227, open Tue-Sat 1330-1530 and 2030-0030, metro Jaume I. One of the most elegant tapas spots in the Born, Santa Maria offers tiny portions of delectable tidbits – sometimes using unusual ingredients like *espardanyas* (sea slugs) – with an excellent and comprehensive wine list. Sleek modern fittings complement the old stone walls.

Bar Hivernacle, Parc de la Ciutadella, T93 295 40 17, open 1000-0100, metro Arc de Triomf. A beautiful, relaxing café-bar set in an elegant iron and glass pavilion built for the 1888 Universal Exhibition; lots of shady palms, a terrace, changing art exhibitions and occasional jazz concerts in summer. *Estrella de Plata*, Pla del Palau 9, T93 319 60 07, open daily except Sun 1300-1600 and 1900-0200, metro Barceloneta. A long, slim bar which is at the vanguard of Barcelona's gourmet tapas bars; it's expensive, but the quality is among the best in the city. There are tables outside overlooking the square in summer.

Euskal Etxea, Plaçeta Montcada, T93 310 21 85, open Tue-Sat 0900-2330, Sun 1245-1530, restaurant Tue-Sat 1330-1530 and 2100-2330, metro Jaume I. Where better to tuck into Basque *pintxos* than the Basque Cultural Centre. There's a large restaurant and exhibition space at the back, but it's most fun crowding around the bar, piled high with an excellent selection of the famous Basque snack. Get a plate from

⭐

**Five of the best:
veggie restaurants**

- *Juicy Jones* (see page 83)
- *La Flauta Mágica* (see page 99)
- *L'Hortet* (see page 112)
- *La Buena Tierra* (see page 151)
- *L'Illa de Gràcia* (see page 168)

the bar staff, help yourself and then count up the cocktail sticks at the end. Come early for the best selection. *El Xampanyet*, C/Montcada 22, T93 319 70 03, open Tue-Sat 1200-1600 and 1830-2330, Sun 1200-1600, metro Jaume I. A classic little bar with old barrels, coloured tiles and marble-topped tables, run by an eccentric but very charismatic family. Simple tapas – salt cod, anchovies and tortilla – are on offer and the house cava is deliciously cool. One of the nicest spots in the city.

Pla de la Garsa, C/Assaonadors 13, T93 315 24 13, open Mon-Sat 1300-1600 and 2000-0100, Sun 2000-0100, metro Jaume I. Set in a converted former stable, this is a beautiful wood and stone bar with classical music. It specializes in simple tapas – *torrades*, cured meats and cheeses – but there is a good fixed-price menu at lunchtimes and in the evenings. *Va de Vi*, C/Banys Vells 16, open daily 1200-1500 and 1700-0100, metro Jaume I. A sophisticated, candle-lit wine bar set in a stone vaulted space beneath a 16th-century palace. There's an excellent, if expensive, wine list and simple, but high-quality tapas – like platters of perfectly cured meats or pungent local cheese. *Sagardi*, C/Argentería 62, T open daily 1200-2400, metro Jaume I. A lively spot with a long wooden bar overlooking a small square. Another of the popular Basque *pintxo* bars and there's an *asador* (grillroom) at the back featuring grilled fish and meat.

La Vinyor del Senyor, Plaça Santa Maria 5, T93 310 33 79, open Tue-Sat 1200-1330, Sun 1200-1600, metro Jaume I. This elegant wine and tapas bar, has an excellent selection of wines, cavas, sherries and moscatell. Bottles line the walls and vines figure on the creamy lampshades. Exquisite and beautifully presented tapas are on offer – from olives stuffed with anchovies to unusual cured meats. In summer, an attractive terrace faces the soaring main façade of Santa Maria del Mar.

Cal Pep, Plaça Olles 8, T93 310 79 61, open daily 1300-1645 and 2000-2400, evenings only on Sun and Mon, metro Barceloneta. Run by the same owner as the nearby *Passadis del Pep* (see page 98), this is one of Barcelona's classics. There's a smart, brick-lined restaurant at the back, but it's more entertaining to stand at the bar as charismatic Pep grills fish and steaks and holds court at the same time. The tapas are of excellent quality.

Café del Born Nou, Plaça Comercial 10, T93 268 32 72, open 0900-2200, metro Jaume I. A spacious, airy café with tables out on a terrace overlooking the old Born market, this is a very mellow spot to while away a morning with the papers. Occasional art exhibitions and relaxing music add to the appeal. *Tèxtil Cafè*, C/Montcada 12, T93 268 25 98, open Tue-Sun 1000-2345, metro Jaume I. Set in the graceful courtyard by the Museu Tèxtil (see page 91), this is a delightful café with a good range of snacks and pastries. *Xador Granja*, C/Argentería 61, T93 319 36 48, open daily except Mon 0830-1230, metro Jaume I. A charming old *granja* with some *modernista* decoration near the cathedral of Santa Maria del Mar, this has a good selection of pastries to dip into your thick hot chocolate.

Cafés
● *on maps, pages 88 and 91*

Shopping

La Mutata, Passeig de la Cadena 10, metro Jaume I. This is a tiny, relaxed bookshop and café just around the corner from the Museu Picasso on Carrer Montcada. It's got a

Books

reasonable selection of art, design and a few coffee table books. *Norma Comics*, Passeig de Sant Joan 9, www.norma-ed.es   metro Arc de Triomf. This is the city's biggest comic shop, with a vast selection of comics from around the world.

Fashion   **Streetwear** at *La Comercial*, C/Rec 50, metro Jaume I. Clothing and accessories from labels like Paul Smith, Energie, Scooter, Satellite and dozens of others. **Leather goods** at *Casa Antich* SCP, C/Consolat del Mar 27-31, metro Jaume I. Traditional luggage with a vast range of bags and suitcases. They can also make leather goods to order. *Las 40 Ladronas*, C/Esparteria 17, metro Jaume I. The boutique of the '40 thieves' is an Aladin's cave of daring, one-off designs made from secondhand clothes. Rummage through the heaps, or pick out an entirely original outfit. *Pisamorena*, C/Consolat de Mar 41, metro Barceloneta. Original women's clothes – feminine but sexy dresses, quirky t-shirts, beaded shoes, scarves. It's impossible to walk out without buying something. *Anna Pobo*, C/Vidrieria 11, metro Barceloneta. This is an elegant boutique with cool, simple designs in linen, and natural fabrics, and a small but discerning selection of shoes and accessories.

Food & drink   *La Mallorquinai*, C/Vdreria 15, metro Barceloneta. This is a delightful bakery and cake shop in La Ribera; don't miss out on the traditional Catalan almond biscuits called *carquinyolis*. *E&A* Gispert, C/Sombrerers 23, metro Jaume I. Just follow your nose to this wonderful old shop established in the 1850s – it's a Mecca for teas, coffees, herbs and spices.

Interiors   *Aspectes*, C/Rec 28, metro Barceloneta. Well-known design shop, featuring furniture and household items by young designers from across Europe. *Homâ*, C/Rec 20, metro Barceloneta. No two pieces are the same at this shop, which creates all kinds of lighting and furniture from unusual materials and has kitted out some of the most fashionable addresses in town. *Ici et Là*, Plaça Santa Maria del Mar 2, metro Jaume I or Barceloneta. Affordable, unusual creations for the home from around the world. *Atalanta Manufactura*, Pg del Born 10, metro Jaume I. Beautiful hand-painted silks, linen and velvet and a few unusual objects for the home; it's part-shop, part-atelier and you can watch the artists at work. *Nayamau*, Pg del Born 12, metro Jaume I. You'd never guess from the outside, but this scruffy workshop supplies some of the hippest bars in the neighbourhood with their extraordinary light fittings and ornaments.

Specialist   Toys and magic at *El Rei de la Màgia*, C/Princesa 11, ww.arrakis.es/~reimagia   metro
shops   Jaume I. An extraordinary shop devoted to magic and magicians, with walls papered with photographs of celebrated magicians. *Kitsch*, Placeta de Montcada 10, metro Jaume I. A virtually life-sized papier mâché model of a grinning gipsy sits at the entrance to this extraordinary shop; inside are even wilder creations.

Transport

Bus   Buses skirt the edge of the small, compact district of La Ribera, El Born and Sant Pere. For Parc de la Ciutadella, take a bus to the Pg de Picasso, the Arc de Triomf, the Pg Pujades or the Pg de Cirumval.lació. Bus no **17** from Pg Joan de Borbó to Avda Jordà, via Via Laietana, Pg de Gràcia, Gràcia and Avda Tibidabo. No **39** runs from Pg Joan de Borbó to Guinardo, via Arc de Triomf, and the Eixample. No **42** from Santa Coloma to Plaça de Catalunya, via Gran Via, Parc de la Ciutadella and Arc de Triomf.

Metro   Line 4 (yellow) to Jaume I, Plaça Urquinaona or Barceloneta. Line 1 (red) to Plaça Urquinaona. Line 1 (red) to Arc de Triomf, Ciutadella-Vila Olímpica.

Taxi   There is a taxi rank near the Arc de Triomf metro station.

Train   Some trains on the local RENFE network (*cercanías/rodalies*) stop at Arc de Triomf and Plaça de Catalunya on their way to or from Sants station.

El Raval

Not so long ago, El Raval was the neighbourhood that everyone avoided – poor, seedy, and desperate. Nowadays, it's the place where everyone wants to be seen – fashionable new bars, clubs, galleries and restaurants seem to pop up almost daily. The slightly edgy atmosphere of the old days still lingers in some streets, but that only adds an extra twist to what is definitely Barcelona's most vibrant alternative scene in fashion, music and art.

A sizeable immigrant community, mainly North Africans and Pakistanis, has grown up, making El Raval one of the most multicultural neighbourhoods in the city, with halal butchers and curry houses rubbing shoulders with old-fashioned modernista *haberdashers and grocers. This barri may be best known for its nightlife, but there are several surprises tucked away, including a* modernista *masterpiece from Gaudí:* **Palau Güell***, the medieval* **Antic Hospital de la Santa Creu***, the prettiest Romanesque church in Barcelona:* **Església de Sant Pau de Camp***, and the glittering new* **Museu d'Art Contemporani***.*

History

El Raval lay well outside the city boundaries until the 14th century, when fields and scattered farmhouses were encircled by the final extension to the city walls. The smelliest and most dangerous industries like brick-making and leather tanning were located here, well away from most of the population. Churches, charitable institutions and hospitals also grew up outside the city walls, where more land was available. When the Catholic church's property was seized and auctioned off after the Mendizabel Laws were enacted in 1837, vast tracts of property became available, particularly in the Raval area. This was also a boom time for the city's industrial manufacturers, who seized the lands and began to throw up factories and apartment blocks. By the mid-19th century El Raval was a dank, fetid slum crammed with squalid buildings, a miserable home to the poor and wretched. Then it was known simply as El Quinto (The Fifth District).

By the late 19th century, the southern part of El Raval, nearest the port, had become the most famous red-light district on the Mediterranean, filled with whorehouses, seedy bars, music halls and cabarets. Jean Genet plied his trade as a rent boy here, Picasso and his impecunious friends rented shabby studios on its fringes, and anarchists and radicals conspired in its miserable attics. Nicknamed the *Barri Xinès* after San Francisco's vice-ridden Chinatown, its heyday was in the 1920s and 30s. Like New York's Harlem, tourists flooded in to slum it at the bars and cabaret halls until Franco put an end to the party.

During the 1970s, the arrival of heroin was causing serious problems and the city hall eventually stepped in to begin the latest regeneration project. This time it has had some success: swathes of the poorest buildings have been replaced with new apartment blocks, the worst of the bars and bordellos have been closed down, and a brand new promenade, the Rambla de Raval slices through its heart.

Sights

The Gothic shipyards, **Drassanes** (see page 196), lie at the southernmost tip of the Raval. A stretch of the 14th-century walls still survives on the **Avinguda del Paral.lel** (known simply as Paral.lel), incorporating one of the fortified

Five of the best: sights in El Raval

- *Palau Güell* (see below)
- *Sant Pau del Camp* (see page 106)
- *Hotel Espanya* (see page 106)
- *Antic Hospital de la Santa Creu* (see page 107)
- *MACBA* (see page 109)

towers of the old shipyard. The Avinguda de les Drassanes, which runs past the entrance to the **Museu Marítim**, is an unlovely 1960s effort to drive some light and space through the old **Barri Xinès**. The grim **Torre Colón**, which looks like a giant Darlek, was planted on the site of a famous old brothel, **Can Manco** (House of the One-Armed Man) at the same time.

Ciutat Vella: The Old City

You should watch out for your bags and don't walk the streets, especially those nearest the port, late at night by yourself

A small square at the meeting point of the Avinguda de les Drassanes and the **Arc del Teatre**, named after Jean Genet, whose novel *Journal de Voleur* (Thief's Journal) memorably charts the depravity and squalor of the Raval in the 1930s. Genet scratched a living as a rent boy and a thief, earning a few extra pesetas to dress in drag at *La Criolla*, perhaps the most famous cabaret of the era, which stood around the corner on Carrer del Cid. The web of streets in this southern section of the Raval are still the poorest, and most intimidating at night, but it's also here that a glimmer of the old **Barrio Xinès** can still be found in a handful of old-fashioned bars – like the Kentucky, the London and Bar Marsella (see page 106) – which haven't changed in decades.

Palau Güell

In 1987 Palau Güell became the first modern building to be declared a World Heritage Site by UNESCO

The Avinguda de les Drassanes continues north until it meets **Carrer Nou de la Rambla**, the main thoroughfare of the southern part of the Raval. To the right, at No 3, stands the Palau Güell, Gaudí's first major commission for the man who was to become his most important patron, **Eusebi Güell**. The palace never really became a home to the Güells, who preferred their comfortable old-fashioned estate in Pedralbes (see page 155). It was appropriated during the Civil War, stripped of its riches and pressed into service as a prison and barracks, and then spent years languishing as the city's Theatre Museum.

In 1886, the big event on everyone's lips was the **1888 Universal Exhibition** (see page 97) and Eusebi Güell wanted to build something extraordinary. He commissioned Gaudí, who was still in his early 30s but had already worked on the Finca Güell in Pedralbes (see page 158), and told him to spare no expense. The young architect took Güell's instruction seriously, using the only the finest wood, marble and stone, and inlaying the specially designed furniture with the most lustrous rare materials.

At that time, this was an unlikely neighbourhood for a bourgeois home, and a passage was built connecting the Palau Güell with the residence on the Rambla. It's possible that the **façade**, an imposing mesh of whiplash iron and ranks of columns, was designed to awe poor passers-by and deter them from thoughts of burglary. The Catalan coat of arms is splayed massively between the two entrance archways, surmounted by a crown and an eagle. The archways allowed visiting carriages to sweep in through one gate and out through the other; the household's carriages were kept in the cavernous basement stables. A solemn staircase leads up to the main apartments, past a large stained-glass window bearing the red and yellow stripes of the Catalan flag.

Public rooms

In the public areas of the palace, guests would wait for admittance to the lofty main salon. The visitor's room boasts a spectacularly ornate carved ceiling in which tiny spyholes were carved so that the Güells could overhear their guests' private conversations. The visitor's gallery is formed by sweeping parabolic arches supported by slender marble columns, probably inspired by the cloister of the Monastir de Poblet, which the young Gaudí had dreamed of restoring. Güell's wife was never happy with the building, and when she saw the windowed gallery, she exclaimed with horror that it looked like a barber's shop. Gaudí's fascination with Mudéjar architecture, especially marked in the Casa Vicens in Gràcia (see page 147) is particularly evident in the richly carved wooden ceilings, which seem to drip as though moulded from wax.

This is the heart of the house, with all the rooms organised around the central hall in true Mediterranean fashion, and surrounded by a series of galleries and miradors. This lavish hall, topped with an arched cosmic dome covered with deep blue honeycombed tiles is overwhelming; thin shafts of light entering through tiny windows symbolize the stars circling the moon. The southern wall is fitted with an enormous cupboard made of exquisitely carved Brazilian hardwood, inlaid with ivory. It unfolds to reveal the private chapel, which was stripped of its sumptuous fittings during the Civil War but retains spectacular panels inlaid with the brilliant white shell of the endangered Caribbean turtle.

Main salon
Güell and Gaudí were intensely religious men; this space was designed to function as the family's chapel as well as its main salon

The salon's acoustics are perfect and the gallery functioned as a bandstand where musicians played on the rare occasions that the Güells threw a party, and the guests danced beneath the heavy paintings of lugubrious saints and martyrs.

Behind the salon is the family's dining room and private sitting room. The heavy grandeur of the public rooms gives way to a more intimate but equally elegant space, with a Japanese-style chimney surrounded by twin serpents, and an undulating carved window seat. This was the back of the house and is therefore less ornate; just the central panel has been decorated with iridescent *trencadís* (broken tiles), and an innovative series of wooden slats act as an enormous sun blind over the gallery, giving it the look of a well-armoured armadillo. The rooms on the second and third floors are not yet open to the public: a narrow staircase leads up to the rooftop terrace.

Private rooms

Despite its sumptuousness, the dim lighting, the heavy religious solemnity and the weight of historical references combine to make Palau Güell a sombre, gloomy experience. The **rooftop** is its antithesis: a rippling terrace with a playful forest of swirling, *trencadí*-covered chimneys, surrounding a lofty central spire covered with knobbly limestone pebbles. This spire is surrounded by parabolic windows and also functions as a lighting conductor, with a tall metal spike surmounted by a wrought iron bat, a legendary guardian of Catalan heroes.

Michelangelo Antonioni used Palau Güell as the setting for his unsettling thriller 'The Passenger' in 1977

■ *Guided tours only, Mon-Sat 1000-1300 and 1600-1900. €2.40.*

Carrer de Sant Pau and around

Carrer de Sant Oleguer (the continuation of Avda de les Drassanes) runs north until it joins Carrer de Sant Pau which marks the base of the Raval's newest promenade, the broad, palm-lined expanse of the Rambla de Raval which sweeps up to Carrer Hospital and was only opened in late 2000. Outdoor concerts take place in summer, including some concerts under the umbrella of the *Festival de Flamenco*, (see page 42), in early May and there's a sprinkling of cafés with terraces in the sunshine.

Rambla de Raval

Ciutat Vella: The Old City

★ Things to do in El Raval

- Climb up to the magical rooftop of Palau Güell (see page 104)
- Visit the great Granja de Viader which hasn't changed in decades (see page 113)
- Visit the Saturday vintage fashion market on the Riera Baixa (see page 114)
- Check out the ultra-hip bar scene (Aurora is a good place to start) (see page 245)

Església de Sant Pau del Camp Heading left down Carrer de Sant Pau, you'll find the tiny church of Sant Pau del Camp, the most important surviving Romanesque church in the city. A Benedictine monastery was established here in 1127, which flourished until the end of the 18th century. The church narrowly escaped demolition thanks to the efforts of the Catalan *Excursionistas*, who had the Gothic and Baroque additions stripped away to reveal the simple Romanesque church at their heart. The remnants of the previous seventh- or eighth-century chapel have been recycled and incorporated into two columns flanking the doorway. The interior was destroyed during the riots of the Setmana Tràgica in 1909 (see page 273), but a chapel containing the tomb slab of Count Guifre Borrell (947-992), who probably founded the church, survived. There's a very pretty cloister, with Moorish-inspired arches and pairs of columns simply carved with a menagerie of mythical creatures, one of the most peaceful and charming spots in the old city. ■ *Wed-Mon 1120-1300 and 1800-1930, Tue 1130-1230.*

Carrer de Sant Pau *The bars are relatively new to the neighbourhood and are a sign of its renaissance as a trendy nightlife area* Just after Carrer de Sant Pau passes La Rambla de Raval, there's another institution from the bad old days: the dusty old **Bar Marsella**, said to have been founded by a homesick Marseillais who introduced the locals to absinthe, which the brave can still order here (see page 245). Further down on the right No 9, the equally dusty **Hotel Espanya**, despite its air of genteel shabbiness, has managed to hold on to some of its original *modernista* fittings: Lluis Domènech i Montaner was responsible for the award-winning design of the dining room, which he remodelled in 1902-03.

Almost opposite the hotel, a narrow street threads up past the vast unfinished hulk of the Baroque **Església de St Agustí**, constructed here after the Augustinian monastery was demolished to make way for the Ciutadella. It overlooks **Plaça de Sant Agustí**, a pleasant dusty square, with tables spilling out from the bar and club *Rita Blue* (see page 113) and a relaxed live music bar, *La Ruta dels Elefants* (see page 238), just around the corner.

Paral.lel *From underneath the metro station a funicular, inaugurated in 1928, sails up to Montjüic (see page 114)* Carrer de Sant Pau leads westwards to Avinguda del Paral.lel which marks the border with Poble secretary and is now a quiet laid-back neighbourhood sprawling up the lower slopes of Montjüic. Built in time for the Universal Exhibition of 1888, it was one of the earliest civic efforts to open up the slums of the Raval, and was intended to be another showcase promenade like La Rambla or Passeig de Colom.

Paral.lel resisted such a haughty role and became instead the backbone of Barcelona's very own Montmartre, the brash, popular music hall district. At the junction with Carrer Nou de la Rambla is a statue of *Raquel Meller*, a Barcelonan cabaret star, whose world famous career began in the clubs of the Paral.lel. The statue stands as one of the last reminders of an era which has long since disappeared. Occasionally, a sentimental passer-by will tuck a bunch of violets into her hand, recalling one of her most famous songs, *La Violetera* (The Violet-Seller). Theatres, bingo halls and cinemas have taken over the old buildings and the last music hall, the much-loved *El Molino*, closed its doors in 1997.

It's just an illusion ★

Gaudí was always seeking ways of allowing natural light to penetrate his buildings: the site of the Palau Güell, squeezed into narrow streets and surrounded by tall constructions, posed some tricky problems. They were solved to some extent by filtering the ambient light of adjoining passages or hallways through stained glass, creating an illusion of natural light. It's hard to tell that they aren't just windows with direct access to the outside.

Carrer de Hospital and around

Running across the top of Plaça de Sant Agustí, Carrer de Hospital forms another of the main arteries of the Raval. On 11 May, the charming *Festival de St Ponç* (Saint Pontius), patron saint of beekeepers and herbalists, is held here. It also marks the northern boundary of the old Barri Xinès; the section beyond this street has always been comparatively prosperous and altogether less seedy. On the left is the 19th-century **Teatre Romeu**, which is considered the cradle of modern Catalan theatre. It came close to demolition in the early 1980s, but the Generalitat stepped in and it is now the **Centre Dràmatic de la Generalitat**.

Here you'll find the greatest concentration of the fashionable new bars and restaurants

Almost opposite the Teatre Romeu is the elegant Renaissance stone courtyard of the Antic Hospital de la Santa Creu (Holy Cross), a massive stone complex built in 1402 after the Consell de Cent decided to bring all six of the hospitals in Barcelona under one enormous roof. The complex, which comprised an orphanage and hospital for lepers, as well as wards for the city's sick and dying, continued its good work until 1926, when the hospital was relocated to Domènech i Montaner's fairytale pavilions near the Sagrada Família (see page 133). The long vaulted wards of the hospital are now the **Biblioteca de Catalunya**, the largest in the city with over a million volumes.

Antic Hospital de la Santa Creu
Gaudí was brought here after he fell under the wheels of a tram in 1926 and everyone took him for an unfortunate tramp

In the late 17th century, the Casa de Convalescència was built for recuperating patients, it's now the **Institute of Catalan Studies**. *Azulejos* (ornate blue and white tiles) line the staircase which leads to the old hospital chapel, now an art gallery. La Capella holds regular workshops, commissions pieces from local artists, and holds shows of the work of contemporary Barcelonan artists.

Carrer Carme culminates in little Plaça del Pedró. At the corner of the square is the humble Romanesque **Església de Sant Llàtzer**. A little further up along Carrer de Sant Antoni Abat is the modest little Església del Carme, built in 1914 to replace an earlier church that was said to rival Santa Maria del Mar in beauty but was sent up in flames in the *Setmana Tràgica* of 1909. If you continue up this street, you'll see the pretty *modernista* **Mercat di Sant Antoni**, designed by Antoni Rovira i Trias (see page 114).

Plaça del Pedro & around

From Plaça del Pedro, walk back along Carrer Carme, a pleasant bustling street with a handful of old *modernista* shops and relaxed café-bars. Branching off to the right is the narrow sloping Carrer de Riera Baixa, an underground fashion Mecca, and a great place to find vintage clothes, dance music and club wear. There's also a street market on Saturdays in summer.

Carrer Carme & around

Turning left onto Carrer des Àngels will lead you up to the vast concrete expanse of **Plaça Àngels**, generally full of whizzing teenagers on skateboards or bikes. The square was named for the 16th-century **Convento de Els**

Ciutat Vella: The Old City

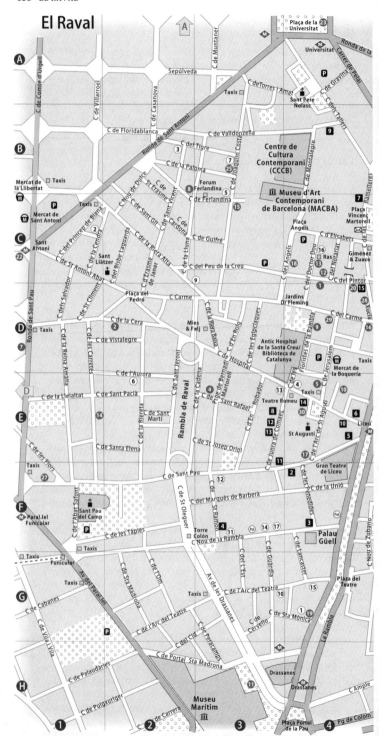

El Raval

● **Eating**
1 Biocenter *D4*
2 Can Lluís *D2*
3 Carles *B5*
4 Casa
   Leopoldo *E3*
5 El Convent *E4*
6 Elisabets *C5*
7 Els Ocellets *D1*
8 Imprevist *B2*
9 Iposa Bar *D4*
10 La Gardunya *E4*
11 La Llotja *H3*
12 L'Hortet *C4*
13 Mamacafé *C4*
14 Méson David *E1*
15 Pla dels
   Angels *C3*
16 Quo Vadis *D4*
17 Romesco *E4*
18 Silenus *C4*
19 Sushi & News *G4*

● **Cafés & tapas bars**
20 Bodega
   Fortuny *D4*
21 Buenas Migas *C5*
22 Els Tres Tombs *C1*
23 Estudiantil *A4*
24 Granja de
   Viader *D5*
25 Granja y Gavà *B3*
26 Kasparo *C5*
27 La Confiteria *F1*
28 Mirinda *D4*
29 Ra *D4*
30 Rita Blue *E4*

○ **Entertainment**
1 Bar Pastis *G4*
2 Jazz Sí Club
   -Café *C1*
3 La Paloma *B2*
4 La Ruta dels
   Elefants *E4*

■ **Sleeping**
1 Ambassador *C5*
2 Espanya *F4*
3 Gaudí *F4*
4 Hostal Morató *F3*
5 Hostal Òpera *E4*
6 Hostal Ramos *E4*
7 Hostería Grau *C4*
8 La Terassa *E3*
9 Méson de
   Castilla *B4*
10 Moderno *E4*
11 Peninsular *E3*
12 Pension
   Venècia *E3*
13 Principal *E3*
14 San Augustin *E4*
15 Turin *D4*

○ **Clubs & bars**
5 Almirall *C3*
6 Aurora *E2*
7 Benidorm *B3*
8 Boadas
   Cocktail Bar *C5*
9 El Café Que
   Pone
   Meubles
   Navarro *C3*
10 Kentucky *G3*
11 London *F3*
12 Marsella *F3*
13 Mendizabel *E3*
14 Milk House *F3*
15 Moog *G4*
16 Nou 3 *C4*
17 Salsitas *F3*

Àngels which flanks one side of the square. It was controversially converted into a municipal library and archive in 1984, and part of it now houses, the **Foment de les Arts Decoratives** (FAD), an influential organisation of architects, artists and designers formed in 1900, which holds temporary exhibitions. It's overshadowed by the huge, gleaming Museu d'Art Contemporani de Barcelona (MACBA).

Museu d'Art Contemporani de Barcelona

Richard Meier's museum landed like a glistening white space ship in 1995, a symbol of the city's dedication to urban renewal and a monument to its preoccupation with contemporary design. The museum has never managed to gain popular acclaim – or the crowds. Nonetheless, under the current directorship of Manuel Borja-Villel, a Tàpies scholar who earned his appointment here after a brilliant stint at the Fundació Antoni Tàpies (see page 122), its fortunes seem to be on the up.

A changing selection of the permanent collection, loosely structured around four periods, is arranged in the first and often the second floor galleries, while the third floor is devoted to temporary exhibitions. Although the permanent collection officially begins after the Civil War, there are some earlier pieces by **Alexander Calder**, **Paul Klee** and Catalan artists like **Leandre Cristòfol**, **Joan Ponç** and **Àngel Ferrant**.

The first period of the permanent collection, which roughly covers the 1940s to the 1960s, is represented by artists like **Antoni Tàpies**, **Joan Brossa**, and **Antoni Saura**. These artists were members of the Dau al Set (seven-spot die) Group, a loose collection of writers and artists who were influenced by the Surrealists, and particularly by Joan Miró, and

1940-60

Related maps
A *Eixample*,
page 122
B *Barri Gòtic, page 72*
C *Port Vell &
Barceloneta, page 198*
D *Montjüic &
Poble Sec, page 176*

Ciutat Vella: The Old City

0 metres 100
0 yards 100

whose works marked an end to the torpor which had settled on the cultural life of Spain after Franco's victory.

Antoni Tàpies' later works caused a greater stir after the dissolution of the Dau al Set Group, when he began his 'material paintings', like *Pintura Ochre* (Ochre Painting, 1959), a stretch of plastered wall scratched and scraped to reveal its many layers. The abstraction of such works is contrasted with the search for order and clarity in **Jorge Oteiza**'s boxy, iron *Desocupación no cúbica del espacio* (Non-cubic disoccupation of space, 1958-59), or the pared down sculpture of *Pablo Palazuelo*.

1960-70 Popular and consumer culture had more of an impact on the art of the 1960s and 70s: there are several fun, kitsch pieces by **Carlos Pazos**, including the mocking *Voy a hacer de mí una estrella* (I'm going to make myself a star, 1975), a series of pouting, celebrity-style photographs. Art was being redefined by international artists like Dieter Roth, Dan Graham and Marcel Broodthaers, who were experimenting with different kinds of media; **Dieter Roth**'s *Schokalenmeer* (1970) is made of crumbling chocolate threaded with strips of typed text.

1980-90 The 1980s and early 90s are marked by a return to painting and its forms of expression; among Catalan artists, **Miquel Barceló**'s paintings and **Susana Solano**'s stark metal sculptures reflect this return to traditional forms. There's an intriguing series of photographs from **Pere Jaume** (who designed the ceiling fresco at the Liceu, see page 64), and don't miss the extraordinary *48 Portraits* (1998) by **Gerhard Richter**, a selection of prints of famous figures taken at random from encylopaedias. Video and digital art has become increasingly predominant in recent years, and many of the temporary shows – like the recent **Tacita Deane** exhibition – are dedicated to artists working with new media. The museum shop, opposite the main entrance, has a good selection of monographs, books on art and design and unusual gifts. Behind it is an attractive café-bar which shares a square with the CCCB (see below) around the corner.

There are several excellent photographic pieces from this period, including works by Anselm Keifer, Jeff Wall, and Suzanne Lafont

■ *26 Sep-24 Jun: Mon, Wed-Fri 1100-1930, Sat 1000-2000, Sun 1000-1500; 25 Jun-25 Sep: Mon, Wed, Fri 1100-2000, Thu 1000-2130, Sat 1000-2000, Sun 1000-1500. €4.80. Guided tours in summer only; Wed and Sat 1800, Sun 1100, www.macba.es*

Centre de Cultura Contemporani

The centre runs several community-based projects and many other activities, including the Sónar Music Festival (see page 44)

Behind MACBA, Carrer Montalegre heads northwards past a colourfully muraled (and graffitied) makeshift football ground. Opposite stands the Centre de Cultura Contemporània de Barcelona, the second prong of the city's institution for contemporary culture (with MACBA as the first), set in the former Casa de la Caritat, a hospice for pilgrims established in the 16th century. What's left of the building dates back to the 18th century, but has undergone dramatic remodelling by the architects of the mirrored Maremàgnum (see page 198) shopping and entertainment complex out in the harbour. There are more mirrors here; one section of the old building was entirely dismantled to make way for a glassy new edifice, with an inclined ridge at the top giving mirrored views of the old city and the pretty Pati de les Dones (Courtyard of the Ladies). The centre hosts eclectic exhibitions on all aspects of contemporary culture. There's also a good bookshop, which has an excellent range of titles with urban themes.

■ *Mid-Jun to mid-Sep: Tue-Sat 1100-2000, Sun 1100-1500; mid-Sep to mid-Jun: Tue, Thu, Fri 1100-1400 and 1600-2000, Wed and Sat 1100-2000, Sun 1100-1900. €4.80. www.cccb.org*

Ciutat Vella: The Old City

Turning left onto Carrer de Valldonzella and then left onto sloping *Carrer dels Tallers* named for the slaughterhouses which stood here since medieval times, when cutting meat was forbidden within the city walls. A detour southwards leads to Carrer Xuclà, which leads in turn to the pleasant little **Plaça Vincenç Martorell**, where the *Café Kasparov* has a shady terrace overlooking the square. This square was built on the site of the old **Casa de la Misericòrdia** (House of Mercy), where abandoned children were left at a revolving door. The nuns would collect them and hang a label around their necks with the date. It's an altogether happier place for children now, with a small playground.

Eating and drinking

Casa Leopoldo, C/de Sant Rafael 24, T93 441 30 14, open 1330-1600 and 2130, metro Liceu. This classic, family-run restaurant has been going since 1939 and not much has changed since – you'll still find solid wooden tables and chairs, dark beams and tile-covered walls. Hearty Catalan dishes made with the freshest market produce are on offer, like *albondigas con sepia y gambas* (meatballs with squid and prawns), an excellent *sopa de pesca* (fish soup) or a range of perfectly grilled seafood and meat. The service is very welcoming and friendly. *Quo Vadis*, C/del Carme 7, T93 302 40 72, closed Sun, metro Liceu. A very elegant restaurant serving a French-influenced menu of new Catalan cuisine; the wild mushrooms, prepared in a number of ways during the mushroom season are a delight, and the *filete de toro* (steak) is simple but wonderful. The wine list is excellent and service is formal but highly efficient.

Can Lluís, C/de la Cera 49, T93 441 11 87, open 1330-1600 and 2030-1130, metro Paral.lel or Sant Antoni. A busy, old-fashioned restaurant very popular with locals, who are pointed towards their regular seats by stern-faced waiters. The menu of traditional Catalan dishes is extensive, with plenty of goat, rabbit and *bacallà* (salted cod), and there's a very reasonably priced *menú del dia* at lunchtimes. There's another branch called *Els Ocellets* at Ronda Sant Pau 55, T93 441 10 46. *El Convent*, C/Jerusalem 3, T93 317 10 52, open 1300-1600 and 2030-2300, *menú del dia* €6, metro Liceu. Just behind the *Boquería* market, this is a popular, cosy place in a rambling old building. Offers Catalan specialities, using produce directly from the market. The *bacallà* (cod) prepared in all kinds of sauces is especially good.

La Gardunya, C/Jerusalem 18, T93 3024 323, open 0700-0800, 1300-1600, 2000 until 1100, *menú del dia* €7.65, metro Liceu. Used to be located in an old inn just inside the *Boquería* market, but it has moved to a slick new home at the back of the market. It still serves imaginative Catalan cuisine using ultra-fresh produce at low prices and, though it's perhaps a little touristy – more multi-lingual menus – there's always a good, lively atmosphere. *La Llotja*, Museu Marítim, Avinguda de les Drassanes, T93 302 64 02, open Mon-Thu, Sun 1400-1545; Fri-Sat 1400-1545 and 2100-2330 metro Drassanes. A beautifully located restaurant tucked away in the courtyard of the museum. Set under the vast stone arches of the Gothic shipyards, with a huge window overlooking a hidden courtyard where you can sit outside in summer. Run by a local food critic and gourmet, it serves excellent Catalan food, including a couple of medieval dishes – like chicken spiced with saffron – to complement the extraordinary setting.

Mamacafé, C/Doctor Dou 10, T93 412 63 16, open Mon 0900-1700, Tue-Fri 0900-0100, Sat 1300-0100, metro Catalunya. Bright colours, bold design and great music have made this a very hip hang-out in the Raval: the menu offers an eclectic selection of dishes from around the world including several vegetarian options. *Silenus*, C/dels Angels 8, T93 302 2680, open Mon 1300-1600, Tue-Sat 1300-1600 and 2100-2345, metro Catalunya. On a small street very close to the Museu d'Art

Expensive
● *on map,
page 109*

Mid-range

Ciutat Vella: The Old City

Contemporani. A cool, arty restaurant serving top-notch international and Catalan dishes – try the almond gazpacho with caramelized apple. It's a long narrow space with pale walls lined with comfy sofas and dotted with changing art exhibitions and projections. Service is relaxed, friendly and knowledgeable.

Cheap *Biocenter*, C/Pinto Fortuny 25, T93 301 45 83, bar open 0900-1700, restaurant 1300-1700, metro Catalunya or Liceu. A long-established vegetarian restaurant with a wholefood shop and delicatessen across the street. This has a good-value *menú del dia* which includes the self-service salad bar, a main course and dessert. *Carles Restaurant*, C/dels Tallers 29, T93 302 25 01, open Mon-Sat 1300-1630 and 1930-2300, metro Catalunya. Another simple, down-to-earth neighbourhood stalwart serving a very good menú del dia in a pretty, peachy little dining area.

Elisabets, C/Elisabets 2-4, T93 317 58 26, open Mon-Thu and Sat 1300-1600, Fri 1300-1600 and 2100-2330, metro Catalunya. Delightful, classic neighbourhood restaurant catering to locals and serving up hearty Catalan dishes at very low prices. The *menú del dia* usually offers several choices and is very good value.

L'Hortet, C/Pintor Fortuny 32, metro Catalunya, T93 317 61 89, open Mon-Thu, Sun 1315-1600, Fri and Sat 1315-1600 and 2100-2300, *menú del dia* Mon-Fri, €7.20 at weekends. Good, imaginative vegetarian dishes and a friendly, cosy atmosphere at this sweet little place in the Raval; no alcohol but you can get delicious fresh juices. There's an excellent-value four-course lunch menu, which is very popular.

Imprevist, C/Ferlandia 34, T93 342 58 59, metro Universitat. This is a large, relaxed, modern café-bar, with funky industrial-style décor, low lighting and orange walls draped in rich fabrics. Plenty to read and occasional live performances – dance, poetry readings, art installations – on the small stage. Downstairs there's a small alcove with a low Japanese-style table – a good spot if there you come with a group. Serves good light dishes – salads, pasta and noodle dishes, falafel platters.

Iposa Bar, C/Floristas de la Rambla 14, T 93 318 6086, open Mon-Sat 1300-0300, metro Liceu. Another of the new, arty café-bars springing up in the Raval. Run by three French friends, it offers an excellent lunch and dinner menu, as well as a selection of tapas and light snacks. There's also a resident DJ and art projected onto a big screen at the back. *Méson David*, C/de les Carretas 63, T93 441 59 34, open daily except Wed 1300-1600 and 2000-2400, metro Sant Antoni. A cheerful, bustling restaurant serving big, very reasonably priced portions of authentic Gallego cuisine. The emphasis is on seafood – try the whole stuffed trout, or the squid cooked in a tomato sauce.

Pla dels Àngels, C/Ferlandia 23 (opposite MACBA), T93 443 31 03, open 1300-1500, 2030-0030, metro Universitat. Bright, modern décor, dark blue walls, dining room has glass-fronted rock garden, big area downstairs, good salads, pasta and some grilled meat and fish. Extremely well priced and beautifully presented on colourful square dishes, good service, excellent wine – try the Tinto Artesano.

Restaurante Romesco, C/Sant Pau 28, T93 318 93 81, open Mon-Sat 1300-2430, metro Liceu. A big favourite with budget travellers and impecunious locals, the Romesco is nearly always heaving. The friendly staff dish up hearty portions of very tasty black beans and rice at very low prices. *Sushi & News*, C/Santa Monica 2bis, T93 318 58 57, open Tue-Sat 1330-1630 and 2030-2430, metro Drassanes. Good sushi and sashimi during the day and a wider choice of Japanese noodles and other dishes at lunchtimes and evenings. A popular spot with students and young hipsters.

Café-bars *Bar Ra*, Plaça Gardunya, open Mon-Sat 0930-0230, metro Liceu. Friendly, hip little
with bar-café just behind the Boquería market; good muffins and juices for breakfast, which
food/tapas you can enjoy out on the terrace. It gets trendier and noisier as the night wears on, and there's a good, eclectic dinner menu with Thai, Mexican and Mediterranean influences. *Bar Estudiantil*, Plaça Universitat 12, T93 302 31 25, open Mon-Fri 0600-0200, Sat-Sun

0500-0300, metro Universitat. A down-to-earth bar serving sandwiches and other snacks, this is a favourite with students at all times of the day. Packed with clubbers on weekend mornings tucking into a big breakfast before collapsing after a night out.

Rita Blue, Plaça Sant Agustí 3, T93 412 34 38, open Mon-Wed 1100-0200, Thu-Fri 1100-0300, Sat 1900-0200, Sun 1900-0200, metro Liceu. The latest in the *Blue* chain, a trendy, colourful spot overlooking the pretty Plaça Sant Agustí, attracting a fashionable, slightly snooty young crowd. Good, well-priced Mexican food and cocktails are on offer and there's an underground bar for when the night really gets going.

Bar Bodega Fortuny, C/Pintor Fortuny 31, T93 317 98 92, open Tue-Sun 1000-2400, metro Catalunya. A hip, colourful conversion changed this old-fashioned *bodega* into a perennially popular hang-out for arty locals. The old wine barrels still line one side of the walls, but there's a lot of chrome and primary colours, too. It opens up onto the street in summer, and there are delicious snacks and light meals are on offer all day and evening.

Bar Mirinda, C/de la Xucluà 7, no phone, open Mon-Sat 0930-0230, metro Liceu. This quirky café-bar down a narrow back street has bright orange plastic chairs out on a small square (just a crook in the street, really) surrounded by colourful graffiti. Inside there's more orange and yellow décor to brighten things up, a mellow, funky soundtrack and good tapas.

Bar Kasparo, Plaça Vincent Martorell 4, T93 302 20 72, open 0900-1000 in winter, until midnight in summer, metro Catalunya. A popular Australian-run café-bar overlooking the playground in the square (it's a good place to bring your kids). There are very tasty sandwiches and some hot snacks on offer, and it's a relaxed place to while away an afternoon in the sun. *Granja y Gavà*, C/Joaquin Costa 37, T93 317 58 83, open daily 2000-0100, until 0300 at weekends, metro Universitat. This is a mellow café-bar, a quiet oasis on a street rapidly filling up with noisy, fashionable bars. A huge carved wooden statue marks the entrance, and there is a delicious menu of crêpes and salads. Occasional poetry readings and live music.

Cafés

Buenas Migas, Plaça Bonsuccés 6 (just off C/Elisabets), T93 412 16 86, Mon-Wed, Sun 1000-2200 Thu-Sat 1000-2400, metro Catalunya or Liceu. There are two branches of this popular *focacceria*, the other one is near the Gothic cathedral at Bajada Santa Clara 2, T93 318 13 89, which has primrose yellow walls, scrubbed wooden tables and friendly staff. There are all kinds of focaccia on offer – with toppings like aubergine and goat's cheese, or without – as well as good cakes and coffee. Very friendly service.

Granja de Viader, C/de la Xucluà 4-6, T93 318 34 86, open Mon 1700-2045, Tue-Sat 0900-1345 and 1700-2045, metro Liceu. This lovely old *granja* has been going strong for more than a century, although much of the décor is left over from the 1950s. It's popular with old ladies enjoying a thick hot chocolate after a hard day's shopping, and the walls are lined with postcards, posters and other memorabilia. It still sells fresh farmhouse produce.

La Confiteria, C/de Sant Pau 128, T93 443 04 58, open Tue-Fri 1000-0300, Sun 1200-2400, metro Paral.lel. A converted turn-of-the century confectioners, this has become a very elegant café-bar with lots of burnished mirrors and red velvet. There are good cakes and snacks during the day, when it's quiet and peaceful. It gets much more lively in the evenings, attracting an arty crowd. *Els Tres Tombs*, 2 Ronda de Sant Antoni 2, T93 443 4111, open daily 0600-2000, metro Sant Antoni. This simple café is where the market traders come for a break while setting up their stalls – it's also the last stop for plenty of clubbers straggling home after a big night out.

Shopping

Bookshops *Ras*, C/Doctor Dou10, metro Catalunya. A very hip bookstore and exhibition space, not far from the Contemporary Art Museum. It specializes in art, design, photography and architecture.

Fashion *Mies & Felj*, C/Riera Baixa 5, metro Liceu or Sant Antoni A great selection of jackets, *Carrer Riera Baixa* dresses, hats, bags and t-shirts. *Recicla Recicla*, C/Riera Baixa 13, metro Liceu or Sant *has lots of clubwear,* Antoni. All kinds of second-hand fashions from original 1950s-style cocktail dresses to *second-hand and* fake fur coats as well as shoes and even some pieces of furniture. **Streetwear** at *vintage fashions* *Giménez & Zuazo*, C/Elisabets 20, metro Catalunya. Ultra-hip women's fashions from this Raval-based designer shop. Bright colours and prints feature in their latest collection and they have just launched BOBA, a new range of 'nice and cheap' t-shirts.

Jewellery **Jewellery** at *Forum Ferlandina*, C/Ferlandina 31, metro Universitat. This original jewellers, just around the corner from MACBA, has a range of unusual contemporary designs in everything from gold to plastic.

Markets *Mercat de Sant Antoni*, C/Comte d'Urgell 1, metro Sant Antoni. Another attractive *modernista* market, the fresh produce stalls are replaced by a second-hand book and coin market on Sundays.

Music There are several music shops along trendy C/Riera Baixa: Edison's at No 9-10 has vinyl *For the latest dance* Lps and singles as well as an eclectic selection of CD's. *Discos Castelló*, C/Tallers 3, *music sounds, head* metro Catalunya. There are several branches of this music shop (including three more *into the Raval* branches along Carrer Tallers) which each specialise in a different kind of music. This is the one to go to if you are looking for classical music. *La Casa*, Plaça Vincenç Martorell 4, metro Catalunya. Highly respected dance music shop with very knowledgeable owners. *Etnomusic*, C/Bonsuccés 6, metro Catalunya. Well-known world music shop with very helpful staff.

Transport

Bus Most buses run around the edge of the compact Raval area. Take a bus to Plaça de Catalunya, La Rambla, Plaça Universitat or Avda Paral,lel.
No.**14** goes from Bonanova to the Vila Olímpica, via the Gran Via, the Rambla, Monument a Colom, and Parc Ciutadella. No **38** goes from Zona Franca to Plaça Catalunya, via Monument a Colom and La Rambla. No **59** from Plaça Maria Cristina to Pg Marítim, via Sarrià, Gran Via, Rambla, Port Vell, and Parc de Ciutadella. No **9** goes from Zona Franca to Plaça de Catalunya, via the Placa Espanya, Gran Via and Placa Universitat.
To get around the Raval neighbourhood, take the smaller *Barribus*, no **220**, which runs between the Mercat de Sant Antoni and the Avda Paral.le via Plaça del Angels and Avda Drassanes.

Funicular The Montjüic funicular leaves from the **Paral.lel** metro station and heads up to Avda Miramar. Single tickets cost €1.50 and return tickets are €2.40. Open Nov-Apr Sat and Sun 1045-2000, Apr-Jun daily 1045-2000, Jun-Oct daily 1100-2300.
Metro Line 3 (green) to Catalunya, Liceu, Drassanes, or Paral.lel; Line 2 (purple) to Sant Antoni or Universitat; Line 1 (red) to Catalunya or Universitat.
Taxi There's a taxi rank in the Placa Universitat, and another opposite the Tourist Information Office in the Plaça de Catalunya.
Train The nearest train station is on Plaça de Catalunya, a 2-min walk from Plaça Universitat (see above).

Eixample

Eixample

118 History

118 Dreta de l'Eixample

119 Sights

119 Passeig de Gràcia and around

119 Museo Egipci

121 Fundació Francisco Godia

122 Fundació Antoni Tàpies

124 Mansana de la Discòrdia

126 Casa Milà (La Pedrera)

127 Around La Pedrera

128 Rambla de Catalunya

128 Diagonal and around

131 Sagrada Família

132 Around Sagrada Família

134 Esquerra de l'Eixample

134 Sights

135 Eating and drinking

138 Shopping

140 Transport

Eixample (pronounced 'Ay-sham-play') means 'extension' in Catalan: this was Barcelona's answer to its chronic overcrowding problems during the 19th century. The Eixample quickly became home to Barcelona's wealthiest families, who lived in sumptuous houses designed by the greatest modernista *architects of the day. The area to the right of the railway line which ran up Carrer Balmes rapidly became the most desirable, and the Eixample was divided in two: the* **Dreta** *(Right), with the greatest concentration of* modernista *buildings and the* **Esquerra** *(Left) which languished on the wrong side of the tracks. The divide remains; the Dreta still has all the sights and monuments, but the Esquerra is getting its own back by gaining the best reputation for nightlife, with a high concentration of gay bars and clubs.*

The Eixample was Gaudí's playground and his delirious imprint is everywhere, from the creamy **La Pedrera** *apartment building to the looming, still unfinished spires of* **Sagrada Família**. *It is still the city's financial and commercial heart, with hundreds of excellent shops, restaurants and bars, and the shopping is among the best in Europe.*

History

By the mid-19th century, the old city of Barcelona was choking behind its thick ring of walls and an extension was needed to deal with the severe problems of overcrowding.

When permission for the demolition of the city walls was finally granted in 1854, the townspeople poured out on to the streets to tear them down with whatever tools they had to hand. Remnants of the old Roman and Gothic wall still exist in Barcelona, but not a stone remains of the loathed Bourbon walls.

In 1859, the city council held a competition for the design of this new extension. Two plans were considered: a fan-shaped design radiating out from the old city, submitted by Antoni Rovira i Trias, and an uncompromising grid design by Ildefons Cerdà. The city council chose the former but, to their outrage, were over-ruled by Madrid, who insisted that Cerdà's plan be implemented.

Cerdà, inspired by the Utopian socialism of Étienne Cabet and the boldness of Haussman's remodelling of Paris, envisioned a modular city of spacious regular blocks formed around airy central gardens in which workers, merchants and the bourgeoisie would live harmoniously side by side. It wasn't long before his socialist dream went up in smoke; Cerdà was edged out of overseeing the project, and the original design was rapidly undermined by greedy speculators, who saw the gardens as a wasted opportunity for making more cash and quickly swallowed them up.

The bourgeoisie had no sympathy with Cerdà's notions of equality, and commissioned the greatest *modernista* architects – among them, Gaudí, Domènech i Montaner, Puig i Cadafalch – to create trophy mansions which would dazzle their neighbours. A wealth of *modernista* monuments sprang up, as architects rose to the challenge of individualising each new mansion with whirls of intricate ironwork, colourful tiles, towers and spires.

Just a few years later, during or after the Civil War, not only did *modernisme* go out of fashion, but no one could afford the upkeep on such grand mansions. However, with the re-emergence of Barcelona as a tourist destination and the enormous popularity of Gaudí, the city recognised the importance of its *modernista* heritage and a typically determined renovation programme is underway.

Dreta de l'Eixample

Bus nos 7, 16, 17, *The Dreta was the Right Eixample in more ways than one; it's the city's most*
22, 24 and 28 *chi-chi neighbourhood, where the best families lived in luxurious homes remodelled by the most prestigious architects. Most of the Eixample's major sights are concentrated on or around the Passeig de Gràcia including what are arguably the most extravagant examples of modernista architecture: **Mansana de La Discòrdia** and **La Pedrera**. Barcelona's most visited monument the **Sagrada Família** is situated to the north of Diagonal which runs through both the left and right Eixample. The grandest modernista mansions, each marked with a plaque, are concentrated in an area now known as the **Quadrat d'Or** (Golden Square). There are also many exhibitions and museums which are worth visiting, including the **Museu Egipci** and the **Fundació Antoni Tàpies**.*

Five of the best: Eixample sights

- *Passeig de Gràcia* (see below)
- *Mansana de la Discòrdia* (see page 124)
- *La Pedrera* (see page 126)
- *Sagrada Família* (see page 131)
- *Hospital de de la Santa Creu i Sant Pau* (see page 133)

Passeig de Gràcia and around

At the heart of the Eixample is the glossy Passeig de Gràcia, a broad boulevard flanked by the former mansions of the wealthy and lined with tall, shady plane trees and twirling wrought-iron lamp-posts and benches designed by Pere Falqués. When the Bourbon walls were still constricting the city, this area was just a rutted track to the outlying village of Gràcia. It was paved over in the 1820s and quickly became a popular promenade which gradually acquired fountains, manicured gardens, dance halls, a railway and an open-air theatre, and was popularly known as the *Camps Elisis* (Elysian Fields).

Passeig de Gràcia sweeps up from Plaça de Catalunya (see page 61) which forms an uneasy bridge between the old city and the new

As the Eixample developed, Passeig de Gràcia replaced La Rambla as the most fashionable promenade for the city's upper classes, and became the backbone of the most desirable section of property in the city. This section contains some of the most dramatic and emblematic architecture in the city, with dazzling constructions on almost every *xamfré* (corner).

Overlooking Plaça de Catalunya at Nos 2-4 Passeig de Gràcia is **Cases Pascual i Pons** (1891), a spiky neo-Gothic creation by the prolific architect Enric Sagnier. Futher up on the right at Nos 4-6 are the vast **Cases Rocamora**, one of the largest *modernista* buildings in the Eixample, which encloses three houses behind a single façade; it looks like a castle, complete with a fairytale turret at the corner of Carrer Casp. On the opposite corner, the **Joierica Roca**, an upmarket jeweller's, breaks out of the *modernista* mould and is housed in a spare rationalist building designed by Josep Lluís Sert in 1934.

Around Plaça de Catalunya
Take the metro to Catalunya then stroll up Passeig de Gràcia and absorb the modernista extravaganza

Across the street, at No 21, is the flamboyant **Union y el Fénix Español** building, commissioned by the insurance company after which it is named and completed in 1931. The insurance company knew what they wanted, and it wasn't *modernista*; instead they took their inspiration from the monumental edifices of 19th-century France and topped the whole thing off with a bronze figure of Ganymede standing astride a soaring phoenix, symbol of eternal life – perhaps an odd choice for a company dealing in life insurance.

Before reaching the architectural climax of **Mansana de la Discòrdia** and **La Pedrera** there are many other ancient artefacts to be found in the wealth of museums on Passeig de Gràcia.

Museu Egipci

Making a small detour, right from the Passeig de Gràcia on to Carrer Valencia, is the excellent Museu Egipci de Barcelona. The museum was established by Jordi Clos whose fascination with ancient Egypt began when he was still a teenager. It is now run under the auspices of the prestigious Fundació Arqueòlogica Clos, which organizes digs in Egypt, runs university programmes and makes purchases for the museum. It moved into this light, airy new building from its previous headquarters on the Rambla de Catalunya in May 2000.

The museum houses an excellent selection of artefacts spanning more than three millennia

The collection begins with a section devoted to the **pharaohs**, rulers with divine blood flowing though their veins, who are commemorated with huge stone statues, and a display of intricate musical instruments adorned with tiny

Eixample

serene-faced figures. There are dozens of **sarcophagi**; the earliest are made of terracotta moulded vaguely into the form of the body within, but they grow steadily more elaborate. One is magnificently carved, with a gold case richly decorated with symbols of protective gods. Burial scenes are dramatically recreated, with cult chapels, mummies – including bizarre x-rays of mummified animals – and tombs.

There's a palm-shaded rooftop café where, like an ancient Egyptian, you can sip an iced tea flavoured with mint

There are images of some of the thousands of **deities** worshipped by the ancient Egyptians, including Teuris – with the body of a hippopotamus, the legs and arms of a lion and human breasts – who was the protector of pregnant women. There is also a rich collection of **ceramics**, some dating back to 3500 BC, and jewellery – gold and silver, glittering with lapis lazuli and cornelian for the rich; painted glass paste for the poor – revealing the astonishing level of craftsmanship that the early Egyptians attained. There's an excellent giftshop with all kinds of related books, games, and souvenirs.

Eixample

Passeig de Gràcia

■ **Sleeping**

1 Alexandra *B1*
2 Avenida Palace *D1*
3 Claris *C2*
4 Condes de Barcelona *B1*
5 Diplomàtic *D2*
6 Gallery *A1*
7 Ginebra *E1*
8 Gran Via *E1*
9 Hostal Neutral *D1*
10 Hostal Oliva *D1*
11 Hostal Palacios *D2*
12 Hostal Windsor *C1*
13 Majestic *C2*
14 Paseo de Gràcia *B2*
15 Regente *C1*
16 Sant Moritz *D2*

● **Eating**

1 El Japonés *B1*
2 Jean-Luc Figueras *A2*
3 L'Hostal de Rita *C2*
4 Madrid-Barcelona *C2*
5 Tragaluz *B1*

● **Cafés & tapas bars**

6 Bracafé *E1*
7 Ciudad Condal *E1*
8 Forn de Sant Jaume *D1*
9 La Barcelonina
  de Vins I Esperits *C2*
10 La Bodegueta *C1*
11 Laie Llibreria *E2*
12 Quasi Queviures *D1*
13 Torino *C1*

○ **Entertainment**

1 Capsa *C2*
2 Casablanca *A1*
3 Casa Elizalde *C2*

○ **Clubs & bars**

4 La Pedrera de Nit *B2*
5 Row Club *A1*

Things to do in the Eixample

- Gaze at Gaudí's wonderful dragon house – the Casa Batlló (see page 125)
- Enjoy a cocktail and live music on the roof of La Pedrera in summer (see page 126)
- Window-shop at the Diagonal's swanky boutiques (see page 138)
- Rediscover some of the 1980s 'design' bars like Nick Havannah's (see page 246)

■ *Mon-Sat 1000-2000, Sun 1000-1400. €5.40, www.fundclos.com The museum offers guided tours with an Egyptologist on Sat at 1000 and 1700 and there are even themed evening tours at weekends, in Catalan, call to arrange in advance; T93 488 01 88. Café: daily except Mon, 1100-2000.*

Fundació Francisco Godia

Next door to the Museu Egipci is the Fundació Francisco Godia, another of the city's fine, privately owned museums. Francisco Godia (1921-90) was an odd combination: a successful racing driver for more than three decades, he drove Maseratis during the Formula One World Championships between 1954 and 1958, and also found time to acquire a dazzling collection of painting, medieval sculpture and ceramics.

There's a small section devoted to Godia's racing days, with cups, medals, black and white videos of famous races and his old hat and goggles. Beyond is a mesmerising gathering of polychrome, gilded statues from the 12th century onwards, including a surreal *Joseph of Arimathea* supporting the limp body of Christ, and a dignified *Seated Virgin*, one of the earliest pieces in the collection, dating back to the second half of the 12th century. The stars of the show are **Jaume Huguet's** burnished, gilded *Mary Magdalene* (circa 1445-55), seated imperiously on a carved throne dressed in regal blood-red velvet and ermine, and the Gothic masterpiece *Virgin of Humility* (circa 1363-73) attributed to **Llorenç Saragossa**, court painter to Pere II the Ceremonious.

The **ceramic** collection is equally sumptuous, although just a few pieces from the vast holdings are usually on show. They have been gathered from all over Spain, and include lustrous 15th-century Manises ceramics with a metallic shimmer. There's also a delightful collection of Valencian ceiling tiles depicting cheerful animals.

Godia also collected **turn-of-the-century art**, including a strong collection of Moderniste and Noucentiste paintings: among them are **Ramon Casas'** society paintings *At the Racecourse* (circa 1905) and **Isidre Nonell**'s haunting study of a *Gypsy Woman* (1905). There is a nightmarish series of paintings by **Joan Ponç**, who was greatly influenced by Klee and Miró. There's an unnerving portrait of Picasso by **Irving Penn** and a cartoon of Pere Romeu, one of the founders of the *Els Quatre Gats* tavern, by **Picasso** himself.

Godia's daughters are expanding the collection by adding works from the late 20th century and some contemporary art: there's a stunning piece by **Lucio Fontana**, *Concetto spaziale, attese* (Spatial concept, expectation circa 1965), a brilliant, vivid blue canvas scored with four slashes, and a beautiful series of black and white photographs by **Robert Mapplethorpe** entitled *Roses* (1988), intense and yet serene. ■ *Daily except Tue 1000-2000. €4.20. Combined ticket available with the Museu Egipci next door, €8.40, www.fundacionfgodia.org*

Eixample

Fundació Antoni Tàpies

Turning left onto Carrer d'Aragó from the Passeig de Gràcia, you can't miss the extraordinary red-brick building topped with what looks like a huge cloud of barbed wire and is in fact a vast sculpture entitled *Nuvol i Cadira* (Cloud and Chair) by Antoni Tàpies, Spain's best-known living artist. The building, known as the Editorial Montaner i Simon, was built in 1880 by Domènech i Montaner for the family publishing house and is one of the earliest *modernista* monuments. It's now been taken over by the Fundació Antoni Tàpies which holds one of the largest collections of Tàpies' works in the world.

There are interesting temporary exhibitions by contemporary artists, often featuring video and installation work, and at least one floor usually shows a selection of works by Tàpies himself. Tàpies early works reveal the sense of isolation and semi-conscious imaginings of his sickly childhood in Barcelona.

Eixample

Eixample

Detailed map
A *Passeig de Gràcia,* page 120

Related maps
B *Gràcia,* page 146
C *La Ribera & Sant Pere,* page 88
D *Barri Gòtic,* page 72
E *La Rambla,* page 62
F *El Raval,* page 108
G *Montjüic & Poble Sec,* page 176
H *Western districts,* page 156

0 metres 200
0 yards 200

■ **Sleeping**
1 Antibes *C4*
2 Balmes *B3*
3 Caledonian *C2*
4 Gran Derby *A1*
5 Gran Havana *C4*
6 Hostal Eden *B3*
7 Hostal Plaza *C3*
8 Pensión Rondas *C4*
9 Ritz *C4*

● **Eating**
1 Beltxenea *B4*
2 Casa Calvet *C4*
3 Cava di Donna Fugata *C5*
4 Domèstic *B3*
5 Ginza *B3*
6 Gorria *C5*
7 Jaume de Provença *B2*
8 La Muscleria *B4*
9 La Tramoia *C3*

10 L'Atzavara *B2*
11 L'Olivé *B3*
12 Mandalay Café *B4*
13 Mezzanine *B3*
14 Rosalert *B5*
15 Semproniana *B2*

● **Cafés & tapas bars**
16 Casa Alfonso *C4*
17 Del Centre *C4*

The psychic automatism and dream states celebrated by the French surrealists, and particularly the Catalan artist Joan Miró, whom he revered, were profoundly influential.

In 1948, he became part of the rather short-lived *Dau al Set* (seven-spot die) group: a gathering of writers and artists including Joan Brossa and Joan Ponç, whose works were the first sign of cultural revival in Spain after the grim 'hunger years' which succeeded Franco's victory. Tapiès is most celebrated for his 'material paintings', which he began after the dissolution of the *Dau al Set* group, adopting radically innovative techniques and media, particularly the use of random objects and matter. There's an excellent library and a small but well-stocked bookshop. ■ *Tue-Sun 1000-2000. €4.20. T93 487 03 15 museu@ftapies.com 15 Library; daily to scholars by appointment only.*

Eixample

18 Horchateria Fillol *C3*
19 Jaízkibel *C5*
20 La Gran Bodega *B3*
21 Paris *A2*
22 Santécafé *B2*
23 Suris *A2*
24 Taktika Berri *B2*
25 Udala *B5*

○ **Entertainment**
1 Antilla Barcelona *B2*
2 Auditori de Barcelona *C6*
3 El Patio Andaluz *A3*
4 Filmoteca de la Generalitat de Catalunya *A2*
5 La Boîte *A2*
6 Luz de Gas *A2*
7 Méliès Cinemes *B2*
8 Teatre Nacional de Catalunya *C6*

○ **Clubs & bars**
9 Agua de Luna Tropical *B1*
10 Apolo 7 *B2*
11 Bare Nostrum *B4*
12 Bar Six *C2*
13 El Otro *B2*
14 Fresa y Chocolate *B2*
15 Fuse *C4*

16 Illusion *A6*
17 Jordy's Cocktail Bar *B2*
18 La Bolsa *A3*
19 La Fira *B2*
20 L'Arquer *C1*
21 Lo-Li-Ta *A3*
22 Mond *A4*
23 Nick Havanna *B3*
24 Zsa Zsa *B2*

Mansana de la Discòrdia

This block, between Carrer Consell de Cent and Carrer d'Aragó, is the most famous stretch of the Passeig de Gràcia: the Mansana de la Discòrdia (Block of Discord), where works by the three most famous *modernista* architects – Gaudí, Domènech i Montaner and Puig i Cadafalch – are nudged up against each other – the 'discord' arising from their dramatically different styles. The three architects were independently invited by three of the city's most influential families to entirely remodel existing buildings.

Casa Lleó Morera
Originally built in 1864, this is one of the oldest houses in the Eixample

Standing at the corner of Carrer Consell de Cent, Casa Lleó Morera was utterly transformed by Domènech i Montaner in 1902. Sadly, much of the beautiful **façade** was destroyed by the luxury leather goods shop, *Loewe*, who ripped out the original ground floor windows and stripped it of much of the original sculptural decoration by Eusebi Arnau. The surviving nymphs bearing symbols of the new age – electric light, photography, the telephone and the phonograph – flit across the façade, thickly clustered with garlands of flowers oozing like piped icing.

The **tribune** on the first floor is supported by a pink Carrera marble column, topped with two lions and a mulberry tree in a play on the family's name (Lleo i Morera); this tribune was the family's showcase, where the ladies would sit and show off the latest fashions to passers-by, and where the fabulously expensive marble column spoke eloquently of the riches to be found within.

Domènech i Montaner gathered a formidable team of craftsmen to remodel the interior of the apartment. **Josep Pey** was responsible for the finely detailed marquetry work on the ceilings and floors, and the pretty mosaic scenes of family outings. The stained-glass artist **Joan Rigalt** created the stunning rainbow-coloured panels in the dining room, with contented cockerels pecking away in front of a delicate landscape of mountains and flowers. Almost the entire set of the exquisite furniture designed for the apartment by Gaspar Homar can be seen at the Museu d'Art Modern (see page 178).

Casa Amatller
Three doors up at No 41, Casa Amatller was the first of the 3 major remodellings on the 'Block of Discord'

Antoni Amatller's fortune was built on chocolate and Puig i Cadafalch built him a fairy-tale house, with a stepped gable covered with shimmering polychrome ceramics, which almost look good enough to eat. Puig was violently opposed to the monotonous regularity of Cerdà's designs for the Eixample and saw this as an opportunity to undermine the dull uniformity of the grid plan. The result was a Catalan Gothic palace, harking back to the glory days of the Catalan empire and playfully surmounted by the colourful Flemish-style pediment.

The entrance **portal** and the windows of the second floor are surrounded by sculptures of scurrying pseudo-medieval creatures which were created by the quirky Eusebi Arnau. These both reflect Amatller's hobbies and celebrate contemporary mechanical advances: a frowning, short-sighted donkey reads studiously while a cloaked rat takes a photograph; rabbits scamper around an iron foundry; and, in a veiled allusion to Amatller's passion for collecting, frogs blow glass while pigs craft ceramics.

The sculptural group just above the doorway depicts the story of St George and the Dragon with a winsome Gothic virgin drooping over the door. Inside, a luminous stained-glass ceiling protects the carriage hall, and the original *modernista* **elevator** still creaks up and down. There are more delightful sculptures near the elevator entrance: a strange little creature crushes the cocoa beans, the second mixes them up and the greedy third has made himself sick.

Eixample

The Casa Amatller functions as the **Centre del Modernisme** where you can get information on the *Ruta del Modernisme* (see page 30), and which offers free guided tours of the three façades of the Mansana de la Discòrdia. There's also a new chocolate and gift shop where you can buy Amatller chocolates prettily wrapped in turn-of-the-century designs.

Next door to Casa Amatller is the fantastical Casa Batlló (1904-06), unmistakably the work of Antoní Gaudí. Originally it was just another undistinguished town house built in the 1870s until Gaudí was commissioned by a wealthy industrialist, Josep Batlló, to entirely refurbish it. Gaudí set about the project with his usual disdain for costs and corner-cutting.

Casa Batlló
The fibia-like columns of the lower façade gave the building its popular nickname 'the house of the bones'

Covered with shimmering, multi-coloured *trencadís* (broken tiles) and culminating in an undulating scaly roof, Casa Batlló gleams like an underwater sea dragon. Theories about the symbolism of the façade abound, but the story of St George and the dragon seems to fit most neatly: The rippling waves of tiny ceramic tiles, and the bone-white pillars which support the balconies, evoke the curling dragon, while his scaly back is formed by the swaying roof ridge. St George is represented by the bulbous cross, or lance, erupting from a thick column, spearing the dragon from on high. The spiky, *trencadí*-covered chimney is the final flick of the dragon's tail.

If you don't buy the dragon story, there are two more theories: the first is that Gaudí was creating an underwater seascape, the second is that the façade is a harlequin mask, and the rainbow-coloured ceramics are a shower of carnival confetti. The only thing that everyone seems clear on is that the little spyhole in the roof enabled Gaudí to keep a watchful eye on the development of La Sagrada Família (see page 131).

The interior of the main apartments are equally theatrical, with swirling organic ceilings like Italian ice-cream. Light slants down the interior patio, which is covered in a haze of deep blue ceramic tiles which fade almost to white at the bottom; another of Gaudí's ingenious measures to scoop in as much light as possible.

When the Casa Batlló was completed, it became the talk of the town, but Señora Batlló, a formidable battle-axe, who had taken a great dislike to the imperious architect who refused to speak anything but Catalan, which she couldn't understand, had him peremptorily dismissed. Nonetheless, the building was a triumph, and Gaudí's fame spread.

Set between Casa Amatller and Casa Lleo i Morera are two dour buildings which look as though the architects deliberately chose to make them as inconspicuous as possible while in such exalted company: the Casa Ramón Mulleras, at No 37, a relatively austere design with discrete rococo-style decoration by Enric Sagnier from 1906, and the Casa Bonet, a nondescript classical-style edifice by Jaume Brossa.

Casa Ramon Mulleras & Casa Bonet

The Casa Bonet now contains the *Regia* perfumery which contains the small **Museu del Perfum** (Perfume Museum) through the doorway at the back. It contains one of the largest collections of scent bottles in the world, from miniature early Greek phials and pearly Roman flasks dating back to the seventh century BC to the latest 21st-century brands. There are Catalan *almorratxa* (handpainted glass pots with lots of tiny spouts), and elaborate 19th-century dressing table sets like the little Pierrot figures which hold pots of perfume and puffs of face powder. Among the dozens of 20th-century brands there are some limited editions including Dalí's design for Elsa Schiaparelli. ■ *Mon-Fri 1030-1330 and 1630-2000, Sat 1030-1300. Free.*

Eixample

Casa Milà (La Pedrera)

There's a little gift shop near the entrance with modernista-style knick-knacks

A little further up Passeig de Gracia, on the right, stands one of the most extraordinary buildings in the world: Casa Milà. The sensation provoked by Casa Batlló spurred another industrialist, Pere Milà i Camps (or rather, his beautiful, spendthrift wife), to commission Gaudí to create another apartment building. Sure enough, controversy ensued; when the French statesman Georges Clemenceau saw it on a brief visit to the city and left swearing that he had 'no intention of returning to a city that could allow such a monstrosity to be built'.

Casa Milà (1906-10) rises like a creamy cliff draped with sinuous wrought iron balconies. It was quickly dubbed La Pedrera (stone quarry) in the press, who lambasted it in cartoons, drawing it as an garage for airships or a giant, oozing cream cake. The windows are gouged like caves into the creamy Montjüic stone, and the balconies undulate like nets of seaweed, full of trapped underwater creatures.

Inside, the apartments sway around two interior courtyards, decorated with murals and iridescent *trencadís* which have been recently restored after years of neglect. A ramp leads down to the underground parking lot, the first in Barcelona, now transformed into a concert hall, and another, lined with columns and overhung with plaster reliefs of sea creatures, sweeps up to the apartments.

The building is now owned by the cultural foundation of the Caixa Catalunya savings bank, who have renovated the upper floors and installed a 1911 model apartment: **El Pis de La Pedrera**. A small exhibition space near the entrance describes the apartment's historical context and shows the way it might have looked around 1911 when the first occupants moved in. There isn't a straight line anywhere, with the walls, ceilings, doorways and windows flowing around the interior patios. Rusiñol made bad jokes about residents keeping snakes instead of cats or dogs as pets in La Pedrera, and a comic poem by Josep Carner recounts a conversation between Gaudí and a resident who couldn't find room for her piano – Gaudí gives it some thought and tells her to take up the violin.

Unusually for the era, these apartments are constructed to allow as much light as possible to flood in, and yet give privacy if necessary. Gaudí was quick to appreciate new modern conveniences like telephones, well-equipped kitchens with gas cookers and private bathrooms. Gaudí himself designed all the finish and detailing, giving the door handles as much of his attention as the façade. Many of the fittings in the apartment are original, including the elegant bedroom suite with its pretty polychrome floral motif, which was designed by the celebrated craftsman Gaspar Homar.

Upstairs, *La Caixa* have thoroughly renovated the attic spaces, where washing was once hung to dry, to reveal the dense rows of bare-brick parabolic arches which look like a dragon's ribcage. A museum, **L'Espai Gaudí**, has been established to provide what is the only systematic overview of the architect's life and works in the city, from the early days of the Casa Vicencs to his unfinished cathedral, the Sagrada Família, revealed through models, photos, drawings and video installations.

A spiral staircase leads up to the climax of the visit, the sinuous **rooftop terrace** which curls around the patios like a dreamscape studded with fantastical bulbous crosses and plump *trencadí*-covered towers; Gaudí's magical response to the building's prosaic need for chimneys, air vents and stairwells. But this surreal vision was only the beginning: Gaudí originally wanted to top the building with a massive 40 ft statue of the Virgin, gazing down towards the sea to which the Milàs demurred. Following the terrible church-burnings of the Setmana Tràgica in 1909, Gaudí was finally persuaded not to erect the statue. As with the Casa Batlló, Gaudí did not remain on good terms with his employers; the Milàs were shocked at the bill he submitted for his work and refused to pay it. The case went to court, Gaudí won and promptly donated the money to a convent. As the art historian Manuel Trens mused: "God is the only master with whom Gaudí finished on good terms".

■ *Daily 1000-2000, guided visits weekdays at 1900, weekends and holidays 1100; €6.01, www.caixacat.es/fund_cat.html La Pedrera de Nit, open Fri and Sat 2100-2400 in Jul and Aug, live music and cocktails on the roof.*

Around La Pedrera

Just down from the La Pedrera is Vinçon, Barcelona's celebrated design emporium, which is set in a palatial *modernista* mansion, built in 1898-99 for the painter Ramon Casas. His friend Santiago Rusiñol lived in the third-floor apartments. It's possible to visit the pretty interior courtyard gardens.

Clustered around the *xamfré* at Consell de Cent and Carrer Roger de Llúria you'll find the earliest buildings in the Eixample. Cerdà designed each of these blocks with gardens in the interior courtyard, but property speculators had more lucrative ideas; one of their earliest commercial endeavours was to convert the interior garden space into a passage flanked with two-storey cottages in the 'English style'.

Take a walk down Carrer Roger de Llúria and look out for the **Passatge Permanyer**, which runs between Carrer Roger de Llúria and Carrer de Pau Claris. On the left is a very pretty, and now extremely expensive, row of cottages painted in ice-cream colours. Also on Carrer Roger de Llúria, down a dim, unobtrusive passage next to a furniture shop at No 56, there's a small urban park, the **Parc de Torre de les Aigües**, with a brick *modernista* water tower in the centre, Josep Oriel Mestres' **Torre de les Aigües**.

One of the delights of the *modernista* movement is that everything was considered worthy of transformation; it wasn't just the bourgeois houses which got facelifts – pharmacies, bakeries and grocers' shops did too. Just a couple of blocks further along at the junction with Carrer Girona, Carrer Consell de Cent is crammed with smart galleries and antique shops. There is a delightfully shabby old *modernista* bakery , *El Forn Sarrat*, at No 74.

Where Passeig de Gràcia meets Diagonal is the **Palau Robert**, a graceful, neo-classical building with small, peaceful gardens, open to the public, and which is now the Catalan government's very helpful information centre. Beyond it, Passeig de Gràcia crosses the broad, fast artery of the Diagonal and fizzles out in a small garden.

Pere Falqués, who designed the elegant lamp-posts-cum-benches which twirl along the Passeig de Gràcia, was also responsible for the sculptural **Casa Bonaventura Ferrer** at No 113. Domènech i Montaner's graceful **Casa Fuster** (1908-11), a little further up on the right, marks the end of the Passeig de Gràcia at No 132. This was one of his last residential projects, completed with the assistance of his son, Pere Domènech, and is much more restrained than you might expect from the flamboyant architect of the Palau de la Música Catalana.

Vinçon

Carrer Roger de Llúria & around

Diagonal intersection

Eixample

Rambla de Catalunya

Another chi-chi boulevard, Rambla de Cataluyna runs parallel to Passeig de Gràcia geographically and culturally

Rambla de Catalunya is another of the glossy hubs of this elegant neighbourhood. Shaded by leafy lime trees, there are dozens of terrace cafés, frequented by the well-dressed, mobile-phone toting locals. The **Casa Dolors Calm** at No 54 was given a pretty *modernista* makeover in 1902 by Josep Vilaseca who designed the bombastic Arc de Triomf, but managed to restrain himself here.

Almost opposite is the **Casa Fargas**, designed by Enric Sagnier for the politician Ramon Trias i Fargas, with a teetering stack of diminishing tribunes. Further up the Rambla de Catalunya at No 77 is the charming *modernista* **Farmacia Bolós**, with a profusion of stained-glass flowers and delicate wrought-iron lamps. At the corner of the Rambla de Catalunya and Carrer Provença at No 100 is *La Bodequeta*, a charming old-fashioned and thoroughly down-to-earth little bar which seems oblivious to the smart boutiques and offices which surround it. Next to it is *Mauri*, a century-old confectioner's with antique wooden fittings and an adjoining café full of perfectly coiffed ladies with shopping bags and lap dogs.

Diagonal and around

If you return to the Diagonal and take a brief detour up to the right, you'll pass **Can Serra** (1903-08) at No 423-25, near the junction with the Rambla de Catalunya. This is a bizarre mixture of Puig i Cadafalch's original *modernista* building, complete with pointy fairytale tower, and a glassy modern building from the 1980s, which now holds the headquarters of the Provincial Council of Barcelona.

Walk back in the opposite direction down the Diagonal to find **Casa Comalat** (1911) at No 442, designed by Gaudí's follower Salvador Valer, who had to come up with ideas for two façades because of the oddly placed plot. The one on the Diagonal is topped by a swirling multicoloured ornamental rooftop and the other, on Carrer de Corsèga, is a tribute to Gaudí's Casa Batlló, with rippling, bony balconies and an undulating roof with a peephole.

Museu de la Música
The collection spans two millennia and contains one of the finest collections of classical guitars

A little further down Diagonal at No 373 is another of Puig i Cadafalch's fantastical neo-Gothic mansions, the **Palau Baró de Quadras** (1906), which is easily spotted by its thick fringe of leering gargoyles, and its row of watery creatures doing service as waterspouts. And if that isn't enough there's also sculptures of the ubiquitous St George and his dragon by Eusebi Arnau. It now contains the Museu de la Música, a treasure trove of unusual and historic musical instruments.

The interior courtyard is charming, with a delicate fountain inhabited by ceramic frogs, and a richly tiled stairway sweeping grandly to the upper storeys. Some of the original stained glass has been preserved, along with a sumptuous ceramic fireplace. There is a wide range of exotic and ancient instruments from around the world; Japanese shakuhachi pipes, exquisitely inlaid Moroccan lutes, ancient Ecuadorian pipes, a delightful collection of 19th- and 20th-century accordions, and an astonishing number of pianos. There's also a collection of personal mementoes from musical heroes like the Catalan cellist Enrique Pau Casals, and the composers Albeniz and Granados.
■ *Tue-Sun 1000-1400; until 2000 on Wed in winter. €3. The museum may be moving to new premises; call in advance to check T93 416 11 57.*

Further down Diagonal, at No 416-420, you can't miss yet another of Puig i Cadafalch's flamboyantly Gothic apartment blocks, conventionally known as the **Casa Terrades** (1906), but always referred to as the Casa de les Punxes (House of Spikes). It's a spectacular building, partly because of its tremendous size, and partly because of its Baron Munchausen theatricality: ranks of pointy gables culminating in wrought-iron spikes with four slim corner-towers topped with mosaic witches' hats. Yet another large mosaic of St George slaying the dragon is emblazoned with the words 'Holy Patron of Catalunya, return our freedom to us'.

Casa de les Punxes

Just at the point where Diagonal meets Carrer Girona, there's yet another sculpture of the *Ictíneo*, Monturiol's 19th-century submarine, proudly claimed by Catalans to be the first in the world. This one, which features a scaled-down model of the submarine jutting out of a cliff of rock, is by Josep Maria Subirachs, the sculptor whose blockish figures on the *Passion* façade of the Sagrada Família have caused such controversy.

Carrer Girona

The statue of the priest-poet Jacint Verdaguer, which sits in the centre of the Plaça Jacint Verdaguer, was erected in 1924, at the height of Primo de Rivera's dictatorship. This caused outrage among Catalanists, who saw their hero of the Renaixença being appropriated by the Madrid centrists. A group of them led by Àngel Guimera, a poet, playwright and editor of the Catalan-language newspaper *La Renaixença*, placed flowers on Verdaguer's grave at the moment when the statue was being unveiled.

Plaça Jacint Verdaguer
This square forms the intersection of Diagonal with Passeig de Sant Joan

Just off the square, at Passeig de Sant Joan 98, is a strange glass cube; this is the entrance to Barcelona's most unlikely museum, the **Museu del Clavegueram** which takes you underground for an enthusiastic, close-up look at the city's sewers and how they have coped through the ages. ■ *T93 209 15 26 for more information.*

A few blocks down Passeig de Sant Joan, another monument to Catalan patriotism stands on the Plaça Tetuan: the wildly lavish **Monument a Dr Bartolomeu Robert**. Doctor Robert came to fame by enthusiastically supporting a bank strike while mayor of the city in 1899: Madrid demanded higher profit taxes in order to fill up its empty coffers after the disastrous campaign in the Americas, but the Catalans had had enough; the banks closed, and business halted. The Madrid government stunned the city by declaring war and although no troops were actually mobilized Dr Robert and his ministers eventually resigned.

Plaça Tetuan

A cascade of Rodinesque allegorical figures swarm upwards from a marble cave which may well have been designed by Gaudí: Dr Robert sits sternly at the top, while Catalunya whispers her advice in his ear; a poetic figure grips the Catalan flag, another wields the sickle of the Reaper's war, while Truth reveals herself and Mercy tends a young sick woman. The work was proudly placed in front of the University on Plaça Universitat, but was put into storage by Franco's toadies after the Civil War. Finally, it was resurrected here in 1985, with a ceremony attended by King Juan Carlos and Queen Sofia.

The history of the Sagrada família: a never-ending story

The Sagrada Família had a gloomy start. It was the brainchild of Josep Maria Bocabella, who was so reactionary that he even refused to eat French food on the grounds that it came from the land of Voltaire and Napoleon. He founded the organisation now known as the Josephines, a dour lot who pursed their lips piously at the decadence of modern society and decided to build an expiatory temple where the faithful could go to pray and beg forgiveness for the sinful hordes.

The first stone of the Templo Expiatorio de la Sagrada Família was laid in 1882, but the first architect quit after a year. Gaudí, who was only 31 and had not yet made a name for himself, was appointed. No one quite knows why, but an old story relates that Bocabella's aunt had a vision in which the temple's architect gazed at her with blue eyes, and when Bocabella met Gaudí's piercing stare (once described as "bolts of lightning") he hired him on the spot. Visions seem to have haunted the

construction of the Sagrada Família – Gaudí is said to have drawn the plans for most of it in a hallucinatory state caused by excessive fasting during Lent.

The project became an obsession and after 1914 he devoted himself solely to its construction. When the money petered out, as happened regularly, he would solicit contributions from unwary passers-by on the street. Dressed in a shabby old suit with his flowing white beard, his eyes still gleamed maniacally and people would cross the street to avoid him. He spent the last two years of his life living ascetically in a shack on the building site. In June 1926, he was crushed under a tram (he always hated trams) and rushed to the Hospital de la Santa Creu, where he was taken for an unfortunate tramp. But when he died two days later, the news spread like wildfire, and ten thousand mourners followed his coffin to its burial place in the crypt of the Sagrada Família.

Palau Macaya

The palace is now an exhibition space run by the cultural foundation of the Caixa Catalunya savings bank

Back up on the Passeig de Sant Joan, just above Diagonal, at No 108, is the Palau Macaya (1901), a delicate white stuccoed building with sharp turrets by Puig i Cadafalch. Eusebi Arnau was responsible for the utterly charming carved capitals, including a plump lady cyclist puffing her way through a forest of giant flowers just by the main entrance. The magnificent Gothic-inspired interior courtyard has remained intact, but sadly none of the other original fittings have survived inside.

Palau Macaya overlooks gardens which run all the way up to the Travesseria de Gràcia and were placed here in the 1920s, forming an elegant, formal promenade. It's possible that the name Passeig de St Joan came into use because local people would come here to have their fortunes told on Midsummer's Eve (the night of St John).

Carrer Sicília & around

Continuing along the Diagonal, there's a late bloom of *modernista* architecture at the corner with Carrer Sicília. This is the **Casa Planells** (1924) by Josep Maria Jujol, Gaudí's indefatigable collaborator and friend, a swirling, undulating apartment block which hints at La Pedrera. On the other side of Casa Planells, on Diagonal and the corner of Carrer Sardenya is the **Escola Ramon Llull** (school), a *noucentista* work by Josep Goday, which is still curiously known as the 'Dog's Convent' after a religious building popular with the neighbourhood pooches which once stood on this spot.

Despite the mourning crowds, Gaudí, his architecture and his ultra-conservative brand of Catholicism were thoroughly out of fashion at the time of his death. Work limped on for a few years but came to an abrupt halt with the start of the Civil War. Anarchists attacked the crypt destroying every plan, model and sketch that they could find, with the intention of ensuring that it would never be completed. The temple languished for decades until finally, in 1952, a group of architects decided to continue the work by raising money through public subscription. Japanese corporations are currently the highest contributors; Gaudí-mania was big in Japan long before it really took off Europe.

In the absence of detailed plans and records, the architects are being forced to conjecture what Gaudí might have envisioned and it this which has caused such controversy. They have pieced together the broken models, examined photographs and early designs and drawn up plans by computer. And yet Gaudí was infamous for his lack of reliance on plans; his buildings changed shape even as they were being constructed, and his early designs are notoriously vague. Purists argue that it is simply impossible to guess Gaudí's intentions.

The current team is directed by Jordí Bonet, the son of one of the temple's original architects, and the sculptor Josep Subirachs. The Passion façade on Carrer de Sardenya is now complete, but has aroused equal amounts of scorn and praise for the distinctly un-Gaudíesque sculptures which adorn it. Gaudí, in the meantime, looks set to become a saint. The Vatican announced that it would consider the case for his beatification in 2000 and the Association for the Beatification of Antoní Gaudí, founded in 1992 by architects, admirers and artists, are getting down to the business of finding out the particulars of his miracles.

Eixample

Sagrada Família

Carrer Sardenya swoops up two blocks to meet Plaça Sagrada Família, where Gaudí's unfinished masterpiece, Sagrada Família, glowers magnificently. Love it or hate it, it's impossible to ignore: the completed towers stand at almost 330 ft high, and the central spire, when finished, will soar an astonishing 590 ft into the sky. The temple is supposedly set for completion in 2026, the anniversary of Gaudí's death, but this seems increasingly unlikely in view of the technical problems surrounding the construction of the vast central tower which need to be resolved.

La Sagrada Família temple is easily the biggest tourist attraction in Catalunya, drawing more than 1,000,000 visitors a year

The cathedral is surrounded by crowds, tour buses, street traders and tour guides trying to keep their flocks in order, and so it's hard to feel any sense of religious awe as you jostle your way through the iron gates at the entrance. Gaudí designed three façades: *Nativity* and *Passion* on either side of the nave and *Glory* forms the magnificent main entrance. Each façade was topped by four spires, symbolizing the 12 Apostles, and the whole temple was surmounted with a vast spire, surrounded by four smaller spires symbolizing Christ with the four Evangelists. Another spire, just to the side of the main one, would symbolize Mary.

Nativity

An ecstatic celebration of life and joy, the nativity façade is deliberately set towards the east, to receive the first rays of the sun

The Nativity façade, almost completed by the time of Gaudí's death, rises up craggily like a vast cave, surmounted with a green cypress tree flecked with white doves of peace. Many of the thickly clustered **statues** were made from life casts – including, apparently, the donkey – and all are precisely symbolic. There's even an anarchist in the act of hurling a bomb and 36 kinds of birds, from an old Catalan song, all individually sculpted. Above them rise towers reminiscent of the jagged cliffs of Montserrat, the Catalan Holy Mountain. Three portals, made from Gaudí's favourite parabolic arches, represent Faith, Hope and Charity.

Inside, you'll find a building site and will have to pick your way past cement mixers and machinery; the **apse** on the right, begun by Villars in a nondescript neo-Gothic fashion, was completed before Gaudí's death, and the **nave** is almost finished. Work has begun on the construction of four huge columns made of basalt and porphyry (the hardest stone) which will eventually support the enormous domed roof.

Passion

The Passion façade dominates the opposing side of the church: the antithesis of the joyful Nativity façade, this is supposed to represent death and sacrifice. Gaudí said he would "break arches, cut down columns, just to give some idea of how bloody the Sacrifice was", but the anguish and torment of his vision are utterly lacking in the present façade. Josep Subirachs' grim, squared-off sculptures are entirely devoid of any emotion or vitality, veering in a mechanical sequence from the Last Supper at the bottom left, to Christ's burial in the top right.

The reactions these sculptures provoke are always extreme: young Catalans seem to love the squared-off forms, so different from Gaudí's fluid sculpture, and yet the art critic Robert Hughes condemned them as "the most blatant mass of half-digested modernist clichés to be plunked on a notable building within living memory". Subirachs completed the façade in 1998, despite fierce opposition from purists, and is now sculpting the apostles above the huge bronze door.

There's a **lift**, with long queues which takes you up the **Passion towers** and the very brave can climb even higher into the blobby spires for an uncanny sensation of stepping out into space, and descend by the tight spirals of the vertiginous staircase.

Underneath, the **crypt** contains Gaudí's tomb and a musty old-fashioned museum devoted to the history of the temple, with drawings, models and photographs and a reconstruction of Gaudí's little den of a work room. Perhaps the most extraordinary exhibit is the strange contraption he used for working out his catenary arches: a series of weighted chains suspended over a mirror.

■ *Entrance on Carrer Sardenya. Daily Nov-Feb 0900-1800, Mar, Sep and Oct 0900-1900, Apr-Aug 0900-2000. €5.12, includes entrance to the museum, www.sagradafamilia.org Passion towers' lift: 1000-1745. €120.*

Around Sagrada Família

Avinguda Gaudí

The nearby parks are good for a picnic and a chance to escape the tourist hordes around the Sagrada Família

The eastern façade of the Nativity overlooks Plaça Gaudí, with a flat lake reflecting the massive temple. This pedestrian walkway, where the Avinguda Gaudí begins, is lined with more of **Pere Falqués'** *modernista* lamp-posts, like the ones which twirl along the Passeig de Gràcia, and there are plenty of shops and cafés. There are a couple of small parks in the neighbourhood, the **Parc Aigües**, a stiff uphill walk, would be nicer if it weren't so close to the noisy

Gaudí – opinions of the Sagrada Família

*La Sagrada Família has caused controversy almost since its inception. **Jean Cocteau**, like most people, couldn't get his head around it: "It's not a skyscraper, it's a mindscraper," he said. There have always been plenty of detractors: **Evelyn Waugh** found La Sagrada Família so depressing he refused to leave his cab to visit it, and **George Orwell** decided it was one of the "most hideous buildings in the world", its "four crenellated spires exactly the shape of hock bottles". When **Picasso**, who despised Gaudí as a reactionary old duffer, went to Paris for the first time, he wrote to a friend "If you see Opisso (another friend who was working on the cathedral)…tell him to send Gaudí and La Sagrada Família to hell…here there are real teachers everywhere". **Pevsner**'s authoritative work Pioneers of Human Design didn't even mention the ascetic Catalan. **Dalí**, on the other hand, adored its "terrifying, edible beauty", but deplored the idea of later interventions and insisted that it be covered with a glass geodesic dome and left as it was at the moment of Gaudí's death.*

Ronda de Dalt, or there's the modern **Jardins Princep de Girona**, with a large pond with a couple of cafés and snack bars. Handily close, tucked away on a narrow street just beyond Hospital de la Santa Creu i Sant Pau, is the **Museu del Còmic i la Il.lustració**: a small museum devoted to the history of comics, and some unusual temporary exhibitions – a recent one looked at medieval comics. ■ *Mon-Sat 1000-1400 and 1700-2000; €3.*

Avinguda Gaudí leads directly to the other enormous *modernista* project of this neighbourhood, the Hospital de la Santa Creu i Sant Pau, with its imposing red-brick entrance pavilion and swirling wrought-iron gates. Catalan banker Pau Gil bequeathed a substantial sum for the endowment of a new hospital complex to be named after Sant Pau. Domènech i Montaner was duly commissioned to work on plans for 46 individually decorated **pavilions**, ingeniously linked by underground passages.

Hospital de la Santa Creu i Sant Pau
The complex was completed in 1930 and has remained a working hospital ever since

By 1911, the money had run out and only eight of Montaner's delightful fairytale pavilions, with their colourful mosaics, had been constructed. By this time, the Hospital de la Santa Creu in the Raval (see page 107) had been going for almost six centuries and its premises and services were equally creaky. It joined forces, and combined names, with the new hospital and building began again, with Domènech's son, Pere Domènech, coming to the assistance of his father.

Visitors are invited to wander freely around the grounds and admire the magical turrets and spires – it's particularly lovely, if ghostly, at dusk. The **entrance hall**, up two grandiose ramps, is vaulted with shallow domes covered with soft pink ceramic tiles, shimmering columns with floral capitals and a huge stained-glass window sending shafts of rippling, rainbow-coloured light. If you climb the garlanded staircase, there are wonderful views sweeping down to the sea.

Eusebi Arnau and Pau Gargallo were in charge of the team of craftsmen who covered each of the pavilions with delightful fluttering angels, musicians and folkloric characters. It's such a charming, whimsical paradise that it almost seems worth being sick. Sadly, the squat prefab additions to the gardens are a sign of the lack of space which is forcing the hospital to consider new premises once again.

Eixample

Plaça de Toros
There are fights during bullfighting season (Apr-Sep, see page 48 for ticket information)

There's another grandiose *modernista* monument in this corner of the Eixample: the Plaça de Toros Monumental. Head back towards the Sagrada Família and turn down Carrer Marina, pausing just to see the huge modern mural with 26 famous personalities including Picasso and of course Gaudí at the corner of Carrer Enamorats and Diagonal.

A strange red-brick structure with a crown of four blue and white ceramic eggs sits at the intersection of Carrer Marina and Gran Via de Corts Catalanes. This neo-Arabic folly, built in 1915 by Ignasi Mas i Morell, is Barcelona's bull ring. There's another bullring, but it has closed down due to lack of demand – even the Monumental doesn't get much business as Catalans don't really like bull-fighting. The large Andalusian population who flocked to the city looking for work in the 1960s manage to keep the tradition alive, but it hasn't taken root with the locals. Inside there's the small, little-visited Museu Tauri with a lacklustre exhibition of bullfighting memorabilia – posters, stuffed heads and costumes through the ages – and a gift shop. ■ *Museum open Mon-Sat 1030-1400 and 1600-1900, Sun 1000-1300. €2.40.*

Esquerra de l'Eixample

Bus nos 6, 7, 54 and 62 run along Gran Via

The Left Eixample was quickly earmarked for industry, rather than bourgeois homes and there are comparatively few sights; much of the space was snapped up by industrialists who needed the room for their factories and the few modernista mansions are smaller and more modest, with some notable exceptions. The left side of the Eixample has a booming alternative nightlife, particularly in the gay district surrounding the junction of Carrer Consell de Cent and Carrer Muntaner.

Sights

Gran Via
This noisy main road cuts through the vast, empty Plaça Universitat which marks the boundary of the Eixample with the old city

There is a sprinkling of *modernista* architecture along Gran Via, although these are generally more modest than the showy mansions of the rich on the Dreta de l' Eixample. At Gran Via No 491, **Casa Golferichs** (1901), constructed by Gaudí's assistant, Joan Rubió i Bellvé, managed to hang on to its gardens before the Eixample grid got too crammed. It's a charming chalet-style house with neo-Moorish decoration; in the 1980s, it was almost pulled down by property speculators. The locals resisted its demolition and it is now a public centre.

A little further along Gran Via at No 475 is **Casa de la Lactància** (1910), topped with a sculptural motif of a queenly figure breast-feeding and surrounded by surprisingly grim-faced parents clutching infants. Originally a nursery, it's now an old people's home, and no one minds if you put your head through to admire the attractive ceramic decoration and skylight of the entrance courtyard.

Parc Joan Miró
Miró planned more sculptures for the park, but died before they could be executed

Tucked in behind the bullring of Les Arenas, near where Gran Via meets Plaça Espanya, Parc de L'Excorxador was built on the site of a former municipal slaughterhouse which existed here until 1979. The park is more popularly known as Parc Joan Miró after the artist whose monumental sculpture *Dona i Ocell* (Woman and Bird) rises up from the pond, thickly encrusted with colourful *trencadís* in homage to Gaudí. Robert Hughes describes it as "a moon calf dropped from Bronindingnag"; the journalist Alexandre Cirici Pellicer called it "a mushroom-woman with the moon for a hat". All this lyricism doesn't faze passing taxi drivers who bluntly refer to it as "a prick with a croissant".

At the top of Carrer del Comte Urgell stands a relic of the old days. The old Escola Industrial Batlló textile mills, encompassing four huge blocks of the Eixample, were converted into the vast Escola Industrial in 1908. The main buildings were designed by Joan Rubió i Bellvé, Gaudí's disciple, who also built the stunning chapel supported with broad parabolic arches which adjoins the residential buildings.

Carrer del Comte Urgell meets Diagonal at the Plaça Francesc Macià, which Plaça Francesc Macià & around has been developed since the 1960s as the centre of the city's new business district and is surrounded by glassy office blocks, business hotels and a huge branch of the Spanish department store, *El Corte Inglés*.

Two blocks down Diagonal, duck briefly along Carrer de Casanova where you'll find another *modernista* fancy, the **Casa Companys** (1911), at Carrer Buenos Aires Nos 56-58. Built by Puig i Cadafalch, it is a simple, but rather pretty white house with a pointy roof, which has been converted into the **Museu i Centre d'Estudis de l'Esport** – a small sports museum with a collection of Catalan sporting trophies and memorabilia, including the ice-pick used by Carles Vallès when he climbed Mount Everest. ■ *Mon-Fri 1000-1400 and 1600-2000. Free. www.cultura.gencat.es/esport/museu.*

At Diagonal No 423 is the **Casa Sayrach** (1918), one of the last *modernista* buildings to be constructed in the Eixample and is certainly the one which most resembles a wedding cake, particularly the interior of the vestibule.

Eating and drinking

Beltxenea, C/Mallorca 275, T93 215 30 24, closed Sat lunch, Sun and Aug, metro Diagonal. A grand restaurant overlooking an immaculately manicured garden, with a reproduction of the *Venus de Milo*, which has a romantic terrace in summer. The Basque cuisine is every bit as magnificent as the surroundings, featuring classics like *merluza koskera a la vasca*, a delicate dish of hake cheeks simmered with clams and parsley. *Casa Calvet*, C/de Casp 48, T93 413 40 12. Open Mon Sat 1300-1530 and 2030-2300, metro Urquinaona. Gaudí designed the building (for which he won an award in 1900) and it retains some beautiful *modernista* touches inside. Fresh, modern Catalan cuisine is on offer, try the smoked foie gras with mango sauce and there's a fabulous array of desserts.

Expensive ● *on maps, pages 120 and 122*

Jean-Luc Figueras, C/Santa Teresa 10, T93 415 28 77, closed Sat lunch and Sun evening, metro Diagonal. A chic, sophisticated restaurant in a neo-classical palace featuring one of the city's most renowned chefs. The highly imaginative cuisine is Catalan/Mediterranean, exceptional wine list and dreamy desserts; try the chocolate *pastel* with spicy bread ice-cream. *Gorria*, C/Diputació 421, T93 245 11 64. closed Mon. Basque-Navarrese cuisine in a traditional, very smart setting. The Pyrenean lamb is mouth-watering, as is the suckling pig. The wine list is equally good and reservations are essential.

Cava di Donna Fugata, Plaça Tetuan, T93 231 77 29. Open daily 1300-1600 and 2000-2400. This new restaurant, with its warm décor has a sunny Sicilian feel. There's an eclectic Mediterranean menu and a particularly good wine wine list. If you just fancy sampling, the original tapas are delicious. *Ginza*, C/Provenza 205, T93 451 71 93. Open daily 1300-16000, 2000-2400, FGC Provença. Smartly decorated but well priced Japanese restaurant in the heart of the Eixample. Try the tempanyaki, when the chef will cook your dish in front of you, and there's also a range of rice dishes, as well as sashimi and sushi. *El Japonés*, Passatge de la Concepció 2, T93 487 25 92. Open 1330-1600 and 2030-2430, until 0100 Thu, Fri and Sat, metro Diagonal. A sleekly designed restaurant, owned by *Tragaluz* across the street with shared wooden benches, bamboo and low lighting.

Mid-range

Eixample

Madrid-Barcelona, C/d'Aragó 282, T93 215 706. Open Mon-Sat 1300-1530 and 2030-2330, metro Passeig de Gràcia. An attractive slick restaurant on two levels. The hip, chatty crowd appreciate the modern, simple Catalan food and low prices. **Mandalay Café**, C/Provença 330, T93 458 6017. Open Mon 1300-1600, Tue-Fri 1300-1600 and 2100-0200, Sat 2100-0300. Set in a former exotic furniture shop, this welcoming restaurant, furnished with cushions and banquettes, features unusual and delicious Pacific Rim/Catalan cuisine. On weekends, trapeze artists and other circus acts perform. **Mezzanine**, C/Provença 236, T93 454 8798. A very romantic spot in the heart of the Eixample offering innovative vegetarian dishes. It isn't cheap, but the food and service are excellent.

L'Olivé, C/Balmes 47, T93 430 90 27. Closed Sun evening, metro Hospital Clínic. A popular, lively restaurant with marble tables and highly polished floors, this serves traditional Catalan dishes, using the freshest market produce. Try the *rap amb all cremat* (monkfish with roasted garlic) or the *amanida de col llombarda amb seitons* (a refreshing salad of marinated red cabbage and small fish). It's a good place to try *calçots*, when in season. There's seafood galore at **Rosalert**, Avda Diagonal 301, T93 207 19 48. Open Mon-Sat 1300-1530 and 2030-1230, until 0130 on Fri and Sat, metro Verdaguer/Sagrada Familia, closed Sun. Huge wicker baskets, laid out on a long counter or in tanks, display the excellent seafood. Take your pick or else select a dish from the extensive menu.

Semproniana, C/Rosseló 148, T93 453 18 20. Open daily except Sun 1330-1600 and 2100-2330, metro Hospital Clínic. Housed in an old print works and wonderfully decked out with flea market finds, Semproniana is an eccentric, fashionable spot serving creative Catalan dishes. Come for the atmosphere and the décor, as the food is not quite as good as the high prices might suggest. **Tragaluz**, Passatge de la Concepció 5, T93 487 06 21. Open 1330-1600 and 2030-2430, until 0100 Thu, Fri and Sat, metro Diagonal. In a very pretty side street off the Passeig de Gràcia, this is a very stylish, split level restaurant with a huge glass *tragaluz* (skylight) which slides open in summer. The food is fresh, simple Mediterranean-style fare, and the downstairs bar has tapas and light snacks all day.

Cheap
Barcelona's experimentalism extends to the inspiring line-up of highly creative menus, combining unusual ingredients to great effect at suprisingly low prices

Domèstic, C/Diputacio 215, T93 453 16 61. Open 1830-0230 (kitchen open until 0100), until 0300 Fri and Sat. metro Universitat. This is a very welcoming hip new bar and restaurant with a resident Brazilian DJ playing mellow sounds. The menu offers some tantalising concoctions; try the delicate avocado and orange salad, or the gamey ostrich steak and finish up with a *xupito* (a shot of sweet Catalan liquer). The bar area is great, with red-painted walls, comfortable armchairs and sofas – sink in and you'll never want to go home. **La Tramoia**, Rambla de Catalunya 15, T93 412 36 34. Open daily 0730-0130, metro Plaça de Catalunya or Passeig de Gràcia. A buzzy *cervecería-brasería* with a long bar area and tables at the back specializing in grilled meats and fish. It's inexpensive and laid back, with a very good-value *menú del dia* and some tasty staples like onion soup and garlic prawns. **L'Hostal de Rita**, C/d'Aragó 279, T93 487 23 76. Open daily 1300-1545 and 2030-2330, metro Passeig de Gràcia. Other branches in the popular chain include **La Fonda**, (see page 83) and **Les Quinze Nits** (see page 66). They don't take bookings and there are always long queues. The food, good simple Catalan favourites and stylish, understated décor draw big crowds of tourists and locals.

La Musclería, C/Mallorca 290. Open 1300-1600 and 2030-2400, Sat 2030-0100, metro Girona or Verdaguer. Big steaming pots of mussels are constantly bubbling away at this friendly café; there's a choice of different sauces – Roquefort, béchamel, romesco. The fixed-price lunch menu is excellent value. **Can Jaume**, C/ Pau Casals 10, T93 200 75 12. Open 1300-1600 and 2100 and 2330. A buzzing, old-fashioned café-bar, popular with students and locals. The fixed-price daily menu is a steal, and there are plenty of solid, traditional home-cooked dishes to choose from – macaroni, escalopes, etc. *L'Atzavara*, C/Muntaner 109, T93 454 59 25. Open Mon-Thu 1300-1600, Fri, Sat 1300-1600, 20.30-23.30, metro. The delicious salads and soups, and a very good-value three-course *menú del día*, as well as the mellow atmosphere mean that there is always a queue here.

Five of the best: top restaurants

- *Agut d'Avingon* (see page 82)
- *Passadis d'en Pep* (see page 98)
- *Jean-Luc Figueras* (see page 135)
- *Ot* (see page 151)
- *Ca L'Isidre* (see page 191)

Café-bars serving food/tapas

Taktika Berri, C/de Valencia 169. Open Mon-Sat 13000-1600 and 2030-2300, metro Hospital Clínic. Another of the popular, ubiquitous Basque *pintxo* establishments; grab a plate, pile it up and the cocktail sticks will get counted up at the end. This one is particularly popular with office workers en route home. *Quasi Queviures*, Passeig de Gràcia 24, T93 317 45 12. Open daily 0830-0100, metro Passeig de Gràcia. This is one of the nicest and most imaginative of the large tapas bars lining this strip of Passeig de Gràcia; with unusual sandwich fillings and cured meats – there's also a small deli and a restaurant serving larger meals at the back. *Café París*, C/de París 187, T93 209 85 30. Open daily 0600-0300, metro Diagonal. This old café has recently had a colourful makeover and it's as popular as ever with a young crowd. It's especially good for breakfasts or late night munchies.

Santécafé, C/Urgell 171, T93 323 78 32. Open Mon-Thu 0800-0300, Fri-Sun 1000-0300. Small, elegantly minimalist café-bar with a good selection of juices and pastries during the day, and cocktails and music in the evenings. DJ sessions from Thu to Sat nights, featuring lounge, nu-jazz and fusion music. It's handily close to the *Filmoteca* (see page 249). *Casa Alfonso*, C/Roger de Lluria 6. Open Mon-Tue 0900-2200, Wed-Fri 0900-0100, metro Urquinaona. This charming, old-fashioned neighbourhood bar has been in the same family since it opened in 1934. There's a delicatessen at the front and a simple menu of sandwiches and light dishes – the desserts and pastries are wonderful.

Café del Centre, C/de Girona 69. Open Mon-Sat 0700-0300, metro Girona. An old gaming hall with battered wooden tables, this popular neighbourhood café is famous for its *torrades*, which arrive on a wooden platter surrounded with delicious toppings. There's live piano music at weekends. *Jaizkibel*, C/Sicilia 180, T93 245 65 59. Open Tue-Sat 0800-0200, closed Sun eve and Mon, metro Verdaguer/Sagrada Familia. An excellent down to earth neighbourhood Basque-style tapas bar, where the bar groans with *pintxos*.

Udala, C/Sicilia 202, T93 245 21 65. Open Tue-Sun 0800-0200, metro Verdaguer/ Sagrada Familia. A traditional, old-fashioned dark wooden bar with a restaurant at the back, this offers a good variety of tapas and *montaditos* (bread with toppings), in an easy-going atmosphere. In the restaurant, try the *cazuelitos* (stews or casseroles) baked in earthenware pots. *Suris Bar*, C/Muntaner 190, T93 201 99 46. Open Mon-Thu 0800-0200, Fri-Sat 0800-0300, metro Universitat. A relaxed, student favourite and a great place to hang out and play pool – especially in summer, when you can cool off in the air-conditioning. Simple bar snacks and tapas are on offer.

La Bodegueta, Rambla de Catalunya 100, T93 215 48 94. Open Mon-Sat 0800-0200, Sun 1830-0100. A charming, old-fashioned little bar lined with bottles, this is tucked downstairs in a cellar overlooking the *xamfré*, where it steadfastly ignores the surrounding smart boutiques. It serves a selection of excellent tapas and does a very good value fixed-price lunch. *La Barcelonina de Vins i Esperits*, C/València 304, T93 215 70 83. Open 1800-0200, metro Passeig de Gràcia. Elegant, intimate little wine bar, with angels scampering across the walls, serving good, if expensive, tapas,

Eixample

accompanied by an excellent and varied wine list. Unusual cured meats are the house speciality, but the desserts are also delicious. *La Gran Bodega*, C/Valencia 193, T93 453 10 53. Open Tue-Sun 1100-0100, metro Universitat/Passeig de Gràcia. Cheerful, popular café with all kinds of tapas where you can try out the local *porró* (Catalan drinking pot), with a long glass spout – it's more difficult than it looks, but you'll have a laugh (and so will everyone else) trying.

Cafés

A great way to beat the heat is to try a delicious orxata (a creamy drink made from chufa fruit)

Laie Llibreria Café, C/Pau Claris 85, T93 302 73 10. Open Mon-Fri 0900-0100, Sat 1000-0100, metro Urquinaona. This was the original bookshop café in Barcelona and it is still one of the nicest; lots of comfy armchairs, plenty of magazines to flick through, and a good range of tasty snacks and light meals, including a reasonably priced fixed-lunch menu (*€9.63*). It's got plenty of choice for vegetarians, too. *Bracafé*, C/Casp 2, T93 302 30 82. Open 0700-2230, metro Plaça de Catalunya. This is a very busy café just around the corner from the Plaça de Catalunya; it has tables outside in summer and a cosy little glassed-in area in winter. The coffee has an excellent reputation, and it's always full with shoppers taking a break.

Café Torino, Passeig de Gràcia 59, T93 487 75 71. Open 0800-2300 (until 0130 Fri and Sat), metro Passeig de Gràcia. Situated in an ideal location on Passeig de Gràcia, the original Café Torino was a famous haunt of intellectuals and bohemians, but it was sadly bulldozed in the 1960s. This reconstruction has lovely carved wooden doors and serves a good selection of sandwiches and snacks, and some very nice cakes. *Forn de Sant Jaume*, Rambla de Catalunya 50. Open Mon-Sat 0900-2100, metro Passeig de Gràcia. Friendly little bakery with fresh croissants and mouth-watering cakes; take out or sit down at one of the tables in the café. *Horchateria Fillol*, Plaça de la Universitat 5. Open Mon-Fri 0700-2330, Sat 0700-1300, Sun 0700-1230, metro Universitat. Revive yourself with an *orxata* or one of the several varieties of *batidos* (milkshakes) on offer. They also do simple, very cheap breakfasts.

Shopping

Antiques

Bulevard des Antiquaris, Passeig de Gràcia 55, metro Passeig de Gràcia. This arcade has more than 70 shops offering all kinds of antiques and bric-a-brac from toys, porcelain dolls to jewellery, paintings and carved picture frames. *Gothsland Galeria d'Art*, C/Consell de Cent 331, metro Passeig de Gràcia. This gallery and exhibition space has an incredible collection of *modernista* art, from beautiful furniture to sculptures and paintings.

Books

Altaïr, C/Balmes 69-71, metro Passeig de Gràcia. This is an excellent, very helpful travel and sailing specialist with a good selection of books, guides and maps covering all aspects of Catalunya and the rest of Spain, many in English. *BCN Books*, C/Roger de Lluria 118, metro Passeig de Gràcia. This is a good resource for English teachers in Barcelona, with an enormous selection of textbooks and teaching materials. There's also a decent selection of novels and reference books. *Llai Libreria Café*, C/Pau Claris 85, metro Urquinaona. The first and one of the nicest bookstore-cafés in the city, this has an excellent selection of books in English and some good guides to the area. It also has a small section dedicated to adventure sports and outdoor activities, although these are mostly in Spanish.

Fashion

The big, international fashions, like Chanel, Prada and Gucci, can be found up in the Eixample

Jean-Pierre Bua, Diagonal 469, metro Diagonal. The original and best-known designer-fashion shop, with the latest from names like Jean-Paul Gaultier, Vivienne Westwood, and Dries Van Noten. There is also a selection of unusual, very stylish bridal wear. *Adolfo Dominguez*, Passeig de Gràcia 32, www.adolfodominguez.com, metro Passeig de Gràcia. Well-known Spanish designer; elegant, spare designs in rich fabrics for men and women.

Armand Basi, Passeig de Gràcia 49, www.armandbasi.com, metro Passeig de Gràcia. Stylish, classic fashion including day and evening wear for both men and women. *Emporio Armani*, Diagonal 490, metro Hospital Clinic. Sleek, minimalist fashion and accessories for men and women from the popular Italian designer. *Josep Font*, Passeig de Gràcia 106, metro Diagonal. Luxurious fabrics, unusual designs and warm colours from this well-known Spanish designer. *Gucci*, Avda Diagonal 415, metro Diagonal. Ultra-fashionable clothes and luxurious leather accessories from shoes to bags.

Groc, Rambla de Catalunya 100, metro Diagonal. Toni Miró is perhaps the best-known Catalan designer around at the moment; find his very creative designs for men and women here. Other labels, shoes and other accessories are also available. *Noténom*, C/Pau Claris 159, metro Passeig de Gràcia. The latest and most unusual designs for both men and women from Helmut Lang, *Comme des Garçons*, *Espé* and dozens of others. Underwear, perfume and accessories are also on sale.

Purificación García, Pau Casals 4, metro Hospital Clinic. This slick Spanish fashion chain has cool urban fashions in high-quality fabrics. *E-male*, C/Consell de Cent 236, metro Universitat. Glamorous, show-off fashion for men; labels include *Millennium III* and local designers. *Discount Outlet*, Stockhouse, C/Balmes 67, metro Universitat. Discounts of up to 70% on designer labels including *Levis*, *Diesel*, *Guess* and *Armani Jeans*. *Stockland*, C/Comtal 22, metro Urquinaona. Offers excellent discounts on end-of-line fashions from labels like *Purificación García* and *C'est Comme ça*. **Streetwear** can be found at *Bad Habits*, C/València 261, metro Passeig de Gràcia. Strikingly original and often androgynous designs from Mireya Ruiz. *E4G*, Via Augusta 10, metro Diagonal or FGC Gràcia. Own-label clothes as well as the latest from Milan, London, Paris and New York.

Escribà, Gran Via de les Cortes Catalanes 546, metro Urgell. This is chocolate heaven, and it's worth coming just to see the incredible window displays – whole landscapes painstakingly created from whirls of different kinds of chocolate. The pâtisserie is equally delectable and there's a branch, with an adjoining coffee shop on La Rambla, in a pretty *modernista* building at No. 83. *Patisseria Maurí*, Rambla de Catalunya 102, Metro Diagonal or FGC Provença. Delicious cakes and chocolates, which are beautifully packaged if you are looking for gifts, as well as a small café. *Queviures Murrià*, C/Roger de Llúria 85, metro Passeig de Gràcia. This is a delightfully old-fashioned grocery store set in a beautiful old *modernista* premises. You'll find a range of farmhouse cheeses, excellent hams, and a good selection of wines and cavas. | **Food & drink**

Mercat de la Llibertat, C/Oreneta, just off C/ Gran de Gràcia, metro Fontana. This market up in Gràcia, piled high with fresh produce, is located in a pretty *modernista* wrought-iron building. | **Food markets**

BD Edicions de Disseny, C/Mallorca 291, metro Passeig de Gràcia. Set in a stunning *modernista* mansion, the BD group was founded in 1972 by the prestigious architect Òscar Tusquets among others. There's a range of exquisite, expensive furniture – both reproduction *modernista* and contemporary designs – and other household goods. *Dos i Una*, C/Roselló 275, metro Diagonal. A selection of high quality crockery, lamps, postcards and t-shirts featuring the best of Barcelona's designers. *Galeries Vinçon*, Passeig de Gràcia 96, www.vincon.com, metro Diagonal. The best-known and most influential design emporium in the city, located right next to La Pedrera, with everything for the home from furniture and lighting to kitchenware and table accoutrements. *Pilma*, Avda Diagonal 403, metro Diagonal. Everything from contemporary furniture to unusual knick-knacks. *Punto Luz*, C/Pau Claris 146, metro Diagonal. An extraordinary lighting shop featuring the designs of Philip Starck and many others. | **Interiors**

Jewellery & leather goods   *Loewe*, Passeig de Gràcia 35, metro Passeig de Gràcia. Perhaps the most famous Spanish fashion house, with a range of beautiful leather clothes, shoes, bags and other accessories for men and women. *Bagués*, Passeig de Gràcia 41, metro Passeig de Gràcia. Founded in 1839, this is still one of the most exclusive and elegant jewellery designers in the city.

Sports goods   *Cuylás Sports*, Via Augusta 37, FGC Gràcia. This is an all-round sports shop, but the emphasis is mainly on tennis and skiing. *La Tenda*, C/Pau Claris 118-130, metro Passeig de Gràcia. Large shop dedicated to climbing, trekking and other mountain activities. *Tomás Domingo*, C/ Rocafort 173, metro Tarragona i Entença. One of the best cycling shops in the city, with a wide range of models and accessories.

Specialist shops   *Botiga Disney*, Avda Diagonal 557, metro Maria Cristina. In the *l'Illa* shopping mall, the Disney store is packed with everyone's favourite characters. *Imaginarium*, Rambla de Catalunya 31, metro Passeig de Gràcia. This is one of an excellent chain of toy shops, with all kinds of toys and books and a magical, very kid-friendly interior.

Transport

Dreta de l'Eixample   **Bus** Note that because of the one-way system routes may change slightly and run on parallel roads depending on the direction of the journey.

Along Passeig de Gràcia No **7** from Zona Universitària to Diagonal Mar, via Diagonal, La Pedrera, Pg de Gràcia, Placa de les Glòries and Poble Nou. No **16** from Pg Manuel Girona to Plaça Urquinaona, via Gràcia, Diagonal, Pg de Gràcia and Plaça de Catalunya. No **22** from Avda d'Esplugues to Plaça Catalunya, via Pedralbes, Sarrià, Tramvia Blau, Gràcia, Pg de Gràcia. No **24** from Carmel to Paral.lel, via Park Güell, Gràcia, Placa de Catalunya, Placa Universitat. **For Sagrada Família** No **10** from Montbau to Pg Marítim, via Sagrada Família and Vila Olímpic. No **19** from Sant Genís to Port Vell, via Hospital Santa Pau, Sagrada Família, Avda Paral.lel and Drassanes. No **33** from Zona Universitària to Verneda, via Diagonal, Sagrada Família. No **43** from Les Corts to Barri-Besòs, via Sants and Sagrada Família.

Metro Line 1 (red) to Catalunya; Line 2 (purple) to Sagrada Família, Monumental; Line 4 (yellow) to Pg de Gràcia, Girona, Verdaguer; Line 3 (green) for Diagonal, Pg de Gràcia, Catalunya; Line 5 (blue) to Diagonal, Verdaguer, Sagrada Família, Hospital de Sant Pau.

Taxi There are several taxi ranks along the Passeig de Gràcia, and another in Plaça de Catalunya.

Train Passeig de Gràcia is a stop on both the regional and national train lines run by RENFE. All trains stop at Sants. Trains depart from here for Sitges and others towns along the coast south of Barcelona. For trains from Plaça de Catalunya, see above.

Esquerre de L'Eixample   **Bus** No **33** from Zona Universitària to Verneda, via Diagonal, Sagrada Família. No **34** from Sarrià to Plaça Virrei Amat, via Diagonal, Sagrada Família. No **54** from Campus Nord to Estació del Nord, via Les Corts, FC Barcelona stadium, Sarrià and the Right Eixample

Metro Line 1 (red) to Universitat, Urgell, Rocafort; Line 5 (blue) to Entença, Hospital Clínic, Diagonal; Line 3 (green) to Diagonal.

Taxi There are several taxi ranks along the Gran Via and another in the Rambla de Catalunya.

Train The nearest train stations are at Passeig de Gràcia, Catalunya and Sants.

Gràcia, Tibidabo & outer districts

Gràcia, Tibidabo & outer districts

144	**Gràcia**
144	History
144	Sights
147	Casa Vicens
148	Park Güell
151	Eating and drinking
153	Shopping
153	Transport
154	**Tibidabo & outer districts**
154	**Sants**
154	**Les Corts**
155	**Pedralbes**

155	Palau Reial
158	Monestir de Santa Maria de Pedralbes
160	**Sarrià**
161	**Parc de Collserola**
162	**Tibidabo**
165	Horta and the Vall d'Hebron
165	Jardins de Laberint d'Horta
166	**Glòries**
166	Eating and drinking
168	Shopping
169	Transport

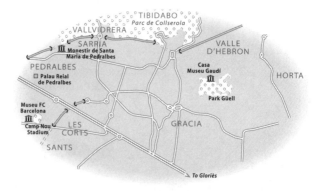

Not all Barcelona's sights are crammed into La Ciutat Vella or the Eixample: on the city's fringes you'll find a string of popular sights. One of the biggest is the **FC Barça Museum** at the **Camp Nou Stadium** in **Les Corts**, dedicated to the team which has been described as "Catalunya's unarmed army".

Much of the city's outskirts are refreshingly free of crowds. To get a sense of what Barcelona is about behind the tourist tinsel, stroll over to lovely old **Gràcia**, once a hotbed of revolutionary fervour, and now a laid-back, liberal town with an excellent nightlife. Or, to get further off the beaten track, head for the hills where you'll find everything from ancient monasteries in **Pedralbes** to hilltop natural parks in **Collserola**, and secret mazes in **Horta**.

Up on the dizzy heights of **Tibidabo**, with the city spread out breathtakingly below, is a giddy, old-fashioned funfair. Getting there is half the fun – trundle up to the top in an old-fashioned tram and funicular railway. On a gentler slope near Gràcia is Gaudí´s dream-like **Park Güell**, a magical landscape which inspired Miró and Dalí. It is guarded by the colourful ceramic dragon which has become a symbol of the city.

Gràcia

The independent town of Gràcia was dragged under protest into the burgeoning city of Barcelona in 1897 and has never quite forgiven its powerful neighbour. It's still a popular district with students, artists, writers, actors, and a sizeable community of Catalan-speaking gypsies, but Gràcia has largely settled down to its role as a mildly bohemian, traditional neighbourhood. Its distinctive charm is best appreciated with a stroll, especially in the evening, when the names of streets and squares – the Mercat de la Libertat, the Plaça de la Revolució and Carrers Progres, Libertad and Fraternitat – evoke its fiercely liberal past.

Gràcia has few big sights, although one of Gaudí's first commissions, Casa Vicens, is tucked down a small street. The spellbinding Park Güell, sprawls on the outskirts of Gràcia, with its fairytale pavilions, forest of stone trees, and birds-eye views out across the whole city. The lively Plaça del Sol is the heart of the neighbourhood's nightlife, with tables out on the square in summer and a buzzing atmosphere all year round. One of the best times to visit Gràcia is in August, for the Festa Major de Gràcia which transforms the streets into a wonderland of streamers, stars and balloons, as everyone vies for the prize of best-decorated street. It's now one of the biggest and most popular festas on the local calendar, although some residents still mutter darkly about being taken over by the no-good Barcelonans.

History

The 'Liberation for Gràcia' movement still has a few supporters and most Graciencs are fiercely protective of their distinct identity

In 1820 Gràcia was little more than a village; by the end of the century it was the ninth largest city in Spain, with a population of more than 60,000. At that time, Gràcia was an infamous hotbed of radicalism – fiery Catalanists, anarchists, liberals, Republicans and proto-feminists thrived, and radical newspapers and journals rose and collapsed almost weekly.

During the grey years of the Franco regime, it became the epicentre of left-wing liberalism for the 1960s generation, who began the trend for the cafés, bars and restaurants which form much of its current attraction, and, for a brief moment it was fashion's favourite during the heady years of the 1980s. There may be less revolutionary fervour on the streets of Gràcia nowadays, but it's become one of the most enjoyable and laid-back neighbourhoods in the city.

Sights

Plaça Rius i Taulet

The symbol of Gràcia's independence has long been the clocktower on Plaça Rius i Taulet, more commonly known as **Plaça del Relotge**, just down Carrer Goya off the neighbourhood's main drag, Carrer Gran de Gràcia. No one can explain why the square was named after the feisty mayor of the 1888 Universal Exhibition, unless it was some kind of a joke – many of the malicious cartoons of the plump little mayor weighed down by his excessive moustaches were first printed on the pages of Gràcia's satirical journals.

The dainty, creamy clocktower, topped with a bell wrapped in a wrought-iron mesh, was built in 1864 by **Rovira i Trias**, the architect of the fan-shaped Eixample plan which was overturned in favour of Cerdà's grid in 1859 (see page 118). The tower was badly damaged in 1871, when locals revolted against conscription and were summarily repressed by the army; the bell tolled, sounding the alarm, until a soldier took a pot shot at it and put it out of action. The looming clocktower became the symbol of *La Campana de Gràcia*, one of the most important satirical weeklies in Catalunya.

The neat local council offices are also a symbol of Gràcia's resistance to Barcelona's authority; designed in 1905 by Francesc Berenguer, Gaudí's faithful friend and collaborator. Their main adornment is the defiant Gràcian coat of arms. Berenguer was Gràcia's unofficial municipal architect and responsible for a great slew of building projects, although many of them were recorded under other names as Berenguer, who had a wife and seven kids to feed, was forced to abandon college before getting his official architect's diploma.

Five of the best: sights in Gràcia ★

- *Plaça de la Virreina* (see below)
- *Plaça del Sol* (see below)
- *Casa Vicens* (see page 147)
- *Park Güell* (see page 148)
- *Mercat de la Llibertat* (see page 153)

Heading away from Placa Rius i Taulet, along Carrer Diluvi, you'll find the heart of the long-established gypsy community. Plaça del Poble Romaní stands on the site of a 19th-century textile factory which once employed 500 people. A single forlorn chimney remains standing, but the surrounding street names – **Libertad**, **Fraternidad**, **Progres** – attest to the feisty, working-class ideals of the locals. Further down Carrer Siracusa is one of Gràcia's newest squares, the modern, concrete **Plaça John Lennon**, which lacks charm but is a favourite with kids.

Plaça del Poble Romani & around *This square is dedicated to gypsy language and culture*

The Plaça del Sol, with dozens of bars and cafés nudging up around the square, fills nightly with knots of people of all ages, bikes, kids and plenty of dogs. The square itself is a bland concrete expanse, unattractively remodelled in the 1980s, but the atmosphere is always lively, and the bars are some of the most genial in the city. Beyond it, just off Carrer Torrent d'Olla, is **Plaça del Diamant**, the setting for **Mercè Rodera**'s popular novel *La Plaça del Diamant*, usually translated as the *Time of the Doves*. It isn't a particularly engaging square, but a Civil War air-raid shelter has recently been discovered here and there are hopes that this will be turned into a Peace Museum.

Plaça del Sol & around *This is the hub of the area's nightlife,* ▶▶ *see bars and clubs page 242*

A couple of blocks away is Plaça de la Virreina, a quiet attractive square lined with a row of simple cottages. The square is named after the widow of the ex-Viceroy of Peru who built the magnificent Palau de la Virreina, now the city's Cultural Institute, on La Rambla (see page 63). Widowed at 19, she spent her husbands ill-gotten gains on philanthropic gestures and donated this land to the city. The village air is completed by the old parish **Església de Sant Joan**, which was virtually destroyed during the church burnings of the Setmana Tràgica in 1909, and restored by the indefatigable Francesc Berenguer. **Casa Rubinat** (1909) one of his finest *modernista* mansions, stands nearby at Carrer d'Or No 44, with a series of balconies edged with lacy wrought-iron and colourful *trencadí* mosaics.

Plaça de la Virreina

Head left up Carrer Torrent de les Flors to find the peaceful, shady Plaça Rovira i Trias. Rovira was perhaps the city's most famous runner-up; his fan-shaped plan for the Eixample was approved by the Barcelona City Council, but their decision was over-ruled by Madrid, who insisted on Cerdà's grid. Rovira's statue sits on a bench by the side of the square, musing over his own plan which is laid out at his feet, so you can judge for yourself.

Plaça Rovira i Trias & around

Gracia, Tibidabo & outer districts

There are a sprinkling of other laid-back neighbourhood squares heading up towards the busy Travessera de Dalt – the prim little **Plaça del Nord** with its old fountain bearing Gràcia's coat of arms, and the **Jardins Mestre Balcells**, named after the founder of Gràcia's own choral society, the *Orfeó Gracienc*. These gardens – which are really little more than a graffitied concrete strip overlooked by some lofty palm trees – are so quiet that a colony of parakeets which have escaped their cages have made it their home.

Around Carrer Gran de Gràcia The oldest section of Gràcia is squeezed between the broad avenues of Carrer Gran de Gràcia and Via Augusta; at the heart of the district stands the

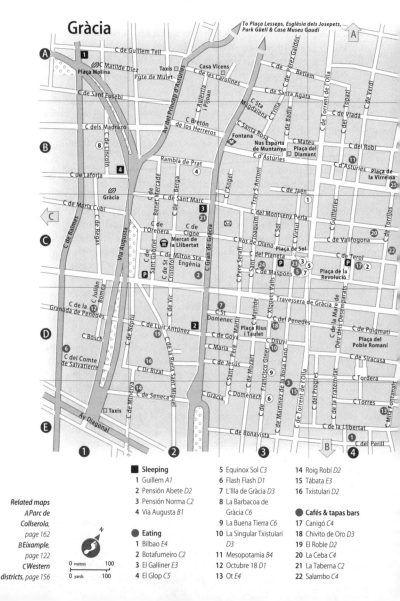

Gràcia, Tibidabo & outer districts

Related maps
A Parc de Collserola, page 162
B Eixample, page 122
C Western districts, page 156

0 metres 100
0 yards 100

■ Sleeping
1 Guillem *A1*
2 Pensión Abete *D2*
3 Pensión Norma *C2*
4 Via Augusta *B1*

● Eating
1 Bilbao *E4*
2 Botafumeiro *C2*
3 El Galliner *E3*
4 El Glop *C5*
5 Equinox Sol *C3*
6 Flash Flash *D1*
7 L'Illa de Gràcia *D3*
8 La Barbacoa de Gràcia *C6*
9 La Buena Tierra *C6*
10 La Singular Txistulari *D3*
11 Mesopotamia *B4*
12 Octubre 18 *D1*
13 Ot *E4*
14 Roig Robí *D2*
15 Tábata *E3*
16 Txistulari *D2*

● Cafés & tapas bars
17 Canigó *C4*
18 Chivito de Oro *D3*
19 El Roble *D2*
20 La Ceba *C4*
21 La Taberna *C2*
22 Salambo *C4*

neighbourhood's oldest market, the **Mercat de Libertat**, which was established in 1875, and given a pretty *modernista* wrought-iron roof in 1893 by Francesc Berenguer. The Gràcia coats of arms of proudly double up as drinking fountains. Two streets to the north is the delightful **Rambla de Prat**, with a cluster of *modernista* buildings showing off their swirling façades, offering tantalising glimpses of elegant staircases and lustrous, carved wooden doors. At No 18, four masks by Pau Gargallo crown the pretty façade of the old **Teatre del Bosc**, refurbished in 1917; Pau Gargallo himself is one of them, joined by his old friend Picasso, Dr Jacint Reventós and the painter Isidre Nonell.

23 Sol Solet *C3*
24 Tetería Jazmín *C3*
25 Virreina *B4*

◯ **Entertainment**
1 Teatre Lliure *C3*
2 Teatreneu *C4*

◯ **Clubs & bars**
3 Café del Sol *C3*
4 Casa Quimet *B2*

5 Eldorado *C3*
6 Gusto *E3*
7 Mond *C3*
8 Otto Zutz Club *B1*
9 Sabor Cubana *D3*

Casa Vicens

Two streets further up again is Carrer de Carolines, a quiet residential street which is the site of Gaudí's first major architectural project in Barcelona, the flamboyant **Casa Vicens** (1883-88), designed for the ceramics manufacturer Manuel Vicens, whose business was advertised by the eye-popping proliferation of sea-green and white tiles. It's an imposing, neo-Moorish red-brick mansion with spiky turrets which was once surrounded by an elegant, fountain-filled garden with a huge triumphal archway and a domed pavilion, which has long since disappeared. At the end of the 19th-century, fascination with the Orient was at its height, and Gaudí wasn't immune to its allure; he pored over designs from India, Persia, the Far East and Africa, choosing decorative elements to adorn his plans.

The house is private, but you can peep into the vaulted smoking room guarded by a couple of winsome cherubs, where a hookah-smoking pasha wouldn't be out of place. Wrought-iron balconies spinning flowers, leaves and fabulous creatures, twist around the windows and doorways, and the garden is enclosed by a fence made from fanning, delicate palm fronds.

Plaça Lesseps

Avinguda Princep d'Asturias snakes up to Plaça de Lesseps, where a small green park has been broken up by a maelstrom of traffic buzzing along several main roads. There's a hint of old Gràcia in the old men who come to play *petanc* (boules) on the dusty earth, disregarding the noise and

Gracia, Tibidabo & outer districts

★ **Things to do in Gràcia**

- Sit out on Plaça del Sol with a beer and some tapas (see page 145)
- Catch a film at the Verdi cinema and have coffee on the Plaça de la Virreina (see page 145)
- Find out what the Eixample might have looked like in the Plaça Rovira i Trias (see page 145)
- Head to the top of Park Güell for wonderful, crowd-free views (see below).

hubbub, and in the ancient **Església dels Josepets** which has squatted here since the 17th century, now squeezed between ugly, modern developments. Sitting pretty, almost opposite the church, is **Casas Ramos** (1906), formed by three delightful *modernista* homes wrapped behind a delicate blue façade swirling with pale flowers.

Continue along the noisy, anonymous **Travessera de Dalt** and turn left up Avinguda Sant Joseph de la Muntanya to reach the fantasy world of Gaudí's Park Güell.

Park Güell

Take bus no 24 or 25 right to the gate if you can't face the steep walk from Gràcia — The whimsical turrets, fabulous *trencadí*-covered creatures, floating balconies and sloping parklands of Park Güell are perhaps the most delightful and varied of Gaudí's visionary creations. Gaudí's benefactor and friend, Eusebi Güell, had visions of an exclusive English-style garden city (which is why Park is spelt with an English 'k' and not a Catalan 'c'), and bought two adjoining plots of land on the scrubby slopes of **Mont Pelat** (Bald Mountain) for the purpose. He proposed dividing the park into 60 lots, and asked Gaudí to design the entrance pavilions, market place and carriage roads which would link the houses. There were few subscribers to this grand, expensive project and only two houses were ever built: **Can Muntaner** for the Güell family and a candy-pink house, **Torre Rosa**, designed by **Francesc Berenguer**, which became Gaudí's last home and which now houses the Gaudí Museum.

Güell had very particular ideas for the park – all building plans had to be submitted to him for approval. The houses were to retain the forest land around them, on pain of a fine for each tree cut down, and there was a torrent of instructions relating to the height, position and access roads for the prospective mansions, which it was categorically ordered were to be used for residential purposes only.

Considering the wealth of rules and regulations, the enormous cost, the park's awkward location – too far from the city for convenience and not far enough away to feel like a country retreat – it seems hardly surprising that the plots remained unfilled. Güell died in 1918 and the empty grounds passed to the city for use as a public park in 1922. It was listed as a UNESCO World Heritage Site in 1984, and in 1995, once the city had started cashing in on its most celebrated son, it had a multi-million peseta restoration, and its shimmering mosaics gleam again.

Pavilions — Two fairy tale pavilions, with their twirling roofs and gleaming coats of multi-coloured *trencadís* (broken tiles) guard the entrance to the park, as sugary sweet as the gingerbread house in Hansel and Gretel. This isn't mere fancy – some of Gaudí's biographers have suggested that the production of a Catalan version of the fairy tale, which was a hit at the Liceu in 1900, was the inspiration behind the whimsical pavilions; the wicked witch lives in the house topped by a poisonous mushroom and the children are protected by the double cross which soars above the one on the left. Prosaically, the pavilions were built to accommodate a house for the park warden, and a waiting room for the expected hordes of visitors which never materialized. Gaudí left no record of his intentions, so no one will ever know for sure.

Beyond the pavilions is a grand flight of **stairs** edged with a fanciful tiled balustrade and divided by a **fountain** of water trickling down the centre; the fountain is guarded carefully by a dazzling **multicoloured dragon** which has become one of Barcelona's best-loved symbols.

The steps ascend grandly to culminate in the astonishing cave-like recesses of the Sala Hipóstila, also known as the 'Hall of a Hundred Columns', even though there are only 86, for the forest of thick Doric columns which support its undulating, mosaic-covered roof. This extraordinary temple was intended to be the market place for the inhabitants of the 60 unbuilt mansions, but was an infinitely more appropriate setting for the charitable concerts which Güell allowed to be held here in the embarrassing absence of market stalls.

Sala Hipóstila

Gaudí's talented collaborator, the architect **Josep Maria Jujol**, was given free reign to colour the vaulted ceiling with every kind of whimsy; the vaults are covered with tiny fragments of the palest china, and a host of spirals, flowers and stars shimmer on the keystones between the arches. Gaudí and Jujol brought left-over *trencadís* from Casa Batlló (see page 125) and instructed their workers to collect all the broken odds and ends that they could find, particularly the deep-blue glass bottles which held rosewater. Such technical eccentricity was met with astonishment from passers-by; one remarked, "What a weird sight! Thirty men breaking things and still more of them putting them back together again!". The hall is spectacularly lit up at dusk, the best time to pick out the patterns of smashed china ware, ceramic dolls' heads and old bottles which compose the rippling surface.

Flights of steps lead up to the rooftop of Sala Hipóstila, which forms a central square and offers beautiful views of the city below. The neverending **serpentine bench**, which wriggles around the square, is thickly encrusted with *trencadís*, which shimmer and change colour in the sunlight like the scales of a monstrous snake or dragon; another product of Gaudí's collaboration with Jujol, it forms a dazzling collage of bizarre symbols, fragments of text, stars, butterflies, moons and flowers which presaged Cubism and Surrealism. Gaudí's trencadí-covered sculptures must have influenced the young Picasso's move towards Cubism.

Miró was spellbound by Park Güell and his paintings were filled with similar symbols

Surrounding the square are **porticoes** and **viaducts**, which hug the slopes and stretch for more than 3 km. The arches and columns are made from unworked stone quarried *in situ*, which seem to erupt organically, swooping overhead like cresting waves; Salvador Dalí, wandering wildly through the park's upper reaches, was filled with 'unforgettable anguish' and the rocky landscapes re-emerge in his surreal dreamscapes. Each of the porticoes is different; the thicker columns seem to suggest the knotted trunks of ancient trees, while others soar smoothly to meet the arch – one of them is supported by a saucy stone female figure, one hand on hip as she uses the other to steady the mountain above her.

Hidden off a pathway near the top of the hill is a stony nub called La Capella (Chapel), the only part of a projected rose-shaped chapel to be completed, but no one has managed to discover a way into the tower. Above it loom three stone crosses, which merge into one if you look towards the Holy Land to the east.

La Capella

Gracia, Tibidabo & outer districts

Gaudí and God's favoured nation

The sheer playfulness and whimsy which characterize Park Güell lend themselves perfectly to the myriad interpretations of the symbolism found there: Gaudí and Güell have been variously depicted as Freemasons, Rosicrucians, occultists and worse; sometimes convincingly but more often not. The few notes and records which Gaudí left behind at his death were burned during the Civil War, so fancy continues to prevail.

One thing is not in doubt: both Gaudí and Güell were profoundly Catalanist. Güell's lifelong friend, Pere Miquel de Esplugues, later wrote that "Güell ordained the use of Park Güell for the enlargement of the Catalan spirit". Gaudí's firmly held Catalanist beliefs were widely known; he rarely left Catalunya, and thoroughly despised the centralism of Madrid: "Our qualities are not those of the centre – and neither are our faults. We can never unite with them." On his presentation to King Alfons XIII, he addressed the nonplussed monarch in Catalan, and in 1914 he was thrown into jail at the age of 71 for refusing to state his occupation in Castilian. Gaudí believed that Catalunya, where a fountain is supposed to have burst from the dry rock at the moment of the Crucifixion, was especially blessed by God.

Park Güell was begun in 1900 when

Catalanism was riding high on a wave of popularity and is crammed with symbolism. The Catalan shield which sits at the base of the steps at the entrance is the most obvious, but there are unmistakable references to Catalunya's glorious past: the Doric columns leading to the 'Hall of the Hundred Columns' are reminiscent of a Roman Temple, a reference to Catalunya's position as the first civilized corner of the Iberian peninsula under the Romans; the roughly hewn stone which supports the porticoes deliberately evoke the sturdy Romanesque churches of the Catalan hinterlands. The creature – a dragon? a lizard? a crocodile? – which clamps itself to the fountain at the entrance has inspired all kinds of speculation about its symbolism: perhaps it's a crocodile which served to remind Eusebi Güell of his student days in the French city of Nîmes, whose emblem was a crocodile flanked by a pair of palms (the mosaic palms which once shaded this creature have disappeared), and was also the city which marked Catalunya's northern boundary at the height of her medieval empire. Or perhaps it's a dragon, a central figure in Catalan folklore, usually speared by St George, but taking on the saint's role as a guardian, carefully watching over the sacred Catalan nation.

Torre Rosa Just off the main esplanade is the modest, pink Torre Rosa, built by **Francesc Berenguer** in order to attract potential plot-buyers. In 1906, Gaudí moved here with his ailing father and his orphaned niece Rossita; his father died in October 1906, and his sickly niece who finally died in 1912 at the age of just 36. Gaudí remained here alone, increasingly wrapped up in his monumental project for the Sagrada Família, until his death under the wheels of a tram in 1926.

Gaudí's house has been transformed into the **Casa Museu Gaudí**. It is a delightful little cottage covered in creamy swirls and topped with a *trencadí* – covered spire surmounted with a cross. The garden is filled with wrought-iron flowers made by Gaudí from cast-off iron railings, and there's a delicious little pergola with parabolic arches which he designed himself. Inside, the modest rooms are filled with plans and drawings, examples of Gaudí's furniture designs for the grand mansions of the Eixample – beautiful chandeliers of coloured glass, plush, gilded benches and monumental, carved wooden cabinets – and a sparse collection of his few personal possessions. His bedroom, which has been conserved much as he left it, contains a narrow bed, a copy of his prayer book and his death mask.

■ *Daily Nov-Feb 1000-1800; Mar, Oct 1000-1900; Apr, Sep 1000-2000; May-Aug 1000-2100. Free. Casa Museu Gaudí daily Nov-Feb 1000-1800, Mar, Apr, Oct 1000-1900, May-Sep 1000-2000. €2.40.*

Eating and drinking

Jaume de Provença, C/de Provença 88, T93 430 00 29. Tue-Sat 1300-1600 and 2100-2330, Sun 1300-1600, closed Aug, metro Hospital Clinic. The décor may be verging on the austere but the cuisine is emphatically the opposite: Chef Jaume Bargués is renowned for his adventurous and imaginative Catalan cuisine – like the lobster tempura served with a poached egg and truffle sauce. The menu also includes a selection of traditional Catalan dishes, faithfully prepared to classic recipes. *Roig Robí*, C/Seneca 20, T93 218 92 22. Open Mon-Fri 1330-0600 and 2100-2330, Sat 2100-2330, metro Diagonal. A very charming and welcoming restaurant, Roig Robí has a very pretty garden terrace in summer. It offers refined Catalan dishes, such as goose with cherries, or *caldereta de rape*, an aromatic monkfish stew.

Ot, C/Torres 25, T93 284 77 52. Open Mon-Fri 1400-1530 and 2100-2230, Sat 2100-2230, metro Diagonal or Joanic. A very fashionable restaurant run by two innovative young chefs which serves inspired variations of Catalan classics. It offers an eight-course set menu which changes monthly, and might include pigeon with a spicy lentil stuffing, or a monkfish, banana and bacon kebab. *Botafumeiro*, C/Gran de Gràcia 81, T93 218 42 30. Open daily 1300-0100, metro Fontana. An outstanding Galician seafood restaurant, with a stunning array of sea creatures on the menu; the excellent value *menu de degustación* is highly recommended, and the wine list is exceptional. There's an attractive, traditional tavern next door which serves fresh oysters and other excellent tapas.

Bilbao, C/Peril 33, T93 458 96 24. open Mon-Sat 1330-1530 and 2000-2330, closed Sun and holidays, metro Verdaguer or Joanic. The menu changes almost daily depending on what's in season and what's good at the market; the food is excellent, immaculately prepared, and you could be sitting down to anything from wild mushrooms to a simply prepared fish *a la plancha* (grilled) that will be deliciously fresh. The new extension is not as atmospheric as the old part, which is lined with dozens of pictures, photographs and sketches.

Expensive
For price categories, see inside cover

La Barbacoa de Gràcia, C/Torrent Flores 65, T93 210 22 53. Open Wed-Sun 1300-1600 and 2000-0100, metro Joanic. A busy, noisy old-fashioned grill house with wooden benches and tables; daily specials as well as an extensive menu, and they also do good *torrades* with lots of different toppings. *La Buena Tierra*, C/de l'Encarnació 56, T93 219 8213. Open Tue-Sat 1300-1600 and 2000-2400. One of the most delightful vegetarian restaurants in the city, set in a charming old house with a lovely garden terrace. The food is always imaginative and the fresh, chilled soups are great in summer.

El Galliner, C/Martínez de la Rosas 71, T93 218 53 27. Open daily 1330-1530 and 2030-0100, evenings only on Tue, metro Diagonal. A pretty, family-run restaurant set in a old pink house, specializes in *bacalao* (cod), served up in more than 40 different ways. There's plenty of other choice on the menu, and the service is very friendly. *Mesopotamia*, C/Verdi 65, T93 237 15 63. Open Mon-Sat 2030-2345, metro Fontana. A trendy new spot, this Iraqi restaurant serves tasty fresh dishes like chicken cooked with rosewater and aubergines in yogurt. Lots of young, arty people and a relaxed chatty atmosphere.

Octubre, 18, C/Julián Romea. Open Mon-Fri 1330-1530 and 2100-2300, Sat 2100-2300, T93 218 25 18. A cosy, romantic restaurant with exposed brick walls and soft lighting which serves fresh, simple French-Catalan dishes; the menu changes regularly but it's worth trying the warm artichokes with foie gras, and saving room for the

Mid-range
● *on map, page 146*

Gracia, Tibidabo & outer districts

fabulous desserts. *Tábata*, C/Torrent d'Olla 27, T93 237 89 46. Open Mon 1300-1600, Tue-Sat 1300-1600 and 2100-2400, metro Diagonal. This elegant restaurant specializes in meat and fish cooked on sizzling *tabas* (hot stone slabs), but there is also a good range of salads and some vegetarian dishes.

Cheap
Flash Flash, C/Granada del Penedès 25, T93 237 09 90. Open daily 1300-0130, bar open daily 1100-0200, FGC Gràcia. Classic 1970s black and white décor with white leatherette seating and black silhouettes on the walls. Best known for its excellent selection of tortillas, it also does great burgers and steaks and attracts a trendy uptown crowd. *Equinox Sol*, Plaça del Sol 14. Open 1300-0100, metro Fontana. A cheap and cheerful Lebanese café with tables outside on the square. It serves great falafel and other pitta sandwiches.

El Glop, C/Montmany 46, T93 213 70 58. Open Tue-Sun 1300-1600 and 2000-0100, metro Joanic. There are now a handful of *Glop* restaurants in the city, including one just down the street at No 49, offering grilled meat and fish and other traditional dishes at very reaonable prices. You can make a meal from the *torrades* (toasted bread with tomato) and assorted toppings, washed down with a jug of local wine. The ceiling opens up in summer, and it attracts a mixed, friendly crowd. *La Singular*, C/Francesc Giner 50, T93 237 50 98. Open 1300-1600 and 2100-2400 closed Wed and Sat lunch. Popular, lively spot for clubbers gearing up for the night ahead. Choose from the snacks and daily specials scrawled up on the blackboard.

Txistulari, C/Doctor Rizal 16, T93 237 13 26. Open daily 1130-0100, *pintxos* are laid out between 1130-1530 and 1900-2300, closed Sun and Mon evening, metro Fontana. Another Basque bar and restaurant with a wooden counter heaving with *pintxos*, and a dining room if you prefer to sit down and eat something more substantial. *L'Illa de Gràcia*, C/Sant Domènec 19, T93 238 02 29. Open 1300-1600, 2100 until 2400, *menú del día* €5.12, metro Fontana. You have to be sure to book this laid-back veggie spot; unusual, imaginative dishes and a good range of home-made desserts, as well as beer and wine.

Café-bars with food/tapas
Sol Solet, Plaça del Sol 21, T93 217 44 40. Open Mon and Tue 1900-0200, Wed and Thu 1500-0200, Fri and Sat 1200-0300, Sun 1200-0300, metro Fontana. One of the prettiest bars in Gràcia, with marble-topped tables, old tiles and paddle fans, and looking out onto the square. An excellent range of unusual tapas are on offer, including several vegetarian options, like the delicious spinach and potato pie, and cous cous salads.

Virreina Bar, Plaça de la Virreina 1, T93 237 98 80. Open daily 1000-0230, until midnight on Sun. Another relaxed bar on a leafy square, with a small church and a village atmosphere, this offers good snacks and sandwiches during the day and is a quiet place to enjoy a chat in the evenings. *Café Salambo*, C/Torrijos 51, T93 218 69 66. Open daily 1200-0230, metro Joanic. Owned by a famous literary agent, this popular, elegant café attracts lots of writers and arty types. It's on two levels, with plenty of tables downstairs and pool tables upstairs. There's a good range of teas, sandwiches and snacks.

El Roble, C/Lluis Antúnez, T93 218 73 87. 0700-0100, closed Sun, metro Diagonal. This is a roomy old-fashioned tapas bar which hasn't changed in decades. There's a rickety, yellowing old sign showing what's on offer, or you can go and inspect the dishes lined up along the counter. Long-aproned waiters dash about the place, and it's a big favourite with locals. *La Taberna del Cura*, C/Gran de Gràcia 83, T93 218 17 99. Open daily 1300-0100, metro Fontana. Attached to a very smart restaurant, the Botafumeiro (see page 151), this old-style tavern with hams dangling from the ceiling offers an excellent range of gourmet tapas and barbecued meats. If you haven't reserved, you can console yourself with some spit-roasted chicken sold at the street stall outside.

La Ceba, C/de la Perla 10. Open Mon-Sat 1300-1600 and 2030-2400, metro Fontana. A popular local bar, it specializes in *truita* (Catalan tortilla). There are more than 50 varieties on offer, with fillings ranging from courgette and aubergine to ham and cheese. **Bar Canigó**, C/Verdi 2, T93 213 3049. Open 1200-0200, closed Sun, metro Fontana. An old-fashioned bar with wooden fittings and burnished mirrors, which hasn't changed in years. It has a popular terrace overlooking Plaça de la Revolució and offers good, well-priced sandwiches and snacks.

Cafés

Chivito de Oro, Plaça Rius i Taulet, T93 218 33 27. Open 0900-0200, closed Mon, metro Fontana. Famous for its delicious *chivitos* (Uraguayan-style sandwiches stuffed with ham and cheese), this delightful neighbourhood bar has a good terrace overlooking the square. *Tetería Jazmín*, C/Maspons 11, T93 210 71 84. Open Tue-Sun 1800-0200, metro Fontana. This delightful Moroccan tearoom has hanging carpets and low-cushioned benches and serves big pots of fresh mint tea accompanied by tiny pastries, and light couscous dishes. If you've had enough of the bar scene and want to relax, this is the perfect spot as it's open 'till late.

Shopping

Markets

Mercat de la Llibertat, C/Oreneta, just off C/Gran de Gràcia, metro Fontana. This market up in Gràcia, piled high with fresh produce, is located in a pretty *modernista* wrought-iron building.

Sports goods

Nus Esports de Muntanya, Plaça Diamant 9, metro Fontana. The name says it all: a treasure trove for mountaineers or anyone interested in adventure sports. *Pro-bike*, C/París 128, metro. This mountain-biking shop has all the equipment and also publishes its own magazine.

Transport

Bus You'll find most bus stops around Plaça Gal.la Placídia and Plaça Lesseps; several buses run along Torrent de les Flors and Gran de Gràcia. Bus Nos **24**, **25** and **28** go right to the gates of the Park Güell.
Nos **16** from Pg Manuel Girona to Plaça Urquinaona, via Gràcia, Diagonal, Pg de Gràcia and Plaça de Catalunya. No **17** from Pg Joan de Borbó to Avda Jordà, via Via Laietana, Pg de Gràcia, Gràcia and Avda Tibidabo. No **22** from Avda d'Esplugues to Plaça de Catalunya, via Pedralbes, Sarrià, Tramvia Blau, Gràcia and Pg de Gràcia. No **28** from Carmel to Plaça de Catalunya, via Parc Creuta del Coll, Gràcia and Pg de Gràcia.

Metro Line 3 (green) to Diagonal, Lesseps, Fontana; Line 4 (yellow) to Verdaguer and Joanic; Line 5 (blue) to Verdaguer, Diagonal.
Taxi There is a taxi rank on the Plaça Gal.la Placídia.
Train There are two FGV train stations which are convenient for Gràcia: Gràcia and Plaça Molina, with services to Passeig de Gràcia and Plaça de Catalunya, and onwards to Avda Tibidabo (for connections with the **Tramvia Blau** and the funicular up **Tibidabo**), **Sarrià**, and **Baixador de Vallvidrera** (for the **Parc de Collserola**).

Gracia, Tibidabo & outer districts

Tibidabo and outer districts

On the fringes of the old city lies a ring of distinct neighbourhoods; some were towns in their own right, before Barcelona gobbled them up, and others are industrial or residential neighbourhoods which grew up more recently and filled in the gaps. Few – besides the giddy peak of **Tibidabo***, with its funfair, the huge* **Camp Nou Stadium** *in Les Corts, and the serene* **Monestir de Pedralbes** *– are on the tourist trail, but all preserve a distinct atmosphere which, if you have enough time, make them worth the trek. Sloping up the hills which circle the city are some of its loveliest parks, including the delightful wilderness of the* **Parc de Collserola** *and the enigmatic, manicured maze at* **Horta***.*

Sants

Ⓜ *Plaça de Sants; Bus no 32* The area around Barcelona's main train station, Estació Barcelona-Sants, sits on the borders of the Left Eixample, and encompasses the two adjoining districts of **La Bordeta** and **Hostafrancs**. The neighbourhood began as a haphazard collection of blacksmith's forges and inns, which grew up to accommodate late arrivals in the days when Barcelona's gates shut at 9pm. By the mid-19th century, it had become an important industrial centre, densely packed with factories, mills and workers' housing, and with a feisty reputation for labour militancy. It was in Sants that *Camí d'Espanya* began; dating from Roman times, the 'Road to Spain' is now formed by Carrer de la Creu Coberta and Carrer de Sants.

Most of the old factories in the district have long been demolished, but the locals have demonstrated their enduring appetite for campaigning – for worker's rights in the 19th century, for schools in the early 20th century, and most recently, for more open spaces – and now there are several notable urban parks in the area. The largest and most popular is **Parc de l'Espanya Industrial** which was designed by Luis Peña Ganchegui and Francesc Rius Camps, and constructed on the former site of the massive **Vapor Nou** factory. In front of the train station is a much less admired public park, the dispiriting, comfortless **Plaça dels Països Catalans**; the architects, Helio Piñonó and Albert Viaplana, were given the undesirable task of creating a public space at the end of a scrubby confusion of roads.

Les Corts

Ⓜ *Collblanc* Les Corts, once a rural village dotted with farmhouses, has been transformed almost beyond recognition. Although hidden away between the gleaming offices and high-rise apartment buildings of the business district, there are still some charming corners which retain the spirit of the past. The main reasons for visiting Les Corts are the FC Barcelona Stadium, **Camp Nou**, or the entertainment and shopping complex of **L' Illa** on the upper section of Diagonal.

Nowadays, Les Corts is synonymous with the **Camp Nou** stadium built for FC Barça, one of the most popular football teams in the world. If you can't get into a game, a visit to **Museu FC Barcelona** is a worthy substitute. Even for those not interested in football, the museum holds an evocative collection of mementoes, cups and footballing paraphernalia which recount the club's fortunes over the past century. The highlight for many fans is the European Cup, won at Wembley in 1992. The club has just bought up some of the auctioned-off stock from Wembley Stadium – goalposts, the royal box, bits and pieces from the locker rooms – in order to recreate the club's triumph in style. There are some delightful models of early stadiums, with little figures hunched along the perimeter walls, bottoms overhanging, giving rise to the nickname *culés* (arses). The side rooms show videos of great triumphs and successes, and a vast collection of old posters, magazines, photos, boots and balls portrays the development of the game and the growing popularity of the team. The visit culminates with a view of the immense stadium from the royal gallery. ■ *Museu FC Barcelona, entrance on Av Aristides Maillol, metro Collblanc. www.fcbarcelona.es Mon-Sat 1000-1830, Sun and holidays 1000-1400. €3.46, including stadium visit. For information on match tickets, see page 48.*

Camp Nou
Bus no 15 goes from Collblanc to Hospital de Sant Pau, via FC Barça stadium, Plaça Francesc Macià and Diagonal

The upper section of Diagonal, the glittering avenue which cuts across the city, is the heart of Barcelona's business district. The area is stuffed with gleaming temples to commerce, business hotels, shopping malls and university buildings. Most of the offices are located around **Plaça Frances Maçia**, where the Avinguda Pau Casals leads to **Parc Turó**, one of the few green corners in an otherwise bland and overwhelming neighbourhood. Created a century ago it's now a small, vaguely melancholy spot, with a pretty lake and a sprinkling of sculptures, including a bust of the tenor *Francesc Viñas* by Josep Clarà, and *La Ben Plantada*, a tribute to the muse of the *Noucentistas*. Kids might enjoy the children's theatre, which has puppet shows, mime artists and musicians in summer.

Western Diagonal

Further up Diagonal is the huge white shopping, entertainment and business complex of **L'Illa**, which looks like an ocean liner (see page 168) and further up, just off the **Plaça Reina Maria Christina**, is the smaller **Pedralbes** Shopping Centre and a huge branch of the *El Corte Inglés* department store.

Pedralbes

North of the western end of Avinguda Diagonal the plush, affluent suburb of Pedralbes used to spill down the once-wooded slopes of Collserola. Today, it's filled with plenty of large, private residences surrounded by lush gardens, most of which date from the latter half of the 20th century, although the biggest attractions for visitors in this neighbourhood date back much earlier.

Palau Reial

Just off Diagonal is the stately mid-19th-century mansion known as the Palau Reial de Pedralbes, surrounded by soothing, elegant gardens. It maintains a serene air despite its chequered history: originally owned by the prominent Güell family until they donated it to the Spanish royal family in 1919, the palace was expanded and refurbished for King Alfonse XIII, who slept here in 1926. With the downfall of the monarchy in 1931, it was passed to the Barcelona city hall and then became the headquarters of the Republican

Palau Reial; Bus no 74 Gràcia

Western districts

Gracia, Tibidabo & outer districts

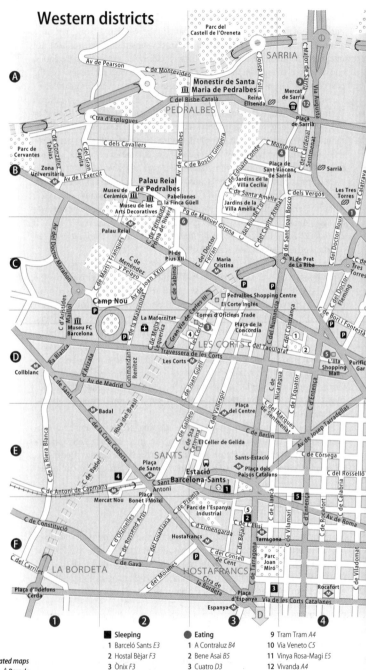

Related maps

A *Parc de Collserola*, page 162
B *Gràcia*, page 146
C *Eixample*, page 122
D *Montjuïc & Poble Sec*, page 176

| 0 metres | 300 |
| 0 yards | 300 |

■ Sleeping
1 Barceló Sants *E3*
2 Hostal Bèjar *F3*
3 Ònix *F3*
4 Pensioón Sants *E2*
5 Roma *E4*
6 Turó de Vilana *B5*

● Eating
1 A Contraluz *B4*
2 Bene Asai *B5*
3 Cuatro *D3*
4 El Vell Sarrià *B4*
5 La Vaquería *D4*
6 Neichel *C2*
7 Pipper's *D5*
8 Satoru Miyano *C5*

9 Tram Tram *A4*
10 Via Veneto *C5*
11 Vinya Rosa-Magi *E5*
12 Vivanda *A4*

● Cafés & tapas bars
13 Casa Fernández & Gimlet Bar *D5*
14 Mas I Mas *D5*

government towards the end of the Civil War. After the war, Franco appropriated it as his private residence while in Barcelona, and finally donated it to the city in 1960.

The palace **gardens** are a delightful, secret oasis, dotted with lily ponds, woods, bamboo forests and shady benches; hidden in one of the glades is a small fountain in the form of a gaping dragon by Gaudí, which was only discovered in 1983, and is a tiny foretaste of the massive beast which flaps across the former main gateway of the Pabeliones Finca Güell, the main estate around the corner on Avinguda de Pedralbes (see page 158).

Palau Reial now houses two quiet museums in separate wings; on the right is the Museu de les Arts Decoratives, an eclectic selection of furniture – exquisitely inlaid writing desks, carved wooden chests and richly brocaded seating – tapestries, glasswork, clocks, fans, jewellery and knick-knacks dating back to the Middle Ages – all handsomely displayed in galleries surrounding the sumptuously decorated oval throne room. The final gallery is devoted to pieces from the 20th century. This being Barcelona, design rules supreme, and includes everything from ashtrays to a mop and bucket. The holdings are enormous and the collections rotate regularly.

Museu de les Artes Decoratives

The opposite wing of the Palace holds the charming Museu de Ceràmica, with an exceptional collection of pieces from the most important Spanish ceramics manufacturers stretching back over the last millennium. There is a beautiful selection of lustrous ceramics from Manises, near Valencia, intricate *mudéjar* pieces from Andalucia and Seville, some colourful, earthy 18th-century tiles from Catalunya with mischievous characters (including the famous little crapper or *cagoner* – see page 76) and

Museu de Ceràmica

Gracia, Tibidabo & outer districts

○ **Entertainment**
1 Auditori Winterthur *D4*
2 Bikini *D4*
3 L'Espai *D6*
4 Renoir-Les Corts *D3*
5 Sal Àtic *F3*
7 El Universal *D5*
8 La Cova del Drac *C5*
9 Lízard *C6*

○ **Clubs & bars**
6 Bubblic Bar *D5*

**Five of the best:
sights in the outer districts**

- *Camp Nou stadium* (see page 155)
- *Monestir de Pedralbes* (see below)
- *Parc de Collserola* (see page 161)
- *Tibidabo funfair* (see page 163)
- *Horta Labyrinth* (see page 165)

occupations, and a couple of 18th-century tiled murals depicting the newly fashionable ritual of drinking chocolate and another of a bloody bullfight. The top floor is devoted to 20th-century ceramics, with a small gallery devoted to works by **Picasso**, **Miró** and the celebrated Catalan sculptor **Josep Llorens Artigas**, who gave Miró his first ceramics lessons.

■ *Museu de les Artes Decoratives: Tue-Sat 1000-1800, Sun and holidays 1000-1500. €3.6, free on the first Sun of the month. Joint ticket available with the Museu de Ceràmica (see below). www.museuartsdecoratives.bcn.es   Museu Ceramica: Same opening hours, www.museuceramica.bcn.es*

Pabeliones Finca Güell

Gaudí's extraordinary Pabeliones Finca Güell were commissioned by Eusebi Güell in 1884, who asked the architect to design the gate, lodge and stables of his family's suburban estate. Gaudí responded with a lavish neo-Moorish concoction which recalls Casa Vicens (see page 147), that he was simultaneously building in Gràcia, decorated with a light filigree of brickwork, and ornamental cupolas studded with tiles.

The stables, to the right of the main gate, adorned by Gaudí's trademark parabolic arches echoed in the shape of the windows, are now home to the **Càtedra Gaudí**, part of Barcelona's architectural school devoted to the study of Gaudí's works. Stretched between these fanciful buildings is an immense, vital dragon whose swooping wings form the main gate, claws spread and tail flapping, with its lunging jaws spread wide enough to swallow a bystander whole. It's impossible not to take an involuntary step backwards when faced with that grimace. This is Hercules' dragon – in **Jacint Verdaguer**'s celebrated poem *L'Atlàntida*: he locates the Garden of the Hesperides of Greek myth in Catalunya, where Hercules has to kill the dragon which guards the magic tree bearing golden oranges. For the Güells, this was interpreted as a flattering allegory of their successful enterprises in Cuba. The gatepost on the right is topped with a delicate, leafy orange tree. Another gate designed by Gaudí survives down on Carrer Manuel Girona, where it has been almost swallowed up by the surrounding banal university buildings.

Monestir de Santa Maria de Pedralbes

Bus no 75 goes from Les Corts to Av Tibidabo via FC Barcelona, Monestir Pedralbes and Sarrià

At the top of Avinguda Pedralbes is the lovely Monestir de Santa María de Pedralbes, established in the 14th century by Queen Elisenda de Montcada, the fourth and last wife of King Jaume II the Just. The king's failing health prompted Elisenda to establish a monastery for her retirement after his death, and she chose *Petras Albas* (white stones), which gave the present neighbourhood its name, as the location in 1326. The king himself considered other options, but the queen, who intended to withdraw from the palace but not from politicking, preferred to remain within easy reach of the court and the convenience of the nearby village of Sarrià. The monastery was built quickly, and yet has survived as one of the purest expressions of Catalan Gothic architecture in the city Jaume II died in November 1327, and the queen moved with her court into her elegant new palace next to the monastery, where she meddled happily in everyone's business until her death in 1364.

Visca el Barça – Up with Barça!

Camp Nou stadium is the largest in Europe, built to accommodate 120,000 fans. And yet getting tickets for a match – particularly with arch-rivals Real Madrid – can be unbelievably tough. The club's unofficial slogan during the last years of the Franco regime – Barça mes que un club *(Barça more than a club)* signalled the extent to which it had become the embodiment of Catalan nationalism; waving the distinctive blue and burgundy colours of the team became a substitute for the banned red and gold standard of Catalunya.

The club is the largest organization in the world, with more than 108,000 members (including – appropriately for a club which has assumed near-religious significance in the eyes of its fans – the Pope). Memberships pass down through generations and babies are signed up only hours after their birth.

Ironically, Barça began as a weekly kick-around for a group of bored Swiss and Englishmen, who established the club in 1899. Hans Gamper, the club's first president, picked the colours because they were the same as his home town of Winterthur. By 1922, Barça had its own stadium and under Franco, the team became the main focus of pent-up nationalist resentment. El Caudillo cosseted his pet team Real Madrid, and FC Barça were instructed to lose matches when the two teams met; during the 1941 cup match, the Barça goal-keeper was suspended for life after waving his cap around each time Real Madrid scored a goal, in order to expose the farce of losing 11-1 to the weaker team. Despite the antics of the Francoist Spanish Football Federation, who ordered that a Falangist and a member of the military attend each

meeting of the board, FC Barça flourished, winning five cups in the early 1950s. Panicked, the Spanish Football Federation found that the signing of the immensely popular player di Stefano was 'illegal' and demanded that Kubala, an amazing player known as the Saeta Rubia *(blond arrow)*, be shared with Real Madrid. These ridiculous, underhand attempts to scupper the Catalan team only served to fortify its fans.

Construction for the new, much-needed stadium in the mid-1950s, was made possible only because the dedicated fans, all of whom had suffered through the hunger years of the 1940s, paid their annual subscriptions up to five years in advance in a dramatic display of faith. The team served not only as a focus for repressed Catalan nationalism, but also to Catalanize immigrants from other parts of Spain who poured into the region in the 1950s and 60s, an unforeseen development on the part of the Falangists.

After Franco's death in 1975 and the re-establishment of democracy, FC Barça went on to win the European Cup Winner's Cup in 1979, 1982, 1989 and 1997, but their most treasured moment came when they won the European Cup at Wembley in 1992.

Their fortunes have wavered in recent years – following Johann Cruyff's inspired coaching, a few disappointing seasons resulted in three managers in four years and the first Spanish manager in more than a decade, the Mallorcan Llorenç Serra Ferrer, who suffered the humiliation of watching his team make an early exit from the Champion's League in his first season. Who knows what the future holds; La Rambla may soon resound with tooting of horns to celebrate another European success.

Gracia, Tibidabo and outer districs

The **convent** still houses a small community of the *Poor Clares*, but a section of it is open to the public as the Museu Monastir de Pedralbes, one of the most serene corners of the city. The unusual three-tiered **cloister**, one of the best preserved in Europe, is a still, contemplative arcade of slender columns, surrounding groves of cypress trees, rose gardens and a small pond. There's a pretty double-decker fountain topped with an angel, where the nuns would wash, and a striking, richly ornamented Gothic well.

Museu Monestir de Pedralbes
The monastery was devoted to a community of nuns from the closed Order of St Clare

The former refectory, infirmary and kitchens are now devoted to a collection of **religious art**. Exhibits include a 16th-century retablo of Mary Magdalen with a sheet of golden hair ascending to heaven, as well as models showing the construction of the convent and its various additions, and liturgical vestments richly embroidered by the nuns. The nuns were buried under the flagstones, apart from the abbesses and Queen Elisanda, who repose in sculpted tombs in a small chapel just off the cloister.

The irregularly shaped **Capella de Sant Miquel** just off the cloister holds **Ferrar Bassa**'s luminous, solemn murals (1346) of the Passion of Christ and the Life of the Virgin, which show the creeping influence of Italian art and the Sienese school in particular. They were completed just two years before Bassa was carried off in the plague epidemic which decimated 14th-century Barcelona. ■ *Tue-Sun 1000-1400. €3.60, free first Sun of the month.*

Col.lecio Thyssen-Bornemisza

The collection is often complemented by visiting pieces from the main Thyssen museum in Madrid

The former nun's dormitories have been remodelled to hold the Col.lecció Thyssen-Bornemisza, a selection of works, mainly but not exclusively Italian, which have been prised from the Museu Thyssen-Bornemisza bequest held in Madrid. The vast room has been beautifully refurbished to show the collection, and many of the later additions which cluttered its original simple lines have been stripped away; the dormitory is now an attractive gallery with a wooden beamed ceiling, marble floors, and the original stucco walls.

There's a shimmering collection of gilded medieval paintings and sculpture, which includes a sweet-faced *Madonna* by **Bernardo Daddi** (circa 1340-45), a strangely ghostly *Nativity* (circa 1325) by **Taddeo Gaddi** and **Fra Angelico**'s lovely masterpiece, the glowing, rosy-cheeked *Madonna of Humility* (circa 1430s). There are some smaller works by **Tintoretto**, **Titian** and **Veronese**, like the latter's blazing *Annunciation* (1570), a couple of paintings by **Rubens**, including the romping, great family reunion *Virgin and Child with St Elizabeth and the Infant St John*, as well as an immaculate, sharp series of portraits of saints by **Lucas Cranach the Elder**.

Later works include **Tiepolo**'s dramatic *Way to Golgotha* (1728) and the histrionic *Expulsion from the Temple* (1760), a selection of airy pieces from **Canaletto**, **Velázquez**'s portrait of *Mariana de Austria* (1655-7), whose peevish expression can just be made out from under her bouffant hair, and **Zurbarán**'s engaging portrait of *Santa Marina* (1640-45), depicted as a sassy, oddly modern young woman. ■ *Tue-Sun 1000-1400. €3, free first Sun of the month, combined ticket with the Museu Monestir de Pedralbes, see above, €4.80, www.museothyssen.org.*

Parc del Castell de l'Oreneta

Behind the monastery, up Carrer Montevideo, the Parc del Castell de l'Oreneta sprawls down the slopes of Collserola. The park is a big favourite with kids, which has a steam train on Sundays, a pony club, a snack bar, lots of picnic areas and and a sports circuit. The castle, preserved only in the name of the park, was destroyed during the Civil War, but enough of the wilderness areas of this former hunting reserve survives to make for pleasant strolling. ■ *Steam train open Sun 1100-1400. €1.20.*

Sarrià

FGC Sarrià, Bus no 14, 30, 34, 66, 70, 72 and 74

Sarrià, which adjoins the neighbourhood of Pedralbes, was the last of the independent townships which circled Barcelona to be annexed and has retained a distinct identity and atmosphere. Sarrià, is equally affluent but a little more charming, with old-fashioned stone houses, narrow streets climbing up the steep slopes, and a sprinkling of pleasant shops, restaurants and cafés. It has no museums or major monuments, but the quiet streets make a pleasant break from the crowds in the city centre.

The main street through old Sarrià is Carrer Major de Sarrià, which has preserved some delightful squares, including the cool **Plaça de Sant Vincenç** surrounded by stone arcades and higgledy piggledy houses, where the *Festival de St Ponç* (Saint Pontius), patron saint of bee keepers and herbalists, is held each year on 11 May. The main square is the central **Plaça de Sarrià**, which just manages to hang on to its villagey air despite the traffic which whizzes by, and is overlooked by the **Església de Sant Vicenç**, built and destroyed dozens of times over the last 1,000 years. Just around the corner from Plaça de Sarrià, on Passeig Reina Elisanda, is the *modernista* covered market, **El Mercat de Sarrià**, built in 1911, with a colourful array of local produce. At the very top of Carrer Major de Gràcia, there's a short passage named for the city's co-patroness, Santa Eulàlia, who is supposed to have lived up here before the Romans got so annoyed with her piety that they killed her.

Vallvidrera

The lovely hill-top village of Vallvidrera was annexed by Sarrià in 1890, before Barcelona engulfed them both a few years later. Set up high on the slopes of Collserola, Vallvidrera has serenely ignored the hectic goings-on in the rest of the city, enjoying its fresh air, wonderful views and calm, peaceful atmosphere. A simple, wooden funicular train joins the town with the Avinguda de Vallvidrera at the bottom of the hill, leaving from Peu Funicular station and making a halfway stop at Carretera de les Aigües, a highly popular jogging and biking spot. Vallvidrera itself has a handful of charming old *modernista* buildings tucked away in its narrow streets (including its whimsical gingerbread funicular station), and an attractive square with a couple of decent café-bars – *Can Trampa* and *Can Josean* – for a snack and amazing views.

Vallvidrera is on the outskirts of Parc de Collserola, it's a pleasant walk, or you can take bus 211 from the main square

Parc de Collserola

The most unexpected delight in Barcelona is this beautiful natural park, which stretches for more than 6,500 ha across the undulating Serra de Collserola, the ring of hills which contain the sprawling city. The highest peak is **Tibidabo** (1,680 ft) where the funfair has been drawing crowds for more than a century, and which is a world away from the quiet woodlands which spread out behind it. Although the park is ringed with towns, it's still possible to completely forget the existence of the bustling city, and stroll, ride or mountain bike through wooded paths, between old *masies* (farmhouses), ancient chapels and half-forgotten springs. ■ *Horse-riding: Severino, Sant Cugat del Vallès, T93 674 11 40.*

Park information, T93 280 3552, www.parccollserola. amb.es

Just opposite the Parc de Collserola information office is a handsome, 18th-century farmhouse, the Vil.la Joana, where the celebrated 19th-century poet Jacint Verdaguer, popularly known as Mossèn Cinto, spent his last days. It is now the Museu Verdaguer, a quiet, shadowy house shaded by tangled wisteria, filled with mementoes of the famous priest who was one of Catalunya's most gifted poets during the great literary revival of the 19th century. He died here in 1902, aged only 57, and his room has been kept as it was on the day of his death, surrounded by eerie photographs of the deathbed

Museu Verdaguer

scene. Busts, photographs and books complete the exhibition. It's a lovely house with long, cool galleries, stone-flagged floors and pretty floral tiling, but still faintly melancholic. ■ *Groups by prior arrangement, Oct-May, Wed 1000-1400 Sat-Sun 1100-1500; Jun-Sep, Wed 1000-1400 Sat 1100-1400 and 1500-1800, Sun 1100-1500. Free.*

Tibidabo

Take the FGC train to Baixador de Vallvidrera, where a flight of shallow steps lead up through the woods to emerge at the park information office

Tibidabo mountain is where the Devil is supposed to have shown Christ the world's treasures spread out at his feet, and tempted him with the words '*haec omnia tibi dabo si cadens adoraberis me*' (All this will I give you if you will fall down and worship me). Not even this astonishing vision of the city curled around the sea in one direction, and the Collserolas undulating gently inland towards Montserrat and the Pyrenees were enough to tempt Christ, but the name stuck, and the views are usually tremendous – at least when a salty blast of sea air lifts the smoggy pall. When the railway and tramline opened at the foot of the hill in the early 1900s, Tibidabo's new career as the city's mountain of fun was launched.

Getting up the mountain is part of the fun take the local train to FGC Avinguda Tibidabo on **Plaça John F. Kennedy**, overlooked by the pretty tiled

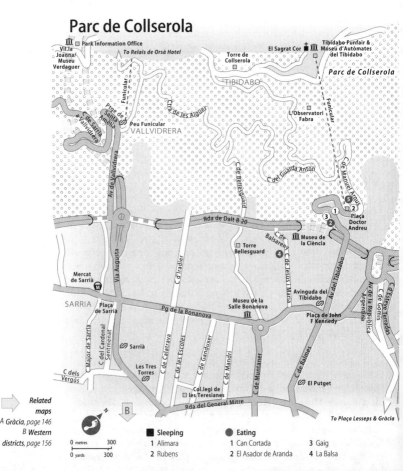

Parc de Collserola

Related maps
A *Gràcia*, page 146
B *Western districts*, page 156

| 0 metres | 300 |
| 0 yards | 300 |

To Plaça Lesseps & Gràcia

■ Sleeping
1 Alimara
2 Rubens

● Eating
1 Can Cortada
2 El Asador de Aranda
3 Gaig
4 La Balsa

tower and cupola of **La Rotonda** (1918), a *modernista* hotel which was converted into a clinic, and is now rather shabby and winsome. The cheerful, refurbished *Tramvia Blau* (see page 170) departs from just outside, clanking its way up past more *modernista* follies along the **Avinguda Tibidabo** and making for the **Plaça Dr Andreu** where it joins the funicular railway for the final ascent. There are a couple of attractive bars and restaurants on the square and a string of flashy clubs and drinking bars with extraordinary views just down the hill (see page 242).

Right on the brow of the hill is the Tibidabo funfair, a cheerful and resolutely old-fashioned funfair, with a small Ferris wheel offering big views, dodgems, a carousel, a house of horrors, shooting galleries and lots of rides for tiny kids. Also inside the Tibidabo funfair is the **Museu d'Autòmates del Tibidabo**, a bizarre collection of early coin-operated fairground machines dating back to the 19th century. Everyone's favourite is the saucy temptress *La Monyos*, named after a famous character who could often be seen swaying along La Rambla, who looks a bit like a man in drag, but tosses her pigtails convincingly and grins broadly. There's also a fiery little recreation of hell, where you can watch the souls being poked into the flames by demons, a mini mechanical ski-station and a host of

Parc d' Attracciones

Gracia, Tibidabo & outer districts

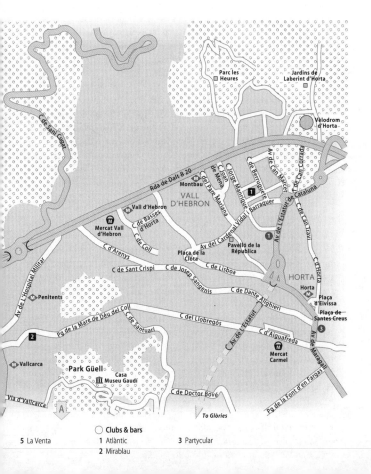

Clubs & bars

5 La Venta
1 Atlàntic
2 Mirablau
3 Partycular

Five of the best: highest viewpoints

- *Globus Turístic hot air balloon* (see page 32)
- *The rooftop of La Seu Cathedral* (see page 74)
- *Spires of the Sagrada Família* (see page 131)
- *The Torre de Collserola* (see below)
- *Cable car across the harbour* (see page 201)

other gizmos and contraptions. ■ *Late Mar-Apr, Fri-Sun 1200-1900; May, Thu-Sun 1200-1900; Jun, Wed-Sun 1200-1900; Jul and Aug, Mon-Thu, Sun 1200-2200, Fri-Sat 1200-0100; early Sep, Mon-Thu 1200-2000, Fri-Sat 1200-2200; late Sep, Sat-Sun 1200-2000. Admission and 6 rides €7.22, free to children under 1 m 10 cm, or €15 for a day pass offering unlimited rides, €4.21 to children under 1 m 10 cm. Price includes admission to the museum.*

El Sagrat Cor

Once at the top, you can admire the views from the funfair or head to the roof of the enormous temple of El Sagrat Cor, which looms theatrically on the peak of the hill like something from a Disney film. A lift sweeps up to the roof, just below the feet of the enormous statue of the *Sacred Heart*, arms solemnly outspread, built to replace Frederic Marès's earlier version which was melted down for ammunition during the Civil War. The views are almost as good from the gallery in front of the church's main entrance, up the main flight of steps. The interior of the church – built as an expiatory temple to 'atone' for Barcelona's sins during the Civil War – is ugly and not worth visiting; the crypt (1911) alone is engaging, a florid *modernista* design by Enric Sagnier, but the rest, completed in 1961, is extremely dull.

Torre de Collserola

A free 'mini-train' plies between the funfair and the tower in summer; otherwise walk, or take the T2 or 211 bus outside the main funfair entrance

From the mountain peak, or pretty much anywhere for that matter, you can't miss the needle-like Torre de Collserola which spikes the horizon. This is the 288 m communications tower designed by **Norman Foster** and built for the 1992 Olympics, which has a glass lift to whoosh you up to the *mirador*, with panoramic views stretching for about 70 km in all directions, and even as far as Mallorca on a good day. ■ *Sep-May Wed-Fri 1100-1430 and 1530-1900, Sat-Sun 1100-1900; June -Aug Wed-Fri 1100-1430 and 1530-2000, Sat-Sun 1100-2000. €3, www.torredecollserola.com*

L'Observatori Fabra

Guided visits are often available; call in advance, T93 417 57 36

The road which passes the Torre de Collserola winds back down to the Plaça Dr Andreu, passing the lovely *modernista* Fabra Observatory, which was built in 1904 by **Josep Domènech i Estapa** at the request of the textile manufacturer Camil Fabra, Marquis of Alella. It's worth noting that the Parc de Collserola information office offers *Nits d'Astronomia* (night-time guided tours) of the stars which you can see from the park.

Museu de la Ciència

Below the observatory, is the big touchy-feely Science museum set in an old *modernista* asylum. The attractions and multi-media exhibits were extremely advanced 20 years ago when the museum was developed, but they've started to look a bit clunky and are currently being substantially overhauled. Most of the descriptions are in Catalan or Castilian, but there are enough doodahs and gadgets to keep most kids happily occupied for hours; there's a special section for children under seven, the *Clik dels nens* (Children's Click); a Planetarium; and a wonderful exhibit called *Toca, toca*! (Touch touch!) which shows kids how to pick up all kinds of peculiar Mediterranean creatures, from sea anemones to starfish. ■ *Tue-Sun and public holidays on a Mon 1000-2000. €3, plus €1.50 for the extra attractions, discounts for kids.*

The asylum inmates were not the first to appreciate the health benefits of the leafy slopes of Collserola; bigwigs had been building their summer houses up here since at least the 1400s when King Martí the Humane had his summer residence built at Bellesguard. In 1900, Gaudí was commissioned to build a private house on the site of the old royal ruins. The result was the Torre Bellesguard, at Carrer Bellesguard No 46, just beyond the Museu de la Ciència, a pointy, elaborate neo-Gothic castle with an immense look-out turret topped with a four-armed cross. Gaudí's design simultaneously recalls the fortified mansions of the Middle Ages, and looks forward to the brand new century.

Torre
Bellesguard
*It's a private house,
but peep at its maze of
vaulted garden walls
from C/Valeta
d'Arquer*

Horta and Vall d'Hebron

Horta was another rural neighbourhood scattered along the slopes and valleys of Collserola, which held out against annexation by Barcelona until 1904. Most of the aristocratic mansions and old farms which had grown up here were largely demolished to make way for apartment buildings during the boom years of the 1960s but it's still possible to glimpse placid squares, sturdy old *masies* (farmhouses) which have stood for hundreds of years, and earthy stone washtubs from the early years of urbanisation.

Horta

Vall d'Hebron lies above the old hub of Horta, named after the monastery which was razed to the ground after the Church was stripped of its property in 1835. Despite the resonant biblical name, this is a bleak corner, largely because of the massive ring road, the **Ronda de Dalt**, which blasts through the neighbourhood. It wasn't always this way; a couple of centuries ago, aristocrats built their mansions on these breezy slopes, far from the filthy city but most of these grand houses are now long gone. More recently, the neighbourhood was the focus of major redevelopment for the 1992 Olympics, when it became the main venue for cycling, archery and tennis.

Across the Ronda de Dalt is the **Vèlodrom d'Horta**, the elegant, award-winning stadium which was originally built for the 1984 World Cycling Championships. The stadium is surrounded by forlorn, sadly neglected gardens, presided over by one of Joan Brossa's visual poems, a tall A-shaped sculpture, which he hoped would signify, tongue firmly in cheek, 'birth, the road of life – with pauses and intonations – and death'.

Just beyond the Vèlodrom is one of the city's most appealing and magical gardens. The Jardins de Laberint d'Horta were begun by the sixth Marquis of Llupià in 1791, who commissioned Domenico Bagutti to draw up plans for an elegant, Italian-style garden for his huge country estate. Lakes, fountains, arbours and formal gardens were created, linked by formal staircases and sprinkled with classical sculptures. At its heart is the delicious **Laberint**, a maze of box wood and yew with a statue of Eros at its centre, which is more difficult to negotiate than you might suppose. The mansion has long gone, but the cypress-shaded walks, oak woods and rose gardens are utterly spell-binding, the perfect respite from the crowds and noise of the city centre. Many of the largest and grandest mansions and gardens were destroyed to make way for the ugly but necessary urban artery of the Ronda de Dalt. Behind the Jardins de Laberint d'Horta, the **Parc les Heures** with its frilly, fussy 19th-century mansion, also survived, and is now part of the University of Barcelona. ■ *Daily Nov-Feb 1000-1800, Mar and Oct 1000-1900, Apr and Sep 1000-2000, May-Aug 1000-2100; €1.70, free on Wed and Sun.*

Jardins de
Laberint
d'Horta

Glòries

To the west of Plaça de les Glòries Catalanes is a massive shopping centre and entertainment complex (see page 168)

The name given to the huge roundabout in the eastern Eixample, marking the intersection of Diagonal with Gran Via, has an ironic ring; the scrubby, dusty Plaça de les Glòries Catalanes could hardly be more dispiriting or less glorious. The city, with its love of a good slogan, is calling the neighbourhood the 'New Eixample' and has commissioned a complex of theatres and auditoriums to drag the shabby old neighbourhood out of its former squalor; the imposing **Teatre Nacional de Catalunya** (see page 233), is a glassy take on the Parthenon designed by Ricardo Bofill and inaugurated in 1997. Opposite stands Rafael Moneo's cool, austere **Auditori de Barcelona**, which opened its doors in 1999. The unprepossessing exterior is made up for by the perfect acoustics of the huge, central 2,300-seat auditorium. Parks and gardens meander between them, but fail to lift the leaden atmosphere.

It's no surprise that the only museum in the neighbourhood is housed in the local morgue and is devoted to funeral carriages; The **Museu de Carosses Funebres** contains an historic collection of funeral carriages and hearses which were in use right up to the mid-20th century. This subterranean museum is rarely visited and it's worth calling or emailing in advance *Mon-Fri 1000-1300 and 1600-1800. Free. Call in advance, T93 484 17 20, www.funerariabarcelona.com*

The flea market is worth a rummage if you get there early enough, but watch out for pickpockets

Glories biggest attraction is a huge, cheerfully tacky **Els Encants Vells**; Barcelona's biggest flea market, sprawling, chaotic and stuffed with all kinds of the usual synthetic tat. It's also the place to find everything from wind-up gramophones to mannequins from the 1970s. There's a whole stall devoted to Franco-era pornography, when all the naughty bits were blacked out. There are few bargains nowadays, and the interesting old stuff is getting outweighed by the kind of stalls you find in every market across the world. ■ *Market held Mon, Wed, Fri, and Sat 0900-2000.*

Eating and drinking

Expensive
There are many award-winning restaurants to choose from, which appeal to the areas' discerning and fashionable clientele

El Asador de Aranda, Avda Tibidabo 31, T93 417 01 15. Open open Mon-Sat 1300-1600 and 2100-2300. FGC Avda Tibidabo. Set in a wonderful Moorish-*modernista* mansion, this is a Castillian restaurant and grill house for confirmed carnivores. The house speciality is roasted lamb served out on the terrace, but there are plenty of other succulent roasted meats and fish on offer. *Gaig*, Passeig Maragall 402, T93 429 10 17. Open 1330-1600 and 2100-2300, closed Sun eve and Mon, metro Horta. The Gaig family opened this classic Barcelonan restaurant for cart-drivers in 1869; it's been in the family for four generations and offers traditional Catalan dishes such as *arròs de colomí amb ceps* (pigeon in rice with wild mushrooms) or rack of lamb with juniper. There's an extraordinary wine cellar and you should leave room for the heavenly chocolate desserts.

La Balsa, C/Infata Isabell 4, T93 211 50 48. Open Mon 2100-2330, Tue-Sat 1400-1530 and 2100-2330, FGC Avda del Tibidabo. Set in an award-winning building surrounded by beautiful gardens, offers Catalan and Mediterranean cuisine such as prawn and salt cod croquettes. *Neichel*, C/Beltrán I Rózpide 16 bis, metro Maria Christina, www.relaischateaux.fr/neichel, T93 203 84 08. Open Tue-Fri 1330-1530 and 2030-2330, Sat 2030-2330. An exquisite, award-winning modern French-Mediterranean restaurant, owned by Alsacien chef Jean Luis Neichel, is set in a modern block in Pedralbes. The award-winning menu includes prawns with a delicate truffle vinaigrette, or loin of lamb in an anchovy and herb crust, and there is a menu devoted entirely to dishes made with black truffles.

Tram Tram, C/Major de Sarrià 121, FCG Sarrià T93 204 85 18. Open daily for lunch and dinner; sun dinner only. Prices above €30. Set in an old Catalan *mas* (farmhouse), just up from the old town of Sarrià, this is one of the city's finest and most imaginative restaurants. The *menú de degustación* is worth going for – it changes regularly, depending on what's in season, but is always a contemporary take on traditional Catalan cuisine.

Via Veneto, C/Ganduxer 10, T93 200 70 24. Open Mon-Fri 1315-1615 and 2045-2330, Sat 2045-2330, metro Maria Christina/FGC La Bonanova. An opulent, Belle Epoque-style restaurant serving creative modern Catalan cuisine to a smart, fashionable clientele; try the duck with spinach and caramelized onions, and finish up with the outstanding chocolate soufflé. The wine list is exceptional and the service excellent, making this the perfect place to splash out.

A Contraluz, C/Milanesado 19, T93 203 06 58. Open 1330-1600 and 2030-2430, Thu, Fri and Sat until 0100, FGC Les Tres Torres. Owned by the same people as trendy Tragaluz (see page 136), this is a delightful and very fashionable restaurant with a pretty candlelit garden terrace. Fresh, simply prepared Mediterranean dishes and fabulous desserts. *Can Cortada*, Avda l'Estatut de Catalunya, T93 427 23 15. Open daily 1300-1530 and 2000-2330, closed Sun eve metro Horta. A lovely 11th-century *mas* (Catalan farmhouse) with a pretty terrace in summer, this is set on the hillside and features classic Catalan home cooking. Try the duck with pears and finish up with *crema catalana*.

El Vell Sarrià, C/Major de Sarrià 93, T93 205 45 41. Open Mon-Fri 1330-1530 and 2030-2330, Sat 1330-1530, closed Sun. FGC Sarrià. This is a very cosy, old-fashioned little spot on a pretty street, with dark wooden beams, fussy lace tablecloths and curtains and a fleet of ponderous waiters with long aprons. The food is hearty Catalan with lots of excellent rice-based specialities and there's an attractive, leafy terrace in summer. *Satoru Miyano*, C/Ganduxer 18, T93 414 31 04. Open Mon 1330-1530, Tue-Sat 1330-1530 and 2100-2330, FGC La Bonanova. A sleek Franco-Japanese restaurant serving excellent sushi and a range of Pacific rim or Mediterranean dishes. It's a coolly elegant spot, with clean minimalist décor. The French desserts are exquisite.

Vivanda, C/Major de Sarrià 121, T93 203 19 18. Closed Sun, FGC Sarrià. Vivanda is a fine old restaurant specialising in sophisticated, elaborate Catalan dishes; it's a very romantic spot with a beautiful leafy terrace garden. *La Vaquería*, C/del Deu I Mata 126, T93 439 35 56. Open Mon-Sat 1300-0100, metro Les Corts. An attractive and unusual establishment set in a refurbished cow shed, this has a piano bar, disco and a straightforward restaurant. It caters to a slightly older crowd who enjoy the 60s and 70s music, and offers very imaginative Catalan-Mediterranean cuisine at surprisingly good prices.

La Venta, Plaça Dr Andreu, FGC Avda Tibidabo, T93 212 64 55, www.restaurantlaventa.com Open daily 1330-1515, 2100-2315, Smart, bustling restaurant with pretty flower-filled terrace at the terminus for the *Tramvia Blau*. Fine dining – classic Catalan cuisine – for about €30. *Vinya Rosa-Magi*, C/Avda de Sarrià 17, T93 430 00 03. Open open Mon-Fri 1330-1600 and 2030-2330, Sat 1330-1600, closed Sun. An utterly charming restaurant in the heights of Sarrià, serving delicate and original versions of Catalan favourites; try the chickpeas in squid ink or the oven baked fish with wild mushrooms.

Pipper's, C/Buenos Aires 42, T93 430 51 54. Open 0900-0130, metro Hospital Clinic. A kitsch old-fashioned bar stuck in the 1970s: it's popular with students and offers good budget meals – Catalan dishes and pizzas – as well as substantial tapas and raciones in a lively atmosphere. *Cuatro*, C/Masferrer 4, T93 330 68 60. Open 1300-1600 and 2100-2300, closed Sun and Wed evenings. A simple, friendly and unpretentious

Mid-range
● *on maps, pages 157 and 163*

Cheap

Five of the best: drinks with a view

- *Tapas Bar Maremàgnum* (see page 198)
- *Atlàntic Bar* (see page 247)
- *Bar Miramar* (see page 247)
- *Mirablau* (see page 247)
- *Partycular* (see page 247)

restaurant serving up delicious great value pizzas, pasta dishes and salads. *Bene Asai*, C/Doctor Carulla 61, T93 434 06 77. Open 1300-1600 and 2100-2300, metro Les Tres Torres. Busy, bustling tiny little Italian trattoria, very popular with a young crowd. There are excellent pizzas and pasta on offer as well as an attractive terrace in summer.

Café-bars with food/ tapas *Casa Fernández*, C/Santaló 46, T93 201 93 08. Open daily 1200-0230, FGC Muntaner. This elegant designer bar and restaurant serves a good range of excellent tapas, and has a wide selection of imported beers. It's most famous for its fried eggs and chips – which may not sound very designer friendly but are served in a dozen different ways. *Mas i Mas*, C/Marià Cubi 199, T93 209 45 02. Open daily 1930-0230, until 0300 on Sun, metro Muntaner. The Mas family have put their stamp across much of the Barcelona scene – they own *La Boîte, Jamboree and Moog* (see page 240) – but this was where they started out. It's a friendly tapas bar, offering reasonably priced snacks in an upmarket, sophisticated atmosphere. There's another branch at C/Còrsega 300, in the Eixample.

Shopping

Fashion *Purificación García*, Avda de Pau Casals 4, metro Hospital Clinic. This slick Spanish fashion chain has cool urban fashions in high-quality fabrics. *Carlos Torrents*, C/Pau Casals 6, metro Hospital Clínic Very swish menswear by upmarket Spanish designers in fashionably minimalist surroundings.

Food & drink *El Celler de Gelida*, C/Vallespir 65, www.mestres-celler.com, metro Sants Estació. There are more than 3,500 labels on offer in this well-respected *celler* near Sants station. *Tutusaus*, C/Frances Pérez Cabrera 5, metro Hospital Clínic, or bus to Plaça Francesc Macia. The best cheese shop in the city with more than 40 varieties of Spanish cheeses alone. *Zemon*, C/de Ganduxer 31, FGC Bonanova. A very upmarket grocers catering to the well-heeled locals, with everything from caviar to a great selection of regional wines.

Leather goods & jewellery *Furla*, Plaça Francesc Macià 5, metro Les Corts, FGC Gràcia. Flagship store offering very stylish bags and shoes in unusual colours and designs. *Nuria Ruiz*, C/Pau Casals 24, FGC Gràcia. Very elegant, minimalist pieces in gold and silver from this Barcelonan designer, beautifully displayed in her workshop near the Turó Park.

Malls & department stores *L'Illa*, Avda Diagonal 545-557, www.illa.es, metro María Cristina. The largest mall in the city, l'Illa looks like an enormous white ship. It's up in the business district along Diagonal, and attracts a wealthy clientele. All the fashion chains are there along with a *FNAC, Decathlon* sports shop, and several trendy fashion boutiques. *Glòries* shopping centre, Avda Diagonal 458, metro Glòries. Soulless and dispiriting, this massive shopping centre still has all the major chains along with a seven-screen cinema. *El Corté Inglés*, Avda Diagonal 617, metro Maria Cristina. Another branch of the well-known Spanish department store with a supermarket and gourmet delicatessan in the basement.

Markets *Els Encants*, Plaça de les Glòries Catalanas, metro Glòries. A vast sprawling flea market with everything from new clothes and shoes at bargain prices, to antique gramophones and paintings.

Transport

Bus No **30** from Sarrià to Plaça Espanya, via Sants. No **32** from Roquetes to Sants station, via Gràcia. No **43** from Les Corts to Barri-Besòs, via Sants. No **78** from Sant Joan Despí to Sants, via Monestir Pedralbes and the Left Eixample. No **109** from Sants to Zona Franca, via Plaça Espanya.

Metro Line 1 (red) Sants Estació, Plaça de Sants, Mercat Nou, Hostafrancs; Line 5 (blue) Sants Estació, Plaça de Sants.

Taxi There is a taxi rank outside the train station.

Train This is the main RENFE train station in Barcelona, with national and international trains as well as regional trains to most areas of Catalunya.

Sants

Bus There are plenty of bus stops on the Plaça Francesc Macià and the Plaça Maria Cristina. Nos **7**, from Zona Universitària to Diagonal Mar, via La Pedrera. No **15** from Collblanc via Camp Nou and Diagonal. No **33** from Zona Universitària via Diagonal and Sagrada Família. No **75** from Les Corts to Avda Tibidabo, via Camp Nou, Monestir Pedralbes and Sarrià.

Metro Line 3 (green) Maria Cristina, Les Corts.

Taxi Both Plaça Francesc Macià and the Plaça Maria Cristina have taxi ranks.

Les Corts & Western Diagonal

Bus No **63** from Sant Just to Placa Universitat, via Monestir Pedralbes, Plaça Francesc Macià and Diagonal. No **74** from Zona Universitària to Sarrià, via Palau Pedralbes and Gràcia. No **75** from Les Corts to Avda Tibidabo, via FC Barcelona, Monestir Pedralbes, Sarrià. And No **78** from Sant Joan Despí to Estació de Sants, via Monestir Pedralbes and the Left Eixample.

Metro Line 3 (green) Maria Cristina.

Taxi This is a largely residential suburb: your best chance of getting a taxi is to hail one on the Diagonal.

Train FGV train station at Reina Elisanda. It's a 5-10 minute walk from here to the Monastery of Pedralbes.

Pedralbes

Bus No **30** from Sarrià to Plaça Espanya, via Estació Sants. No **70** from Bonanova to Sants, via Plaça Maria Cristina. No **74** from Zona Universitària to Sarrià, via Palau Pedralbes and Gràcia.

Metro Line 3 (green) Maria Cristina. It's quite a walk into Sarrià from here.

Taxi This is a quiet neighbourhood, but you can usually find taxis on Plaça Sarrià.

Train FGV train stations at Sarrià, Tres Torres, La Bonanova.

Sarrià

Bus Take bus nos **30** and **66** to get the funicular which takes you up to Vallvidrera. Bus no **211** runs between Tibidabo and Vallvidrera.

Funicular The funicular (run by the FGC, www.fgc.catlunya.net) runs from Peu del Funicular to the top of Vallvidrera via Carretera de les Aigües. FGC run connecting trains from Peu del Funicular station to Plaça de Catalunya (lines S1 and S2).

Taxi You can usually find taxis in the main square.

Vallvidrera

Funicular FGC train from Plaça de Catalunya to to Baixador de Vallvidrera on the Barcelona-Terrassa/Sabadell line (lines S1 and S2).

Parc de Collserola

Bus No **17** from Pg Joan de Borbó to Avda Jordà, via Via Laietana, Pg de Gràcia, Gràcia and Avda Tibidabo. No **58** from Avda Tibidabo to Plaça de Catalunya, via Gràcia and Plaça Universitat. No **75** from from Les Corts to Avda Tibidabo, via FC Barcelona, Monestir Pedralbes, Sarrià.

Tibidabo

Gracia, Tibidabo & outer districts

Funicular Runs from the Plaça Andreu to the top of the hill at Plaça Tibidabo. A single ticket costs €1.80 and a return is €2.40. It runs end-Sept to early June: Sat, Sun and public holidays 1030-1930; in May also Thu and Fri 1000-1800; Jun-Aug Mon-Fri 1030-2230, Sat and Sun 1030-1330.

Metro Line 3 (green) Vallcarca is the closest.

Taxi There is a taxi rank outside the FGV station Avda Tibidabo.

Train FGV station Avda Tibidabo. The stop for the Tramvia Blau (which in turn connects with the funicular up Montjüic) is just next to the Rotonda building and visible from the station exit.

Tram Tramvia Blau: The 'Blue Tram' runs from Plaça Kennedy, just by the FGC train stop, Avinguda del Tibidabo, up to the Plaça Andreu. It costs €1.65 one way and €2.40 for a return ticket. It runs about every 15-30 minutes between 0900-2130, weekends only in winter (mid-Sept to mid-May) and daily in summer.

Horta & Vall d'Hebron **Bus No 27**, from Roquetes to Plaça Espanya, via Pg Vall d'Hebron, Gràcia, the Eixample and Gran Via. No **60** from Zona Universitària to Plaça de les Glòries, Pg Vall d'Hebron. For **Jardins de Laberint d'Horta**, take bus nos **27**, **60** and **73** down Pg de Hebron and get off at the Vèlodrome.

Metro Line 3 (green) vall d'Hebron, Montbau; Line 5 (blue) Horta.

Taxi There are usually some taxis near the Plaça Evissa.

Glòries **Bus** No **7**, from Zona Universitària to Diagonal Mar, via Diagonal, La Pedrera, Pg de Gràcia, Plaça de les Glòries and Poble Nou. No **56**, from Collblanc to Besòs-Verneda, via Plaça de Sants, Plaça Universitat and Plaça de les Glòriès.

Metro Line 1 (red) Glòries, Marina.

Taxi It's usually possible to hail a taxi from near the roundabout; if not, get one from outside the Glòries shopping centre.

Montjuïc

Montjüic

174 Montjüic

174 History

174 Sights

178 Palau Nacional

184 Poble Espanyol

184 Anella Olímpica

186 Fundacío Miró

188 Castell Montjüic

189 Around Passeig Santa Madrona

190 Poble Sec

191 Eating and drinking

192 Transport

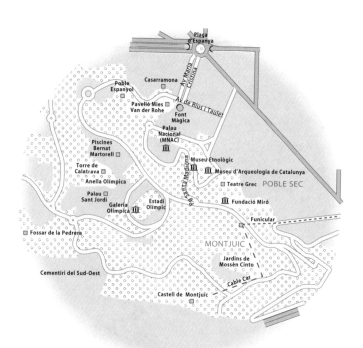

*The ancient promontory of Montjüic rises up to the west of the city, overlooking the sea. The Laietanos worshipped here long before the Romans arrived and Hercules is said to have kicked his heels up along its slopes. There are all kinds of stories about the unusual name: perhaps the Romans named it for Jove (Mons Jovis) or else for the Jews (Mont Jeu) after a Jewish cemetery found near the fortress at the top. Whatever the legends, it has been Barcelona's favourite playground since her inhabitants were cramped behind the old ring of the city walls. The **International Exhibition of 1929** changed the face of the hill dramatically, throwing up palaces and monuments and landscaping gardens, beginning the spate of building works which culminated with the **Anella Olímpica** (Olympic Ring), a string of dazzling sports complexes built for the 1992 Olympics. The next phase of improvements, including a lake and more parklands on the hill's scrubby southern side, is set to be completed in 2004, when Barcelona will host its next big event, the **Universal Forum of Cultures** (see page 210). On its eastern slopes is the attractive, relaxed working class neighbourhood of **Poble Sec**, a straggle of narrow streets wriggling away from the brash strip of Paral.lel and the old cabaret and theatre district.*

Montjüic

*Most of Montjüic's biggest monuments were built for the 1929 International Exhibition, and some of the biggest crowd-pullers back then are still the biggest draws today – like the fabulously kitsch **Font Màgica**, a dancing fountain show, and the **Poble Espanyol**, a cheerfully gaudy recreation of an idealized Spanish village. The vast, monolithic **Palau Nacional** is now the setting for the most remarkable and beautiful collection of Romanesque art in Europe – an unsettling yet mesmerising series of murals collected from churches scattered throughout the Pyrenean valleys. The 1929 International Exhibition also provided some of the sports facilities for the 1992 Olympics, including the **Estadi Olímpic** (Olympic stadium) and the wonderful outdoor swimming pools, the **Piscines Bernat Martorell**. One of the loveliest museums in Barcelona is the luminous **Fundació Miró**, which holds concerts and temporary exhibitions as well as a spectacular collection of Miró's works. From the mountain, you can swing over to Barceloneta in a cable car, or take a slightly less scary ride to the very top of the mountain for wonderful views out across the harbour.*

History

International Exhibition of 1929

At the end of the 19th century – as at the end of the 20th century – Barcelona was gripped by a fervour for all things new, and intent on showing the world what Catalans could do. The Universal Exhibition of 1888 demanded a sequel, and plans were made to enact it on the slopes of the city's favourite mountain. Financial problems, politics and social turmoil put the plans on ice for several years, but an exhibition was finally planned for 1917. It was intended to showcase the young, feisty electricity industry (which was lobbying hard), as well as offer an overview of Catalan and Spanish arts and crafts.

The celebrated landscapist Jean Forestier was commissioned to transform the scrubby slopes of Montjüic into elegant parklands, and Puig i Cadafalch was put in charge of overseeing the project. As the political situation grew increasingly fraught, the exhibition was continually postponed. When Miguel Primo de Rivera came to power in 1923, he began stamping out regionalism wherever he could find it and that included Barcelona: Puig i Cadafalch was ousted, but the idea for the exhibition suited Rivera's ambitions.

When the International Exhibition finally took place in 1929, it was on a scale unimagined by the original progenitors of the idea, with four sections devoted to industry in general, agriculture, the arts and sport. The architecture was puffed up and wildly overblown. Most of it remained after the exhibition was dismantled and the palaces and pavilions converted into museums and trade exhibition venues. Some of its structures formed the basis for the mountain-top Anella Olímpica .

Sights

Plaça d'Espanya & around

Plaça d'Espanya is the main transport hub for Montjüic

The starting point for the 1929 International Exhibition was the circular **Plaça d'Espanya**, surrounded now by whizzing traffic. In the centre is a huge fountain, built for the exhibition by Gaudí's collaborator, Josep Maria Jujol. The fountain brims with symbols of Spain's rivers and is topped by carved stone said at the time to represent 'Spain's constant sacrifice for civilization'.

Things to do in Montjüic

· Party till dawn at La Terrrazza behind the Poble Espanyol (see page 184)
· Watch a film in the Bernat Martorell outdoor swimming pool (see page 185)
· Catch some contemporary music or dance at the Fundació Miró (see page 186)
· Try the best orxata in the city at the Orxateria Sirvent (see page192)

Just off the Plaça is the red-brick neo-Arabic **Arenes** bull ring, long retired from hosting *corridas* and now rather dismal and scruffy. The Beatles sang here in 1966; a key event in the gradual liberalization of Spain during the last years of Franco's repressive regime. Just visible behind it, on Carrer Llançà, is the **Casa de la Papallona** (1912), a simple *modernista* apartment block whimsically crowned with a huge ceramic butterfly.

The main esplanade of the exhibition was Avinguda Maria Cristina.The entrance is flanked by two enormous towers, supposed to look like Venetian campaniles but more reminiscent of prison watchtowers. Two pompous porticoed palaces, both built for the exhibition, run along the avenue: on the left is the **Palau del Treball** and on the right is the **Palau de Comnuicacions i Transports**, both now used for trade fairs. Halfway along is Josep Llimona's statue of the *Foundry Worker,* given to the city to mark the Dia del Treball (Labour Day, 1 May) in 1930. **Avinguda Maria Cristina**

At the end of the avenue is the **Font Màgica** (Magic Fountain), one of the stars of the exhibition and an example of monumentalism at its most absurd. It's best appreciated during the fabulously kitsch sound and light shows in which jets of fruity-coloured water leap and dance to the sounds of Tchaikovsky and Abba. ■ *Shows 23 Jun-23 Sep; fountain 2000-2400; musical events Thu-Sun and holidays 2130-2330.*

At the start of Avenida Marqués de Comillas is the Pavelló Mies Van der Rohe; a cool, glassy reconstruction of Ludwig Mies Van der Rohe's monument to rationalist architecture that was built for use as the German pavilion during the International Exhibition. Amid the thick sprawl of the exhibition's ostentatious monumentalism the small German pavilion stood out for the purity and clarity of its lines, and its prescient, deliberate fuzzing of the interior and exterior spaces. Van der Rohe chose the site and the expensive materials – onyx, marble, chrome and glass, all reflected sharply in twin pools – and designed everything including the furniture; his classic *Barcelona Chair* is the prize exhibit inside. ■ *Daily Nov-Mar 1000-1830 and Apr-Oct 1000-2000. €3, www.miesbcn.com For information on exhibitions and events call T93 423 40 16* **Pavelló Mies van der Rohe** *The pavilion is now home to the Fundació Mies van der Rohe, which hosts conferences, poetry readings and art exhibitions*

Just across from the Pavelló Mies van der Rohe is the Casaramona: a red-brick *modernista* fancy topped with a pointed witch's hat. A former textile mill designed by Puig i Cadafalch in 1913, the mill has been expensively converted into yet another exhibition space for the ubiquitous Fundació la Caixa – the savings bank with acultural foundation renowned throughout Spain. ■ *For information on forthcoming exhibitions, call T90 222 30 40.* **Casaramona**

Montjüic

Montjüic & Poble Sec

Montjüic

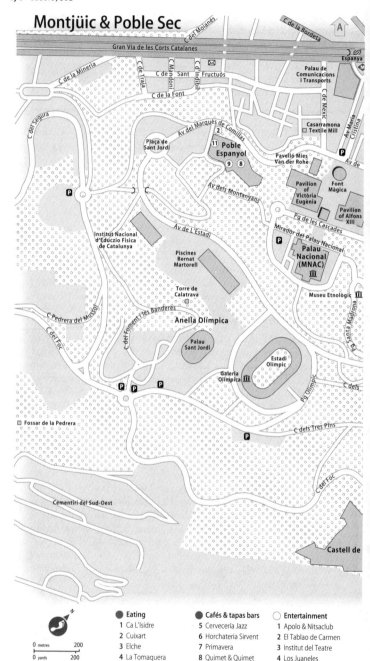

Gran Via de les Corts Catalanes

C de la Mineria
C de Traia
C de Mandoni
C de Sant Indíbil
C de Sant Fructuós
C de la Font

C del Moianès
C de la Bordeta

Espanya

Palau de Comunicacions i Transports

Casarramona Textile Mill

C de Mexic
C de María Cristina

Av del Marqués de Comillas

Plaça de Sant Jordi

Poble Espanyol

Pavelló Mies Van der Rohe

Av de

Av dels Montanyans

Pavilion of Victòria Eugènia

Font Màgica

Pavilion of Alfons XIII

Pg de les Cascades

Av de L'Estadi

Institut Nacional d'Educzio Física de Catalunya

Piscines Bernat Martorell

Mirador del Palau Nacional

Palau Nacional (MNAC)

Torre de Calatrava

Museu Etnològic

C Pedrera del Mussol

C del Foment i les Banderes

Anella Olímpica

C del Foc

Palau Sant Jordi

Galeria Olímpica

Estadi Olímpic

Pg Olímpic

C dels

Fossar de la Pedrera

C dels Tres Pins

C del Foc

Cementiri del Sud-Oest

Castell de

A

N

0 metres 200
0 yards 200

Eating	Cafés & tapas bars	Entertainment
1 Ca L'Isidre	5 Cerveceria Jazz	1 Apolo & Nitsaclub
2 Cuixart	6 Horchateria Sirvent	2 El Tablao de Carmen
3 Elche	7 Primavera	3 Institut del Teatre
4 La Tomaquera	8 Quimet & Quimet	4 Los Juaneles

Montjuïc

5 Mercat de las Flors
6 Tinta Roja

○ Clubs & bars
7 Barcelona Rouge

8 Discothèque
9 La Terrrazza
10 Miramar
11 Torres de Avila

Related maps
A Western
districts, page 156
B El Raval, page 108

★ Five of the best: sights in Montjüic

- *Font Màgica* (see page 175)
- *MNAC* (see page 178)
- *Torre Calatrava* (see page 185)
- *Fundació Joan Miró* (see page 186)
- *Funicular to Poble Sec* (see page 192)

Palau Nacional

The dour, monolithic Palau Nacional, looming from the Montjüic hilltop, looks exactly like the kind of palace a dictator would commission – an impression only intensified by the rays of light, like searchlights, which radiate out from it at night, just as they did back in 1929. On either side of the thoughtfully constructed elevators leading up to the Palau Nacional are the **Alfons XIII and Victòria Eugènia** pavilions (1923-28). Built according to Puig i Cadafalch's designs they are delightful, creamy concoctions with swirling ornamentation and frilly little towers.

The Palau Nacional is now home to the Romanesque and Gothic collection of the **Museu Nacional d'Art de Catalunya** (MNAC). In 2003, the holdings of the Museu d'Art Modern, currently in the Parc de la Ciutadella (see page 96) are set to join the rest of MNAC's collection in newly refurbished galleries, allowing visitors to see the best of Catalan art in one setting. There are two very detailed and very expensive guidebooks in English, one for the Romanesque section and one for the Gothic section.

Romanesque section

If you don't have time to visit each of the 21 rooms, head for rooms 5, 7 and 21

The undisputed star of the show is the unique collection of Romanesque art, one of the finest in the world, which includes 26 mesmerizing **mural groups** brought from the tiny churches of the Catalan hinterlands. The murals are displayed on reconstructed church interiors, and are lit in order to intensify the shadows. The collection is laid out in loose chronological and stylistic order, with good English explanations and plans and models explaining exactly where the murals would have been placed in their original contexts.

There's a cafetería just off the Sala Oval – you'll need to take a break from all those staring eyes

Room 1: A small introductory room, containing coins and tombstones with Latin, Hebrew and Arabic inscriptions, serves to outline the three main influences of the period, and a magnificent, richly coloured mural of the *Maiestas Domini* (Christ in his Glory) from the Església de Sant Pere in Seu d'Urgell; this theme is commonly depicted on the vaulting of apses in churches of the period. Here, a splendidly calm Christ is surrounded by the four Apostles and the symbols of the four Evangelists: the angel for Matthew, the lion for Mark, the ox for Luke and the eagle for John.

Room 2: The paintings of the Església de Sant Joan de Boí date back to around 1100, and are shown in a space which recreates their original setting. They are among the earliest extant mural groups and enough remains to get an astonishing glimpse of how they must have overawed the first congregations; the fiery demons of hell torment a terrified, lost soul on one wall, St Stephen is being viciously stoned to death close by, and the Seven-headed Beast of the Apocalypse leers monstrously at the end of the south aisle.

The increasing influence of Italian painting from Lombardy – where Romanesque architecture originated – is in evidence

Room 3: The paintings of Italy's Pedret Circle are shown here together. They are of an extraordinarily high quality and have a very complex iconography; one of the finest pieces in the museum's collection is the panel depicting the parable of the wise and foolish virgins from the Església de Sant Quirze in Pedret, in which the wise virgins, with their glowing black eyes, are rewarded by a seat at the heavenly banquet with Christ the bridegroom. The foolish virgins trip around in extravagant finery – earning the contempt of thrifty Catalans. The apse from Santa Maria d'Àneu shows resplendent, terrifying seraphim, with the three requisite sets of wings, two of which are fantastically

Romanesque art

As Romanticism, with its idealization of the medieval period, swept Europe, the Catalans were rediscovering their cultural identity. Architects like Puig i Cadafalch looked for inspiration to the glorious days of the Catalan Empire during the Middle Ages, and excursionistas were heading off to the Pyrenean valleys and mountains, discovering a lost heritage of Romanesque churches.

Many of them were built after the Moors had swept through, small but emphatic monuments to the 'true' religion, blazoned with huge murals depicting biblical events – Eyes stare out dramatically from every wall; the eyes of Christ in Majesty, the Virgin's serene gaze, the hundreds of eyes clustered thickly on the wings of the seraphim, the seven eyes which stare out of depictions of the Lamb of God. The message is clear: there could be no escaping the all-seeing eyes of heaven.

During the 11th and 12th centuries Catalans were rich. Gold was the currency of most transactions and their wealth is apparent; today pigments like lapus lazuli – the most expensive of all – add a lustrous glow to the murals, and the artists themselves were some of the most sophisticated that Catalan gold could buy.

As the art of the medieval period became increasingly sought after, other Europeans and wealthy Americans began to strip the Romanesque churches on the French side of the border. Finally, the Board of Museums in Barcelona panicked when they discovered that the paintings from the church of Santa Maria in Mur had ended up in the Museum of Fine Arts in Boston.

Adamant that the unique artworks of the Catalan churches would not leave the region, the board decided in the early 20th century to remove the murals from their often decrepit homes, and in 1934, they were given a permanent home in the Palau Nacional.

studded with eyes, busy purifying the words of the prophets Elijah and Isiah with burning coals.

Room 4: This room is devoted to the iconography of Jesus and Mary in a description of Romanesque churches, with several versions of common themes. The apse from Marmellar which seems to depict the Ascension of Christ, is remarkably unsophisticated, with clumsy, skeletal figures that you might have sniggered at if they weren't so grotesque. There are several portrayals of the favourite theme, Christ in Majesty, including one from the apse of Santa Maria de Ginesterre, surrounded by some particularly grim-faced Apostles. In contrast, the blazing baldachin panel (an ornamental canopy placed above the altar) from Sant Martí in Tost (12th century) has been executed with luminous clarity and seems strikingly modern. The delicate *Virgin* (circa second half of the12th century) from Geris one of the most beautiful sculptures in the collection.

Room 5: The paintings from the Església de Sant Climent in Taüll are among the most important examples of Romanesque art in Europe; The most striking figure in the whole collection is the masterly figure of Christ in Majesty which looms dramatically in the apse, staring down with huge, hypnotic eyes that could surely see into the heart of any sinner. The disembodied Hand of God points out of an ethereal white circle, fingers stretched in blessing, and the Lamb of God, sporting seven eyes, gambols on the opposite arch. This room also contains several interesting pieces of liturgical furniture, including a delicate spherical reliquary: a small urn containing relics which was hidden inside the altar.

Room 6: Architectural sculpture in Catalunya reached heady new heights in the 12th and 13th centuries; this selection of carved capitals and stone blocks from *voussoirs* (archways) shows the development of the art, as early

Montjuïc

simple geometric patterns and stiff figures gave way to more naturalistic depictions of leering devils and fabulous beasts.

Room 7: The paintings from the Boi valley parish Església de Santa Maria in Taüll are the most complete set in the museum; a blazing, richly coloured series which reaches its apotheosis in the splendid depiction of Mary as the Seat of Wisdom in the apse. There are fragments of a gruesome, and entirely surreal Last Judgement on the west wall; the Archangel Michael solemnly weighs up souls in his big scales, and those that have been condemned to the flames writhe in choreographed agony, tormented by devils while David and the surreal giant Goliath fight it out on the other side of the column. Some original 'graffiti' – animals, labyrinths and mazes etched by bored monks – has been preserved on the columns.

The Boí valley was declared a World Heritage Site in 2000 for the richness of its Romanesque churches

Room 8: The next room is dedicated to religious imagery, with dozens of lovely polychrome virgins, and some dramatic crucifixes, including the mesmerizing *Batlló Majesty* sculpted around the middle of the 12th century, which has conserved its rich blue and red polychromy. It's one of the most important pieces in the collection and it represents Christ triumphing over death.

Room 9: Another beautiful mural group, this time from the Església de Sant Pere in Sorpe, shimmer with gilt and reflect emerging Byzantine influences. The highlight is the finely detailed scene of the Annunciation: the Virgin spins grimly as the Angel appears to her with news of her impending fate, neither of them looking too happy about it.

Room 10: The next small alcove displays the altar frontal from the Església de Sant Quirze e Santa Julito Durro, one of the most surreally gruesome depictions of saints and martyrs being boiled, speared, and even sawn in two with all the calm of a magician's assistant.

The workers in Estaon tried hard to copy the Pedret style

Room 11: The apse paintings from Estaon and Surp show the influence of the celebrated workshops of the Pedret Circle (seen in Room 3). In the church dedicated to Santa Eulàlia Estaon's failure to pull off the Pedret style is apparent. Santa Eulàlia stands next to the Virgin in the baptism scene, and there are some wonderful hunting scenes – a hunter with his dog, and a vicious-looking wild boar are among the characters.

Room 12: The paintings from the apse of Sant Miquel in Engolasters form part of the Santa Coloma Circle in Andorra. They have been executed with a charming ingenuousness; Christ in Majesty beams down on his smiling companions as though delighted to see everyone looking so happy.

Room 13: Byzantine influence became increasingly marked in Romanesque painting from about 1200; the best examples are the murals from Andorra la Vella and an altar frontal from Baltarga, which display Byzantine influence in the finely detailed features and modelling of the faces and the almost sculptural depiction of the bodies and drapery.

Room 14: The paintings from the atrium of the glorious Romanesque Església de Sant Vicenç in Cardona were executed well into the latter part of the 12th century; Christ floats above in the bubble of the mandala in his customary position. Beneath are the remains of a depiction of the Ascension and a gruesomely realistic flagellation scene. The painting of the Defence of Girona was added much later; it was commissioned by the canny Viscount of Cardona, who preferred to be remembered for this heroic gesture rather than his earlier uprising against the king.

Many of the pieces preserved here were made in Limoges, famous for its enamel workshops

Room 15: This room is devoted to metalwork and enamels. There's an exquisitely rendered Eucharistic Dove, which would have been suspended to show the presence of the Holy Spirit during the Eucharist, and a beautiful crozier (a bishop's staff) with a minute depiction of the Archangel Michael slaying the dragon on the handle.

Room 16: Little remains of the paintings from the apse of Sant Cristòfol in Toses, but the remnants show the transition between the Romanesque and Gothic styles. The iconography is still purely Romanesque – Christ in Majesty surrounded by the symbols of the Evangelists – but the painted crossbeams were a new feature.

Room 17: The Frontal of the Archangels is a deliciously anecdotal piece executed with remarkable delicacy. In one panel, a sly demon tries to trick the Archangel Michael while he weighs up souls in his scales, in another he slays the dragon. The Archangels Raphael and Gabriel carry a joyful soul up to heaven in what looks like a bedsheet, and a hunter who tries to kill the ox representing Michael in his sanctuary manages to shoot himself in the eye.

Here the move towards the Gothic is further demonstrated

Room 18: As new styles and methods were beginning to emerge, the last painters of the Romanesque era were still clinging to the old themes; the altar panels from Orós use the central figure of Christ in Majesty surrounded by the Evangelists and Apostles, but the bold black outlines are reminiscent of the leading used in stained-glass windows.

Room 19: The Rigagorca workshop active in the late 13th century, and painted elaborate altar panels using backgrounds of stucco reliefwork covered with silverleaf and painted to resemble gold. Much of the silverleaf has deteriorated, but the stories still glow vigorously; the Frontal from Chía depicts St Martin on his deathbed, covered with the gold and scarlet striped flag of Catalunya.

The Rigagorça masters were celebrated for their use of bright colours and anecdotal style

Room 20: The Monestir de San Pedro in the Castilian town of Arlanza was almost ruined when the monasteries were disentailed in 1836. The decorations now held by MNAC were probably used to ornament a secular hall, perhaps used as a royal residence. There's a magnificent griffon, with glaring eyes and lions' claws, and a whole host of fabulous, dancing creatures.

Room 21: The last section of the Romanesque collection is devoted to the paintings from the chapterhouse of Sigena (Aragón), they were sadly almost destroyed by fire in 1936, stripping them of their rich polychromy. The smoke has reduced all the once-vibrant reds, golds and greens into sludgey browns and greys, but they are still magnificent. They exhibit a marked Byzantine influence and were probably executed by English artists, who may have learned their techniques at the court of Sicily where the king of Catalunya had taken an English bride.

Montjuïc

The 13th to the 15th centuries were Catalunya's glory years, when her ships ruled the Mediterranean and her empire was dramatically expanded. The merchants and the cities became increasingly important, and the arts flourished, reaching new heights of accomplishment with the work of painters like **Jaume Huguet** and **Bernat Martorell**. Influences from France, Italy and Flanders were absorbed into the local tradition, and mural painting gradually fell out of fashion. **Altarpieces** became the latest fashion, giving the painters a chance to show off their capacity for rich detailing, although, in Catalunya at least, many of the altarpieces were almost as large as murals.

Gothic section

The Gothic collection is less magical than the Romanesque, but equally magnificent

Room 1: Most of the museum's examples of secular art have been gathered into the opening room, which is dominated by the lively mural paintings that originally came from Palau Berenguer (now the Museu Picasso). The merchants of Barcelona were getting steadily richer and more powerful, and they liked to display their wealth in showy, chivalric murals such as this one, which relates the Catalan's victory over the Saracens in 1229.

The MNAC holdings are predominantly religious, but secular art and architecture were undergoing massive transformation

Room 2: Early pieces of Gothic religious art from Aragon, Navarra and Castile are shown together in this section: in the retablo of St Peter the martyr, the saint poses manfully despite the huge gash in his head. Around 1300, the

Dominicans and other mendicant orders were enormously popular; in the Panel of St Dominic, the virginal saint is surrounded by depictions of his life and miracles, indicating the increasing emphasis on narrative during the Gothic period.

The earliest Gothic works in Catalunya display the importance of line over colour, which characterized early Gothic art, and gave rise to the name Linear Gothic

Room 3: The Panel of St Michael, attributed to the Master of Sorigerola, is made up of several panels relating to aspects of the saint's life: the devil plays his silly games during the Weighing of the Souls, and St Michael wrestles and defeats the dragon in the final panel. A Jewish tombstone commemorating a celebrated Jewish sage and community leader indicates the political importance of the Jewish community during the period, but the jealousy and fear which boiled over into vicious attacks on Jews, particularly in the latter part of the 14th century, is evident in the panels from Vallbona de les Monges, which depict the Jews trying to interrupt the Christian message of salvation.

Rooms 4 and 5: The next sections present sculpture from the second half of the 14th century and the early 15th century, revealing a greater attention to detail and emphasis on naturalism. Statues of the Apostles were often placed around the large doorways of Gothic churches; four have been gathered here, and the statue of St Paul with waving golden hair is easily the most accomplished. There's also a unnerving Head of Christ (circa 1352) which has become separated from the rest of the body over the years, only adding to its painful grimace, and a spectacular altarpiece of the Virgin and Anthony the Abbot sitting under spires which are strangely reminiscent of the knobbly towers of the Sagrada Família while devils scuffle with lightening shooting out of their necks.

The next rooms are devoted to Italian painting and its significant effect on local Catalan art

Rooms 6 and 7: A dazzling, gilt panel which forms part of a triptych, the other two panels are usually on display in the Col.lecció Cambó, depict the Presentation of Christ in the Temple, with breathtakingly realistic detail, particularly in the faces attributed to the anonymous Master of the Cini Madonna, who is thought to have worked in the Rimini area. A pretty, if rather dopey-looking, Virgin of Perafita also displays a minute attention to detail in the hang of her draperies and the clasp of her cloak.

The Catalan miniaturist Ferrer Basser visited Italy, and encountered the works of Giotto and other artists from Siena, returning with a wealth of new ideas which began to infuse local artistic techniques. One of the loveliest pieces here is **Pere Serra**'s *Virgin of the Angels and Saints* (1385), a tender portrait of the Virgin and the infant Jesus holding a bird on a piece of string and surrounded by heavenly musicians. There's a truly sublime statue of the Madonna who seems to be absent-mindedly caressing a toe – it's a very acute portrait of motherhood.

One of the earliest of the Spanish kingdoms to accept the International Gothic style was Valencia

Room 8: The courtly style dubbed International Gothic spread across Europe around 1400. A uniform style and technique had suddenly become established. Several pieces are gathered here but the finest is undoubtedly the luminous Altarpiece of St Barbara (circa 1410-25), attributed to **Gonçal Peris Sarrià**. Barbara's imprisonment by her father, her flight and the transformation of the treacherous shepherd and his flock into marble for his betrayal are all energetically depicted.

Room 9: In Catalunya, the International Gothic was eagerly embraced by painters like Lluís Borassà, Gueraur Gener and Joan Mates; the latter's *Saint Sebastian and Crucifixion* (1417-25) is a good example of the style, with the saint dressed in the latest fashions in the and holding the instrument of his martyrdom, the bow and arrows. There's a touching *Madonna Nursing the Child* (circa 1415-25) by **Ramon de Mur** whose work may well have had an impact on Bernat Martorell. There's also a charming, light-hearted sculpture of a village *festa* by **Pere Sanglada**.

Montjuïc

Room 10: In 1976, the widow of Pere Fontana i Almeda donated 13 Gothic panels to the museum on condition that they be hung together; they include a glorious altarpiece panel by Lluís Borassà and Gueraur Gener from the Monestir de Santes Creus. There's also a bizarre depiction of Saint Michael the Archangel (circa 1435-45), in which the saint is wearing an outfit of contemporary silver armour and battling with a beast which would have been at home in one of Dalí's nightmarish landscapes, with its ragbag collection of limbs and heads from a dozen different kinds of demon.

Room 11 and 12: The following rooms are devoted to one of the most brilliant periods in Catalan art and the work of the three outstanding painters of the time: **Bernat Martorell**, **Lluís Dalmau** and **Jaume Huguet**. The subtlety and delicacy of Bernat Martorell's altarpieces were profoundly influential; there are two here, one depicting Saint Vincent and the other John the baptist and John the Evangelist. His works reveal the increasing Flemish influence which dominated the arts in Spain from the 1440s. Lluís Dalmau's altarpiece *Madonna of the Councillors* (1443-45), which was commissioned by the Consell de Cent, clearly shows the influence of Van Eyck in the extreme naturalism of the portraits (particularly the smug councillors) and in the minutely detailed Gothic interior. A whole room glitters with Jaume Huguet's beautiful work; there's a lushly gilded retablo of Saint Michael glowing with his triumph over the dragon, and another of a rather gloomy St George and the princess.

Room 13: A selection of pieces from around Lleida show the enormous influence of Jaume Huguet's work; **Pere Garcia de Benabarre**'s *Virgin and Four Angels* (circa 1470) is a delicate portrait in which the Holy Infant wears a talisman of red coral to ward off evil spells, like all the new born babies of the period, and there's a monumental series of panels from the Vergos workshop which had close ties with Huguet.

Room 14: Two of the most accomplished painters outside Catalunya were **Fernando Gallego**, represented by an unusual Epiphany scene (circa 1480-90) and the Cordoban painter Bartolomé Bermejo, whose *Resurrection* (circa 1480) is an hallucinogenic vision of Christ emitting golden rays as he steps from the tomb.

Flemish influence had taken a hold on art throughout Iberia by the late 15th century

Room 15: The last room devoted to Catalan art is a collection of works attributed to the anonymous **Master of Seu d'Urgell**, including fragments of some prettily landscaped decorative panels for the cathedral organ in Seu d'Urgell; they are very different from many of the preceding works, and foreshadow the emergence of a more figurative language in the early 16th century.

Room 16: MNAC has an extensive collection of paintings from Valencia and Aragon, including a delightful panel of Saint Margaret serenely spearing a bloody dragon by **Jaume Baço**, better known as Jacomart, and a glowing altarpiece of the Epiphany by **Joan Reixac**.

Room 17: By the time Lluís Dalmau was commissioned to paint his magnificent Madonna and the Councillors (in room 11), the councillors were giving him exact instructions about what outfits they wanted to be wearing in the painting and even the expressions they wanted to be shown on their faces. In this collection, the donor, usually a kneeling figure, peeps out of the folds of saints' draperies, or tugging on his skirts, as in the panel of Saint James attributed to Ramon Solà II, and the pieces can often be dated according to the increasing size of the donor figure.

An early ancestor of portraiture, the figure of the donor grew in importance during the Gothic period

Room 18: The other ancestor of portraiture was funerary art; this richly diverse collection shows how the early stylized depictions of the deceased gave way to increasingly naturalistic portraits. The richest and most important members of the congregation were buried in magnificently sculpted tombs as near as possible to the presbytery, while the commoners had to make do with the cemeteries.

Room 19: The cult of the Virgin throughout Europe reached spectacular new heights during the Gothic period, with a proliferation of churches devoted to her. From her childhood with St Anne to her coronation as Queen of Heaven, this collection shows her in all her guises – one of the loveliest examples is a rare French ivory sculpture from the first half of the 14th century.

Tucked away in a couple of rooms at the end of the Gothic section is the small collection of works from the 15th-18th centuries, mostly donated by the Catalan politician Frances Cambó. There are two striking pieces by **Zurbarán** – a luminous still life, and a florid *Immaculate Conception* – and a luscious, fleshy *Allegory of Love* by **Goya**. There's a swirling portrait of St John the Baptist and St Francis of Assisi having a chat in the desert by El Greco, and a selection of 17th-century Flemish paintings by **Pieter de Hooch**, **Pieter Quast** and **Willem Drost**, and a gleefully lecherous portrait of an old man ogling a young maiden by **Lucas Cranach the Elder**. There's also a **Rubens** of the portly Countess of Arundel, and a **Fragonard** of the Abbé de Saint Nou frivolously dressed *a l'espanyola*.

■ *Tue-Sat 1000-1900; Sun and holidays 1000-1430. €4.80, free on the first Thu of the month, www.mnac.es*

Poble Espanyol

The 'Spanish Village', is a gloriously tacky collection of traditional architectural styles from around the country

After all the high art at the MNAC, there's the pure kitsch of Poble Espanyol to look forward to, reached via Avinguda Marqués de Comillas or along the Avinguda Montanyans. The entrance way is marked by a couple of fake medieval-style copies of the towers in the Castilian town of Avila, which were turned into the most over-the-top designer bar in Barcelona by Alfredo Arribas and Javier Mariscal (see page 241) in the 1980s.

Inside, there's an arcaded Plaça Mayor, a pretty little Barrio Andaluz, a Catalan village, and streets copied from villages all over Spain, from Extremadura to the Basque lands. Plenty of bars, cafés, restaurants, everything from Cuban to vegetarian, and art and craft shops will part you from your money very quickly, and there's also a chance to catch the *Barcelona Experience*, an audio-visual potted history of the city which is also shown in English.

There are plenty of traditional dance and music performances on the main square, and one of the city's hottest clubs: **La Terrrazza Discothèque** is held just behind the village. The flamenco *tablao* (see page 250) is geared towards tourists, but is pretty enjoyable nonetheless, with some remarkable performers and if you get a ticket in advance, you won't have to pay the entrance fee.
■ *Sep-Jun Mon 0900-2000, Tue-Sat 0900-0200, Sun 0900-2400; Jul-Aug Mon 0900-2000, Tue-Thu 0900-0200, Fri-Sat 0900-0400, Sun 0900-2400. €5.87.*

Anella Olímpica

Avinguda Marqués de Comillas continues to wind up the hill, past the circular little Plaça Sant Jordi with its equestrian statue when it becomes the Avinguda de l'Estadi, and the entrance to the Anella Olímpica (Olympic Ring): the string of sports complexes used in the 1992 Olympic Games. Bofill's dismal pseudo-classical building for the **Institut Nacional d'Educazió Fisica de Catalunya**, is the first of the Olympic commissions, a very dull affair with a bold sculpture by **Rosa Serra** called *Tors Olímpic* at the door.

The enormous stadium which looms further along the Avinguda de l'Estadi was built in 1929. The stadium is home to Barcelona's 'other' football team, Espanyol – getting tickets is much easier than for Camp Nou (see page 48). It was destined to become the central stadium for the Popular Olympiad; a kind of people's Olympics aimed to prove to Hitler that he couldn't run the show. Ironically the Civil War broke out on the day before the games were set to begin.

The main entrance to the stadium is the Marathon Gate which commemorates Lluís Companys, President of the Generalitat and enthusiastic supporter of the Popular Olympiad, who was executed by firing squad in 1940. **Pau Gargallo**'s original 1929 sculptures – *Charioteers*, and *Riders Giving the Olympic Salute* – were restored to the positions for which they were designed above the Marathon Gate. The external structure of the stadium was retained during the radical alterations necessitated by the 1992 Olympics – the new architects, Federico Correa and Alfonso Milà, dropped the level of the central arena by 11 m in order to pack in more visitors, and added a rather ugly metal canopy.

Estadi Olímpic
The Catalans beat Bolton Wanderers at the stadium's inaugural football match

The stadium contains the **Galeria Olímpica**, where the star exhibit is a massive inflatable **Cobi** – Mariscal's ultra-kitsch mascot for the Games – and you can relive the highlights of the Games through videos, photos and displays. There's an exhibit of some of the outrageous costumes, scenery and props used for the opening and closing displays. Some of the high-tech equipment used by the athletes is also on display. ■ *Oct-Mar Mon-Fri 1000-1300 and 1600-1800, holidays 1000-1400; Apr-May Mon-Sat 1000-1400 and 1600-1800, holidays 1000-1400; Jun Mon-Sat 1000-1400 and 1600-1900, holidays 1000-1400; Jul-Sep Mon-Sat 1000-1400 and 1600-2000, holidays 1000-1400. €2.40. www.fundaciobarcelonaolimpica.es*

Galeria Olímpica

Montjuïc

An elegant, pure white tower pierces the city's skyline; this is the soaring Torre de Calatrava sculpture by the Valencian architect Santiago Calatrava, which looms above the circular Plaça d'Europa. It came second in the competition for a communications tower on Collserola (won by Norman Foster, see page 164) and sadly no one much liked it when it came to rest here. The *trencadí* decoration around the base is a deliberate nod to Gaudí.

Torre de Calatrava
The sculpture doubles up as a massive sun dial, with a graduated base showing the hours

The ranks of tall towers which line the esplanade leading to the Olympic swimming pools, glow eerily and rather beautifully at dusk. The Piscines Bernat Martorell, built for the 1970 European swimming championships and given a stunning makeover for the Olympics, are among the best places for a swim in the city, with special evening film sessions during the *Festival del Grec* (see page 44).

Piscines Bernat Martoll

Behind the swimming pools, south of the main esplanade is the undisputed star of the Estadí Olímpic, the Palau Sant Jordi, a spare, elegant design by the Japanese architect Arata Isozaki, with an ethereal, undulating roof. Outside the main entrance, there's an enchanting forest of concrete trees with swaying stainless steel branches, a sculpture by the architect's wife **Aiko Miyawaki** entitled *Change*.

Palau Sant Jordi

Fundació Miró

The Foundation contains the most important and comprehensive gathering of Miró's works in the world

Continuing down the Avinguda de l'Estadi, you'll arrive at the luminous, pure white Fundació Joan Miró. Established in 1971, the foundation houses more than 7,000 drawings, sketches and notes, about 200 paintings, and another 4,000 engravings, books, ceramics and tapestries.

The building was designed by Josep Lluís Sert, a long-term friend and colleague of Miró's, who used as his model the airy building for the Fondation Maeght in the south of France to which Miró had contributed a whimsical sculpture path. Both buildings are designed to complement and respect the surrounding environment and to allow as much natural light as possible to flood the galleries. The airiness and lightness which sweep through the building make it an utterly delightful, contemplative space – if possible it is best to avoid it during term-time when hordes of school groups descend on it.

There are excellent commentaries in English, an illustrated English guidebook, and an audio-guide which you can hire at the ticket office. There's also a wonderful programme of activities – from contemporary music and theatrical performances, to puppet shows for kids. There's a good gift and book shop and the foundation also an attractive café with a terrace in which to muse on Miró's work.

The **opening rooms** hold some of Miró's huge **tapestries**, including one created specially for the foundation – *Tapestry of the Foundation*, (1979), with a huge figure of a woman dancing ecstatically beneath a star and moon, and the whimsical *Textile of the Eight Umbrellas* (1988) inspired by childhood memories of field workers who would take umbrellas to shield themselves from the sun. In a glassed-off space just off the tapestry gallery is **Alexander Calder**'s mesmerizing *Mercury Fountain,* dedicated to the mercury-mining town of Almaden, with thick, globules of shimmering mercury slowly dropping from scoop to scoop. It was created for the Spanish Pavilion of the World Fair in Paris, which took place in 1937 at the height of the Spanish Civil War; Picasso exhibited his bitter, monumental painting *Guernica*, but Miró's own contribution, a massive, intensely Catalan painting of *The Reaper* was lost and has never been recovered.

1917-30
During the war years, a growing colony of exiled artists brought new stimuli to local painters, including Miró

Several of Miró's earliest drawings reflect the inspiration he drew from the countryside around Montroig (near Tarragona) where he spent long summers with his grandparents. Many of the drawings, including a very funny scene at *The Chiropodist,* have been preserved. There are some lovely, almost **impressionistic** early landscapes glowing with bright Fauvist colours from this period. *Carrer de Pedralbes* (1917), a skewed, glowing street, shows him dabbling with Cubism, and *Chapel of Sant Joan d'Horta* (1917), with its rich colouring and broad brushstrokes, is **Fauvist** in inspiration. His first exhibition was held at the Galeries D'Arnau, but met with ridicule and scorn from most critics, although Rusiñol wrote him a congratulatory letter that he kept all his life.

In 1921, Miró moved to Paris where he joined André Breton's surrealist movement, and his work moved away from figurative representation towards suggestion, poetry and **abstraction**. In *The Wine Bottle* (1924), the bottle floats in front of a sharp, mountainous landscape, peered at by a mustachioed snake and a dizzy dragonfly. Increasingly, objects float weightlessly in space – as in *The White Glove* (1925), and *The Music-hall Usher* (1925) – as Miró stripped away the unnecessary in pursuit of the essence.

He began to experiment with **automatism**, dipping his brush in petrol and sweeping them over the pages of his drawing book: "The blotches on the surface put me in a proper state and so provoked the birth of shapes: human figures, animals, stars, the whole sky, the moon and the sun' he later wrote, although he worked meticulously on the balance of the composition and every painting was the culmination of carefully prepared sketches. This combination of spontaneous creation and careful labour is the perfect illustration of the Catalan virtues of *rauxa* and *seny* – delerium and common sense – which infuse Miró's work.

The 30s saw more experimentation as Miró sought new methods of expression; he produced collages and objects and in the early 1930s he designed costumes and sets for the Ballet, namely **Russes**'s production of *Romeo and Juliet*.

1930-40

In 1932, Miró produced a series of 12 small paintings in jewel-bright colours, including *Flame in Space and Naked Woman* (1932), in which the figure of a woman – who was to appear again and again in his work – was the central theme. Balance and harmony between colours and forms are paramount.

He never forgot his earthy **Catalanism**; *Man and Woman in Front of a Pile of Excrement* (1935), shows two figures, enormous feet planted firmly on Catalan soil, gesturing lewdly with their bulging genitalia in front of a turd raised up as though looking on with interest. Miró was completely fascinated by hair, which sprouts on snakes, in stars and on genitalia throughout his works.

In 1937, **Civil War** broke out in Spain and Miró was devastated; he took his family to Normandy, where his work began to reflect his 'profound desire to escape...night, music and the stars began to play an increasing role'; he produced posters for a campaign to help the Republicans and painted his enormous, iconic *Reaper* for the World Fair in Paris. The poetic series of *Constellations* – of which the foundation holds one, *Morning Star* (1940) – date from this period. Delicate lines trace between the floating symbols, suggesting an interconnectedness between the earth and the sky, flooded with wheeling stars. The series was created without sketches.

Miró was simultaneously working on an infinitely bleaker set of works which required much more intense preparation: the *Barcelona Series*, which were published after the war with the help of his friend Joan Prats. These dramatically austere lithographs feature the same birds, female figures and starry skies of the *constellations*, but are grimly stripped of colour. These characters from Miró's personal cosmology would reappear countless times in later works in all media, as he honed and refined his peculiar sign language.

The constant themes of the **post-war years** were woman, birds and stars – as in *Woman dreaming of escape* (1945), and *Woman and birds at daybreak* (1946). In 1956, he moved to his new studio in Mallorca (also designed by Sert) and began reworking some of his earliest sketches, including an early self-portrait. The minute detailing and precision of the earlier portrait is super-imposed with a bold, almost cartoonish amorphous figure; just one eye is singled out with a careful circle of red. Miró's sign language was constantly being refined and his paintings became increasingly gestural and impulsive – like *Woman in a pretty hat* (1960), in which there are just two isolated spots of colour, and *Figure in front of the sun* (1968). This almost Zen-like urge to strip things to their essence is beautifully illustrated in the series of paintings he made after a visit to Japan, including the spare, luminous *The Day* (1974). There are some spectacular **sculptures** from this later period, including the soaring white *Solarbird* (1968), blazing against a brilliant blue background,

1940-74
The collection closes with a permanent gallery in homage to Miró, which includes pieces by Léger, Chillida, Duchamp and Ernst

Montjuïc

the delightful bronze *The bird makes its nest in the fingers in flower* (1969), and one of his first clay pieces, the *Double-sided Stele* (1956). There are more sculptures on the roof terrace.

■ *Oct-Jun Tue-Sat 1000-1900, Thu 1000-2130, Sun and holidays 1000-1430; Jul-Sep Tue-Sat 1000-2000, Thu 1000-2130, Sun and holidays 1000-1430, closed Mon except public holidays; €4.80, www.bcn.fjmiro.es*

A short walk beyond the Fundació Miró brings you to the **funicular** station which trundles down to the Diagonal. ■ *Nov-Apr Sat and Sun 1045-2000; Apr-Jun daily 1045-2000, Jun-Oct daily 1100-2300. Single tickets cost €1.50 and return tickets are €2.40.*

Castell Montjüic and around

Avinguda Miramar
At Plaça Armada the cable car swoops across the bay to Barceloneta: 8.43 euros for a return or 4.21 euros for a single

Avinguda Miramar, snakes along to Plaça Armada. There's a rather nondescript bar out here which nonetheless enjoys spectacular views out across bay, especially lovely at dusk. The pretty **Jardins de Miramar** are very pleasant for strolling, dotted with sculptures by **Josep Clarà** and a delightful *La Pomona* (Fruit Goddess) by Pau Gargallo. Just below the Miramar are the **Jardins Costa i Llobrera**, a dusty maze of thousands of species of cactus, including a plump pincushion kind known as 'mother-in-law's chair'; this is one of the largest cactus gardens in Europe, although years of neglect have taken their toll.

Museu Militar
The only statue of Franco in the city is here, swiftly moved from the city's parade ground after his death

Castell Montjüic is now the rather dull and dusty Museu Militar which hit the news when it was discovered that Francoist and neo-Nazi objects were being offered for sale in the gift shop. There is a large collection of weaponry – muskets, lances, swords, and crossbows – and armour spanning five centuries, much of which was collected by Frederic Marès (see page 73). There are portraits of the count-kings of Catalunya, dozens of maps, flags, models, medals and a massive collection – more than 23,000 – of lead soldiers. Tombstones and fragments of memorial stones attest to the melancholy presence of a medieval Jewish cemetery.

The views from the ramparts are wonderful, but it's hard to shake the sense of the castle's bloody past; the gardens lead to Marès' statue to the Little Drummer Boy of El Bruc, whose drum rolls echoed off the mountains and persuaded the French they were surrounded by a much larger enemy during the battle of 1808. Beyond it, there's a small balcony overlooking the infamous **Cementiri de Santa Elena** where the firing squads did their terrible work.

Fossar de la Pedrera

The quarry which became the communal grave of those shot by Franco's forces at the end of the Civil War was converted into a memorial garden in 1986: the Fossar de la Pedrera sits on the scrubby southern flank of the mountain, a quiet, undulating path which twists between cypress groves dotted with sculptures and pillars recalling the names of the dead. A mausoleum commemorates Lluís Companys, who was caught by the Nazis in Belgium in 1940, brought here and shot. ■ *Nov to mid-Mar 0930-1630, mid-Mar to Oct 0930-1930. €1.50.*

Cementiri del Sud-Est

Just below the old quarry is another monument to the dead, the Cementiri del Sud-Est, which was inaugurated in 1883 when there was no more room for ostentatious tombs in the old cemetery in Poble Nou (see page 209). It's a mini-*modernista* city of the dead, sprawling up the mountain and looking out over the sea, stuffed full of elaborate tombs and monuments, including the

Castell de Montjüic

At the brow of the hill, where beacons were once lit to guide sailors into port, stands the once-despised Castell de Montjüic. When the Bourbons finally broke the Barcelonan resistance in 1714, they wasted no time turning the city into a fortress; the vast Citadel was erected on one side of the city, and the old fort on top of Montjüic was rebuilt and expanded for use as a prison and torture centre, a role it continued to play until after the Civil War.

In 1842, and again the following year, General Espartero bombarded the city from behind its walls; in 1896, there were vicious reprisals after a wave of anarchist bombings, and suspects were rounded up and brought for torture during the so-called 'Montjüic Trials' – five were tortured to death; five more citizens were shot by firing squad after the terrible events of the Setmana Tràgica in 1909 – including the anarchist Francesc Ferrer i Guàrdia who hadn't even been in the city at the time, provoking outrage from the whole of Europe. He is remembered by a monument of a naked man holding a flame in a small square near the Palau Nacional.

Thousands of Falangist prisoners were shot during the Civil War, and thousands more were executed after it during Franco's vicious purge of Catalan resistance, including the former President of the Generalitat, Lluís Companys; their bodies were flung into a mass grave on the southern flank of the hill (see below). In a gesture of mind-boggling inappropriateness, the Caudillo donated the fortress to the city in 1960.

tomb Josep Puig i Cadafalch designed for the Amatller family, which mimics the stepped gable he gave their mansion in the Passeig de Gràcia. There are few visitors and the florid but largely abandoned monuments are slowly crumbling on the sun-baked hillside.

Back up at the top of the hill, just beneath the Castell de Montjüic, the Jardins de Mossèn Cinto sprawl along the slopes and are especially lovely in spring. Lazy terraces drip water and there is a pretty pond with a sculpture by **Ramon Sabí** with some rousing lines by the priest-poet Verdaguer after whom the gardens are named. The gardens spread down behind the funicular station and meet the Avinguda Miramar.

Jardins de Mossén Cinto

Around Passeig Santa Madrona

After leaving Jardins de Mossén Cinto, turn left, back towards the Fundació Miró, and swing right down the Passeig Santa Madrona; named for the tiny 18th-century chapel dedicated to Santa Madrona and the last survivor of the handful of chapels which once dotted the hillside. The saint has been adopted by the *barri* of Poble Sec (see page 190), which creeps up the eastern flank of the hill.

Just beyond the back of the Palau, in the crook of the Passeig Santa Madrona, you'll find the Museu Etnològic, set in a squat 1970s building with huge concrete friezes of stolid people and animals. The extensive holdings from Africa, Oceania, Asia, South America and Spain are shown on a rotating basis – there is simply too much to show at one time, but the short, temporary exhibitions are usually the most interesting. Among the main holdings, there are plenty of ghoulish objects from South America – shrunken heads from the Amazon, and a Peruvian head-deformer – and some exquisite Indian and Nepalese religious sculpture, as well as a particularly strong collection of objects from Morocco,

Museu Etnològic

but the presentation is usually worthy rather than engaging. ■ *Tue and Thu 1000-1900, Wed, Fri-Sun, holidays 1000-1400. €3, www.museuetnologic.bcn.es*

Teatre Grec Below the museum, just to the right, steps lead down to **La Rosaleda**, one of the oldest gardens on Montjüic, and just beyond them is the Teatre Grec, an amphitheatre inspired by a model in Epidaurus and built over an old quarry for the 1929 International Exhibition. It's the main venue for the *Festival del Grec*, the city's main performing arts festival which is held in June and July (see page 44).

Museu d'Arqueològia de Catalunya At the end of Passeig de Madrona, there's another crop of fanciful pavilions left over from the 1929 International Exhibition. The first of them was the pavilion for the graphic arts, inspired by the Italian Renaissance, with cream and red arcades and a monumental entrance, which is now the Museu d'Arqueològia de Catalunya.

It was beautifully modernized and enlarged in the 1980s, and the holdings, which date back to the Palaeolithic period, are attractively arranged around a star-shaped central hall. The collection begins with copies of early cave paintings – dramatic hunting and battle scenes – discovered in the Pyrenenean regions. There are recreations of Neolithic and Iron Age burial sites, and several galleries devoted the Majorcan Taliaotic culture. Among the pieces from the Carthagian settlement on Ibiza is the *Dama d'Evissa*, a remarkable 4th-century sculpture of an elaborately dressed and bejewelled figure doing a double 'thumbs up' gesture, which was discovered in the necropolis. There's a whole gallery devoted the findings from the Greek colony of Empuriés, and an extensive collection of Roman work including original floor mosaics, funerary *steles*, a huge statue of the Asclepius, the Roman god of healing, and several glimmering mosaics. The enormous statue of Priapus is coyly hidden almost out of sight. ■ *Tue-Sat 0930-1900, Sun and holidays 1000-1430. €2.40, www.mac.es*

Ciutat del Teatre Just beyond the pavilion is a square which was once known as the *Widow's Square*, because lonely women once used to be 'consoled' in its shadowy recesses. Just across the road is the old **Palau de l'Agricultura**, which is being refurbished to house the Teatre Lliure, as part of the city's controversial plans to bring many of its major theatrical institutions together in the Ciutat del Teatre (Theatre City).

Behind it is the **Mercat de las Flors**, another hangover from the 1929 International Exhibition, which did its duty as a flower market before being transformed into a theatre and performance space (see page 234). Inside, the main auditorium has a remarkable frieze by Miquel Barceló, one of the city's best known artists, on the cupola. These buildings look inward onto the pretty **Plaça Margarida Xirgù**, now dominated by the spanking new, glassy building for the Institut del Teatre (see page 234) which is to hold a new museum of Performing Arts ■ *For more information, call T93 227 39 10, or visit the website www.diba.es/iteatre*

Poble Sec

The web of streets between Montjüic and Paral.lel are part of the easy-going, traditional neighbourhood of Poble Sec. It is a poor district which grew up rapidly during the industrial years of the late 19th century, an extension of the older slums of Raval. The barri is dotted with old-fashioned bars and restaurants – as well as an increasing number of hip ones.

Heading down Carrer Lleida and turning right onto Carrer França Xica, (little France), you will find one of the oldest and least changed streets in the neighbourhood. It crosses Carrer Creus dels Molers, named for the *molers* (stone masons) who used to quarry the famous pale Montjüic stone.

Poble Sec means 'Dry Town'; the factories that sprouted up sucked up the water from the springs of Montjüic, and it wasn't until 1894 that the neighbourhood finally got its first street fountain, which still exists, on the corner of Carrer Margarit just off Carrer França Xica and Carrer Elcano. The poor factory workers were so delighted, they celebrated with a big street party. The nearby square on the corner of Carrer Magalhães and Carrer Blasco de Garay, is still known as **Plaça Sortidor** (Fountain Square) despite all official attempts to change it. There is a sprinkling of old-fashioned bars on the square, including the unofficial club house of the Poble Sec football club.

Head downhill to the Paral.lel and walk seawards along the broad street which was once the centre of the city's vibrant, vulgar but much-loved cabaret district. On the right loom the enormous chimneys of the old electrical power station, which have been preserved in a small park – **Parc de les Tres Xemenies**, wedged between some glassy new office buildings. This is where the neighbourhood kids hang out on rollerblades and skateboards. Further down on the left of the Paral.lel is the attractively mouldering stretch of the 14th-century walls which finally encircled the old city.

Eating and drinking

Ca L'Isidre, C/Flors 12, T93 441 11 39. Mon-Sat 1330-1600 and 2030-2330, metro Paral.lel. Tucked down a narrow side street, the entrance of this celebrated family-run restaurant proudly displays a photograph of the owners posing with King Juan Carlos, who is said to be a big fan of the classic Catalan cuisine on offer. Try the *cabrit*, goat marinaded and roasted slowly in a wooded oven, or the succulent loin of lamb. The heavenly desserts are made by the daughter of the family.

Expensive
● *on map, page 176*

Cuixart, C/Vila i Vilà 53, T93 441 30 78. Open 1300-1545, Tue-Sat 1300-1545 and 2100-2345, metro Paral.lel. An atmospheric, neighbourhood restaurant specializing in *bacalao* (salt cod) and other traditional Catalan recipes. There's an outdoor terrace in summer, and a very good value *menú del día*. *Elche*, C/Vila i Vilà 71, T93 441 30 89. Open daily 1300-1630 and 2000-2430, metro Paral.lel. A popular, lively restaurant named after a town near Alicante; it specializes in rice dishes, particularly paella and has been going strong since 1959.

Mid-range

La Tomaquera, C/de Margarit 58, no tel. Open Tue-Sat 1330-1530 and 2030-2330, metro St Antoni or Paral.lel. A resolutely no-nonsense restaurant serving up great grilled meats with garlic sauce, specialities like snails or torrades with different toppings, and great home made desserts. Much of the appeal of the place come from the gruffly charismatic owner-chef – he refuses to have a telephone installed, and won't serve Coca Cola.

Cheap

Quimet & Quimet, C/Poeta Cabañas 25, T93 442 31 42. Open Tue-Sat 1200-1600 and 1900-2230, Sun 1200-1600, metro Paral.lel. A small, traditional *bodega* usually packed with crowds; it's got one of the best selection of wines in the city, and a range of excellent tapas to match. *Cervecería Jazz*, C/Margarit 43, no tel. Open daily except Sun 1800-0200. Mellow jazz music, a good range of international beers and excellent sandwiches make this a very relaxed spot. *Bar Primavera*, C/Nou de la Rambla 192, T93 329 30 62. Open daily 1000-1900, until 1700 in winter, metro Paral.lel. A delightful and very peaceful outdoor spot halfway up the slopes of Montjuïc.

Café-bars with food/tapas

Montjüic

Cafés   *Horchateria Sirvent*, C/del Parlament 56, T93 441 27 20. Open Mon-Sat 1000-0300, Sun 1200-2400, metro Paral.lel. This narrow little *horchatería* has been going for more than 80 years, and is generally considered to serve up the best horchata in the city. Lean up against the counter, or take away.

Transport

The main transport hub for this area is the **Plaça Espanya**.

Bus Note that few buses go up Montjüic: bus nos **13** and **50** go to Poble Espanyol; only bus no **50** carries on to the Anella Olímpica, the Fundació Miró, the funicular station for Paral.lel, and the cable car station for the top of Montjüic. The small **Barribus No 221** covers the streets of Poble Sec, and has a circular route beginning at the Mercat Sant Antoni. Take bus no **55** for the Ciutat del Teatre and Museu d'Arqueologia.

Ferrocarril Plaça Espanya is one of the main stations for suburban FGV (*Ferrocarrils*) trains run by the Catalan government www.fgc.catalunya.net. Trains depart for **Montserrat** (line R5) from this station, and to **Colònia Güell** (lines S4, S8, R5, R6).

Funicular Montjüic funicular leaves from the Paral.lel metro station and heads up to Avda Miramar. Single tickets cost €1.50 and return tickets are €2.40. Open Nov-Apr Sat and Sun 1045-2000, Apr-Jun daily 1045-2000, Jun-Oct daily 1100-2300.

Metro Line 1 (red) to Espanya; Line 3 (green) to Paral.lel (for the funicular), Poble Sec, Espanya.

Taxi There's a big taxi rank on Plaça d'Espanya.

Teleféric/Cable cars

Teleféric de Monjüic: The cable car ride begins at the funicular station on Avda Miramar and heads up toward the castle right at the top. Open Jun to mid-Sep, Mon-Fri 1115-2000, Sat-Sun 1115-2100; mid-Sept to Oct daily 1130-1945 and 1600-1930; Nov-May weekends only 1115-2100. Tickets cost €2.85 single and €4.06 return.

Teleféric de Barceloneta: The cable car runs from the Miramar station in Montjüic at the end of Avda Miramar down to Passeig de Joan de Borbó in Barceloneta, with a pause at the tower near the new World Trade Center. Open daily mid-Oct to Feb 1030-1730, Mar to mid-Jun and mid-Sep to mid-Oct 1030-1900, mid-Jun to mid-Sept 1030-2000. Ticket prices are hefty: €8.43 for a return or €4.21 for a single.

El Litoral

7

194

El Litoral

196	**Port Vell**		205	Transport
196	Plaça Portal de la Pau		206	**Vila Olímpica**
198	La Rambla de Mar		206	History
200	Palau del Mar		207	Sights
201	Eating and drinking		208	Eating and drinking
202	Shopping		208	Transport
202	Transport		209	**Poble Nou and Diagonal Mar**
203	**Barceloneta**		209	History
203	History		210	Eating and drinking
203	Sights		210	Transport
204	Eating and drinking			

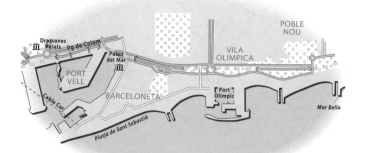

The seafront (el litoral) in Barcelona was the main focus for the frenzy of cleaning, construction and redevelopment which heralded the 1992 Olympic Games. The **Port Vell** (Old Port) was utterly transformed, its decrepit warehouses demolished or revamped, and its streets widened and studded with palm trees and sculptures: now, yachts and gin palaces bob in the harbour, smart restaurants have spread their awnings onto broad boulevards, and the walkways are filled with craft markets and street hawkers. Behind all the tourist gimmicks and laminated menus of Port Vell sprawls the old fishermen's neighbourhood of **Barceloneta**, a shabby, atmospheric district of narrow streets and modest houses brightened with cheerful geraniums and still sprinkled with traditional bars serving fresh seafood tapas. Beyond Barceloneta stretch the city's six beaches, not especially lovely, but buzzing with an enduring populist fizz and always packed in summer. They edge past the brash, glitzy new **Port Olímpic** development with its clutch of shops, restaurants and bars, and culminate at the seafront of another quiet old worker's district, **Poble Nou**, which is being totally revamped to host the city's Universal Forum of Cultures in 2004 – Barcelona's next excuse to dress itself up and show off.

Port Vell

Port Vell (Old Port), once a scruffy working port surrounded by dark, dirty warehouses, has been revamped beyond recognition; 'Barcelona obert a la Mar' (Barcelona open to the sea) was the catchphrase of the city-driven project to utterly transform Barcelona's waterfront in time for the Olympic hordes in 1992. The grimy beaches and sagging buildings were swept away or swept clean in a huge regeneration project.

*At the foot of La Rambla, the symbolic **Monument a Colom** towers over the **Drassanes** shipyards and leads to **Rambla del Mar** and the quays of **Moll d'Espanya**, dominated by the **Maremàgnum** entertainment Mecca, and **Moll de la Fusta**. The old dockside access road is now the grand **Passeig Joan de Borbó**, an elegant, broad promenade, which sweeps past the pleasure port, crammed with yachts and gleaming cruisers from all over the world. At the top is the **Palau del Mar**, an old warehouse complex which now houses the **Museu d'Història de Catalunya**.*

Plaça Portal de la Pau

Monument a Colom
This is the world's largest statue of Christopher Columbus

Right at the bottom of the Rambla stands the enormous Monument a Colom, which enjoys a bird's-eye view of the city. The statue was made from iron provided by melted-down cannons from the fort at Montjüic and erected in 1888, just in time for the first Universal Exhibition in 1888. It was immediately popular thanks to the unusual addition of an interior lift which still swoops visitors up to a viewing platform in the globe at Columbus' feet. These feet were recently shod in honour of the monument's marriage to New York's Statue of Liberty in 1992, a characteristically madcap idea from the Barcelonan conceptual artist Antoni Miralda. One of the outsized shoes is on view at the **Museu de Calçat** (see page 76). The monument is always being overhauled and is often surrounded by an untidy mush of fences and scaffolding, but it is rarely closed, despite the evidence. ■ *Colom interior lift: Oct-May Tue-Sat 1000-1400 and 1530-1830, Sun 1000-1900, Jun-Sep daily 0900-2100. €1.40.*

Port Authority

At the seafront here you'll see the frothy cream cake Port Authority building, overlooking the tiny fleet of *Golondrines*: elegant, double-decker sightseeing boats which offer cruises around the bay (see page 32). It faces the grand **Duana** (Customs House), with a fleet of beady-eyed griffons taking wing from the roof. In the little plaça which is squeezed between them, you can rummage through the antique and junk stalls which appear on Saturdays and Sundays (0800-2000).

Drassanes Reials
The often overlooked Museu Marítim is housed in these medieval shipyards

Just off the Plaça del Pau are the magnificent Drassanes Reials, the vast medieval shipyards which form the largest and most important civil Gothic structure in the world. By the end of the 13th century, the House of Barcelona was firmly linked with the Crown of Aragon. This powerful confederation harboured grand expansionist dreams; over the next two centuries great swathes of the Mediterranean would submit to their military might, including Sicily, the Duchies of Athens and Neopatria, Mallorca, Ibiza, Sardinia and Naples.

The old shipyards west of Montjüic could no longer cope with demand and work began as early as 1243 on a replacement. By the beginning of the 17th century, 30 galleys could be comfortably accommodated; a century

Things to do by the sea

- Hire a tandem and cycle along the seafront (see page 39)
- Swing up in the cable car to Montjüic (see page 201)
- Watch the sun set as DJs play on Mar Bella beach (see page 204)
- Get some fresh seafood tapas at a backstreet bar in Barceloneta (see page 204)

later, that number had increased to forty – and if that still seems unimpressive, wait until you see the tremendous size of the 16th century galley ship which dominates the interior of the Drassanes.

The galley ship is the focal point of Barcelona's excellent and very entertaining **Museu Marítim**, which has been housed in the Drassanes since 1941. Under the vast arches of the medieval warehouses, the monstrous galley ship – a replica of the Royal Galley of John of Austria – dwarfs everything else in the museum: even the towering arches, spanning more than six metres and rising to a height of 13 metres, seem puny in comparison. The galley is more than 60 metres long and carries 236 oars, each weighing 180kg, pulled by an unfortunate slave – usually an 'infidel' or convict – whose fate was to be shackled to his place at the oar for twenty-four hours a day, sleeping, eating and sometimes dying in one spot. The galley was built to lead the Holy Alliance against the Infidel Turks in the Battle of Lepant in 1571, one of the very last battles to use galley ships.

Elsewhere in the museum, there's a fine collection of **ships' figureheads**, including the sweet-faced *Blanca Aurora*, carved to ward off the evil eye and ensure good fortune for the ship and her crew. There's also an absorbing collection of beautifully illuminated **medieval maps**, mainly from Mallorca, which depict a world perceived as a single land mass surrounded by a sea filled with monsters. You can explore the interior of a 19th-century sailing ship, or head for the museum's newest addition, the interactive *Great Adventure of the Sea*, a favourite with kids; get caught in a storm in Havana, wander through a huge ocean liner, or investigate one of the world's first submarines, the *Ictíneo*, invented by **Narcís Monturiol** in 1859 (see page 200). ■ *Daily 1000-1900. €5.40.*

Beyond the Museu Marítim, the cranes still loom over the Moll de Barcelona. This is where the cruise ships dock and the ferries for Italy depart – it's the focal point for the city's determined efforts to put itself firmly on the shipping map. At its tip is the circular **World Trade Center**, which was plagued by a lack of finances for years, but has finally opened its doors to shops, restaurants and a swanky hotel which is slated to open in early 2002.

In the middle of the Moll de Barcelona, the ungainly **Torre de Jaume I** is one of the stops on the cable car which swings from Montjüic to Barceloneta (see page 201). You can take the lift to the top for a bird's eye view of the new harbour development, if you don't want to take the cable car – but be warned that the ongoing building works are likely to mean its closure, at least temporarily.

Plans are afoot to extend the **Zona Franca** industrial district and create a 'Logistics Park' with new, improved port, road, rail and air links, to entice yet more ships. The commercial zone will remain confined to the Zona Franca, but the cruise ships and pleasure boats will have a new entrance to the harbour by the end of 2001. In 2000, the vast, gleaming **Puerta de Europa** opened, a spectacular drawbridge which links the old breakwater with the land.

Moll de Barcelona
The port can already receive nine cruise ships simultaneously – more than any other city except Miami

El Litoral

La Rambla de Mar

This floating wooden walkway begins near the Port Authority building

The crowds sweep down from the Ramblas and onto the undulating Rambla de Mar, which opens wide for boat traffic, and leads to some of Barcelona's most popular attractions: the **Maremàgnum** shopping centre; the IMAX cinema, and the aquarium. The glassy Maremàgnum building is stuffed full of boutiques selling everything from clothes and souvenirs to novelty condoms and jewellery. Upstairs, there are plenty of snack bars and restaurants, many with terraces overlooking the yacht-filled harbour, as well as a couple of hugely popular clubs.

El Litoral

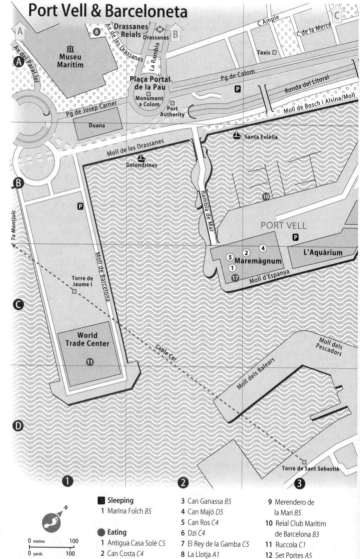

Port Vell & Barceloneta

Related maps

A *El Raval*, page 108
B *La Rambla*, page 62
C *Barri Gòtic*, page 72
D *La Ribera & Sant Pere*, page 88
E *Vila Olímpica & Poble Nou*, page 206

0 metres 100
0 yards 100

■ **Sleeping**
1 Marina Folch *B5*

● **Eating**
1 Antigua Casa Solé *C5*
2 Can Costa *C4*
3 Can Ganassa *B5*
4 Can Majó *D5*
5 Can Ros *C4*
6 Dzi *C4*
7 El Rey de la Gamba *C5*
8 La Llotja *A1*

9 Merendero de la Mari *B5*
10 Reial Club Marítim de Barcelona *B3*
11 Ruccola *C1*
12 Set Portes *A5*

The **IMAX** theatre offers everything from dinosaurs to dolphins in 3D and surround sound, and you can see the real thing (well, dolphins anyway) at **L'Aquàrium** next door. It is the largest aquarium in Europe, with dozens of exhibits and a new special interactive centres for kids. The highlight is the enormous central tank, which you can coast through gently on a conveyor belt to a shmaltzy soundtrack as rays, sharks and glinting shoals of silvery fish wheel overhead. ■ *Jul and Aug 0930-2300, Jun and Sep 0930-2130, Oct-May Mon-Fri 0930-2100 Sat-Sun 0930-2130. Admission €9.33.*

El Litoral

● **Cafés & tapas bars**
13 Can Paixano *A5*
14 El Lobito *B5*
15 El Vaso de Oro *B6*
16 La Cepa *C5*
17 Maremàgnum *C2*

18 Taverna Can Ramonet *B5*

○ **Entertainment**
1 Irish Winds *C2*

○ **Clubs & bars**
2 Insòlit *C3*
3 Luz de Gas *A4*
4 Mojito Bar *C3*
5 Nayandei Disco & Nayendei Boite *C2*

Moll d'Espanya

At the tip of the Moll, Roy Lichtenstein's sculpture, Barcelona Head, looks out cheerfully over the crowds

Another walkway, the Moll d'Espanya, will take you back to land, past a replica of *Ictineo II*, **Narcís Monturiol**'s second submarine which was tested in Barcelona harbour. Monturiol (1819-85) was a tireless worker for the rights of the downtrodden, editing a stream of magazines which championed equal rights and exposed the hideous conditions inside the factories of Port Vell. In 1857 he began work on his first submarine – the *Ictíneo*, which was to be followed by a new improved version – *Ictíneo II*. Praise was forthcoming, but unfortunately the cash was not. Monturiol, crippled with mounting debt, died, forgotten and miserable. Ironically, less than a century later, no less than six submarines would be found on the streets of Barcelona, watery monuments to his idealism and invention.

Moll de la Fusta

Running parallel to the Passeig de Colom is the seafront Moll de la Fusta; the 'wood quay' was earmarked for development during the heady years of the 1980s, when the city was gripped by design fervour and the need to get smartened up for the Olympics; some of Barcelona's wildest bars and clubs, like the infamous *Octopussy*, were located down here, but they were closed down a couple of years ago to make way for a new tourist information centre and an extension to the maritime museum. So far nothing much has happened, apart from the huge grinning lobster, by Barcelona's adopted enfant terrible, **Javier Mariscal**, waves from an abandoned bar – no one quite knows what to do with it. Moored up along the Moll de la Fusta is the beautifully restored turn-of-the-century sailboat, the **Santa Eulàlia**, which belongs to the Museu Marítim (admission to the boat is included in museum admission).

Passeig de Colom

One of the houses on Plaça d'Antonio Lopez is said to have lodged Cervantes, creator of Don Quixote

The broad, palm-lined Passeig de Colom runs parallel to the Moll de la Fusta and marks the line of the old sea ramparts. Its former maritime importance is hinted at by the remaining handful of shabby shipping offices and ship's chandlers. The imposing neo-classical building which flanks **Placa d'Antonio Lopez** looks far too grand for its humdrum role as the city's main **Edificio de Correos** (post office). Built in 1926, its grand columns are topped with allegorical figures by the *noucentiste* sculptor **Manuel Fuxà**, and inside, barely discernible in the gloom, there are more *noucentiste* murals.

The grandest building on the whole of Passeig de Colom stood only a matter of weeks: Domènech i Montaner's **Hotel Internacional** was built in just 53 days for the Universal Exhibition in 1888 (see page 97) – all five storeys and 1,600 rooms – and was destroyed in 1889 in order to redevelop the site. The press had a field day with the hotel's daring floating foundations, and drew cartoons of it sinking into the sands or sailing regally out to sea.

Palau del Mar

There is a taxi rank at the top of Passeig Joan de Borbó

The former warehouse complex at the top of the Passeig Joan de Borbó has been carefully renovated and refurbished to become the grandly named Palau del Mar, which houses a string of elegant restaurants as well as the engaging **Museu d'Història de Catalunya**, a huge, gleaming museum devoted to the story of Catalunya's fortunes from prehistory to the present.

The exhibits are divided chronologically and thematically; from *Roots*, where the non-squeamish can watch prehistoric man hunting and skinning a rabbit; through *Birth of Nation*, which describes the extension of Catalunya's medieval empire and gives visitors the chance to try on some armour and admire themselves in mirrors; up through the *Electric Years* of the early 20th century, where you can take a tram ride through the Barcelona of the 1920s, and onto an exhibit on the Civil War, complete with sound effects and a recreated bomb shelter.

The last years of Catalunya's history are presented under the tactfully titled display 'Undoing and New Beginnings', which covers the nation's fortunes under the Franco regime and its subsequent re-emergence. The first floor holds large, usually very interesting temporary exhibitions.

The multi-media presentations make any visit entertaining but there is a lack of information in English and so it's worth getting hold of a the English guide at the excellent gift shop which also has an interesting range of unusual gifts from local designers, as well as the usual posters and t-shirts.

■ *Tue-Sat 1000-1900, Wed until 2000, Sun and holidays 1000-1430. €3, http://cultura.gencat.es/museus/mhc*

Museu d'Història de Catalunya
The museums' top floor café terrace offers fabulous views of the yachts bobbing in the harbour and out to sea

Outside the Palau de Mar, a **craft market** sprawls around the marina at weekends, selling unusual hats, jewellery and painted glassware. There are plenty of bars and restaurants lining the port, including a converted boat, the **Luz de Gas** – a tad tacky but fun – and the long Passeig Joan de Borbó has the bright cheerful air of a smaller seaside town, with flip flops and ice cream being sold from small neighbourhood shops. The old fishing port lies just beyond the Marina, overlooked by a simple brickwork clocktower which dates back to 1772.

The Passeig Joan de Borbó culminates in the scruffy little **Plaça del Mar**, where you'll find the **St Sebastià** swimming pools, with indoor and outdoor pools, gym, sauna, restaurant and café, if you can't manage to squeeze yourself onto the beach nearby. This beach was the site of the first mixed bathing establishment in the city, surrounded by some pretty louche bars and cafés and even boasted a casino during the 1920s.

Around Passeig Joan de Borbó

El Litoral

Just across from the swimming pool is the Torre de Sant Sebastià where cable cars begin their terrifying journey over the harbour and up to Montjuïc. The cable car was first mooted to provide another means of access to the 1929 International Exhibition on the slopes of Montjuïc, but financial problems delayed its construction until two years after the exhibition had closed. It's worked erratically ever since, closing intermittently for long periods until the next instalment of funds could be found. The continuing work on the World Trade Center will probably lead to its closure, at least temporarily, so it's worth catching while you can. ■ *Daily mid-Oct to Feb 1030–1730, Mar to mid-Jun and mid-Sep to mid-Oct 1030-1900, mid-Jun to mid-Sep 1030–2000. €8.43 for a return trip to Montjuïc or €4.21 for a single, and €6 for a return to the World Trade Center. You can pay €3.61 to take the lift up the tower and admire the views.*

Torre de Sant Sebastià

Eating and drinking

Ruccola, World Trade Center, Moll de Barcelona, T93 508 82 68.1300-1600 and 2000-2345, metro Drassanes. Newly opened up in the World Trade Centre, Ruccola has been getting excellent reviews in the city's magazines. The cuisine is a well-balanced

Expensive
● *on map page 198*

mix of traditional Catalan favourites and international influences, and it's become very popular with the fashionable crowd.

Mid-range *La Llotja*, Museu Marítim, Avinguda de les Drassanes, T93 302 64 02. Open Mon-Thu and Sun 1400-1545, Fri and Sat 1400-1545 and 2100-2330, metro Drassanes. A beautifully located restaurant, La Llotja is tucked away in the courtyard of the Museu Marítim (see page 197). It's set under the vast stone arches of the Gothic shipyards, with a huge window overlooking a hidden courtyard where you can sit outside in summer. Run by a local food critic and gourmet, it serves excellent Catalan food, including a couple of medieval dishes – like chicken spiced with saffron – to complement the extraordinary setting. *Reial Club Marítim de Barcelona*, Moll d'Espanya, T93 221 6256. Open Mon-Sat 1330-1600 and 2100-2330 and Sun 1330-1630, metro Barceloneta or Drassanes. With a terrace overlooking the sea of yacht masts in the harbour, this is a fine restaurant serving innovative Catalan cuisine with interesting international influences. Try the langoustine kebabs with parmesan and dress as though you own a yacht, even if you don't. The service is extremely friendly and welcoming, and few people realize that you don't have to be a member to eat here.

Café-bars **with food/** **tapas** *Tapas Bar Maremàgnum*, Moll d'Espanya, T93 225 81 80, open Mon-Thu and Sun 1100-0100, Fri-Sat 1100-0200, metro Barceloneta or Drassanes. Brash, cheerful tapas bar (part of the chain) which is redeemed by the fabulous views across the harbour and back to the city.

Cafés *Cava Universal*, Plaça Portal de la Pau 4, T93 302 61 84, open daily 0900-2200, metro Drassanes. Simple, unassuming little bar just at the foot of the Monument a Colom; good, reasonably priced *bocadillos* and great views.

Shopping

Malls & **department** **stores** *Maremàgnum*, Moll d'Espanya, www.maremagnum.es, metro Drassanes. This glassy mall right in the middle of the port development is good for souvenir shops and small fashion shops. There are also dozens of restaurants, bars and clubs.

Markets *Fira de Brocanters*, Moll de Drassenes, Port Vell, metro Drassanes. Open Sat and Sun 1100-2100. So-called antiques laid out on a few tables just in front of the Columbus monument. Don't expect any bargains, but you might get a few laughs from some of the bizarre items that pop up.

Transport

Bus No **17** from Pg Joan de Borbó to Avda Jordà, via Via Laietana, Pg de Gràcia, Gràcia and Avda Tibidabo. No **36** from Paral.lel to Plaça Congres, via Drassanes, Pla del Palau and Poble Nou. No **40** from Trinitat Vella to Port Vell, via Gran Via and Arc de Triomf. **Metro** Line 3 (green) for Drassanes, the bottom of the Rambla. **Taxi** There's a taxi stand on Pg de Colom near the Estació de França.

El Litoral

Barceloneta

While tourists sit under canvas umbrellas and sip their cocktails in between visits to the beach, the shabby little neighbourhood of Barceloneta just behind it goes about its business undisturbed. The best time to appreciate it is during the **Festa Major de Barceloneta**, *at the end of September, when the lumbering figure of Bum Bum (a take off of Prosper Verboom) careers down the narrow streets popping off a cannon and showering sweets onto the following children, and fireworks fly in the evenings, watched from boats in the harbour. People don't come to Barceloneta for the sights. This old-fashioned neighbourhood has just two attractions, but they are among the best in the city – the old* **fishermens' bars** *serving fresh seafood tapas, and the sandy* **beaches** *packed with cheerful crowds.*

History

In the early years of the 18th century, a great swathe of La Ribera was demolished and homes, businesses and neighbourhoods were ripped apart, leaving thousands homeless and broke, forced to live in the crude shacks which grew up on the triangle of marshy land which edged the seafront. The engineer of the citadel, a Frenchman with the explosive name of Prosper Verboom, came up with plans for a new housing development built on reclaimed land to provide homes for the dispossessed in 1715 but it wasn't until 1753 that another military engineer, Juan Martín Cermeño, finally put the plan into action.

The original design was in line with the latest principles of urban planning, a grid-like development crossed by 15 narrow streets, crossed with five broader avenues, with a central market place and a parade ground to ensure that no one escaped the repressive presence of the military. The buildings were to be two storeys tall and the narrow blocks would ensure that every apartment had windows overlooking the street; of course, these regulations were completely ignored, and the houses rose dizzyingly, so that light and air could not penetrate to the streets and lower floors.

During the 19th century, poor dockers and fishermen lived in unspeakable misery, eloquently described in **Eduardo Mendoza**'s *La Ciudad de los Pródigos* (City of Marvels), in the run-down buildings, cut off from the rest of the city by the grubby, noisy railway tracks and access roads to the docks right up until the 1990s. As the old buildings mouldered away or were destroyed by bombing during the Civil War, they have been replaced by anonymous apartment blocks, and the delightful *xiringuitos* (makeshift snack bars), started up by fishermen's families in the 19th century, were swept away in the pre-Olympic reforms. Still, most of these reforms have only touched the fringes of the old neighbourhood, leaving its unassuming, down-to-earth heart intact.

Sights

Just off the Passeig Joan de Borbó is the little **Plaça de Barceloneta**, where the modest **Església de Sant Miquel** has stood since 1755. Dedicated to Barceloneta's patron saint, it's a simple, tentatively Baroque edifice, which managed to survive the church-burnings of the Civil War. The sleepy, central **Plaça del Font** has retained a few remnants of the past – a couple of the original two-storey houses at Nos 30 and 32, and a pair of old washtubs around the corner on Carrer Andreu Dòrria. The square is commonly known as the *Plaça del Mercat* for the delightful, bustling covered market which was rebuilt in

El Litoral

1884 and is one of the oldest in the city.

On the other side of the Plaça del Mercat, on **Carrer Maquinista**, is the oldest tavern in Barceloneta, *Can Ramonet*, now a smart restaurant and tapas bar. There are plenty of earthier, scruffy local bars where you can pick up some freshly caught fish and a draught of good, rough wine (see page 205). At the end of Carrer Maquinista, on the edge of the neighbourhood, is the **Parc de la Barceloneta** where there's a very pretty, *modernista* red-brick and tile water tower, **Torre de les Aigües**, designed by Domènech i Estapa in 1905, but which is currently shrouded in scaffolding.

Down at the tip of Barceloneta is the Passeig Marítim, an early attempt to drive some light and air into the suffocating neighbourhood, and the site of the **Somorrostro**: a chaotic shanty town where the flamenco dancer Carmen Amaya was born (commemorated by a fountain on the Passeig Marítim), and which was only finally destroyed in 1966. At the end of the Passeig Marítim is the vast **Hospital del Mar**, originally an establishment devoted to curing sufferers of the bubonic plague. It grew haphazardly into a hospital and was remodelled for use as the Olympic hospital in 1992, when an attractive light-filled esplanade lined with slender columns looking out over the sea was added.

The beaches were dramatically cleaned up in time for the 1992 Olympics

The **Platjas** (beaches), which extend for several kilometres from the **Platja Sant Sebastià**, at the end of Passeig Joan de Borbó in Barceloneta, all the way to the **Platja Nova Mar Bella** near the Besos River, are not the most beautiful nor the cleanest on the Mediterranean, but they are fun, easy to get to, packed with people, and conveniently lined with cafés and snack bars. You can rent a sun-lounger for about €3 if you want to work on your tan for a while, but if you'd prefer something more active, stroll along to **Mar Bella** beach where you can get sailing and wind-surfing lessons, or hire snorkelling equipment. The crowds thin out slightly the further you walk.

The city is well aware that the proximity of the Mediterranean constitutes a large part of Barcelona's attraction for tourists; palm trees and sculptures, like **Rebecca Horn**'s towering *Homage to Barceloneta*, a leaning sculpture which echoes the buildings of the old neighbourhood, now line the esplanade and there's an attractive boardwalk popular with cyclists and roller-bladers.

Eating and drinking

Expensive
● *on map page 198*

Antigua Casa Solé, C/Sant Carles 4, T93 221 51 12. Open Tue-Sat 1300-1600 and 2000-2300, metro Barceloneta. This is a very pretty restaurant set in a 19th-century building with breezy blue and white tiles and lots of flowers. Apparently, the *sarsuela* (local fish stew) was invented here and it's still a great place to try traditional Catalan fish recipes. The service is impeccable and there's a good wine list.

Mid-range

Merendero de la Mari, Plaça de Pau Vila 1, T93 221 31 41. Open Mon-Sat 1300-1600 and 2030-2330, Sun 1300-1600. An elegant restaurant set in the arcades of the beautifully renovated Palau del Mar, with an airy terrace shaded by canvas umbrellas. Excellent, imaginative seafood dishes include the salt cod puffs and black noodles with clams, but the desserts are well worth saving room for.

Can Costa, Passeig Joan de Borbó 70, T93 221 59 03. Open daily 1230-2400, metro Barceloneta. The Costa family ran one of the best beachside *chiringuitos/xiringuitos* before the harbour area was redeveloped; now they run a very busy restaurant offering good, fresh fish and a list of changing daily specials. *Dzi*, Passeig Joan de Borbó 76, T93 221 21 82, open daily 1300-1600 and 2000-2400, metro Barceloneta. Good, fresh and imaginative Chinese cuisine and a terrace overlooking the harbour in summer. There are also some Singaporean and Thai dishes – try the beef sautéed with mango

El Litoral

or the sea bream with prawns.

El Rey de la Gamba, Passeig Joan de Borbó 46-48, T93 222 56 40, open daily 1200-2430, metro Barceloneta. Well known seafood restaurant with great views over the harbour, the *King of the Prawns* is a tad touristy and over-priced but still offers a good selection of very fresh seafood dishes: pick your victim from the tanks first or choose from the menu. *Can Majó*, C/Almirall Aixada 23, T93 221 58 18. Open Tue-Sat 1300-1600 and 2000-2330, Sun 1300-1600, metro Barceloneta. This is one of the best-known seafood restaurants in Barcelona, and specializes in classic Catalan fish dishes – it's a great place to try traditional recipes like *suquet* or the *sarsuela*. It's a favourite among local chefs, and there's an outdoor terrace on the upper level.

Can Ros, C/Almirall Aixada 7, T93 221 45 79. Open daily 1300-1700 and 2000-2400, metro Barceloneta. A well-established Barceloneta favourite, serving good standards like the paella or *arrós negre*. There are also some delicious starters including steamed mussels and clams in tomato sauce. *Set Portes*, Passeig de Isabel II 14, T93 319 30 33. Open daily 1300-0100, metro Barceloneta. A very famous old restaurant, with frilly net curtains, a piano and aproned waiters, the 'Seven Doors' has been dishing up tradi-tional Catalan cuisine since 1836. The clientele is now fairly touristy, but the food retains its excellent reputation, particularly the house speciality, *paella de peix* (sea-food paella). Ask for the shells to be left on the seafood for maximum flavour.

Cheap *Can Ganassa*, Plaça de la Barceloneta 4-6, T93 221 67 39. Open daily excluding Wed 1230-2330 (bar opens 0900 food served from 1230), metro Barceloneta. This is a popu-lar local bar-restaurant overlooking the neighbourhood's central square; the *menú del dia* is good value and there is a selection of tapas and sandwiches too. The house speci-alities are mussels and *torrades* (bread rubbed with tomato and olive oil and smoth-ered with delicious toppings).

Café-bars with food/tapas
▶▶ *Go to page 242 for bars and clubs*

El Lobito, C/Ginebra 9. Open Mon-Sat 1200-1600 and 2100-2400, metro Barceloneta. Another bustling, old-fashioned spot, this has a bar piled high with seafood tapas and is popular with local fishermen. *Can Paixano*, C/Reina Cristina 7, T93 310 08 39. Open 0900-2230, closed Sun, metro Barceloneta. A very popular, endearingly scruffy bar with simple snacks like toasted sandwiches and a good, cheap cava. *El Vaso de Oro*, C/Balboa 6, T93 319 90 98. Open 0900-2400, metro Barceloneta. A long narrow bar where you'll have to fight for a space (standing room only); the tapas are fantastic and they brew their own beer, so the crowds pour in.

Bar Restaurante La Cepa, C/Almirante Cervera, T93 221 80 70. Open 0900-0000, metro Barceloneta. Simple, neighbourhood bar with a couple of tables out on the street serv-ing very decent tapas – good *sardinas a la plancha* (grilled sardines), *pulpo a la gallega* (squid in tomato sauce) and paella. *Menú del dia* at €6.50, including wine, dessert and bread. *Taverna Can Ramonet*, C/Maquinista 17, T93 319 30 64. Open 1000-1600, 2000-2400, closed Aug, metro Barceloneta. This is the oldest tavern in Barceloneta, set in a pretty pink two-storey house covered in flowers – established in 1763, and run since 1963 by the same family. Have a glass of wine from one of the barrels, tapas heaped up on wooden barrels, smart (expensive) seafood restaurant at the back.

Transport

Bus No **45** from Horta to Passeig Marítim, via Hospital Santa Pau, Catedral de la Seu and Port Vell. No **57** from Cornelià to Pg Marítim, via Sarrià, Gran Via, La Rambla, Port Vell and Parc de la Ciutadella.
Taxis Pla del Palau and at the top of the Pg Joan Borbó near Palau del Mar.
Metro Line 4 (yellow) for Barceloneta.

El Litoral

Vila Olímpica

*The Vila Olímpica (Olympic Village) was supposed to be the highlight of the new developments in the run-up to the 1992 Games. But, despite a stunning shore-side site, the involvement of famous architects, plenty of money and even bigger ideas, the project has been a wash-out. This is a dehumanised space – concrete, treeless and overlooked by the monolithic towers of the **Mapfre** insurance offices and the **Hotel des Arts Barcelona**. It's no surprise that no one stops as they scuttle on down to the beaches. The only success story of the Olympic Village is the brash, fun-filled **Port Olímpic** development, which is tacky and neon-lit but good fun in summer. A stroll east towards the beaches of **Bogatell** and **Mar Bella** is worthwhile – it's a little less hectic, and there's a sailing school with DJs out on the beach in the evenings.*

History

Until Barcelona was nominated to host the 1992 Olympic Games, the area between Barceloneta and Poble Nou was a vast conglomeration of docks, abandoned warehouses, tired old factories and miserable slums linked by a grimy railway track. This decidedly unglamorous stretch of land became the site of the city's biggest and most ambitious architectural project: the brand new development of the Vila Olímpica (Olympic Village). The village included housing for 2,000 athletes, a church, offices, service buildings, parks and gardens, a port development and massive regeneration of the seafront and beaches.

El Litoral

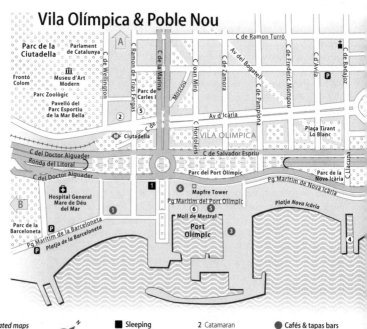

Vila Olímpica & Poble Nou

Related maps
A *La Ribera & Sant Pere, page 88*
B *Port Vell & Barceloneta, page 198*

0 metres 200
0 yards 200

■ **Sleeping**
1 Arts Barcelona

● **Eating**
1 Agua

2 Catamaran
3 El Cangrejo Loco
4 Els Pescadors
5 La Taverna de Cel Ros
6 Lungomare

● **Cafés & tapas bars**
7 El Tio Ché
8 Xiringuito Escribá

The city's finest architects – Oriol Bohigas, Josep Martorell, David Mackay and Albert Puigdomènech – were commissioned for the project: all of them were previous winners of the prestigious FAD architectural awards and, buoyed by the design fervour which flourished in Barcelona during the 1980s, everyone had high hopes. These hopes were echoed in the Olympic Village's other name, *Nova Icària*, named for the idealistic, socialist colony of Icaria which briefly existed here during the 19th century. But, like the doomed Icarians, what Barcelona finally got was a disappointment.

Sights

The Olympic Village is a bland, sterile mini-city of boxy, uninspired buildings, sliced by endless relentless roads which ignore the needs of a pedestrian community. The concrete parks are brutal, and there is barely a café or shop in sight. The apartment buildings were slated to become low-cost housing, until speculators smelt money and sold them off as expensive holiday homes. The supposed '**triumphal arch**' which marks the entrance to the Village on Avinguda d'Icària looks like a giant motorway toll booth, and the tortured metal sculptures which line the street in front are grim, forbidding excuses for trees. Even the soaring towers – one is the fabulously luxurious **Hotel de Arts Barcelona** (see page 261) which wasn't completed until after the Olympic Games and the other, the **Mapfre** tower, is full of offices – can claim only to be the tallest skyscrapers in Spain.

Ciutadella-Vila Olímpica

Most of the parks are cold and ugly, filled with depressingly large sculptures and fountains, too much concrete and not enough trees – even when the beaches are teeming, no one seems to want to escape the crowds in them. A few come to visit the **Parc de Carles I** for the mooning 6-metre-high statue by the Basque sculptor **Eduardo Úrculo**, which has quickly become known as *El Culo de Úrculo* (Úrculo's Arse).

The streets may be empty in the Vila Olímpica, but down at the **Port Olímpic** there's plenty going on. Besides the marina and sailing school (see page 50), there's a massive leisure complex stuffed with cafés, restaurants and shops, which is now one of the most popular nightspots and weekend destinations in the city. Above it flaps **Frank Gehry**'s huge sculpture of a shimmering copper fish.

Continuing along the seafront, just behind the **Platja Nova Icària**, is the nicest of the new parks, the **Plaça Tirant lo Blanc**, named for the bawdy 15th-century satirical novel by Joanot Martorell, a small, circular red-brick space. Between the beaches of **Bogatell** and **Mar**

El Litoral

○ **Entertainment**
1 Garatge Club
2 Icaria Yelmo Cineplex
3 Razzmatazz

○ **Clubs & bars**
4 Base Nàutica de la Mar Bella
5 Luna Mora
6 Pachito

Bella is the **Base Náutica de Mar Bella** (see page 248) where you can hang out and listen to DJs in summer or hire out a boat for the day. It's also the unlikely setting for an outpost of the celebrated *Escribà* confectionery business, the *Xiringuito Escribà*.

Eating and drinking

Mid-range
● *on map, page 206*

Agua, Passeig Marítim 30, T93 225 12 72. Open 1330-1600 and 2030-2430, until 0100 Thu, Fri and Sat, metro Barceloneta. A slick, stylish restaurant with tables overlooking the sea, this is one of the nicest and most romantic beachside spots. It specializes in rice dishes, often with an unusual twist (try the wild rice with greens and ginger) but there are plenty of good meat and fish dishes. *El Cangrejo Loco*, Moll de Gregal 29, T93 221 05 33. Daily 1300-0100, metro Ciutadella-Vila Olímpica. The 'Crazy Crab' was started by the owners of Botafumeiro (see page 151), and offers excellent, very reasonably priced paellas and other seafood dishes. The menú de degustación is a bargain. It's a big, bustling cheerful place on two levels with a terrace right by the shore, but it's always full and you may wait a while for service. *Lungomare*, C/Marina 16-18, T93 221 04 28. Open Mon-Sat 1300-1600 and 2030-2400, Sun 1300-1600, metro Ciutadella-Vila Olímpica. At the base of the Mapfre skyscraper, this is an Italian restaurant with a good selection of tasty meat and pasta dishes – a haven in this neighbourhood if you don't like fish .

Cheap

La Taverna de Cel Ros, Moll de Mestral 26, T93 221 00 33. Open daily excluding Thu 1300-1700 and 2000-2400, metro Ciutadella-Vila Olímpica. A very unpretentious place in the midst of the bustle of the Port Olímpic, this is popular with local sailors and port workers. There's a good value lunch menu too. *Catamaran*, Platja de Bogatell, no tel. Open summer Tue-Sun 1030-0100 , winter Fri-Sun 1200-1600, metro Llacuna or Ciutadella-Vila Olímpica. A beachside *chiringuito/xiringuito* out on the beach at Bogatell, this is a simple, unassuming spot with good tapas and grilled fish at very reasonable prices.

Café-bars
with food/
tapas

Catamaran, Platja de Bogatell, no tel. Summer Tue-Sun 1030-0100, winter Fri-Sun 1200-1600, metro Ciutadella-Vila Olímpica or Llacuna. A *chiringuito* or beach bar serving good, seafood tapas out on the terrace; full meals are served at the back. *Xiringuito Escribà*, Platja de Bogatell, open Tue-Thu 1300-1600 , Fri-Sun 1300-1600 and 2100-2300 in winter, Tue-Sun 1100-0100 in summer, metro Ciutadella-Vila Olímpica or Llacuna. This is a very popular place with a well-deserved reputation for excellence. It is run by the celebrated *Escribà* confectioners, and serves delicious seafood tapas followed by truly mouthwatering desserts. There are some simple full meals – fresh grilled fish or *arròs negre*, a Catalan rice dish made with seafood and cooked in squid ink.

Transport

Bus Most buses in this area run along the Pg Marítim and nearby Carrer Tralawney, and the Avda Icària: **No 10**, from Montbau to Pg Marítim, via Sagrada Família and Vila Olímpica. No **14** from Bonanova to Vila Olímpica, via Gran Via, La Rambla, Monument a Colom and Parc de la Ciutadella.
Metro Line 3 (yellow) Ciutadella-Vila Olímpica.
Taxi It can be hard to get a taxi around here: try outside the Hotel des Arts and near Port Olímpic.

El Litoral

Poble Nou and Diagonal Mar

*The old working-class neighbourhood of Poble Nou, which stretches behind the beaches of **Bogatell** and **Mar Bella**, is an old-fashioned, sleepy neighbourhood with few tourist sights but plenty of eccentric charm. It had a brief flicker of glamour a few years ago when artists and designers moved into the old factories, but many have moved out in the face of rising rents. But, fittingly, for a neighbourhood once known as 'the barri where the people are born old', its most extraordinary sight is the **Cementiri de l'Est**.*

*Diagonal Mar (just where the Diagonal meets the sea) is to become the venue for its loftily titled **Universal Forum of Cultures in 2004** (see page 210). A former slum district, Barcelona city council has decided to focus its regeneration of the neighbourhood. The work is already underway on the site, which will feature landscaped gardens, more beaches, a boating lake, a new location for the city zoo, currently bursting out of its cramped quarters in the Parc de la Ciutadella, and a high-tech business park.*

History

Poble Nou began as a port in the 13th century, but expanded rapidly in the 19th century, when textile mills, factories and workers' housing were thrown up in a flurry of industrial activity. A hotbed of anarchism, socialism and Republicanism from the start, it embraced the idealism of the Icarian community during its brief heyday, but paid heavily for its political leanings after the Civil War. Industries moved out and into the Zona Franca, leaving a forlorn landscape of derelict towers and chimneys. Its fortunes revived briefly during the 1980s and early 1990s, when artists like Javier Mariscal set up their workshops and studios in the abandoned buildings, but many of them have moved out again as the old factories were replaced with anonymous apartment blocks.

Rambla Poble Nou This is a pretty, leafy Rambla, quieter than the one in the city centre, but still lined with some attractive *modernista* homes as well as one of the oldest *orxaterias* in Barcelona, *El Tió Ché* (see page 210) where you can slurp up a refreshing *orxata* or *granizado* in surroundings which have survived virtually unchanged for decades. The neighbourhood's low-key Festa Major is held here in mid-September, when street parties and parades shatter the usual calm.

Plaça Prim One of the most engaging corners of Poble Nou is Plaça Prim, surrounded by the crumbling remnants of old factories, but which still manages to present a white-washed villagey charm, complete with old mulberry trees – and an excellent, very romantic fish restaurant, *Els Pescadors* (see page 210).

Cementiri de l'Est Barcelona's oldest cemetery is crammed with the ornate tombs and mausoleums of the city's grandest 19th-century families. Hidden among the weeping angels, pinnacles and miniature chapels is the burial place of Anselm Clavé, who triggered the fervour for choral societies in the mid-19th century. In the newer section is a pale statue of *El Bes de La Mort* (the Kiss of Death), a drooping marble youth being embraced tenderly by the Grim Reaper, which, bizarrely, won an award for erotic funerary art. Just behind it is the gipsy burial corner, where a life-size statue in a glass box surrounded with red roses commemorates the death of a handsome young gypsy in sunglasses with touching kitsch.

El Litoral

Barcelona presents...

Barcelona, never behind the door when it comes to dressing up and showing off, has decided that its next project is to be the **Universal Forum of Cultures in 2004**. The Universal Exhibition of 1888, the International Exhibition of 1929 and the 1992 Olympics were all used as a means of underpinning grandiose regeneration schemes for the less salubrious sections of the city, and the city's latest scheme for the run-down area of Poble Nou is no different. The Universal Forum of Cultures is set to take place between 23 April (the day of Sant Jordi, Catalunya's patron saint) and 24 September (the feast of La Mercé, the biggest celebration in the city, and aims to promote cultural diversity, world peace and a sustainable urban environment. The glistening modern park which will host the Forum will be partly constructed on reclaimed land and some of the buildings will use solar power, in order to press home the environmental theme, and a Virtual Forum linked with points all over the world will celebrate the spirit of cultural diversity. Parts of the scheme are all ready taking shape – the Feria d'Abril already takes place there – and the neighbourhood is a hive of busy activity.

For more information and to see a model of the scheme, visit the exhibition held at the Ajuntament.

Eating and drinking

Expensive

● *on map, page 206*

Els Pescadores, Placa Prim, T93 225 20 18. Metro Poble Nou. An utterly charming white washed restaurant with a terrace overlooking a pretty square shaded by two huge mulberry trees. It's very much off the beaten track and is surrounded by abandoned buildings, yet that makes the square itself seem almost magical, especially in the evenings. This is one of the city's best known seafood restaurants (although they also offer some delicious vegetarian options), with traditional dishes like *fideuà* (a kind of paella made with noodle rather than rice) and *arròs negre* (rice with seafood cooked in squid ink).

Cafés

Tio Ché, Rambla de Poblenou 44, T93 309 18 72. Summer 1000-0200 and winter Tue-Thu 1000-1300 and 1700-1900, metro Poble nou or Llacuna. A famous old *horchatería* overlooking Poblenou's pretty, tree-lined rambla, where you can cool down with a creamy *horchata* or *granizado*. There's ice-cream and *turron* (a kind of nougat) too.

Transport

Bus Poble Nou is served by relatively few buses, and there is no main hub.
No 6 from Pg Manuel Girona to Poble Nou, via Sarrià, Diagonal, Gran Via, Monumental bull ring and Estació del Nord. **No**36 from Paral.lel to Plaça Congres, via Drassanes, Pla del Palau and Poble Nou. **No** 40 from Trinitat Vella to Port Vell, via Gran Via and Arc de Triomf.
Metro Line 3 (yellow) Bogatell, Llacuna, Poble Nou.
Taxi The main taxi rank in Poble Nou is on the Rambla Prim.

El Litoral

Trips from Barcelona

Trips from Barcelona

214	**North of Barcelona**
214	**The Costa Brava**
215	Cap de Creus
216	Ins and outs
217	**Girona**
219	La Garrotxa
220	**Figueres**
221	Ins and outs
221	**Noguera Palleresa Valley**
222	Ins and outs

223	**West of Barcelona**
223	Montserrat
224	Wine routes
225	Monestir de Santa María de Poblet
226	Ins and outs
227	**South of Barcelona**
227	Sitges
228	Tarragona
230	Ins and outs

Catalunya packs a lot into a small space. Bounded by the Pyrenees to the north and the Mediterranean coast to the east, the Catalan interior veers dramatically from endless wetlands, to sudden volcanic eruptions, or waterfall-studded cliffs.

To the north of the city is the spectacular jagged coastline of the **Costa Brava**. In July and August, the resorts heave and throb but there are places to escape, especially the wild **Cap de Creus** which Dalí made his home. Further north, **Girona**, has a perfectly preserved old quarter and lively nightlife. East of Girona is the hazy, pocked volcanic landscape of the **Garrotxa** region around **Olot**.

Out to the west of Barcelona are the eerie jagged peaks around **Montserrat**, Catalunya's holy mountain. Medieval monasteries dream silently in the quiet wine producing villages of **Poblet** where wine has been produced for millennia.

Just south, Sitges is a fun-loving seaside town which goes wild during Carnival, and the long, sandy beaches of the **Costa Daurada** are lined with some cheerfully tacky resorts. The southern tip of Catalunya is swallowed up by the haunting, flat wetlands of the **Ebre Delta** (Delta de l'Ebre).

If you've got more time, head for the hills. The **Pyrenees** are wilder, craggier, and altogether less civilised. Trek across the hauntingly beautiful National Park of **Aigüestortes**, raft down the powerful **Noguera Palleresa** river, or ski or snowboard at one of a dozen resorts.

Trips from Barcelona

North of Barcelona

The Costa Brava

The Costa Brava, officially runs from **Blanes** *to Portbou on the French border. This appropriately named 'wild coast' was the first of Catalunya's costas to fall for the siren call of mass tourism in the 1950s and 60s, and is now clogged with bumper-to-bumper traffic and over-development. Some towns have escaped the cranes – like* **Tossa de Mar**, *arty, whitewashed* **Cadaqués,** *out at the tip of the windswept* **Cap de Creus**, *and the tiny beaches around* **Palafrugell**.

Blanes & around Blanes is the first of a string of towns devoted to package tourism on a grand scale. Boat services ply the bays between **Calella** and **Palamós** during the summer season and are a good way to avoid the really built-up beaches and towns,for timetable information, contact *Crucetours*, T909766091, or *Viajes Maritimos*, T908936476. Between Blanes and brash, brassy **Lloret de Mar** there's the pretty cove of **Santa Cristina**, with a series of well-marked botanical trails and a lovely old hermitage. It's a steep walk down if you come by road but the summer boat service (see above) will take you there effortlessly. There's a smart hotel and a couple of beachside cafés which are open in summer only.

Tossa de Mar & around
In summer, a glass-bottomed boat makes a tour of the surrounding coves; tourist information www.tossademar. com T972 340 108

Tossa de Mar, hugging a small cove dotted with tiny boats, and overlooked by the ruins of a fortified village, is generally considered the first truly charming town along the Costa Brava. But, even Tossa has succumbed to the big bucks offered by property developers – it's worth squinting to avoid the sight of the dreary new section of the town which has taken over one end of the harbour. The **Villa Vella**, perched on the **Cap de Tossa**, is the only medieval fortified village left standing in Catalunya, with a tumbledown church and several old stone houses contained within an imposing – and astonishingly intact – circle of walls and towers.

Sant Feliú de Guíxols, the next large town up the coast, is a pleasant old port with a long sandy beach and an attractive Passeig Marítim dotted with *modernista* mansions. **Sant Pol** and **S'Agaró** have much nicer beaches than over-developed, neon-lit **Platja d'Aro** and **Palamós**.

Palafrugell
Palafrugell is a lively cork-manufacturing town, with a slew of *modernista* buildings, and a colourful Sunday market. There are bus connections to a handful of fishing villages which have grown into busy resorts squeezed between some pretty coves – **Aigua-xel-lida**, **Tamariu**, **Llafranc** and whitewashed **Calella de Palafrugell**, where you can listen to the *havaneras* (old sea shanties) brought back from Cuba, and try *cremat*, (coffee flambéed with rum). There are great views from the **Sant Sebastià lighthouse**.

Begur & around
Lofty Begur, with its fancy mansions and its old walls studded with grim stone keeps, is set just inland. Just north is the fortified village of **Pals**, with spectacular views across the surrounding countryside and an over-preserved old quarter known as *El Pedró* which has been colonized by snooty second-homers. **Sa Riera** has broad sandy beaches and good views across to the Illes Medes, and delightful little **Sa Tuna** has been saved from package tours because of its remote, pebbly beach.

The small archipelago of the Illes Medes was once a haven for pirates and smugglers; now a marine reserve with a wealth of aquatic creatures living in and around the rare coral. It's now a very popular spot for water sports with several diving companies (*La Sirena*, T972 75 09 54), based in the mainland resort of **L'Estartit**. Contact the tourist office: Passeig Marítim, T972 75 89 10, for further details. This area is the heartland of the **Empordà** region, well known for its fine regional cuisine which often combines meat and seafood in unusual ways – pig trotters stuffed with prawns is a local favourite.

Illes Medes
They are so popular in high season that there are more shoals of divers than fish

Back on the coast, L'Escala is a prosperous resort, popular with Spanish families and renowned for its excellent seafood, which still retains a small fishing fleet. Caterina Albert (1869-1966) lived here for many years; her novel, *Solitude*, which appeared in 1905, under the pen name of Victor Català, scandalized its readers with its daring and frank portrayal of female sexuality.

Close by are the **ancient ruins** of Empúries, founded around 600 BC and possibly the first and certainly one of the most important Greek colonies in Iberia. Many of the artefacts discovered on the site are displayed in the small museum, but most of the important ones have been taken to the Museu d'Arqueològia in Barcelona. ■ *Pedestrian access to the ruins is via the beachfront in high season, from the Figueres road at other times; 1000-2000 in summer, 1000-1900 in winter; €2.40, audio commentary €3.60.*

L' Escala & Empúries

Cap de Creus

The jagged peaks of the Cap de Creus, formed by the final thrust of the Pyrenees, have slopes narrowly ridged with olives, corktrees and pale stone walls which once supported rows of vines. The cape has been designated a natural park and offers a variety of activities from hiking and scuba diving to fishing and bird-watching; artificial platforms have been introduced to try to coax back the ospreys which vanished two decades ago, but there are plenty of other species – more than 200 – of bird life to enjoy. It's a strange region – brooding, insular, and still strewn with forgotten dolmens, shepherds' huts and ancient ruins. From the **Verdera watchtower** at the tip of the peninsula, there are stunning views back over the Cap's twisted rocks, stripped of plants and moulded into surreal shapes by the winds.

Exclusive, arty Cadaqués, right out at the tip of Cap de Creus, was once known as the 'St Tropez of the Costa Brava'. Steep, crooked streets lined with gleaming whitewashed cottages meander down to the bay, and it's stuffed full of smart restaurants, art galleries and craft shops – but all this charm comes with a hefty price tag. There's a classical music festival in the summer, and it's a good base for visiting the natural park (see page below).

Cadaques
The magnificent trans-Pyrenean walking trail, the GR11, begins here

Unsurprisingly, the area's most famous resident, Salvador Dalí, surely the greatest exponent of weirdness ever, was drawn here for many years. His favourite house, long abandoned but now partly refurbished, is in the tiny bay of **Port Lligat**, next to Cadaqués, and can be visited in small groups. The house is a surprise; furnished mainly by Gala, his wife and muse, it is a very private series of simple, whitewashed rooms and terraces linked with stairways. Dalí's house was obviously conceived as a refuge and doesn't even have a spare bedroom. Although the house is relatively simple Dalí did insist that Gala's private boudoir was constructed in the same shape as a sea urchin and the bizarre acoustics mean that even the dullest conversation is given a purring, sensuous edge. The swimming pool is shaped like a keyhole, overlooked

Trips from Barcelona

by surreal artworks, including a statue of the Michelin man, and there's a fat, stuffed boa over the canopied seating area. ■ *Call in advance: T972 25 10 15, open 14 Mar-14 Jun; €7.80, guided tours only.*

At the **Parc Natural Cap de Creus** you can explore remote coves and walking trails, hike, walk, birdwatch, snorkel, scuba-dive and take boat trips. The park information office is at Casa de l'Abat, Monestir de Sant Pere de Rodes, 17489 El Port de la Selva, T972-193191, www.gencat.es/darp, www.cbrava.es/girona

Port de la Selva

Try to visit the monastery in the morning sunshine, it can be cold and gloomy in the afternoon

Around the coast, comfortable whitewashed Port de la Selva is refreshingly humble after haughty Cadaqués. A twisting road winds up and up to the lofty **Monestir de Sant Pere de Rodes**, clamped grimly against the mountainside and often lost in wreaths of mist. This was once a Dominican monastery with lands stretching across the whole peninsula and beyond during the height of its influence in the 13th century. There is some excellent walking to be had around the monastery; a 20-minute scramble up the steep hillside will take you to the solid remnants of the Castle of **Sant Salvadera de Verdera**, commanding the highest peak and offering more breathtaking views.

Ins & outs

Getting there There are regular trains to **Blanes** and **Figueres** from Barcelona. *SARFA* buses, T93 265 11 98 run from the bus station in Figueres to most coastal destinations along the **Costa Brava**. They also run connecting services from **Palafrugell** to the surrounding villages. *Barcelona Bus*, T93 232 04 59, runs regular services from Barcelona to **Figueres**, and *SARFA* buses run direct services from Barcelona to **Cadaqués**. There are local buses from **Blanes** to **Tossa de Mar** and **Lloret de Mar**, but note that you will have to get the bus from the train station, 2 km outside Blanes, into the centre of town.

Sleeping

For hotel price categories, see inside cover

D-E *Planamar*, Paseo del Mar 82, La Platja d'Aro hotelplanamar@yahoo.com, T972 81 71 77. Right on the beach with good facilities for watersports, plus a pool and gym. **E** *La Marina*, C/Ciutat de Palol 2, La Platja d'Aro, T972 81 71 82. Good facilities including a pool. **E** *Hotel les Illes*, C/Illes 55, L'Estartit, T97 275 12 39, F972 75 00 86. Modern hotel near the port; geared towards divers. **E** *El Roser*, Plaça Església 7, L'Escala, T972 77 02 19, F972 77 34 98, rosaescala@teleline.es Attractive, old-fashioned hotel with a popular restaurant. **E** *Hotel Rosa*, S Pedro Martin 42, Blanes, T97 233 04 80. Modern hotel not far from the beach with a pool. **F** *Moré*, C/Sant Elm 9, Tossa de Mar, T972 34 03 39. Basic but cheap. **F** *Fonda L'Estrella*, C/de les Quatre Cases 13, near Plaça Nova, Palafrugell, T/F972 30 00 05. Charming, simple rooms around a courtyard. **F** *Pensión Vehi*, C/Església 5, Cadaqués T972 25 84 70. Just four basic rooms – the cheapest place to stay in town.

Eating & drinking

Expensive *Carles Camós – Big Rock* Barri de Fanals 5, Platja d'Aro, T972 81 80 12. Closed Sun nights, Mon and Jan. This is a splendid restaurant with a big reputation set in a rural farmhouse. If you can't make it home after a big blow out, there are five large rooms and a swimming pool. *Cala Montjol*, Roses T972 15 04 57. Closed Mon and Tue except in summer. One of the most celebrated restaurants in Spain, with a magnificent setting looking out over the Mediterranean.

Mid-range *Casa Nun* Passeig Marítim, Cadaqués. This is a tiny, charming little fish restaurant run by a fisherman and his family, with tiled walls hung with local watercolours and a kitchen sandwiched between two dining rooms. The food is fresh, imaginative and informally served. It's worth going à la carte to try the fish caught that morning, but there is a *menú del dia* at around €15. *Can Flores II*, Esplanada del Port s/n, Blanes, T97 233 26 33. Good, cheerful fish restaurant overlooking the port. *Can Toni*, Carrer Garrofers 54, Sant Feliu de Guixols, T97 232 10 26. Cheery, traditional restaurant serving local delicacies – try the dishes with *bolets* (wild mushrooms) when in season.

Cheap *Fonda Caner*, Carrer Pi iRalló 14, Bégur, T97 262 23 91. A great place to try local Empurdan specialities – local game like rabbits and partridge, as well as snails and the dishes made from rice grown in the area.

Girona

Girona, Catalunya's second city and Spain's richest, sprawls languidly around the confluence of the Rivers Ter and Onyar, 36 km inland from the Costa Brava. The expansive modern city, with its leafy avenues lined with galleries and a hand-ful of modernista *mansions, lies on the west side of the Onyar; on its eastern bank is the shadowy huddle of the ancient city which grew up around an early Iberian settlement. A ribbon of ochre-painted houses, once attached to the city walls, hang over the river and behind them lies a medieval web of crooked alleys and narrow passages built on top of the Roman colony.*

A long-established **university town***, the big student population adds some zip to the city's nightlife and the arcaded streets and the placid squares of the old city are lined with trendy shops, bars and restaurants. Girona's main sights are the lofty, central* **cathedral** *with the* **Banyes Àrabes** *(Arabic baths) below, the* **Església de Sant Feliu** *and the rewarding* **Archaeological Museum***. Within easy reach of Girona are the poised and well-preserved towns of* **Besalú** *and* **Banyoles***. Heading west of Besalú is the countryside region known as* **La Garrotxa***, pocked with the grassy crates of long-extinct volcanoes.*

During the Middle Ages Girona was home to a large and influential Jewish community, who established an important school of Jewish mysticism, the *Cabalistas de Girona*, during the 12th and 13th centuries. The undisputed master of the Cabala was Moses Ben Nahman, or Nahmanides, who was born in Girona in 1194 and became the Grand Rabbi of Catalunya. As the community grew, so did local resentment which bubbled up periodically into outright violence: in 1391, a mob tore through the Call and slaughtered forty inhabitants. The Jurats stepped in and maliciously imprisoned all the Jews in the old Roman fortress. The Call was gradually sealed off and became a ghetto; Jews were forced to wear identifying clothing, and city residents were prohibited from renting them houses or market stalls in any of the streets surrounding the quarter. Anti-semitism was on the rise throughout Spain and finally, in 1492, the Jews were expelled from the country.

History

Trips from Barcelona

Just off the Carrer de la Força, the Centra Bonastruc Ça Porta, built on the old Synagogue of Girona is being painstakingly restored. It houses an institute of Jewish learning, as well as the fascinating new **Museo de los Judeos en Catalunya** which describes the development of the Jewish community from the first mention of El Call in 898, and offers an interesting insight into the beliefs and practices of the Cabalistas. ■ *May 15-Nov 14 Mon-Sat 1000-2100, until 1800 in winter, Sun and holidays 1000-1400.* €*3.32, T97 221 67 61.*

Centra Bonastruc Ça Porta
A combined ticket which allows entrance to all of Girona's museums is available for 4.80 euros

Further up the city's History Museum is housed in a sturdy 18th-century mansion. The most gruesome sight is the **Capuchin Cemetery**; the Capuchins dissected the bodies of dead monks on perforated benches and buried them in vertical tombs. ■ *Tue-Sat 1000-1400 and 1700-1900, Sun 1000-1400.* €*1.66.*

Museu d'Història de la Ciutat

Plaça de la Catedral & around Just beyond the History Museum, flanked by the 18th-century **Casa Pastors** (law courts) and the imposing Gothic **Pia Almoina** (almshouse), the street opens up to the lovely Plaça de la Catedral where a broad flight of steps sweep up to the imposing cathedral. It's one of the grandest in Catalunya, with an elaborate Baroque façade topped with a frilly belltower. The present **Catedral** was begun in 1312, but a century later Guillem Bofill added a single, daring nave in defiance of a committee of architects who swore it wouldn't work; it's the largest in Europe, with an audacious 23-m span. The delicate Romanesque **cloister** with its charming carved capitals was left over from the previous cathedral which occupied the spot, as is the Romanesque belltower, the **Torre de Carlemany**, which was incorporated into the new construction as a buttress. The **Museu Capitular** holds a fine collection of religious art, including a powerful 12th-century tapestry depicting the Creation, and the *Còdex del Beatus*, exquisitely illuminated by Mozerabic miniaturists during the 10th-century.

The former **Episcopal Palace**, tucked behind the cathedral, now houses Girona's **Museu d'Art**, an eclectic collection of painting, sculpture, furniture, glass and gold and silver-work from the Visigothic period until the 19th century, displayed in cavernous vaulted halls. There are two notable Gothic retablos, including a particularly fine piece from **Bernat Martorell**, and paintings from **Joaquim Vayreda** of the Olot School and the bohemian dandy, **Santiago Rusiñol**. ■ *Daily except Mon, Jun-Sept 1000-1900, Oct-May 1000-1300 and 1500-1800.* €1.80.

Below the cathedral is the **Portal de Sobreportes**, the ancient Roman entrance to the city, and the final exit for condemned prisoners who went to their deaths in the square beyond. To the left stands the **Església de Sant Feliu**, which was built over an old Christian cemetery, and where legend has it that the city's martyred patron saint, Sant Narcìs, met a sticky end. The Gothic belltower had its spire blasted off by a bolt of lightning in 1581, but still manages to poke its head above the red-tiled rooftops.

Behind the church are the **Banys Àrabs** (Roman baths) which were built on a Roman model, perhaps by Moorish craftsmen, in the 13th century. The loveliest area is the *frigidarium* (cold water pool), which is subtly illuminated by a skylight supported by a ring of slim columns. ■ *Apr-Sep Tue-Sat 1000-1900, Sun 1000-1400, Oct-Mar Tue-Sun 1000-1400.* €1.20.

Monestir de Sant Pere de Galligants Girona's main street, Carrer del Pujada Rei Marti, leads from the Plaça de la Catedral across the Riu Galligans – a small tributary of the Onyar, to the Monestir de Sant Pere de Galligants, a sober 12th-century monastery which now houses the **Museu d'Arqueològia de Catalunya**. The holdings date from the Paleolithic to the medieval period, attractively displayed in the former church. Out in the pretty **cloister** are medieval relics, including more than a dozen Hebraic funerary stones. From here, you can climb up to the **Passeig Arqueològic** for a panoramic stroll across the top of the old city walls (daily 1000-2000) with sweeping views out across the rooftops and the Ter valley. ■ *Museum: Jun-Sep Tue-Sat 1030-1330, 1600-1900; Oct-May 1000-1400, 1600-1800.* €1.80.

Banyoles & Besalu The small quiet town of Banyoles, 18 km north of Girona, sits peacefully beside a placid lake full of plump carp. It was chosen to host the rowing competitions during the 1992 Olympics, sparking a host of new developments along the lake side. The new areas are not especially attractive – although you can hire a boat, take a cruise, or potter about in a pedalo – but the old city has remained largely unspoilt, and there is some pleasant walking around the lake to pretty villages. The hub of the old town (Vila Vella) is the arcaded **Plaça Major**, an agreeable leafy square with plenty of cafés, where a lively local market has been held on Wednesdays for almost 1,000 years.

Besalú, another 14 km north of Banyoles, is a perfectly preserved medieval town with a handsome 11th-century bridge complete with fortified gatehouse; so artful are its immaculate cobbled streets, lined with impossibly picturesque houses, that it looks suspiciously like a stage set. Medieval squares are overlooked by Romanesque churches like the handsome 11th-century **Monestir de Sant Pere**, and the more elaborate 12th-century **Església of Sant Vicenç**, which overlooks a flower-filled square.

La Garrotxa

West of Besalú, the countryside of the region known as La Garrotxa has been designated a natural park, **Parc Natural de la Zona Volcanical de la Garrotxa**. You can visit extinct volcanic craters, beech forest, medieval villages like **Sant Pau**, bird watch and go on nature trails. Medieval **Olot**, the region's main town was flattened by a volcano in the 15th century. You can relive it in the excellent little audio-visual presentation at the park information office, set in a tranquil mansion in a pretty duck-filled **Jardí Botànic** (botanical park) on the edge of Olot. ■ *Avinguda Santa Coloma s/n, 17800 Olot, T972 266 202, www.gencat.mediamb/pn The office has plenty of maps and information on the lovely walking trails which criss-cross the park.*

Garrotxa regional information office, T902 119 337, www.agtat.es

Olot is a surprisingly vibrant little city lined with handsome townhouses from the 18th and 19th centuries. The surrounding, hazy landscape of forested, misty cliffs rising up from lush grasslands edged with neat stone walls inspired the 19th-century artists of the *Olot School*, and you can check out their work at the excellent **Museu Comarcal de la Garrotxa** . The founder of the movement was Joaquim Vayreda i Vila (1843-94), who painted lyrical landscapes suffused with a soft green light and developed an important following of painters and sculptors. The collection is not entirely restricted to the works of the *Olot School*; one of the most dramatic paintings here is **Ramon Casas'** powerful *La Carga* (The Charge, 1899). ■ *Daily except Tue 1100-1400, 1600-1900, Sun 1100-1400. €1.80.*

Olot
This town was an inspiration to the 19th-century painters, and still celebrated for the local food

Getting there Girona is very well served by buses and trains from Barcelona; trains leave regularly from Sants and Pg de Gràcia, or take the *Barcelona Bus*, T93 232 04 59, from Estació del Nord. **Olot** and **Besalú** are linked by regular direct buses from Barcelona with *Garrotxa Exprés*, T90 217 71 78, and *TEISA*, T97 220 48 68, runs services from the corner of C/Pau Claris and C/Consell de Cent for **Girona**, **Besalú** and **Olot,** with more regular services from Girona.

Ins & outs

C *Mas Salvanera*, s/n, Mas Salvanera, Beuda (8 km from Besalú), T972 59 09 75, F59 08 63, www. salvanera.com The perfect place to get away from it all – a lovely 17th-century stone farmhouse on a sunny hillside with just eight thoughtfully decorated rooms and a pool. **C-D** *Mirallac*, Paseo Darder 50, Banyoles, T972 57 10 45, hrmirallac@terra.es Right on the lake with large bright rooms and a pool. More expensive in summer.
   E *Hotel Peninsular*, C/Nou 3, GironaT972 20 38 00. After a recent makeover, this has become a delightful place to stay with light, airy rooms and great rooftop views. **E** *Pensión Bellmirall*, C/Bellmirall 3, Girona, T97 220 40 09. Charming little pensión with friendly owners in the heart of the old city. **E** *Fonda Comas*, C/Canal 19, Besalú, T972 57 01 27. Nicely located in the old town with a homely, cheap restaurant

Sleeping
For sleeping price codes, see inside cover

Trips from Barcelona

downstairs. **E** *Siqués*, Av. President Companys 6-8, Besalú, T972 59 01 10, F972 59 0110. Large, traditional stone guesthouse with a pool and an excellent local restaurant. **E** *Les Turros*, Gloria Mota, Argelaguer (7 km from Besalú), T97 268 73 50. Lost in the middle of a forest, this is a wonderful, simple little refuge with just four rooms; sit around an old wood burning stove, and enjoy a home-cooked dinner cooked by the charming owner. Price includes dinner.

F *Pensión Narmar*, C/Sant Roc 1, Olot, T972 26 98 07. Spotless budget rooms in the centre of town, with a good cheap restaurant and pâtisserie downstairs. **F** *Albergue Juvenil*, C/Ciutadans 9, Girona. T972 21 80 03. Well-equipped youth hostel in the old town.

Eating & drinking
Many fondas (guesthouses) and hotels (see above) have good, traditional restaurants offering tasty local dishes

Mid-range   *Celler de Can Roca*, Ctra Taialà 40, Girona, T97 222 21 57. You wouldn't think so from the outside, but this is one of the finest restaurants in Catalunya, and a great place for a treat. *Quatre Estacions*, Paseo de la Farga s/n, Banyoles, T97 257 33 00. Excellent local cuisine using the freshest local produce. They've got a great range of local liqueurs as well. *Les Cols*, Ctra de la Canya s/n, Olot, T97 226 92 09. Delightful restaurant in a traditional stone *mas*, with a menu based on the excellent regional produce.

Cheap   *Cipresaia*, C/General Fournas 2, Girona. T97 222 24 49. Fashionable, arty hang-out with decent food. *Pont Vell*, C/Pont Vell 28, Besalú, T97 259 10 27. Set in a medieval house overlooking the old bridge, this restaurant serves dishes based on recipes which date back to the middle ages. *La Terra*, C/Bonaire 22, Olot, T97 227 41 51. This friendly veggie restaurant is a welcome surprise. Open lunchtimes only. *Can Ginabreda*, C/ de Mieres, Porqueres. T97 257 49 62. Changing exhibitions by local artists, and tasty regional cuisine in this friendly little spot on the edge of a forest.

Figueres

The rugged landscape north of Figueres forms part of La Albera, the easternmost Pyrenean range, a wild and sparsely populated region scattered with dolmens and menhirs. Once you get past the ugly industrial sprawl on the outskirts, Figueres is a likeable, down-to-earth provincial town which would be entirely unremarkable but for its most famous son: Salvador Dalì, whose bizarre **Teatre-Museu Dalí** *strikes a flamboyant pose in the centre of the city. Catalans have always suspected that the Tramontana wind which rages through the city has affected the Figuerans in the head, but Dalí was undoubtedly the battiest of them all.*

Teatre-Museu Dalí
Dalí considered Figueres the 'spiritual centre of the world'

The Teatre-Museu is topped with a huge glass-latticed dome like a fly's eyeball, and surrounded with giant boiled eggs and leaping androgynous figures; the walls are covered in squidgy protuberances, which, from a man who had a special toilet installed in order to better inspect his excrement and then wrote a book about it, can only be turds. His scatological obsessions have their roots in the earthy Catalan culture which puts a *Cagoner* (Crapper) just downwind of the manger in the traditional Nativity scene which decorates good Catalan homes at Christmas.

Inside, the museum contorts itself around a central courtyard strewn with old bones and skulls, in which a naked singing diva sprouts out of a Cadillac with a snake and a thorny rose; rooms and passages lead off into unexpected dead ends, and recesses hold classical statues with drawers for stomachs, or a velvet curtain providing a lush backdrop to an old fish skeleton. ■ *Daily Jul-Sep 0900-1915 and 2230-0030 in Aug; Oct-Jun Tue-Sun 1030-1715 Jul-Sep €7.20. Oct-Jun €6. www.salvador-dali.org*

Dalí, Diary of a Genius

"I dream of two gentlemen. One is naked and the other is naked too. They are going towards two completely symmetrical streets. Each horse, with the same leg raised at the same time, goes into its respective street, but one street is full of light shining of objectivity, and the other one is limpid like in The Betrothal of the *Virgin by Raphael and its background is even more crystalline. Suddenly, one of the streets is submerged by a confusing fog which becomes thicker and thicker until it forms an impenetrable, lead-like abyss. Both gentlemen are Dalí. One gentleman is the Dalí of Gala. The other one is a Dalí who would never have met her."*

The third point of the so-called Dalí Triangle (Triangle Dalinià) is the 12th-century Castell de Púbol, that Dali gave to his wife and muse Gala, who would frolic here with her young lovers and demand that her husband made appointments to see her. The castle houses a collection of the paintings and drawings which Dalí gave Gala to decorate it, and there's a selection of Gala's haute couture finery upstairs. ■ *The castle is situated 22 km southeast of Figueres, T97 248 86 55; 15 Mar-1 Nov, group visits are accepted during the rest of the year with prior notice; 15 Mar-14 Jun and 16 Sep-1 Nov open 1030-1715; 15 Jun-15 Sep 1030-1915.*

Castell de Púbol
The lovely gardens are filled with elephant sculptures, more gifts from Dalí to his wife

Getting there   There are regular trains to **Figueres** from Sants and Pg de Gràcia. *Barcelona Bus* (T93 232 04 59) run direct service to Figueres. Figueres **tourist information**, T97 2 50 31 55.

Ins & outs

C *Mas Pau*, Avinyonet de Puigventós. Ctra de Figueras a Besalú Km 4, T97 254 61 54, F97 254 63 26, maspau@grn.es   Wonderful four-star comfort in a converted 17th-century stone farmhouse, with lovely gardens and a pool. **C-D** *Hotel Durán*, C/Lasauca 5, Figueres. T972 50 12 50, duran@hotelduran.com   A classic Empordan hotel with an exceptionally good restaurant specializing in regional cuisine.
   D-E *Hotel Empordà*, Cra N-II, Figueres. Km 763, T972 500 562, F972 509 358, hotelemporda@hotelemporda.com Lots of chintz and dowdy décor in the rooms, but it's the restaurant that draws the crowds; one of the very best in Catalunya. **D-E** *España*, C/Junquera 26, Figueres. T972 50 08 69. Comfortable, friendly pensión a little out of the centre with an old-fashioned restaurant serving good local dishes.

Sleeping

Some of the hotels listed have good restaurants. **Cheap** *La Dita*, C/Muralla 7, Figueres. T97 251 11 20. Good vegetarian and Italian dishes and a *menú del dia* at €7.80. *Presidente*, C/Ronda Firal 33, Figueres, T97 250 17 00. Delicious local and French food.

Eating & drinking

Trips from Barcelona

Noguera Palleresa Valley

If you have the time to take a slightly longer trek to the north-western fringes of Catalunya, the Pyrenees are studded with steep valleys, timeless stone villages of slate-roofed houses and powerful rivers: the most powerful of them all is the Noguera Palleresa, which has become a paradise for rafting and adventure sports. The biggest centre for these activities is **Sort**, *surrounded by the ski resorts of* **Espot**, *which is the western gateway to the preternaturally beautiful* **Parc Nacional d'Aigüestortes i Estany de Maurici**.

Sort

For details of all tour operators, call the tourist information office, T973 62 11 30

The streets of Sort are lined with tour-operators and outdoor shops, offering an incredible array of activities in the surrounding canyons and valleys. Every year in late June or early July, there's a festival of *Raiers* (Rafters) who scud down the river on simple rafts made of lashed-together branches just as the old timber pilots used to do. 'Sort' means luck, and the locals seem to have it in spades – the town has produced a suspiciously high number of lottery winners. Northeast of Sort is the ski resort of **Port-Ainé,** a smallish ski station which has a good range of pistes. Further up the valley, there's another ski resort at **Super Espot**, above the small village of Espot.

Parc Nacional d'Aigüestortes i Estany de Maurici

Call the park information office, T973 696 189, or check www.gencat. mediamb/pn/cparcs

This is Catalunya's only national park, a spellbinding, forbidding landscape of lush meadows flecked with scores of crystal-clear lakes and surrounded by jagged, forested peaks. There are hikes for walkers of all fitness levels, and it's also an excellent destination for serious climbers; the park information offices are usually staffed with full-time wardens during the summer, and it is worth calling in advance to ensure a place. Jeep taxis will drop you off at the park boundaries, or you can avoid the road and walk along the GR11, where you can make the short stroll to the **Estany de Maurici**, a still, clear lake of hallucinatory beauty, looked over by the strange stone eruptions of **Els Encantats** (The Enchanted Ones). Legend has it that two hunters and their dog sneaked off one Sunday morning instead of attending mass; they were lured deeper into the mountains by an elusive stag when a bolt of lightning shot down from the heavens and turned them into stone. For experienced walkers, there's a spectacular trek, about 10 hours from **Espot to Boí**, right through the park from east to west. Close to the park there are three major ski resorts (at **Super Espot, Boí-Taüll** and **Baquèira-Beret** – another is planned for the **Sallente** area near **Capdella**) and whitewater rafting at **Sort**.

Vall d'Aran

Tourist information, T973 64 01 10, www.valldaran.com

The road (C-142) continues its tranquil journey along the Noguera Pallaresa Valley and then begins to climb up to the dizzying pass of the **Port de la Bonanaigua,** which at more than 2000 m, is one of the most spectacular in the Pyrenees. This is the beginning of the verdant Vall d'Aran, the only Atlantic valley in the eastern Pyrenees, it has preserved a distinctly French character audible in the local language, *Aranès*, a mixture of Gascon French, Catalan and even the odd Basque word thrown in for good measure.

Just beyond the Port de la Bonanaigua is the ultra-chic ski resort of **Baquèira-Beret**, where the Spanish royal family like to belt down the pristine slopes. The downhill skiing is best for intermediate and advanced skiers. For information call T973 639 010.

The capital of the Vall d'Aran is **Vielha**, a lively mountain town bursting with distinctive Aranese stone houses, with their stepped gables, slate roofs, and carved wooden balconies. It's becoming increasingly smart, thanks to the droves of French visitors who have triggered a spate of fashionable shops, galleries and restaurants crammed along the medieval streets.

Ins & outs

Getting there For Parc Nacional d' Aigüestortes, take a bus from **Barcelona** or **Lleida** to **Espot** with *Alsina Graells*, T973 268 500. You'll have to walk the last 7 km from the main highway to the village, or you can wait for a jeep taxi (2.60 one way). There are two early buses to **Vielha**, one travelling via **Sort**, from the Estació del Nord with *Alsina Graells* T93 265 68 66.

Sleeping

For sleeping price codes see inside cover

D *Pessets*, C/Diputación 3, Sort, T973 62 00 00, F973 62 08 19. There's nowhere cheap to stay in town, but this functional modern hotel has nice views, a decent restaurant and good facilities including a pool and tennis. **D** *Besiberri*, C/El Fuerte 4, Artíes T973

64 08 29. A chalet-style hotel by a stream with delightful owners; delicious breakfasts. **E** *Roya*, Ctra Parc Nacional s/n, Espot T973 62 40 40. Unassuming hotel with an excellent restaurant. **E** *Ctra Puerto de la Bonanaigua*, km 114, Valencía d'Aneu, T973 62 61 24, F973 62 61 07. Friendly, family-run mountain hotel with pool in a charming, unspoiled town. **E-F** *Vielha Casa Vicenta*, C/Reiau 7, T973 64 08 19. Charming little pensión; rooms without bathrooms are cheaper.

Expensive *Casa Irene*, C/Mayor 3, Artíes, T973 64 43 64. One of the finest restaurants in the whole region, run by the charismatic Irene España, and well worth a splurge. **Cheap** *Fogony*, Av Generalitat 45, Sort, T973 62 12 25. A haven for gastronomes, this offers elegant cuisine at surprisingly modest prices. *Pensió La Palmira*, C/Marineta s/n, Espot T973 62 40 72. A well priced *menú del día*. *Roya*, Ctra Parc Nacional s/n, T973 62 40 40. The best dining experience in Espot is to be had at this understated hotel restaurant. *Nicolas*, C/Castèth 10, Vielha, T973 64 18 20. Delicious local specialities and rustic decor.

Eating & drinking

West of Barcelona

Fifty kilometres northwest of Barcelona, on the plain of Les Vallès, nothing impedes the view of the jagged pinnacles of the massif of **Montserrat**. *Gazing serenely over the whizzing highways, they are so romantically out of place that it's hard not to believe that someone didn't paint them in. Less than an hour's train ride west of Barcelona, lie a string of tumbledown wine-producing villages, hidden in hilly folds. Catalan cava, the home-grown bubbly, is mostly produced in the valleys of the* **Alt Penedès** *region. The* **Monestir de Poblet** *is surrounded by beautiful forest and was once the richest and most powerful religious house in Catalunya.*

Montserrat

The monastery vied with Santiago de Compostela as a place of pilgrimage during the Middle Ages, and floods of pilgrims still pour in to touch the sacred **La Moreneta**, the miraculous polychrome wooden statue of the Black Virgin and Child which presides over the altar of the gloomy basilica. Legend has it that it was originally carved by St Luke and that St Peter later hid the statue in a cave, where it was discovered by shepherds in 880. The biggest pilgrimage takes place on 27 April and there's another on 8 September. The *Escolania*, a children's choir which is one of the oldest in Europe, sing daily at 0100 and 1910 in the basilica.

Gaudí's designs for the Sagrada Família were inspired by the peculiar silhouette of the pinnacles of the massif

The monastery also has a museum divided into three sections, which displays a dull collection of Catalan art from the 19th and 20th centuries, a more interesting selection of Spanish, Flemish and Italian Old Masters, and a collection of archaeological treasures from Mesopotamia, Egypt and Palestine. An audio-visual display offers an interesting glimpse of the daily life of the community of monks who still live here. The bus-loads of tourists, jostling crowds, souvenir stalls, and the 1960s cafeteria have largely stripped the area around the monastery of any sense of spirituality or contemplation, but if you head out into the surrounding natural park it doesn't take long to lose the crowds.

There are two funiculars: the funicular Sant Joan heads up to the top of the massif for spectacular views, and another (often out of service), drops down to the tiny chapel of **Santa Cova**, built to celebrate the discovery of La Moreneta. Trails of various lengths and difficulties lead from both of them and wind across the park. One trail leads to each of the romantically abandoned 13 hermitages

For information, check out www.abadia montserrat.net

Trips from Barcelona

The Wines of Catalunya

Catalunya has been making wine since the 5th century BC. The Romans thought of it as plonk (although it was swigged in all corners of their empire) and it took almost two thousand years for its reputation to improve. Now, Catalunya is one of the most up-and-coming wine-producing areas in Spain, with a very wide variety of red, white and rosé wines. But of course it's best known for the sparkling wine, cava, produced locally by the méthode champenoise.

Wine areas

There are eight demarcated areas in Catalonia assigned a Denominació d'Origen *(D.O.)* and administered by Catalonia's own Institute of Wine – INCAVI. Each area has a Consejo Regulador *which* controls different elements such as the grape varietals permitted and the manufacturing processes for the different wines, along the lines of the French AC and the Italian DOC systems. In Catalonia the areas are: Empordà – Costa Brava, Alella, Pla del Bages, Penedès, Tarragona, Conca de Barberà, Costers del Segre, Priorat and Terra Alta, plus a D.O. Cava. The latter functions in much the same way as the sub-regional denominations, but is not tied to a single geographical area.

There are eight main wine-growing areas which have been designated as Denominació d'Origen, *like the French and Italian models, each producing distinctive wines. The Alella region makes mostly very good dry and sweet whites but also some delicious red wines; the Conca de Barberà region produces excellent cava and whites; the producers of the Ampurdán on the Costa Brava make simple reds and rosés; the area of Costers del Segre produces red, rosé, whites and cavas; Tarragona produces a range of wines, both red and white as well as Paxarete, a very sweet traditional chocolatey-brown wine. The wines of the Priorato D.O. are unusual and pricey, reflecting the difficulty of cultivating the hilly land, and the wine of the Terra Alta is usually light and fresh. Undoubtedly the most famous wines come from Penedés, which is the largest and the most important wine area in Catalunya, and include the vast range of wines made by the enterprising Torres family.*

and chapels which are scattered around the mountain. Experienced rock climbers can tackle some of the sheer cliffs. ■ *Museum: summer 1000-1900; winter 0900-1800. Contact the tourist information office for natural park details, Plaça de la Creu s/n, T937 777 777 ext 7586.*

Wine routes

Villafranca de Penedès
For wine tour information, contact the tourist office on Carrer Cort 14, T93 892 03 58

Well over half the land of the Alt Penedès region is given over to cava production, and vines snake trimly across the hills as far as the eye can see. The main centre for cava production is **Sant Sadurní d'Anoia**, where the two giants of the cava world, *Freixenet* and *Codorniú*, have flung open their swirling *modernista* doors for tours. (Visit the tourist office for a complete list of wineries who offer tastings and tours). In the small hamlets surrounding Villafranca de Penedès, still wines are produced, including the excellent range from the indegatigable *Torres* family. There's a delightfully eccentric wine museum, the **Museu del Vi**, set in a Gothic palace, which gives an overview of the history of wine-making in the area, with old-fashioned dioramas, lumbering ancient equipment, racks and racks of *porróns* (Catalan wine jugs), and a queasy collection of local art and stuffed birds. At the end of the visit, head for the recreated *bodega* downstairs to try a couple of the local wines, which should put you in the mood for lunch. ■ *Oct-May 1000-1400 and 1600-1900, Sun 1000-1400; Jun-Sep, Tue-Sat 0900-2100, closed Mon. €2.40, including a small tasting.*

Heading south, the motorway thunders down towards Tarragona, and on to the wine lands of El Priorat. **Reus**, a few kilometres west of Tarragona, is a very handsome city bursting with *modernista* mansions, many of which were designed by Domènech i Montaner. These villages are hidden in the folds of steep hillsides thickly laced with vines that produce some notoriously strong wines. The largest of the wine-producing towns of Priorat is **Falset**, which has a swirling *modernista* bodega by César Martinell, one of Gaudí's acolytes, which is known as the 'Catedral del Vino', and the ruins of an ancient castle. ■ *For information call T977 82 70 06. Oct-May Tue-Sat 1000-1330 and 1500-1730; Jun-Sep Tue-Sat 1000-1330 and 1600-1930, Sun 1000-1330. €1.80.*

El Priorat
Tourist information,
Reus: T977 34 59 43,
www.reus.net
Falset: T977 83 10 23,
www.priorat.org

Monestir de Santa María de Poblet

On the outskirts of the small village of Poblet is the magnificent Monestir de Santa María de Poblet, founded in 1151 by Ramon Berenguer III in gratitude for the success of his campaign to rid Catalunya of the Moorish invaders.

It became the first and most important of three sister monasteries known as the **Cistercian Triangle**, imposing reminders of the power of Christianity and the sovereign. It was a favourite retreat and resting place of a long line of count-kings, many of whom were buried here; Alfonso II was the first, as early as 1196, but the monastery was officially declared a Royal Pantheon in the 14th century.

Poblet, 70 km west of Vilafranca de Penedès, was named for the line of populars which run along the river

Thanks to the munificence of the kings, Poblet became the richest and most influential monastery of Catalunya – but all the wealth led inevitably to corruption and, by the late Middle Ages, Poblet had become a byword for scandal and dissipation on a spectacular scale. It was destroyed in the early 1800s when the church was stripped of its property under the Mendizabel laws. The ruins mouldered for decades, but became a haunting symbol of an empire lost to the romantic innocents of the late 19th century. Gaudí was one of many who dreamed of its reconstruction, which was finally carried out after the Civil War.

The monastery is spectacularly set in a tranquil, golden valley, a vast complex sprawling behind glowering battlements and fortifications. A community of monks now live here, and one of them will guide you around the monastery's stirring collection of beautifully renovated buildings; at the heart of the complex is the peaceful Romanesque **cloister**, rimmed with delicate arcades and the stone tombs of long-forgotten monks, and containing an octagonal pavilion with a huge stone fountain. Leading off the cloister is an echoing, vaulted Gothic chapter house, the library with its brick parabolic arches which must have inspired Gaudí, an enormous wine cellar, the old kitchens lined with copper pots and pans, and the austere wood-panelled refectory.

The glorious main church is austerely unadorned in the Cistercian tradition; apart from a tremendous Renaissance alabaster retablo which fills the apse behind the main altar. But the prize here is the collection of royal tombs exquisitely wrought in alabaster which flank the altar; they were desecrated by the rampaging mob in 1835, but Frederic Marès, the eccentric sculptor and obsessive collector (see page 73), was responsible for their reconstruction in 1950.

■ *Mar-Sep Mon-Fri 1000-1230 and 1500-1800; Oct-Feb daily 1000-1230 and 1500-1730. €3, guided tour only.*

A few miles away is Montblanc, an enchanting medieval town completely encircled by sturdy turreted walls which time – and tourists – seem to have passed by. Montblanc prospered during the Middle Ages, when it had a substantial Jewish community who lived in the tangle of streets between the lovely

Montblanc

Gothic **Església de Santa Maria** and the humble little Romanesque **Església de Sant Miquel** lower down the hill. The best time to come is during the *Setmana Medieval* which kicks off on the feast day of Sant Jordí (23 April), and is an exuberant week-long festival of medieval song and dance. The **Plaça Major** is pretty and always animated, particularly for the evening *paseo*, when families gather at the lively cafés spilling out onto the square. The **Museu Frederic Marès**; holds a typically eccentric selection of painting and sculpture from the 13th to the 19th centuries, including some beautiful carved polychrome statues from the 14th century. ■ *Jun-Sep: Tue-Sat 1000-1500 and 1600-2000, Sun 1000-1400; Oct-May, Sat and Sun only. Free.*

Ins & outs

Getting there From Barcelona, there's a daily *Julià* bus, T93 490 40 00, to **Montserrat**, but the train-cable car option is much more thrilling. Take the FGC train (line R5) from Plaça d'Espanya to **Aeri de Montserrat**, where the cable car swoops up to the monastery. There are two all-inclusive tickets available: the *TransMontserrat*, €17.73, which includes metro, train, cable car, and Sant Joan funicular and the *Tot Montserrat*, €31.55, which includes metro, train, cable car, Sant Joan funicular, entrance to the museum and lunch at the self-service café.

To tour the **wine region** properly you will need your own transport; most of the wineries are scattered around lots of small villages which are rarely connected by the local bus network. Otherwise, there are regular trains from Sants to **Vilafranca de Penedès** via **Sadurni d'Anoia**. For **Reus**, change at **Tarragona**.

The nicest way to get to **Poblet** is by train from Sants to **L'Espluga de Francoli**, and walk the final lovely 3 km to the monastery. Otherwise, there are regular buses between **Tarragona** and **Lleida** which will drop you right outside the monastery gates. Trains from Sants via Pg de Gràcia also stop at **Montblanc**.

Sleeping

Most of the hotels below have excellent restaurants

A-B *Domo*, C/Francesc Macià 4, Vilafranca de Penedès. T938 17 24 26, F938 17 08 53. Four-star comforts including jacuzzi and sauna. **C** *Abat Cisneros*, T93 835 02 01. Run by the monks, this is where newly married couples stay on a visit to get La Moreneta's blessing. They also have a cheaper hostal, *El Monestir*.

C Hotel Gaudí, C/Arabal Robuster 49, Reus T977 34 55 45. Central, with newly renovated rooms. **C-D** *Sol I Vi*, Ctra San Sadurni-Vilafranca, Km 4, Sadurni d'Anoia, T938 99 32 04. This lovely stone farmhouse, 4 km outside Sadurni, has been very prettily converted and even has a pool. The owners can organize tours to the surrounding vineyards. **C-D** *Pedro II El Grande*, Plaça del Penedès 2, Vilafranca de Penedès, T938 90 31 00, recepcion-h.pedro3@ctv.es Modest, central but slightly dour.

C-D *Masia del Cadet*, Les Masies de Poblet, L'Espluga de Francolí, T977 87 08 69, F977 87 04 96. A beautifully renovated 15th-century farmhouse, with a fine restaurant and very friendly owners. **D-E** *Del Senglar*, Plaça Montserrat Canals, L'Espluga de Francolí, T977 87 01 21, F977 87 01 27, www.hostalsenglar@worldonline.es A real charmer, with old wooden beams and a lovely garden with a pool. The restaurant in excellent, and they hold barbecues on Sat evenings in Aug. **E** *Hs dels Àngels*, Plaça Angels, Montblanc T977 86 01 73. An attractive little pensión in the heart of the town, with a nice, reasonably priced restaurant.

Eating & drinking

The food is truly terrible and very over-priced on Montserrat – bring a picnic

Mid-range *Can Sola de Pla*, Can Solá 7, Matadepera, T93 787 08 07. A good local restaurant set in a beautifully converted old stone farmhouse. *El Molí de Mallol*, Muralla Santa Anna 2, Montblanc. T977 86 05 91. Lovely old watermill clinging to the ancient walls; delicious traditional dishes and fine views. *Masia Bou*, Ctra Lleida Km 21.5, Valls. T977 60 04 27. Justly described as the *Palace of Calçotadas*, this is the best place to try Valls' wonderful speciality. *Menú de calçotada*: €21. *Fonda Neus*, C/Marc Mir15-16, Sadurni d'Anoia. T93 891 03 65. Stalwart country favourites at this delightful local restaurant. *Cal Ton*, C/Casal 8, Vilafranca de Penedès, T93 890 37 41. Hearty traditional Catalan cuisine accompanied by an extensive wine list. *La Glorieta del Castell*, Plaça del Castell, Reus T977 34 08 26. The most famous restaurant in town. Three floors with rustic decoration and fine Catalan dishes. *El Cairat*, C/Nou 3, Falset, T977 83 04 81. More classic Catalan cooking, including homemade pasta, from this welcoming little restaurant, which uses the very freshest local produce.

Cheap *Casa Joan*, Placa Estació 8, Vilafranca de Penedès T93 890 31 71. Recipes from all over Spain are used here; the food's good, prices are reasonable and staff are very friendly. *El Pigot de Arbolí*, C/Trinquet 7, Arbolí T977 81 60 63. You won't do better than this friendly spot close to Siurana – the staff are happy to recommend dishes.

South of Barcelona

Just south of Barcelona, the Garraf Massif drops dramatically into the sea, creating a spectacular coastline of steep cliffs overlooking tiny coves. Beyond the massif stretch sandy beaches and a string of bustling seaside towns. Further south is the **Costa Daurada** *(Golden Coast) with long sandy beaches and a string of brash resorts. The highlight of the whole coast is the seaside party town of* **Sitges** *which has become a gay mecca and gets packed with trendy Barcelonans for much of the year. A little further down the coast is* **Tarragona**, *once the most important city in Spain under the Romans, now surprisingly lively and refreshingly untouristy. Most of the towns have marinas offering sailing and diving facilities. At the southernmost tip of Catalunya are the wide, flat marshlands of the* **Delta de l'Ebre**, *where the huge River Ebre finally meets the sea.*

Castelldefels, which started out as a tourist resort, has effectively become a suburb of Barcelona, but it has long golden beaches and some fine seafood restaurants. There is a wide variety of watersports available by the Canal Olímpic. Just beyond Castelldefels is **Garraf**, a charming seaside town with a great beach and a colourful port packed with seafood *tascas*. Gaudí designed the striking *Celler de Garraf* for the Güell family in 1888, a pointy, fairytale *bodega* attached to an old keep.

Castelldefels

Trips from Barcelona

Sitges

The belle of the whole Costa Garraf is undoubtedly Sitges, just a 30-minute train ride from Barcelona. It is a handsome whitewashed town clustered around a rosy church out on a promontory. Sitges has a big reputation for partying which began when the *modernista* painter Santiago Rusiñol (one of the founders of *Els 4 Gats* in Barcelona, see page 281) set up home here in the 1890s; beaches, bars and the certainty of a good time are what draw the hordes of trendy Barcelonans.

Tourist information, T93 894 42 51, info@sitgstur.com

Since the 1960s, it's also become a hugely popular gay resort and the westernmost beaches furthest from the old town are predominantly gay. There is something going on in Sitges almost every month and it's best to visit when a *festa* is in full swing. The *Carnaval* celebrations in February/March are among the biggest and wildest in Spain, largely thanks to the gay community who have taken the event into their own hands. In June the streets are carpeted with flowers for Corpus Christi, and the town's *Festa Major*, dedicated to Sant Bartomeu, at the end of August, is a riot of traditional parades with Giants, Fatheads, and Dragons (see page 42). The long sandy **beaches** are invariably crowded, and right at the westernmost end are a couple of pretty wild nudist beaches, one of which is gay.

Cau Ferrat

There is a combined ticket available to Sitges' three museums at 4.80 euros, valid for one month

Cau Ferrat (Den of Iron) was the home of *modernista* painter Santiago Rusiñol, one of the founders of Els 4 Gats in Barcelona, now it's a fascinating museum. Two little fishermens' cottages, leaning over a sheer cliff in the heart of the old town, were expensively and flamboyantly renovated, the walls painted a glowing azure blue and hung with paintings by all Rusiñol's friends including Picasso, and then the place was crammed with a fantastical hoard of Catalan ironwork.

Rusiñol's home was always filled with artists, musicians and writers, and he organised five *modernista* festivals between 1892 and 1899 to celebrate the new ideas that were being expounded – the wild antics which accompanied these festivals gained the town a heady reputation for bad behaviour which it has been cultivating ever since. ■ *Summer 1000-1400 and 1700-2100; winter Tue-Fri 1000-1330 and 1500-1830. €3, free first Wed of the month.*

Museu Maricel

Next door to the Cau Ferrat, is the Museu Maricel with a collection of art from the medieval period to the early 20th century displayed in a lovely light-filled old mansion hanging over the sea. On the top floor there's a small naval museum with models and plans. ■ *Tue-Fri 0930-1400 and 1600-1800, Sat 0930-1400 and 1600-2000, Sun 0930-1400; entrance €3, free first Wed of the month.*

Tarragona

Tourist information, T977 24 50 64, turisme@tinet.fut.es

The Romans established a military base here at the end of the third century BC which played an important role in the conquest of the Iberian Peninsula. They liked it so much that they decided to make it the capital of Hispania Citerior, and built temples, baths, an amphitheatre, a circus and a forum, bequeathing a spectacular series of Roman monuments which are among the most extensive in Spain. Nowadays, it's a lively, industrious city with a shadowy, picturesque old quarter curled around the imposing Gothic cathedral, and a busy working harbour lined with great seafood restaurants.

Casc Antic

The old city lies north of the Rambla Vell, a handsome promenade which culminates in the **Balcó del Mediterrani** (Balcony of the Mediterranean) with beautiful views over the amphitheatre, the **Platja del Miracle** and out to sea. The old Roman walls which still ring much of the old city have been converted into an attractive walkway known as the **Passeig Arqueològic**, which winds along the Roman walls built in the third century BC. ■ *Oct-May Tue-Sat 1000-1330 and 1630-1830, Sun 1000-1400; Jun-Sep Tue-Sat 0900-2100, Sun 1000-1400, €1.80.*

Cathedral

Tarragona's serene cathedral is a perfect example of the transition from Romanesque to Gothic. Construction began at the end of the 12th century and was completed in 1331. A wide staircase sweeps up to the main façade with an imposing Romanesque portal surrounded with 13th-century sculptures of the Virgin and the Apostles surmounted by a vast rose window. The **cloister** has delicately carved columns featuring a world of fabulous creatures, including one which depicts the story of the clever cat who outwitted the mice by playing dead and then leaps up from his own funeral to gobble them up. ■ *Mid-March to Jun, Mon-Sat 1000-1300 and 1600-1900; Jul to mid-Oct Mon-Sat 1000-1900; mid-Oct to mid-Nov Mon-Sat 1000-1230 and 1500-1800; mid-Nov to mid-March Mon-Sat 1000-1400; €1.80.*

On the edge of the old town, just off Plaça del Rei, the light and airy Museu Nacional Arqueològic holds an excellent collection of artefacts gathered from the archaeological sites which provide a vivid picture of life in Imperial Tarraco. ■ *Jun-Sep Tue-Sat 1000-2000, Sun and holidays 1000-1400; Oct-May Tue-Sat 1000-1330 and 1600-1900; €1.80.*

Museu Nacional Arqueològic

This museum is housed in the Praetorium tower, once home to Augustus and Hadrian, and later the Kings of Aragón who built a castle on top of the Roman ruins. Computer-generated images of the Roman city give a sense of its magnificence two millennia ago. A glass lift swoops to the roof for dizzying views across the rooftops of the old town, and it is also linked by vaulted underground passages to the Circus, which was built in the first century AD to hold chariot races. ■ *Jun-Sep Tue-Sat 1000-2000; Oct-May Tue-Sat 1000-1730; Sun all year 1000-1500; €1.80.*

Museu de la Romanitat
Next door to the archaeological museum

Down by the Platja del Miracle, the ancient Amphitheatre held games of a bloodier kind, where gladiators and wild animals fought to the death. Three Christian martyrs were tortured to death here in 259AD, and a basilica was erected to them in the sixth century on the site of their martyrdom. ■ *Jun-Sep Tue-Sat 1000-2000, Sun 1000-1400; Oct-May Tue-Sat 1000-1300 and 1600-1700, Sun 1000-1400; €1.80.*

Amphitheatre

The lower town holds the prosperous modern extension to the city, but also contains a fascinating collection of Roman remains at the Museu i Necròpolis Paleocristians. Roman law forbade burials within the city walls, and the necropolis, still scattered with amphorae, plinths and inscribed tablets, was established well outside the ancient city. ■ *Jun-Sep Mon-Sat 1000-1300 and 1630-2000, Sun 1000-1400; Oct-May Mon-Sat 1000-1330 and 1500-1730, Sun 1000-1400; €1.80.*

Museu i Necròpolis Paleocristians

Between Salou and Tarragona is this massive **theme park** with heart-stopping rollercoasters like the *Dragon Khan* (the biggest in Europe), log flumes and a great virtual underwater ride called the *Sea Odyssey*. It's popular enough to have its own train station. ■ *Winter 1000-2000, summer 1000-2400; one-day admission €28.90, call T902 20 22 20 for more information or check the website www.portaventura.es*

Universal Studios Port Aventura

Cambrils, just down the coast, is smaller and less hectic. It's an unassuming resort town set back from a large harbour which still has a working port and an excellent selection of seafood restaurants.

Cambrils

The area has been designated a natural park in order to protect the 300 species of bird which have made these wetlands their home, including flamingoes, herons, marsh harriers and a wide variety of ducks. **Amposta**, the largest town in the region, is also the least attractive and **Deltalebre** or seaside **Sant Carles de la Ràpita** make more attractive bases. There are several nature trails, hides for committed bird-watchers and boat-trips down the river and out to sea are offered from Amposta and Deltelebre. There's a spellbinding if harsh beauty in the immense expanse of wetlands, the vast sky, and the wild beaches scattered with driftwood, and even in the height of summer you are almost guaranteed to find yourself alone.

Delta de L'Ebre
Call the tourist office for information on the natural park: T977 74 01 00

Trips from Barcelona

| Ins & outs | **Getting there** There are regular local buses from Estació-Sants to **Sitges**, approximately every 20 mins. There are local and express trains from Estació-Sants down the coast to **Tarragona** and beyond; the more expensive, plusher *Euromed* trains cost more and are no faster. For the **Delta de l'Ebre**, take a train to **Amposta**, **Camarles** or **Ampolla** where buses and riverboats head to the to the park information office at Deltalebre and on to the mouth of the river. For **Sant Carles de la Ràpita**, you'll have to take a train to **Tortosa** and get a bus from there. |

| Sleeping | **C** *Hotel Romàntic*, C/Sant Isidre 33, Sitges, T938 94 83 75, F938 94 81 67. Set in a lovely 19th-century mansion with a garden terrace; popular with gay visitors. **C-D** *Caspel*, Carrer Alfonso V 9, 43840 Salou, T977 38 02 07, F977 35 01 75, www.caspel-dourada.com Very friendly owners, a pool, and a perfect location close to the beach. |

D *El Xalet*, Isla de Cuba 33-35, Sitges T 938 11 00 70, F938 94 55 79. Delightful little hotel in a *modernista* villa. **D** *Lauria*, Rambla Nova 20, Tarragona, T977 23 67 12, F977 23 67 00, info@hlauria.es Very pleasant, well-located hotel with pool. **D** *Camíllela*, s/n Av Canal, Delta L'ebre, T977 48 00 46, F977 48 06 63, www.dsi.es/delta-hotel Traditional style house which has been recently converted for rural tourism; the friendly owners can organize boat trips and horse-riding in the surrounding Ebre Delta.

E *Juanito Platja*, Pseo Marítimo s/n, 43540, Sant Carles de la Rápita, T977 74 04 62, F977 74 27 57. Modest hotel near the beachfront. **E** *Pensión Marsal*, Placa de la Font 26, 43000, Tarragona, T977 22 40 69. The best value cheapie in the city: nicest rooms overlook the square. **F** *Hostel Mariangel*, C/de les Parellades 78, Sitges, T938 94 83 75. Popular budget choice.

Camping There are plenty of campsites at most of the seaside resorts, although many are only open from Apr to Sep. Campsite north of the Sitges, *El Rocà*, T93 894 00 43. If you want to camp around **Sant Carles de la Rápita**, bring mosquito repellent. There are two official campsites in the Deltalebre: *L'Aube*, Urbanització Riumar, T977 44 57 06, or the slightly more expensive *Riomar*, Urbanització Riumar, T977 26 76 80, which has a pool. There's a good campsite right on the beach at Puerta Romana, *Gavina*, T977 80 15 03.

| Eating & drinking | **Mid-range** *Maricel*, Paseo de la Ribera 6, Sitges, T938 94 20 54, www.maricel.es One of the best seafood restaurants in town. *Merlot*, C/Cavallers 6, Tarragona T977 22 06 52. Classic restaurant in a *modernista* townhouse, serving French and Mediterranean cuisine. The café downstairs is very good value. *Casa Gatell*, Psg. Miramar 26, Cambrils, Salou, T977 36 00 57. Seafood overlooking the port from the Gatell family of chefs. |

Cheap *El Celler Vell*, C/Sant Bonaventura 21, Sitges T938 11 19 61. Good Catalan food and a laid-back atmosphere, *menú del dia* at around €6.60. *Morros*, Carrer Rafael de Campalans, Torredembara T977 64 00 61. Well known local seafood restaurant with a well-priced *menú del dia* at €17.90. *Faristol*, C/Sant Martí 5, Altafulla T977 65 00 77. Friendly restaurant with a nice terrace which also rents rooms from €24. *Bufet el Tiberi*, C/Martí d'Ardenya 5, Tarragona T977 23 54 03. Stuff yourself Roman style for less than €12. *Desembocadura Riu Ebre*, T977 26 75 03. Right at the mouth of the Delta de L'Ebre river, serving local dishes made with rice grown in the delta.

Entertainment and nightlife

9

Entertainment and nightlife

233 Theatre

234 The Barcelona music scene

234 Classical and opera

236 World music

237 Contemporary music

238 Clubs

242 Bars

248 Cinema

249 Cinemas

249 Dance

Theatre

Madrid may be the traditional home of Spanish theatre, but Barcelona has made **experimental theatre** its own: the first theatre group in this tradition was established in 1898 by Adrià Gual, who set up the *Theatre Intim*, an amateur group devoted to 'artistic theatre'.

During the Franco era, the performing arts suffered repression and censorship, but, despite these obstacles, or because of them, depending on your point of view, experimental theatre began to really take off in the 1960s. In 1960 Ricard Slava set up the influential *Escola d'Art Dramàtic Adrià Gual*; in 1962, Albert Boadella founded *Els Joglars*; and in 1967, Sitges established its annual festival of international theatre which became a key meeting place for underground playwrights to interact with experimental troupes. At home, shows were closed down and performers imprisoned, but abroad these theatre groups were causing a stir. Their work travelled well, because the widespread use of multi-media, mime and choreography crossed linguistic barriers.

The grandaddy of the experimental theatre groups is *Els Juglars*, which is still going strong, and has lost none of its bite nor its relish for satire – its latest victims have been Jordi Pujol, President of the Generalitat, and Dalí. The *Els Comediants* group has been running for almost as long, and although, again, the emphasis is on physical theatre, their work evokes a simpler, child-like vision of the world. The explosive *La Fura dels Baus* got a world-wide audience at the opening ceremony of the Olympic Games in 1992, and can always be relied upon to cause mayhem and chaos. *El Tricicle*, a three-man mime team, incorporate circus performances into their spectacular acts, and *Dagoll-Dagom* have created their own distinctive brand of anarchic musical shows. Among the best known artists is *La Cubana*, who were a hit at the Edinburgh Festival a couple of years back, and pull off dazzling, inventive shows using all kinds of media with a satirical edge.

At the other end of the spectrum, the prestigious *Lliure* theatre was founded in 1976 and specializes in an international repertory of **classical** and **contemporary** drama performed in Catalan. It is set to move from its home in Gràcia to the new Ciutat de la Teatre in Montjüic but this arrangement has caused some tension within its ranks. The construction of the Bofill-designed Teatre Nacional de Catalunya has been a key player in drawing crowds to the theatres since 1997, and manages to balance overtly commercial productions with some more interesting performances. The **Ciutat de la Teatre** opened in 2001, and is the latest project in the city's ambitious drive for redevelopment. The 'Theatre City' offers student spaces, the Theatre Museum, the Theatre Institute and the Mercat de las Flors Theatre.

Teatre Poliorama, La Rambla 115, T93 317 75 99, www.teatrepoliorama.com Advance tickets also sold through *Servi-Caixa*. A Generalitat-owned theatre, this theatre shows everything from innovative drama to musicals. *Teatre Principal*, La Rambla 27, T93 301 47 50. Standing on the site of the city's first theatre. It's seen better days but still manages to offer a varied programme of serious drama, music and opera.

La Rambla & Plaça de Catalunya
on map, page 62

Teatre Malic, C/Fusina 3, T93 301 70 35. Advance sales also through *Tel-entrada*. Tiny basement theatre which puts on all kinds of shows, including some English-language productions.

La Ribera
on maps, pages 88 and 91

Teatre Nacional de Catalunya (TNC), Plaça de les Arts 1, T93 306 57 00, www.tnc.es Advance tickets also sold through *Servi-Caixa*. Inaugurated in 1997, this Ricardo Bofill designed building is the flagship of the city council's efforts to smarten up the grim Glòries district. Performances range from high quality drama to contemporary dance.

Gràcia & outer districts
on maps, pages 146, 157 and 163

Entertainment & nightlife

Sala Beckett, C/Alegre de Dalt 55 bis, Gràcia, T93 284 53 12, www.teatral.net/beckett Advance sales also through *Tel-entrada*. Founded by the Teatro Frontizero group, which includes the eminent contemporary playwright José Sanchis Sinistierra. Interesting new theatre and contemporary dance. *Teatre Lliure*, C/Montseny 47, Gràcia, T93 218 92 51, www.teatrelliure.com Advance sales also through *Tel-entrada*. One of the most prestigious theatres in Catalunya which has produced some of its leading actors and directors. It will shortly be moving to the refurbished Palau de l'Agricultura in Montjuïc as part of the city's Ciutat del Teatre complex.

Montjuic & | *Institut del Teatre*, Plaça Margarida Xirgú, T93 227 39 00, www.diba.es/iteatre Student productions in Barcelona's theatre school, which has been given elegant new premises in the Ciutat del Teatre. The work is always interesting and very inexpensive. *Mercat de las Flors*, Plaça Margarida Xirgu, Montjüic, C/Lleida 59, T93 426 18 75, www.bcn.es/icub/mflorsteatre Advance sales also through *Tel-entrada* and Palau de la Virreina. This recently converted space has become one of the main venues for the *Grec festival*, (see below), and puts on productions from some of the city's most innovative performers. Excellent contemporary dance as well as cutting edge drama.

Poble Sec

on map, page 177

Festivals | *Festival d'Estiu Grec* Jun-Aug, Barcelona, T93 301 77 75, bi@bcn.es, www.grecbcn.es
Teatre Internacional Jun, Sitges, info@sitgestur.com, www.sitgestur.com
Tàrrega, Fira del Teatre al Carrer, T97 350 00 39, www.firatarrega.com

The Barcelona music scene

Classical and opera

A passion for music runs deep in Catalunya: almost half of the composers now working in Spain were trained by the **Liceu Opera House**; the *Conservatorios* of Barcelona, Girona and Terrassa are among the most important in the whole country; and, in the province of Barcelona alone, there are no less than 48 musical festivals. Among the outstanding musicans of the last century are Isaac Albéniz (1860-1909), the composer and pianist, Pau Casals (1876-1973), the famous cellist, conductor and composer, and the opera stars Montserrat Caballé and Joseph Carreras.

Over the last few years, there has been a sudden increase in both the number and quality of the musical venues on offer in the city: the **Liceu Opera House**, which had been destroyed by fire in 1994, finally reopened in 1999; the city's new concert hall **L'Auditori** in Glòries opened in 1997; and the Palau de la Música Catalana has begun the work which (it is hoped) will finally improve the appalling acoustics and provide a new 600-seat space for chamber music. The **Palau de la Música Catalana** is also home to the *Orfeó Català*, the best known of the choral groups which can be found in almost every Catalan town and village (see page 95).

There is always plenty going on in the musical calendar, although Catalan tastes don't appear to have changed much since the mid-19th century and Wagner and Beethoven still feature heavily. Works by contemporary Catalan composers are occasionally featured alongside more traditional programming. For a taste of what contemporary composers in Catalunya are cooking up, make sure you catch the *Festival de Músiques Contemporànies* held at **L'Auditori**, www.auditori.org The Fundació Miró (see page 186) and CCCB (see page 110) often host concerts by contemporary composers.

Classical music festivals in Catalunya

Apr/May: Sabadell,
Cicle d'Òpera a Catalunya, T93 725 67 34
May: Festival de Música Antiga,
T90 222 30 40, www.lacaixa.es/fundació/
index.htm
Jun-Aug: Barcelona,
Festival d'Estiu Grec, T93 301 77 75,
bi@bcn.es, www.grecbcn.es
Jul: Arsèguel,
Trobada d'Acordeonistes del Pirineu,
T97 362 08 04, www.alturgell.ddi.net
Jul: Cantonigròs,
Festival Internacional de Música,
T93 201 77 11, www.osona.com
Jul/Aug: La Seu d'Urgell, **Festival de
Música Joan Brudíeu**, T97 335 00 10
Jul/Aug: Torroella de Montgrí,
Festival Internacional de Música,
T97 276 06 05, jjmmtdm@ddgi.es,
www.ddgi.es/tdm/fimtdm.html
Jul/Aug: Cadaqués,
Festival Internacional de Música,
T93 301 95 55, trito@bcn.servicom.es
Jul/Aug: El Vendrell,
Festival Internacional de Música

Pau Casals, www.elvendrell.net
Jul/Aug: Peralada,
Festival Internacional de Música
Castell de Peralada, T93 280 58 68,
www.festivalperalada.com
Aug: Santes Creus,
Festival Bach, T97 723 34 12
Aug/Sep: Vilabertran,
Festival Internacional de Música de
l'Empordà, T97 250 01 17
Aug/Sep: Vilanova i la Geltrú,
Festival Internacional de Música
Popular i Tradicional, T93 815 45 17,
fimpt@solblau.net/fimpt
Aug and Dec, Llívia,
Festival Internacional de Música,
T972896313, www.llivia.com/festival
Sep: Puig-reig, **Festival Internacional de
Cant Coral**, T93 822 15 00
Sep: Vic, **Mercat de Música Viva**,
mmvv@osona.net, www.ajvic.es
Oct: Tortosa,
Festival de Música Felíp Pedrell,
www.altanet.org/tortosa, www.idece.es

Gran Teatre del Liceu, La Rambla 51-59, T93 485 99 00, www.liceubarcelona.com The (almost) faithful reincarnation of the celebrated opera house has become extremely popular, so getting hold of tickets can be difficult. There's now a subterranean extension which offers recitals, talks, children's puppet shows and other events, usually related to the main programme. *Sala Cultural de la Caja de Madrid*, Plaça de Catalunya 9, T93 301 44 94. Concerts almost nightly (recitals and chamber music) in this small, idiosyncratic space, many of which are free.

La Rambla & Plaça de Catalunya
on map, page 62

Palau de la Música Catalana, C/Sant Francesc de Paula 2, T93 295 72 00, www.palaumusica.org Advance sales also from *La Caixa* and *Servi-Caixa*. The acoustics may be terrible, but the triumphant *modernista* setting make any performance worthwhile.

Barri Gòtic
on map, page 72

Casa Elizalde, C/de Valencia 302, T93 488 05 90. A pretty, smallish venue which hosts small ensembles, choral music concerts and occasionally shows art exhibitions.

L' Eixample
on map, page 120

Auditori Winterthur, Auditori de l´Illa, Avda Diagonal 547, Les Corts, T93 290 10 90, www.winterthur.es Advance ticket outlets depend according to the production. A small, ultra-modern venue which hosts chamber concerts and small ensembles.

Gràcia & outer districts
on map, page 157

Entertainment & nightlife

World music

There is always plenty going on in Barcelona, from impromptu performances in shabby bars, to huge concerts with all the big names. **Jazz** is traditionally very strong in the city, with an excellent, well-established jazz festival which hits the city in October and takes over most of the bars and clubs. There are a couple of music schools with an excellent reputation – one of them, the *Taller de Música*, also runs a jazz café which is a great place to catch new acts. The greatest Catalan jazz musician of recent times was the pianist, the late Tete Montoliu, but other local artists include Lucky Guri, Lluis Vidal and Laura Simó.

The **folk** tradition in Barcelona never really had a chance to get off the ground. During the 1960s and 70s a new wave of artists began writing songs which were often politically inspired and usually sung in Catalan which became known as *cança*: the best known performers are Lluís Llach, who often sings with Maria del Mar Bonet, as well as Joan Manuel Serrat, Núria Feliu and Raimon.

The Andalusian immigrants and their children ensure that the **flamenco** tradition retains its energy, and although the flamenco scene is bigger in Madrid and Andalusia, it's pretty intense in Barcelona too with some excellent Catalan performers like Mayte Martín or Miguel Poveda who are admired throughout Spain. Also in the flamenco tradition is the homegrown *Rumba Catalan*, first popularised by Peret, a gypsy from El Raval, and an infectious mix of flamenco and latin rhythms; don't miss a performance by *Sabor de Gràcia*, if you get the chance.

Latin music has a massive following, partly due to the huge numbers of South Americans who live here, and partly because of the soaring popularity of salsa and tango all over Europe in the last decade. There are dozens and dozens of places to take classes, from pumping neon-lit clubs to tiny intimate dance halls which take you back to turn-of-the-century Buenos Aires. **African** music, thanks also to the large expatriate population, is surprisingly big in Barcelona and well worth checking out.

Barri Gòtic
on maps, pages 72 and 77

Jamboree, C/Plaça Reial 17, T93 301 75 64. One of the most popular jazz clubs in the city, this subterranean joint is always packed. The programme includes jazz, blues, funk and hip-hop and the Sunday night blues night is the best way to finish up the weekend. After performances, the club opens up to become a late-night club. *Harlem Jazz Club*, C/Comtessa de Sobradiel 8, T933100755. One of the most dynamic jazz clubs in the city, small but atmospheric, with very creative programming.

Los Tarantos, Placa Reial 17, T93 318 30 67. A popular venue for flamenco performances; there's a pretty touristy flamenco tablao, but the club also invites the best performers from a host of other genres – jazz, flamenco, tango, salsa, and Catalan folk. Later the club joins with the adjoining *Jamboree* (see below) to form one big nightclub. *La Macarana*, C/Nou de Sant Francesc 5, T93 317 54 36. Anything could happen at La Macarena; you might be treated to a brilliant set from visiting flamenco performers, or the regulars who mooch around the bar might give you a cursory set. It's best to go with someone from the city who knows the spot, or the suggested 'drink for the artists' could clean you out.

La Ribera
on maps, pages 88 and 91

Ribborn, C/Antic de Sant Joan 3. Friendly, small club featuring live jazz and blues in a mellow setting. (See page 244). *Little Italy*, C/Rec 30, Ribera, T933197973. Live jazz over supper at this New York-style club.

El Raval
on map, page 109

Jazz Sí Club-Café, C/Requesens 2, T93 329 00 20. This club is run by the music school down the road, and offers impromptu performances from the musicians who gather there, as well as a diverse programme of live music each night, ranging from Cuban folk to soul, and jazz to rock. *La Paloma*, C/Tigre 27, T93 317 79 94. This beautiful old dance hall started life in 1902, and still retains its plush fittings and elegant atmosphere. Ballroom dancing, tango and salsa are on offer, but at weekends it hosts the *Bongo Club*, one of the hippest dance clubs in the city (see page 239). **Bar Pastis**, C/Santa Mònica 4, T93 318 79 80, (see page 245). Tiny, atmospheric throwback to the heyday of the Barri Xinès, you can get a taste of the old days on Sunday nights, when cabaret singers warble plaintively.

Luz de Gas, C/Muntaner 246, T93 209 77 11. Set in a stunning turn-of-the-century music hall, Luz de Gas offers a mixed programme, with different acts performing each night. The selections runs from soul, jazz and salsa to rock and pop. **Antilla Barcelona**, C/Aragó 141, T93 451 21 51. Big, boisterous very popular salsa club with great live bands, free salsa lessons and a 'salsateca' on Fri and Sat nights. **Sala Àtic**, C/Tarragona 141-147, Eixample, T93 426 84 44. Big-name salsa and merengue bands and a massive dancefloor.

L' Eixample
*on maps,
pages 120 and 122*

La Cova del Drac, C/Vallmajor 33, Zona Alta, T93 200 7032. Some of the biggest names in Barcelona jazz can still be heard in this club, although its glory days are over. There's also a late-night club at weekends, and poetry readings earlier in the week. **Teatreneu**, C/Terol 26-28, Gràcia, T93 285 79 00, (see page 241). Live world music and jazz in this down-to-earth, friendly little club, part of the Teatreneu complex, which also includes a theatre and restaurant.

Gràcia & outer
districts
*on maps pages 146,
157 and 163*

Los Juaneles, C/Aldana 4, T93 208 13 89. Hidden away in Poble Sec, this club is popular with gipsies and a mishmash of experienced dancers and beginners who want to learn Sevillanas (classes on Thu nights). **Tinta Roja**, C/Creu dels Molers 17, Poble Sec, T93 443 32 43. Step through the doorway of this wonderful cabaret club and you're suddenly in Argentina. There are live tango performances at weekends, and plenty of dancing during the week. Tango lessons are given on Tue.

Montjuïc &
Poble Sec
on map, page 177

Irish Winds, Maremàgnum top floor, Moll d'Espanya, Port Vell, T93 225 81 87. Popular, boisterous Irish bar with live Celtic music and folk.

El Litoral
*on maps,
pages 198 and 206*

Festival Internacional de Jazz de Barcelona Oct/Nov, Barcelona, T93 481 70 40, www.project-plastic.com
Festival de Jazz de TerrassaTerrassa, T93 786 27 09, jazzcava@ilimit.es www.jazzterrassa.org
Festival de Jazz de la Costa Brava, July/Aug, Palafrugell, T97 230 02 28.

Festivals

Contemporary music

Although most bands in the Spanish charts are from the UK or the United States, Catalan **rock and pop** are holding their own in Barcelona. One of the biggest Spanish rock bands, *Mojinos Escozios*, has two Catalan members and all of them live close to the city. *Rock Català*, which is rock like everywhere else but sung in Catalan, is very popular with bands like *Sau*, *Els Pets*, *Sopa de Cabra* and *Lax 'n' Busto* having regular gigs at clubs across the city. Lighter and poppier are bands like Los *Fresones Rebeldes*, or the hip hop group *7 Notas 7 Colores*.

For more information
on the unmissable
Sónar Festival,
T93 442 29 72,
www.sonar.es

The Barcelona music scene, like most others European cities, is dominated by **DJ culture**; to get a feel for what's going on, pick up a copy of the Spanish dance music mag, *Dance De Lux*, and don't miss the incredible *Sónar festival*, a huge three-day celebration of multimedia music and art which culminates in the intense, manic, but unforgettable *Sónar* night. The *BAM* festival which runs at the same time as the *Festa de la Mercé* (see page 44) is a great way to catch some alternative sounds.

Entertainment & nightlife

Clubs like *Jamboree* and *Luz de Gas* (see above) offer a real mix bag of performances, and are always worth checking out. There are always plenty of venues covering everything else, from tiny, ultra hip bars with the latest in electronica to huge crowded *salas* with mainstream rock and pop. Pick up flyers at music shops to discover some of the less well-known venues.

Barri Gòtic
on map, page 72

Sidecar Factory Club, C/Heures 4-6, T93 302 15 86, (see page 243). In the corner of the Plaça Reial. Indie-pop concerts as well as lots of local bands and an alternative performance night on Tue, with everything from poetry readings to video art.

La Ribera
on maps, pages 88 and 91

Abaixadors Deu, C/Abaixadors Deu 10 pral, (see page 244). An elegant café-bar on the first floor of an old palace, this offers an eclectic mix of live music from flamenco to pop, as well as poetry readings, film events and dance performances. *Magic*, Passeig Picasso 40, T93 310 72 67. All kinds of bands, mainly local, in this sweaty club in La Ribera. Some excellent foreign guests also appear, and there's a constant stream of northern European guitar groups. *Astín*, C/Abaixadors 9, Ribera T93 442 96 69, (see page 239). Ultra-trendy, 'industrial space-cum-corridor' featuring the very latest in experimental music and pop.

El Raval
on map, page 109

La Ruta dels Elefants, C/Hospital 48, Raval, no phone, (see page 244). Small, laid-back bar with an eclectic offering of live music – everything from kitsch cabaret acts to reggae and local indie-pop bands.

L'Eixample
on map, page 122

La Boîte, Diagonal 477, Eixample, T93 319 17 89, www.masimas.com (see page 240). This was the first live music bar to be overhauled by the indefatigable Mas brothers and puts on a varied bill of live jazz, blues, funk and soul. Sunday nights are dedicated to jump 'n' jive and swing, and the basement venue opens up as a club when performances are over.

Gràcia & outer districts
on map, page 157

Bikini, C/Deu I Mata 105, Les Corts, T93 322 00 800, (see page 240). Three spaces offering a wide variety of salsa, pop and rock.

Montjüic & Poble Sec
on map, page 177

Apolo, C/Nou de la Rambla 113, T93 441 40 01. One of the best-known live music venues in the city, with a varied programme of concerts including pop and rock, reggae and world music.

El Litoral
on map, pages 198 and 206

Garatge Club, C/Pallars 195, Poble Nou, T93 309 14 38. Indie-pop, speed-metal and psychodelia from local and foreign bands. *Razzmatazz*, C/Almogavers 122, Poble Nou, T93 272 09 10. *Zeleste* went bust in 2000; Razzmatazz has re-opened in the newly refurbished rock venue, with a good programme of mainstream rock and pop, and two dance floors.

Clubs

La Rambla & Plaça de Catalunya
on map, page 62

Karma, Plaça Reial 10, T93 302 56 80. Open daily excluding Mon midnight-0500, metro Liceu. You can't miss the queues or the bouncers for this club right on the Plaça Reial. It gets packed and sweaty, and the music is standard rock with the odd surge of house. It's mainly popular with students and hammered tourists. *Jamboree*, Plaça Reial 17, T93 301 75 64, www.masimas.com Open daily 2230-0530, metro Liceu. This jazz, blues and soul club featuring live bands (see page 236) also has a late night club: after about 0100, the crowds pour in to enjoy the R&B, soul and funk which plays until dawn. There's free entrance to the *Taranto* for Latin and flamenco sounds.

Five of the best: hottest clubs and bars

- *Astin* (see below)
- *Café Royale* (see below)
- *Dot* (see below)
- *La Terrrazza* (see page 241)
- *Havannah's* (see page 246)

New York, C/Escudellers 5, T93 302 70 26. Open 2230-0530, metro Drassanes. Popular with students, this big, ex-sex club has two levels; hang out on the sofas of the mezzanine, with a balcony overlooking the main dance floor, or mingle with the crowd thrashing it out below to a very mixed bag of Britpop, reggae and home-grown hits. And, of course the night always ends with the Sinatra classic. *Café Royale*, C/Nou de Zurbano 3, T93 317 61 24. Open Tue-Thu 1700-0230, until 0300 on Fri and Sat, metro Liceu. A very hip, sleek bar and club just off the Plaça Reial, with big sofas to lounge in, and two dance floors playing the best in soul, jazz and funk.

Dot, C/Nou de Sant Francesc 7, T93 302 70 26. Open daily 2200-0230, until 0300 on Fri and Sat, metro Drassanes. One of the trendiest, and smallest, clubs around, Dot has a minuscule dance floor, with groovy lighting, cult films and wall projections. The varied line up of DJs, including resident DJ Kosmos, provides the latest sounds from across the spectrum of dance music.

Astin, C/Abaixadors 9, T93 301 00 90, www.nitsa.com/astin.htm Open Thu-Sat 2230-0330, metro Barceloneta/ Jaume I. A small, chrome-filled, ultra-hip new bar and club run by the Nitsa crew (see page 241) , playing the very latest pop, house and breakbeat. Guest DJ sessions and concerts. *El Foro*, C/Princesa 53, T93 310 10 20. Open Sun, Wed, Thu 1330-1630 and 2100-2400 Fri-Sat 1330-1630 and 2100-0400, metro Jaume I. Restaurant, bar and club in lofty, warehouse-style premises. At weekends it becomes the *Galazy* nightclub after restaurant hours.

Nao Colón Club, Avda Marqués de l'Argentera 19, T93 310 48 59. Open Fri, Sat and nights before holidays 2200-0300. Opposite the Estacío de França, this new bar and club plays funk, soul and latin jazz to an up-for-it crowd. Guest DJs and some cool visuals. *Luz de Luna*, C/Comerç 21, T93 310 75 42. Open Tue-Sun 2200-0300, until 0430 on Thu, until 0500 on Fri and Sat, metro Jaume I. Small, lively salsa club with a tiny, packed dance floor of very polite dancers. Every now and then the DJ throws in a Spanish pop tune which gets everyone up and dancing. There are free salsa classes Tue-Thu nights. *Little Italy*, C/Rec 30, T93 319 79 73. Open 1300-1600, 2100-2400, closed Sun. Metro Arc de Triomf. Restaurant and live jazz venue, featuring live acts most Wed and Thu.

Bongo Lounge at La Paloma, C/Tigre 27, T93 301 68 97 Open Thu 0100-0500 and Fri 0230-0500, metro Universitat. Late on Thu and Fri nights, this old-fashioned, much-loved dance hall clears away the ballroom dancers and gets hit by the Dope brothers, Barcelona's latest DJ stars, whose mix of funky electronica and Latin sounds have made it one of the best nights out in the city.

Milk House Café, C/Nou de la Rambla, T93 301 02 67. Open 1700-0300, metro Liceu. Glassy, neon-lit ultra-cool bar, café and gallery which might be the only place in barcelona where you can see 'projections of multi-chromatic plasma' (those swirly bits on the walls and ceiling). White minimalism, lots of arty types and DJ sessions from 1900 playing laid-back deep house and lounge. *Moog*, C/Arc del Teatre 3, T93 301 72 82, www.masimas.com Open daily 2330-0500, metro Drassanes. Two floors and two vibes – retro 70s lounge upstairs and techno and house on the packed, sweaty dancefloor downstairs, with guest DJS regularly featuring on Wed nights.

Barri Gòtic *on maps, pages 72 and 77*

La Ribera *on maps, pages 88 and 91*

El Raval *on map, page 109*

Entertainment & nightlife

Salsitas, C/Nou de la Rambla 22. Open 0900-0300 Sat and Sun, restaurant Mon-Fri 1300-1600, 2000-2400, Sat and Sun 0900-2400. Super stylish tunnel-like white space, with a restaurant at the back, that has probably had its finest moment as fashion's favourite. It's pretty pretentious – the entrance doors are covered with velvet curtains and guarded by bouncers. But it's still enormously popular with hip young kids in their finest clubwear, who come for *Club 22*, one of the biggest club nights in the city which gets going from Wed-Sun after midnight.

L' Eixample
*on maps,
pages 120 and 122*

Lo-Li-Ta, C/Tuset 13, T93 272 09 10. Open Fri and Sat 0300-0600, metro Diagonal. A slick new club with plush booths surrounding the dance floor, this features the latest in techno, deep house and electropop from *Djd*!; there's a relaxed chill out space and regular appearances from guest Djs. **La Boîte**, Diagonal 477, T93 319 17 89, www.masimas.com Open daily 2300-0530, metro Diagonal. Owned by the Mas brothers, who also run *Moog*, (see page 239) and *Jamboree*, (page 236). This is a live music venue (see page 238) and club which pulls in crowds from across the city. The music is mainly mainstream soul, funk and house, but Saturday nights are getting more experimental with guest DJs adding something new to the mix.

Row Club, C/Roselló 208, T93 215 65 91. Open 2300-0400, until 0500 on Fri and Sat, metro Diagonal. One of the best nights out in the city, this regular Thu-night club is hosted by the organizers of the Sonar festival (see page 44) and the music runs from house and techno to the latest experimental sounds. **Fuse Restaurant and Club**, C/Roger de Llúria 40, T93 301 74 99. Restaurant open from 2030 and club from midnight Fri and Sat, metro Girona or Plaça de Catalunya. Fuse calls itself a 'laboratory of sensations'; there's a smart restaurant serving Japanese and Mediterranean fusion cuisine, lots of self-consciously hip video art, and club nights are held on Fri and Sat from midnight.

Mond Club (in the Sala Cibeles), C/Còrsega 363, T93 272 09 10. Open Fri 1230-0600, metro Diagonal. Run by the *Mond Bar* in Gràcia (see page 246), this Fri night club devoted to pop and techno pop is set in a beautiful old dancehall. The stage has attracted a string of celebrity DJs, including Jarvis Cocker from Pulp and *Massive Attack*'s Daddy G. **Luz de Gas**, C/Muntaner 246, T93 209 77 11. Open 2300-0400, metro Hospital Clínic. Every night has a different theme at this beautiful Belle Epoque dance hall – blues, folk, soul, salsa, funk, jazz of a consistently high standard. Thu nights are soul nights with regular Monica Green, and there's a regular programme of international artists.

Antilla Barcelona, C/Aragó 141, T93 451 21 51. Open 2300-0400 until 0500 on Fri and Sat, metro Hospital Clínic. One of the best salsa/Latin venues in the city, with great live bands and a big cheerful crowd. Lots of plastic palms and neons only add to the atmosphere and there are free salsa classes Mon-Thu at 2330. (Fri and Sat nights – *salsateca*).

Gràcia &
outer districts
*on maps,
pages 146, 157
and 163*

Bikini, C/Deu i Mata 105 (in *L'Illa* shopping centre), T93 322 00 05, www.bikinibcn.com Open 2400-0430, until 0530 on Fri and Sat, closed Sun and Mon, metro Les Corts. The original legendary Bikini was bulldozed to make room for the *L'Illa* shopping centre. The club has been recreated in the shopping centre and offers three different spaces: *Espai BKN* is a club playing funk, house, disco and 80s pop; *Espai Arutanga* is a Latin room with a broad selection of Latin sounds; and *Dry Bikini* is a cocktail bar which also serves sandwiches and snacks. Call or check the website for details of live music events.

El Universal, C/Marià Cubi 182 bis, T93 201 35 96, open 2300-0430, FGC Muntaner. An attractive club on 2 levels, although it's no longer so hip with the fashion crowd.

Entertainment & nightlife

There's a dance floor downstairs and a plush little salon upstairs. It often features live music, but the standard fare is pure house. *La Cova del Drac*, C/Vallmajor 33, T93 200 70 32. Open Thu-Sat 2000-0530, Tue 2000-0530, FGC Muntaner. Live jazz followed by dancing at this upmarket club, catering to a slightly older clientele who enjoy the 60s and 70s sounds. Occasional poetry readings and other events.

Five of the best: places to eat and dance ★

· *Future* (see page 100)
· *Bar Ra* (see page 112)
· *Fuse* (see page 240)
· *Salsitas* (see page 240)
· *Suborn* (see page 244)

Illusion, C/Lepant 408, T93 347 36 00. Open Fri and Sat midnight-0600 Fri, Sun 1900-midnight, metro Alfons X. This long-established warehouse-style club has recently revamped the Sun night club scene with its T-Dance Sessions. Featuring the newest electronic music, outrageous floorshows from drag queens and go go dancers, it's also got a terrace which opens up from spring. It's a huge hit, drawing crowds from across the city, but Fri and Sat are still most popular with teenagers. *KGB*, Alegre de Dalt 55, Gràcia, T93 210 59 06. Open Thu-Sat 2100-0500, live music 2100-0030, metro Joanic. Another big warehouse club, this doesn't really get going until very, very late. Techno sessions from resident DJs Tone-T, Martian and Moisés start about 1am and get faster and busier as the night draws on. Occasional live concerts are held.

Otto Zutz Club, C/Lincoln 15, T93 238 07 22. Open Tue-Sat 2300-0600, FGC Gràcia. Although no longer at the cutting edge of the club scene, Otto Zutz is still a great night out, with three floors, eight bars and galleries overlooking the dance floor and an expensively dressed crowd trying hard to look cool. Guest DJs and occasional live music. On Wed nights, the club organizes dinners – be sure to reserve in advance. *Teatreneu*, C/Terol 26-28, T93 285 79 00. Open Tue and Wed 2030-2230, Thu-Sat 2030-2400, Sun 1800-2400, metro Fontana. Part of the *Teatreneu* complex, which also includes a theatre and restaurant, this is a friendly, easy-going haunt with live jazz and blues.

Nitsaclub (Club Apolo), C/Nou de la Rambla 113, T93 441 40 01, www.nitsa.com Open Fri-Sat 2400-0600, metro Paral.lel. The *Nitsaclub* takes over when the gigs have ended at the Club Apolo (see page 242), another converted ballroom; this big weekend party is very popular so be prepared for massive queues. The main dance floor features hard techno, breakbeat and house, but the two smaller rooms off the upper gallery are mellower. *Torres de Avila*, Poble Espanyol, Avda marqués de Comillas, T93 424 93 09, www.welcome.to/torresdeavila Open Fri and Sat 2430-0700, metro Espanya. The ultimate designer bar, this one was stamped by Javier Mariscal, the darling of Barcelona's design scene in the 80s and 90s. Tucked just inside the main entrance to the Poble Espanyol (a copy of the medieval entrance gates in Avila), it's got 'more design per square metre' than anywhere else in the city.

Montjüic & Poble Sec
on map, page 177

Los Juaneles, C/Aldana 4. Open Thu-Sat 1000-0530, metro Paral.lel. A traditional Andalucian bar, this is popular with gipsies and locals, who enjoy some tapas and a glass of wine before heading for the dance floor to dance sevillanas. There are classes on Thu evenings from 2100-2200. *La Terrrazza*, Poble Espanyol, T93 423 12 85, www.nightsungroup.com Open May-Oct only; Thu-Sun and days before bank holidays 2400-0600, metro Espanya. The biggest summer party in the city, La Terrazza is a hugely popular and posey outdoor venue, where you can chill out under the pine trees or prance on the podiums to excellent dance music played by an impressive list of guest DJs. Massive queues and a strict door policy.

Entertainment & nightlife

Discothèque, Poble Espanyol, T93 423 12 85, www.nightsungroup.com Open Oct-May only Thu-Sun and days before bank holidays 2400-0600, metro Espanya. When the temperatures drop, the party at Terrrazza comes indoors. It's still a spectacular night, with an outrageous crowd, go go dancers at the top of the towers, drag queens and bunny girls: there's a big dance floor downstairs with house and dance, and a chill out zone upstairs when you need a break. *Tinta Rojo*, C/Creu dels Molers 17, T93 443 32 43 Open Tue-Sun 1700-0130, until 0300 on Fri and Sat, metro Poble Sec. A wonderfully atmospheric shabby-chic old bar with decorated with flea market finds, swathed in red velvet and covered in tango posters and postcards; through the gilded doors at the back, there's an art exhibition and theatre. There are unmissable Argentine tango performances on Fri and Sat nights at 0030.

Apolo, C/Nou de la Rambla 113, T93 441 40 01, www.nitsa.com Open Fri-Sat 2400-0600, metro Paral.lel. This old dance hall just off the Paral.lel is one of the most established live music venues in the city: gigs cover everything from pop and rock to reggae and world music. They also host the weekly *Cinema Ambigú* on Tue nights from 2030, featuring alternative films in VO (original version), info at www.retinas.org

El Litoral
on maps, pages 198 and 206

Sala Razzmatazz, C/Almogàvers 122, T93 320 82 00. Open Fri and Sat 0100-0500, metro Marina or Bogatell. Razzmatazz, newly and very expensively opened in the old Zeleste premises,is a popular party spot at weekends with three spaces catering to all musical tastes: indie, house and techno in the Razz Bar; what you'd expect in the Pop bar; and 'the darkest sounds of the Barcelona night' in the Temple Beat Room. Call or check the music press for gig information. *Pachito*, Moll Mestral, Port Olimpic, T93 221 32 89. Open daily 1700-0500, metro Ciutadella-Vila Olímpica. Thumping house and techno from this outpost of the Ibizan club. *Luna Mora*, C/Rámon Trias Fargas, Port Olímpic, T93 221 61 61. Open Thu-Sat 2300-0500, metro Ciutadella-Vila Olímpica. Slightly more upmarket club on two levels. The Atrium serves up house, dance and techno and upstairs in the Racons de Nit you'll find 60s and 70s pop.

Nayandei Disco and Nayandei Boite, Maremàgnum ground floor, Moll d'Espanya, T93 225 80 10. Open 2230-0500, metro Drassanes. A disco-bar and club next to each other in the Maremagnum; the music tends to 60s and 70s music in the Boîte and the latest mainstream pop in the Disco. *Insòlit*, Maremàgnum 1st floor, Moll d'Espanya, T93 225 81 78, www.insolit.ex Restaurant and cyber-café open 1230-2400, club open 2400-0430, metro Drassanes. Set on two levels with terraces overlooking the sea, this restaurant and cyber-café becomes a club after midnight featuring techno, house and tribal music. *Mojito Bar*, Maremàgnum ground floor, Moll d'Espanya, T93 352 87 46. Open 1700-0430, metro Drassanes. One of dozens of bars in the Maremagnum complex, this offers Caribbean cocktails, a happy, party atmosphere and a constantly packed salsoteca downstairs. Free salsa lessons on Mon nights.

Bars

La Rambla & Plaça de Catalunya
on map, page 62

Glaciar, Plaça Reial 3, T93 302 11 63. Open daily 1600-0300, metro Liceu. An institution on the Plaça Reial, laid-back Glaciar bar has big wooden tables, a good selection of beers and a large terrace out on the square. It's popular with locals and tourists alike, who are often serenaded by passing musicians and drunks on the square – but, as with most of the bars on the square, you should keep an eye on your bags. *Boadas*, C/Tallers 1, T93 318 95 92. Open Mon-Thu 1200-0200, Fri-Sat 1200-0300, metro Catalunya. Elegant, classy Art Deco cocktail bar which began life in 1933; celebrity drinkers, including Miró, have left sketches and mementoes along the walls.

Fonefone, C/Escudellers 24, T93 317 14 24. Open daily 2200-0230, until 0300 on Fri and Sat, metro Drassanes. A relative newcomer, Fonefone has impeccable design credentials with wacky retro-inspired lighting and geometric patterns everywhere. Two spaces, one green, one red, offer a different ambience to enjoy the latest in breakbeat, house and drum 'n' bass. *El Ascensor*, C/Bellafila 3, T93 318 53 47. Open daily 1800-0300, metro Jaume I. This isn't easy to find, tucked down a backstreet behind the Ajuntament. But there is no mistaking it when you get there, as the entrance is through an old demounted lift. Small marble-topped tables and wicker chairs make it a pleasant place to settle in for a *copa* (although the service is not great), but at least the music is jazzy and laid back.

Barri Gòtic
on maps,
pages 72 and 77

Bar Malpaso, C/Rauric 20, T93 412 60 05. Open daily 2130-0230, until 0300 Fri and Sat, metro Liceu. Just down an alley behind the Plaça Reial, this is a groovy, red-painted little bar with decks playing an eclectic range of music, and a few punters dancing under the revolving disco ball. It's got a friendly, buzzy atmosphere, the drinks are cheap and it's a popular student haunt. The guest DJ nights on some Wed (call for information) are especially good. *Padam Padam*, C/Rauric 9, T93 302 11 31. Open 2030-0200, metro Liceu. A small, gay-friendly bar with changing art exhibitions on the wall, and a friendly crowd chatting amiably as Piaf and Brel warble away in the background. *El Paraigua*, C/Pas de l'Ensenyança 2 (just off Plaça Sant Miquel). Open 2030-0200, metro Jaume I. A dimly atmospheric little bar set in an old *modernista* umbrella shop. Good cocktails and classical music make it a relaxing spot in the early evening.

Pilé 43, C/N'Aglà 4, T93 317 39 02. Open daily 1900-0200, until 0300 on Fri and Sat, metro Liceu. A new, brightly-lit, hyper-fashionable bar filled with retro furniture, lights and knick-knacks – everything you see and sit on is for sale. The friendly owner also has a second-hand clothes shop in Carrer Riera Baixa (see page 114) *Margarita Blue*, C/Josep Anselm Clavé 6, T93 317 71 76. Open Mon-Wed 1100-0200, Thu-Fri 1100-0300, Sat 1900-0200, Sun 1900-0200, metro Drassanes. This colourful, spacious cocktail bar covered with eccentric lighting (lightbulbs fitted with mini-angel wings) and artworks, is one of three in the trendy Blue chain. The Mexican food is good, and the cocktails excellent. It's a fun place for dinner and can get pretty crowded with big happy groups. There's another branch, El Taco de Margarita, around the corner at No 1 on pretty Plaça Medinaceli, T93 318 63 21, open Mon-Fri 0800-0300, Sat and Sun 1900-0300.

Shanghai, C/Àgla 9, no tel. Open 1900-0200, metro Liceu. This intimate little bar, tucked down a narrow street off busy Calle Escudellers, has an underground feel with its dim, red lighting and regular crowd of young hipsters. There's an excellent sound system, good cocktails and friendly bar staff. *Sidecar Factory Club*, C/Heures 4-6. T93 302 15 86. Open 2200-0300, metro Liceu. This basement bar and live music club on the corner of the Plaça Reial has been here for years. It's covered in old memorabilia – a petrol pump, an old sidecar, vintage advertisements – and it gets packed out with a mainly studenty crowd.

Ovisos, C/Arai 5, no tel. Open daily 2200-0230, until 0300 Fri and Sat, metro Liceu. Overlooking the teeming Plaça George Orwell, this is a hugely popular narrow little bar, which serves excellent, imaginative food. It's always packed with hip young kids and the music is mainly ambient, garage and house.

Plàstic Café, Paseig del Born 19, T93 310 25 96. Open 2200-0230, metro Jaume I. Another of the lively, ultra-hip bars around the Paseig del Born, this one also has occasional live gigs. *Bier Art*, Placeta Montcada 5, T93 315 14 47. Open Tue-Sun 1230-1630, 1930-0030, Mon 1930-0030, metro Jaume I. This newish beer garden tucked away at

La Ribera
on maps,
pages 88 and 91

Entertainment & nightlife

the end of the Carrer Montcada has a dizzying, if comprehensive, array of beers from around the world, and stylish, minimalist décor.

Borneo, C/del Rec 49. Open 2000-0300 daily, metro Arc de Triomf Mellow, laid-back but hip bar on one of the Born's coolest streets; just a few tables, big windows for posing, and occasional guest Djs. *Lola*, C/Asses 20, no tel. Open 0830-0300, closed Sun, metro Jaume I. Small, friendly bar with laid back, friendly staff and a complete absence of attitude. *Gimlet*, C/Rec 24, T93 310 10 27. Open 2000-0300, closed Sun. Metro Arc de Triomf. Classic, very stylish cocktail bar which draws the ultra-hip crowd as well as plenty of celebrities (not that anyone would deign to notice), the preferred haunt of Barcelona bar owners who come to enjoy a perfectly mixed Manhattan or a Whisky Sour.

Suborn, C/de la Ribera 18, T93 310 11 10. Open 2000-0300, metro Barceloneta. Suborn's dance floor is tiny but that doesn't put anyone off: it's enormously popular and gets jampacked with a happy crowd late on. There's a terrace overlooking the Ciutadella Park early in the evening, when tapas and light meals are on offer. *Barroc*, C/Rec 67, T93 268 46 23. Open Mon-Fri 1800-0300, Sat and Sun 1900-0300, metro Barceloneta. Funky disco-bar with velvet curtains and floating cherubs; another popular, packed place, it's on a bar-lined street just off the Passeig de Born. There's a pool table and pin ball machine, if you manage to get near them. *Lola*, C/Asses 20, no phone, open 0830-0300, closed Sun, metro Jaume I. Small, friendly bar with laid back, friendly staff and a complete absence of attitude.

Abaixadors Deu, C/Abaixadors 10, T93 319 64 92. Open Wed-Sun 2100-0300, until 0400 on Fri and Sat, food served between 2100-0200, metro Jaume An elegant arty space on the first floor of an old mansion; head (quietly, or the bouncer will frown at you) through the courtyard and up the stone staircase. There's a sophisticated bar serving light suppers – salads, carpaccios and daily specials – and a small theatre which has poetry readings, eclectic dance and music performances early in the evenings and hosts the Lounge Social Club from 2300. *Palau Dalmases* (*Espai Barroc*), C/Montcada 20, T93 310 06 73. Open Tue-Sat 2000-0200, Sun 1800-2200, metro Jaume I. Set in a beautiful 17th-century palace near the Picasso Museum, this 'Baroque space' drips with candelabra, heaped platters of fruit and herbs, and glowering oil paintings. If you're in the mood for some old-fashioned decadence, sink onto a plush chaise longue and sip a frighteningly expensive cocktail to the strains of classical music.

Pitin Bar, Pg/del Born 34, T93 319 50 87. Open daily 1200-0300, metro Barceloneta noon-0300 daily. Pitin has been going for years and years, unaffected by changes in fashion, and yet managing to stay cool without any effort. It's a split level bar with a tiny spiral staircase, decorated with all kinds of junk and lit with fairy lights. There's outdoor seating on Plaça Commercial, and a great vantage point just by the door for watching the world go by. *Ribborn*, C/Antic de Sant Joan 3, T93 310 71 48. Open Wed-Sat 1900-0200, until 0300 on Fri and Sat, Sun 1800-0300, metro Barceloneta. A relaxed, thoroughly unpretentious bar with simple tapas and *pa amb tomaquet* (Catalan tomato bread) down a small side street; there's a small stage with a piano which often features live music, usually jazz, funk and blues. *Pas del Born*, C/Calders 8, T93 319 50 73. Open 1100-0300, from 1800 on Wed and Sat, metro Barceloneta. A wonderful little café-bar with a long marble counter and checked lino floor which puts on trapeze shows to packed audiences at weekends.

El Raval
on map, page 109
La Ruta dels Elefants, C/Hospital 48, no tel. Open 2000-0200 daily, metro Liceu. Very close to the Plaça San Augustin, this is a popular, laid-back bar with African art all over the walls, an upbeat, friendly atmosphere and live music most nights – you never

know what you might get, from old fashioned cabaret or flamenco guitar to teenage rock or reggae. Don't look up – a fleet of plastic insects crawl across the ceiling.

Bar Pastis, C/Santa Mònica 4, T93 318 79 80. Open 1930-0230, metro Drassanes. Down a narrow street near the Santa Monica Arts Centre at the bottom of the Rambla, this bar is a hangover from the raffish era of the Barrio Xines. Originally opened in the 1940s, it had a makeover in the 1980s but it's still covered with the drunken artwork of the first owner, and the sounds of Piaf and Brassens still float out onto the street. You can catch live music – French-style chansonniers, usually – on Sun evenings. *Boadas Cocktail Bar*, C/Tallers 1, T93 318 95 92. Open 1200-0200, until 0300 on Fri and Sat, metro Catalunya. A classic cocktail bar from the 1930s, which has preserved its elegant atmosphere along with its beautiful Art Deco fittings. The cocktails are excellent and the walls are lined with mementoes from celebrity visitors.

Benidorm, C/Joaquim Costa 39, T93 317 80 52. Open Mon-Thu, Sun 1900-0200, Fri-Sat 1900-0230. This is a tiny, funky little space decked out with eccentric furnishings – a baroque bench, 70s wall paper – and has a miniature dance floor complete with disco ball. Great DJs, electric atmosphere and jokey, friendly staff. *Aurora*, C/Aurora 7, T93 422 30 44. Open daily 2000-0300, metro Liceu. Tiny, ultra-trendy little bar which keeps on going until lunchtime the following day at weekends; its decorated with attractive, flea market finds, slide projections, and the music is soulful and funky. Weekends are always wild, but it's also great early on or on a quiet night of the week when you might have the place to yourself. *Nou 3 Café*, C/Doctor Dou 12, T93 412 08 47, www.ctv.es/ ebano/nou3.htm Open daily 1900-0230, metro Catalunya or Liceu. Friendly, simple café-bar and gallery, with changing exhibitions and curious light fittings. The food is pretty simple – salads, cheese and cured meats – but the staff are delightful.

El Café Que Pone Meubles Navarro, Carrer de la Riera Alta 4-6, Cell 607 188 096. Open Thu-Sun 1700-0200, metro Universitat. A big, airy café-bar set in a converted furniture shop (as the name suggests) which is aiming for a New York-warehouse feel. Filled with mismatched old sofas in zebra prints or leatherette, its got a mellow retro air and fills up with a fashionable, arty crowd. Sink into an armchair and order a snack with your cocktail – sandwiches, cheese, cured meats or New York cheesecake.

Bar Almirall, C/Joaquim Costa 33, no tel. Open Mon-Thu 1900-0230, Fri and Sat until 0300, closed Sun, metro Universitat. One of the oldest bars in the city, the Almirall was founded in 1860, and has managed to preserve its distinctive swirling Modernista woodwork. It's a relaxed, friendly place with comfy sofas, lazy wooden paddle fans, and a mellow atmosphere – one of the nicest places in the city to come if you want to chill out or chat with friends. *Bar Mendizabel*, C/de la Junta de Comerç, no tel. Open Mon-Thu 1900-0230, Fri and Sat until 0300. This is a bizarre colourfully tiled counter bar stuck in the wall next to the Theatre Romea. It's a friendly place where you can stand at the bar and sip a fresh juice or a beer, or sit across at the tables on the tiny square. *London Bar*, C/Nou de la Rambla 34, T93 318 52 61. Open Tue-Thu, Sun 1900-0400, Fri-Sat 1900-0500, metro Liceu. A classic, narrow old-fashioned bar which dates back to 1910 and is now a lively, popular hang-out for locals and ex-pats. Live music at weekends – no entrance but drinks prices go up.

Bar Marsella, C/Sant Pau 65, T93 442 72 63. Open Mon-Thu 2200-0200, metro Liceu. Another survivor of the Barri Xinès, the big, dusty, bottle-lined Marsella was started by a homesick Frenchman. The smell of absinthe hits you as soon as you walk in; get there early to grab a battered, marble-topped table under the lazy paddle fans and soak up the atmosphere. *Kentucky*, C/Arc del Teatre 11, T93 318 28 78. Open Tue-Sat

2100-0300, metro Drassanes. A throwback to the red-light days of the Barri Xinès, the Kentucky hasn't changed much since the 60s when it was a popular hangout for US sailors. Popular mainly with a mix of foreigners and locals, it's still got an old juke box, and an irrepressible sleazy charm.

L' Eixample
on maps,
pages 120 and 122

La Fira, C/Provença 171, no tel. Open Mon-Thu 2200-0300 until 0430 Fri and Sat, metro Hospital Clínic or FGC Provença. One of the most original bars in town, this spacious 'bar-museum' is stuffed with fairground memorabilia; get a drink or a bucket of popcorn from a bar decked like a circus tent or a funfair stall and then find yourself a Dodgem or a Waltzer. *El Otro*, C/Valencia 166, T93 323 67 59. Open 2230-0300, metro Hospital Clínic. Relaxed, local bar catering to a laid-back, arty crowd. Regularly changing exhibitions, resident DJs and occasional live concerts. *Jordy's Cocktail Bar*, C/Casanova 91, T93 451 88 23. Open Mon-Sat 0130-0230, Metro Universitat. This classic cocktail bar is a throwback to Chicago at the turn of the century, with palms, bow-tied waiter, and very well mixed cocktails.

Apolo 7, C/Comte de'Urgell 106, T93 451 01 19. Open 1800-0300, closed Mon, metro Urgell. Covered in Tintin memorabilia, this is another one of Barcelona's bizarre 'bar museums'. Still, it's a fun night out even for people who couldn't care less about Hergé's creations. *Bare Nostrum*, C/Consell de Cent 384, T93 265 25 26. Open 1900-0300. Big, studenty bar with eclectic music and lots of games – pool, darts, and table football. *Bar Six*, C/Muntaner 6, T93 453 00 75. Open 2000-0300, from 2100 on Sun, closed Mon, metro Universitat. Knock back a couple of shots at this super-slick designer bar with plush red velvet sofas and dim lighting where the music will put you in the mood to party. *La Pedrera de Nit*, C/Provença 261-265. Open Fri and Sat 2100-2400 in Jul and Aug, metro Diagonal. Sip a cocktail and check out the live music and stunning views across the city from the undulating rooftop of Gaudi's creamy apartment building, the Casa Milà (see page 126), better known as La Pedrera (The Quarry).

Nick Havannah, C/Roselló 208, T93 215 65 91. Open 2300-0400, until 0500 on Fri and Sat, metro Diagonal. One of the original and best-known design bars, Nick Havannah's is furnished with Philip Starck classics and covered in massive video screens. The Thu night Row Club is currently one of the hottest party scenes in the city (see page 240). *Fresa y Chocolate*, C/Comte Borrell 221, T93 439 02 32. Open 2000-0500, closed Sun, metro Diagonal. Cuban rhythms and cocktails at this friendly bar named after the classic film. *Agua de Luna Tropical*, C/Viladomat, T93 410 04 40. Open Wed and Thu 2200-0400, Fri and Sat 2000-0400, Sun 2000-0400, metro Hospital Clínic. Salsa club for serious dancers; if you're not quite there yet, there are classes on Wed nights in salsa, merengue and cha-cha-cha. Fri is reserved for dancers, and the club becomes a massive salsoteca on Sat and late on Sun.

L'Arquer, Gran Via 454, T93 423 99 08. Open 1900-0230, until 0330 on Fri and Sat. Another of the slick designer bars which dot the Eixample; this one, oddly, has an archery range. There's a good range of tapas, too. *Zsa Zsa*, C/Rosselló 156, T93 453 85 66. Open 2200-0300, closed Sun, FGC Provença. One of the most elegant of the designer bars, with a sophisticated, expensively dressed clientele who pose and sip cocktails. *La Bolsa*, C/Tuset 17, T93 202 26 35. Open daily 0830-0300, metro Diagonal. Drinks prices go up and down depending on demand.

Gràcia &
outer districts
on maps, pages 146,
157 and 163

Café del Sol, Plaça del Sol 16, T93 415 56 63 Open 1300-0200, until 0230 Fri and Sat, metro Fontana. This is a very mellow spot during the day, with creamy white walls showing changing art exhibitions. There's a good selection of tapas on Sun mornings and a delightful terrace out on the square in summer. DJ sessions on Fri and Sat nights. *Mond Bar*, Plaça del Sol 21, T93 457 38 77. Open daily 2100-0300, metro Fontana. A small, slinky bar on the lively Plaça del Sol, with soft lighting, plush sofas, chilled out house, lounge and trance and a friendly, laid-back crowd. *Casa Quimet*, Rambla del Prat 9, T93 217 53 27. Open 1830-0130, closed Mon, metro Fontana. Known as the 'guitar bar', there are more than 200 lined up along the walls, along with pictures of celebrities and friends. The bar has been going since 1939 and attracts a mellow, hippyish crowd.

Eldorado Bar Musical, Plaça del Sol 4, T93 237 36 96. Open 1800-0230, until 0300 on Fri and Sat. A noisy bar with a terrace on Plaça del Sol, the Eldorado is stuck in a rock time warp. Still, there's a pool table and a cheerful, friendly crowd. *Gusto*, C/Francisco Giner 24, metro Fontana. Hip, minimalist music bar not far from Plaça del Sol; guest DJ sessions on Fri and Sat nights from 11pm playing a wide selection of sounds from funk, soul and drum 'n' bass to house and pop. *Sabor Cubana*, C/Francesc Giner 32, T93 217 35 41. Open 2200-0300, closed Sun. Lively Cuban bar serving great cocktails to a happy soundtrack of Caribbean rhythms.

Atlàntic Bar, C/Lluís Muntadas 2, T93 418 71 61. Open 2200-0300, until 0430 on Fri and Sat, FGC Avinguida del Tibidabo then taxi uphill. Truly stunning views out across the city from this converted Modernista tower which has been deliriously decorated with angels and mermaids. Popular with the moneyed uptown kids, the music is usually mainstream pop, but the outdoor terrace makes it worth the taxi ride. *Bubblic Bar*, C/Mariano Cubí 183-185, T93 414 54 01. Open Thu-Sat 2300-0300, FGC Muntaner. Another designer bar catering to the slick pijo uptown kids throwing their parents' money around; funk, house and pop are on the menu and there's a very sleek terrace.

Gimlet, C/Santaló 46, T93 210 53 06. Open daily 1900-0230, until 0300 on Fri and Sat, FGC Muntaner. A classic 1930s style bar, mixing impeccable cocktails including the eponymous Gimlet. It's popular with a smart, stylish crowd and has an overflowing terrace in summer. *Lízard*, C/Plato 15, T93 414 00 32. Open Thu 2200-0230, until 0330 Fri and Sat, FGC Muntaner. Another swish, upmarket bar; this one plays excellent music from house and swing beat to acid jazz and attracts a fashionable crowd. *Los Tilos*, Pg. Dels Til.lers 1, T93 203 75 46. Open 1600-0400 until 0500 on Fri and Sat. Wonderful views across the city from the terrace of this relaxed bar high up in Pedralbes. An elegant, sophisticated crowd and varied music.

Mirablau, Pza Dr Andreu s/n, T93 352 87 46. Open 1100-0500, FGC Avinguida del Tibidabo then taxi uphill. The Plaça Dr Andreu is where the Tramvia Blau stops and the funicular climbs up Tibidabo; the Mirablau bar is a swanky, elegant spot with a terrace overlooking the whole city, perfect for a cocktail. Tapas are on offer during the day and there's a disco at night. *Partycular*, Avda Tibidabo 61, T93 211 62 61. Open Wed and Thu 1830-0230, Fri and Sat 2400-0330, FGC Avinguida del Tibidabo then take a taxi uphill. A lovely converted mansion high on the hill; big rooms make it very atmospheric in winter and in summer, the extensive gardens are dotted with bars giving fabulous views out across the city.

Barcelona Rouge, C/Poeta Cabañas 21, T93 442 31 42. Open 2300-0400. Ring for entry to this intimate, and very slick bar, with lots of big sofas and tables (everything is red, of course). The cocktails are excellent, and very popular with the laid-back, cool crowd; the music can be anything from electronica to nu-jazz, but it's always pleasingly mellow. *Bar Miramar*, Avda Miramar, T93 442 31 00. Open daily exc Wed 1000-2400 in winter, until 0200 in summer. Metro Paral.lel, then funicular to Montjüic. This bar is nothing special at all – but worth a visit for the stunning views down over the port and out to sea.

Montjuic &
Poble Sec
on map, page 177

Entertainment & nightlife

El Litoral
on map, pages 198
and 206

Base Nàutica de la Mar Bella, Platja de la Mar Bella, Avda Litoral s/n, T93 221 04 32, www.basenautic.net Open Mar-Oct 0900-2300 daily. Out near Poble Nou, the sailing school at Mar Bella beach has a snack bar with DJs spinning from early in the morning. Some big names have guested here, and it is worth looking out for one-off all night parties in summer. **Luz de Gas**, Port Vell (outside the Museu d'Història de Catalunya). Open summer only 1100-0100, metro Barceloneta. This refurbished old boat overlooking the yacht masts in the harbour is a fantastic spot for breakfast or an evening cocktail. Touristy, but so is almost everywhere around here. The music is mainly Latin, and it gets packed in the evenings.

Irish Winds, Maremàgnum top floor, Moll d'Espanya, T93 225 81 87. Open 1100-0400, until 0500 Fri and Sat, metro Drassanes. Popular Irish theme bar with live music and an outdoor terrace. **Boadas**, C/Tallers 1, T93 318 95 92. Open Mon-Thu 1200-0200, Fri-Sat 1200-0300, metro Catalunya. Elegant, classy Art Deco cocktail bar which began life in 1933; celebrity drinkers, including Miró, have left sketches and mementoes along the walls.

Cinema

The Catalans have long been at the cutting-edge of **avant garde cinema**; the lushly named Fructuós Gelabert was its earliest exponent, back in the 1890s, and almost all the major Spanish film companies were based in Barcelona during the early 20th century.

Under Franco, the arts were subjected to severe censorship, but the 1960s and 70s saw a stream of Catalan directors creating challenging, **experimental films**; look out for works by Francesc Bertriu, Pere Portabella and Vicente Aranda. Post-Franco, there was a spate of films which dealt with exclusively Catalan subjects, but the Barcelonans, in their drive to put their city firmly on the international cinematic map, have learned the hard way that stories have to appeal to a broader audience. The veteran director Ventura Pons' latest venture, *Food of Love*, marks his English-language debut and is intended for an international audience. Set partly in Barcelona, it is the latest of many big-name productions to use the city as a backdrop, including Almodover's Oscar-winning *Todo Sobre Mi Madre* (All About My Mother), and Susan Seidelman's *Gaudí Afternoon*. Other films currently being filmed in Barcelona include Peter Greenaway's *The Tulse Luper Suitcase* and Luis Sepulvedra's *Nowhere*, starring Harvey Keitel.

Catalan-language films are nonetheless holding their own in the relentless **commercial** market of the film world; *Pau i El Seu Germà* (Pau and his Brothers) was selected for the 2001 *Cannes film festival*, a fine achievement despite the lukewarm reviews. The city's film commission, the *Barcelona Plató*, are hoping to make the city the new European capital of sci-fi and fantasy films, drawing on the numerous outstanding special effects companies who are based here; one of the biggest players is *Filmax's Fantastic Factory*, whose much-anticipated horror flick *Darkness*, directed by Jaume Balaguero, was also shot in Barcelona. Achieving this vision will not be all plain sailing; already there is furious debate about the choices being made by Catalan production companies – do they decide to make a good film, or make a film that sells. Luckily, being Catalan, most think they can do both.

All the cinemas
listed show original
version (VO) films

Cinema-going is very popular in Barcelona, with plenty of cinemas to choose between – from dazzling multi-screen complexes, to art-house film theatres in dusty converted dance halls. Monday is traditionally the cheapest night for cinema tickets. Check for the *VO* symbol next to cinema listings in newspapers, the weekly listings guide *La Guia del Ocio* , or in the free *Metro* newspaper distributed free in metro

Entertainment & nightlife

stations during the week. Ticket prices are always lower than in most other big cities, usually about €3.61-4.81.

During the *Grec festival*, there are screenings at the **Piscina Bernat Picornell** (see page 49) and some of the museums offer film events: check out MACBA (see page 109) and CCCB (see page 110). The **Cine Ambigú** on Tuesday nights at the **Sala Apolo** is a very trendy venue for unusual independent films. There's a women's film festival, *Mostra Internacional de Films de Dones de Barcelona*, run by the Filmoteca (see below) in early June, but the biggest event on the Catalan film calendar is the *Festival Internacional de Cinema de Catalunya*, held in Sitges (for more information, call T92 419 36 35, or www.sitgestur.com, info@sitgestur.com).

Cinemas

Maldà, C/del Pi 5, Barri Gòtic, T93 317 85 29. Atmospheric little cinema set in an 18th-century palace, showing a weekly double-bill.

Barri Gòtic
on maps, pages 72 and 77

Capsa, C/de Pau Claris 134, T93 215 73 93. Small cinema which occasionally shows VO films. *Casablanca*, Passeig de Gràcia 115, Eixample, T93 218 43 45. Art-house cinema with two screens and very uncomfortable seats. *Filmoteca de la Generalitat de Catalunya*, Cinema Aquitania, Avda Sarrià 31-33, Eixample, T93 410 75 90. The Catalan government funds the *Filmoteca* which offers an overview of the history of cinema, with a constantly changing series of films devoted to themes, directors or countries. *Méliès Cinemes*, C/Villaroel 102, T93 451 00 51. A newish 2-screen cinema offering cult and art-house films.

L' Eixample
on maps, pages 120 and 122

Renoir-Les Corts, C/Eugeni d´Ors 12, Les Corts, T93 490 55 10. A comfortable, well-equipped 6-screen cinema which usually offers at least 2 films in English. It also offers the best facilities for disabled people. *Verdi*, C/Verdi 32, T93 237 05 16 and Verdi Park C/Torrijos 49, T93 328 79 00. Both Gràcia. Two attractive cinemas in Gràcia showing shows international and Spanish art and independent films.

Gràcia & outer districts
on maps, pages 146 and 157

Icaria Yelmo Cineplex, C/Salvador Espriu 61, Port Olímpic, T93 221 75 85. Set in a mall near the Port Olímpic, this massive cinema complex shows most of its films in English.

El Litoral
on map, page 206

Dance

The dance scene in Barcelona, like most branches of the performing arts in this city, is celebrated for its innovation and experimentation. **Contemporary dance** developed earlier and more consistently in Barcelona than in other parts of Spain: in the 1920s, the self-taught dancer Tórtola Valencia was causing a stir with her strange character studies, and for more than 40 years, Anna Laeras's school of dance offered classes in American jazz and modern which helped mould the city's first generation of dancer-choreographers.

In 1974 the *Ballet Contemporani de Barcelona*, the city's first modern dance company, was founded by Ramón Solé and produced a new wave of dynamic independent choreographers. The tradition of modern dance in the city was consolidated by the establishment of a programme at Barcelona's Institut de Teatre in 1980, the only one of its kind in the country. As dance groups travelled abroad, they picked up new influences, techniques and perspectives form other countries which were incorporated into their work.

For information on dance courses and performances, contact the Associació dels Professionals de Dansa de Catalunya; T93 268 2473, www.dancespain.com or contact the Palau de la Virreina (see page 63)

Entertainment & nightlife

Barcelona still has the largest concentration of established dance companies in Spain, producing some of the most striking and exciting dance in Europe. Names to look out for include *Cesc Gelabert*, a group run by the dancer of the same name whose architectural background is reflected in the pure sculptural lines of the dancers; *Danat Dansa* are renowned for their exuberance and sheer energy; *Mal Pelo* (bad hair) are known for their quirky, touching portraits; *Mudances*, founded by Angels Margarit, use exquisite imagery; Juan Carlos García trained with Galotta in France and Merce Cunningham in the USA before returning to Barcelona to form the remakable *Lanónima Imperial* company; Toni Mira's astute musicality and clever imagery are well known. All of these artists are internationally renowned.

If contemporary dance is where it's at in Barcelona, lovers of other forms of dance won't be disappointed. **Classical ballet** fans will have to make do with companies from other parts of Spain or elsewhere in Europe, as there is no resident company in Barcelona. There has long been talk of establishing a Catalan Ballet company at the **Liceu**, but nothing has been decided.

Flamenco may be Andalusian, but the workers who flooded here in the 1950s and 1960s have kept the tradition alive in the city, and it's often possible to see some great visiting performers. There's a *Festival de Flamenco* in early May – the cultural centre at the Palau de la Virreina will be able to give you details of events. The *tablaos* are mainly for tourists, but can be a fun night out anyway. **Tango** and **salsa** have enjoyed growing popularity all over Europe during the past decade or so, and there are plenty of places to learn as well as to watch.

Watch out for special events at some of the museums and cultural institutions like ' the **CCCB** and **MACBA**, and try to catch the three-day dance festival in mid-September or the dance programme *Dansa + a prop*, which offers a range of dance performances in several venues every three months. Some theatres (see page 233) host dance performances; check the programme at **El Mercat de les Flors**, the **Teatre Nacional**, **Teatre Lliure** and the **Sala Beckett**. There are always dance events in the summer *Grec festival* (see page 44), which usually feature the best of local talent.

Entertainment & nightlife

Barri Gòtic
on map,
page 72

Los Tarantos, Placa Reial 17, T93 318 30 67. Popular, touristy flamenco *tablao*, but this venue has the added attraction of a late-night club and other performances (see also page 236).

Eixample
on map,
page 122

El Patio Andaluz, C/Aribau, T93 209 33 78. Very touristy: Two shows nightly and a karaoke bar upstairs.

Gracia &
outer districts
on map, page 146

L'Espai, Travesssera de Gràcia 63, Gràcia, T93 414 31 33, www.cultura.gencat.es Advance sales also from *Servi-Caixa*. The only venue in the city with a dedicated dance slot; performances are almost always of contemporary dance, but they occasionally also have performances of contemporary music.

Montjuic &
Poble Sec
on map, page 177

El Mercat de les Flors, Montjüic (see theatres above) Some of Barcelona's leading contemporary dance companies, as well as Spanish and International companies perform here. *El Tablao de Carmen*, Poble Espanyol, T93 325 68 95. Set inside the 'Spanish village', this is a pricey flamenco joint geared towards coachloads of tourists, but features very high-class acts, and if you book in advance you won't have to pay the entrance fee into the Poble Espanyol.

Sleeping

10

Sleeping

253 **Hotels**

253 **Ciutat Vella**

253 La Rambla and
Plaça de Catalunya

254 Barri Gòtic

255 La Ribera

256 El Raval

258 **Eixample**

260 **Gràcia**

260 **Tibidabo and outer districts**

261 **El Litoral**

261 **Campsites**

262 **Apartment hotels**

262 **Youth hostels**

Accommodation price codes

AL	*over €210*		**D**	*€50-75*
A	*€150-210*		**E**	*€30-50*
B	*€110-150*		**F**	*under€ 30*
C	*€75-110*			

Hotels

Ciutat Vella

AL *Ducs de Bergara*, C/Bergara 11, T93 301 51 51, F93 3173179, www.hoteles-catalonia.es Set in an 18th-century mansion, just around the back of the *Triangle* shopping mall), the Ducs de Bergara has had a multi-million peseta facelift and is now one of the glitziest hotels in the city. Some of the old fittings remain – there's a beautiful *modernista* reception area and a stunning old stone staircase leads up to the bar. The rooms are large, light and very well-equipped with roomy marble bathrooms, and there's a very attractive roof terrace with a smallish pool. **AL** *Le Meridien Barcelona*, Ramblas 111, T93 318 62 00, F93 318 77 76, www.meridienbarcelona.com Before the *Hotel Arts de Barcelona* (see page 261) stole its thunder, this was Barcelona's swankiest hotel. It's still a favourite with visiting opera stars thanks to its superb location right on the Ramblas, and there's a fine restaurant and all the luxury trimmings. **AL** *Rivoli Ramblas*, Ramblas 128, T93 302 66 43, F93 301 93 44, www.rivolihotels.com This elegant old hotel was given a stylish makeover for the Olympic games; the rooms are colourfully decorated with a sympathetic mixture of traditional and modern design. Among the amenities are the *Blue Moon* cocktail-piano bar, a well-equipped gym and a delightful rooftop terrace.

La Rambla & Plaça de Catalunya
■ *on map, page 62*

B *Ramblas Hotel*, Rambla 33, T93 301 57 00, 93 412 25 07, www.ramblashotels.com This hotel is set in a pretty 18th-century building; all the recently renovated rooms are comfortable and spacious but those on the upper floors have terraces with great views over the harbour and back towards Montjuïc. **B** *Oriente*, Ramblas 45-47, T93 302 25 58, F93 412 38 19, www.husa.es The Oriente was built in the mid-19th century and incorporated the ruins of an ancient monastery; it's lost most of its former glamour, although there are glimmers of it in the old ballroom and dining room. Neither the plain rooms nor the erratic service merit the high prices (about €114 for a double room), but the location and the atmosphere of faded grandeur almost make up for the lack of charm.

C *Continental*, Rambla 138, T93 301 25 70, F93 302 73 60, www.hotelcontinental.com George Orwell wrote some of the pages of *Homage to Catalonia* between the walls of this welcoming, century-old hotel. It's surprisingly good value for the location and outer rooms have balconies overlooking the Ramblas. **C** *Hotel Internacional*, Rambla 78-80, T93 302 25 66, F93 317 61 90. Tucked in next to the *Mercat de la Boquería*, the Hotel Internacional is usually draped with football flags and beered-up guests. Rooms are simple but adequate although the recent price hikes mean it's no longer a bargain. **C** *Hotel de l'Arc*, Rambla 19, T93 301 97 98, F93 318 62 63. This is a basic, rather functional hotel tucked away at the seedier end of La Rambla. The facilities are pretty good for the price and it's a quick walk to the harbourside restaurants and bars.

D *Cuatro Naciones*, Rambla 40, T93 317 36 24, F93 302 69 85, www.h4n.com Built in 1770, this was La Rambla's first hotel; it's glory days are long gone but there's still a hint of faded grandeur in the air. Rooms are functional but the price is right for the location.

Sleeping

Five of the best: cheap sleeps

- *Hostal Benidorm* (see below)
- *Hostal Galerías Maldà* (see page 255)
- *Hostal Jardí* (see page 255)
- *Hostal Eden* (see page 259)
- *Hostal Plaza* (see page 259)

E *Pension Ambos Mundos*, 10 Plaça Reial, T93 318 79 70, F93 412 23 63. This attractive little pension is situated above the laid-back bar of the same name on the square; there are a dozen pleasant, tiled rooms with bathrooms, and some have balconies looking out over the square. It's popular with young backpackers and there's a big communal sitting-room.

E *Hotel Roma Reial*, Plaça Reial 11, T93 302 03 66, F93 301 18 39. A bright, friendly hotel in the corner of the buzzy Plaça Reial, this offers decent rooms, and a bar with terrace on the square. It's popular with backpackers and, like all the accommodation on the square, is best for night owls who wont mind the noise.

F *Hostal Benidorm*, Rambla 37, T93 302 20 54. A friendly guesthouse with very well-priced rooms right on the Ramblas. Some of the rooms on the top floor have extraordinary views of Gaudí's wonderful roof on the Palau Guell (see page 104).

F *Pension Las Flores*, Ramblas 79, T93 317 16 34 This tiny pension is hidden up a narrow staircase off the Rambla. The owners are very kind and friendly and the rooms are spotless, but can get very stuffy in summer. Some have bathrooms, and those at the front have balconies overlooking the prettiest, flower-filled section of La Rambla. Prices have leapt recently.

Barri Gòtic
■ *on map,*
page 72 and 77

There are hundreds of hotels in all categories crammed into the narrow streets of the old city. They are perfectly placed for the sightseeing and buzzing nightlife of the atmospheric maze which forms the nucleus of the Gothic City, but the cheaper hotels will also be pretty noisy and you might have to choose between rooms with balconies overlooking the streets, or quieter darker rooms at the back of the buildings.

This is the best
place to head
if you are arriving
late at night

A *Grand Hotel Barcino*, 6 C/Jaume I, T93 302 20 12, F93 301 42 42, www.gargallo-hotels.com Luxury, convenience, and a good location for a more or less reasonable price make this an interesting choice despite the lack of atmosphere; suites are available with a jacuzzi and the nightlife of the Barri Gòtic is on your doorstep. **A** *Colón*, Avinguda de la Catedral 7, T93 301 1404, F93 317 2915, www.hotelcolon.es A discreetly luxurious hotel in a fantastic location facing the Gothic cathedral, the aristocratic Colón has all the amenities including a piano bar and restaurant; the upper rooms have terraces, and all are decorated with classic elegance. **A** *Hotel Gótico*, C/Jaume I 14, T93 315 22 11, F93 315 21 13, www.gargallo-hotels.com Conveniently located in the heart of Barri Gòtic, this is a sleek hotel set in an old palace which caters mainly to business people. Some rooms have balconies overlooking the bustle and prices are reasonable for four-star comforts in this location.

B *Suizo*, 12 Plaça del Angel, T93 310 61 08, F93 310 40 81, www.gargallo-hotels.com, comercial@gargallo-hotels.com This is a dignified, traditional hotel handily placed for the main sights of the Barri Gòtic. It faces the noisy Via Laietana but the nicest rooms overlook the narrow passage called Baixada Llibreteria. There's a beautiful old bar and all the rooms have been recently refurbished. **B** *Adagio*, C/de Ferran 21, T93 318 90 61, F93 318 37 24, book@adagiohotel.com Recent renovations including sound-proofing in all the rooms still don't quite add up to the price of this hotel; still, the staff are friendly, the rooms are clean and well-equipped and the location is very handy for the main sights and nightlife of the old city. **B** *Metropol*, C/Ample 31, T93 310 51 00, F93 319 12 76, www.hoteles-hesperia.es This graceful 19th-century hotel is very

Sleeping

convenient for the nightlife of the harbour area and the Barri Gòtic. It was given a major overhaul for the Olympics and combines modern design with some traditional fittings.

C *Nouvel Hotel*, C/de Santa Anna 20, T93 301 82 74, F93 301 83 70 A pretty *modernista* hotel on a busy shopping street in the heart of the old city, this has gleaming wooden fittings, marble floors and shimmering candelabra. The rooms don't live up to the allure of the public areas and some are a little small, but others have delightful swirling balconies looking over the hubbub below. The staff are very friendly and welcoming.

D *Hostal Jardí*, Plaça de Sant Josep Oriol 1, T93 301 59 00, F93 318 36 64. Book well in advance if you want to get a room at this extremely popular hostal; the nicest rooms overlook the leafy Plaça del Pi, one of the main hubs of the old city. The simpler, less expensive rooms at the back look out onto a patio. **D** *Hostal Lausanne*, Avinguida del Portal de l Àngel 24, T93 302 11 39. A very pleasant family-run hostal with a very pretty tiled entrance, this has 17 simple rooms and an attractive communal sitting room. It's situated on a bustling shopping street, just around the corner from Plaça de Catalunya. **D** *Hostal Palermo*, C/de la Boquería 21, T93 302 40 02 An attractive, recently refurbished hostal with deep red floor tiles, modest, well-kept rooms, and a communal lounge area. **D** *Hostal Rembrandt*, C/Portaferrisa 23, T/F93 318 10 11 Spotless, attractively decorated rooms and a pleasant communal patio area make this a good cheap option. **D** *Hostal Rey Don Jaime I*, C/Jaume I 11, T/F93 310 62 08, www.atriumhotels.com This hostal has an excellent central location just off Plaça Sant Jaume, perfect for enjoying the nightlife of the Barri Gòtic and the Born. Most rooms have balconies overlooking the bustling street – the ones at the back are quieter but less atmospheric.

E *Hostal Layetana*, Plaça de Ramón Berenguer III el Gran 2, T93 319 20 12 This is a well-kept, friendly hostal in a pleasant 19th-century building. There are 20 clean, neat rooms, some of which overlook the strip of old Roman walls, but the traffic zooming down the Vía Laietana means that ear plugs are essential. **E** *Hostal Levante*, Baixada de Sant Miquel 2, T93 317 95 65, www.hostallevante.com Clean, functional rooms set over two floors in an attractive old building; the Levante is popular with foreign students living there long-term and can be a bit noisy. **E** *Hotel Call*, C/Arc de Sant Ramon de Call 4, T93 302 11 23. Simple, plain hotel tucked down an atmospheric side street near the cathedral. The rooms are basic but clean and all have en suite facilities.

F *Hostal Galerías Maldà*, C/del Pi 5, T93 317 30 02. This can be a bit difficult to find, as it's hidden away up a dark staircase in the labyrinth of the *Maldà* shopping arcade, but you'll be glad that you made the effort. The rooms are simple, sunny and very good value, and the owner is friendly and helpful. **F** *Pensión Vitoria*, C/de la Palla 8, T/F93 302 08 34. A popular little pension not far from the leafy Plaça del Pi. One bathroom serves nine rooms, but there are two doubles with en suite facilities. The simple rooms are light and airy and most have balconies.

For youth hostels in the area, see page 262

There are no really grand hotels in this district as yet, but you'll find plenty of reasonably priced, friendly smaller hotels and *pensións*. It's a good base for the sights and nightlife of the trendy Born area, as well as the leafy Parc de la Ciutadella.

La Ribera
■ on maps, pages 88 and 91

C *Hotel Park*, 11 Avinguda Marquès de l'Argentera 11, T93 319 60 00, F93 319 45 19. Built in the early 1950s by the celebrated architect Antoni de Moragas, the Hotel Park was renovated in 1990 by Moragas' son using the original plans. It's a narrow, slim hotel with good-sized balconies looking out towards Barceloneta, an exquisite interior wraparound staircase and comfortable, well-equipped rooms. **C** *Hotel Urquinaona*,

Sleeping

Ronda de Sant Pere 24, T93 268 13 36, F93 295 41 37, www.barcelonahotel.com/urquinaona This recently revamped former hostal is now a very well equipped modern hotel, offering lots of unexpected extras like Internet access. The rooms all have satellite TV and air-conditioning, and the prices are extremely reasonable for the standard of the facilities.

D *Hostal Fontanella*, Vía Laietena 71, T93 317 59 43. This friendly, cosy little hostel is located very close to the Plaça Urquinaona. The traffic can be a bit of a problem, but the owner is very welcoming and looks after her guests very well. The rooms are simple, but clean and thoughtfully equipped with combs, toothpaste and soap. It's in a slightly safer area than some and is particularly popular with young women. **D** *Hotel Oasis II*, Pla del Palau 17, T93 319 43 96, F93 310 48 74. This is in a great location if you want to party in the Born district or in the Port Vell. Run by friendly management, it's popular with young backpackers and can be a bit noisy, but the rooms are good value. Some have balconies overlooking the action on the square. **D** *Hotel Triunfo*, Passeig de Picasso 22, T/F93 315 08 60. A small quiet, attractive hotel set in an arcade overlooking the Parc de la Ciutadella. Rooms are spotless and well-equipped with en suite bathrooms, TVs and air-conditioning. It's very well situated for the buzzing nightlife of the Born district which is just around the corner.

E *Pensión Lourdes*, C/de la Princesa 14, T93 319 33 72. A well-priced, pleasant hostal with basic rooms, some with en suite facilities and some without. It's also handily placed for the main sights of the Born district. **E** *Hostal de Ribagorza*, C/Trafalgar 39, T93 319 19 68, F93 319 12 47. Strictly speaking, this family-run pensión is in the Eixample, but it's very close to the *Palau de la Música Catalana* and the nightlife of the Born. There are only 11 rooms, some with en suite facilities and some without, but all have Tvs.

El Raval
■ *on map, page 109*

This is rapidly becoming the hippest neighbourhood in the city, with dozens of trendy new bars, galleries and clubs opening up all the time, and there are lots of decent places to stay which offer good deals for such a central location. That said, the Raval hasn't yet shaken off its unsavoury reputation, and it's still the kind of neighbourhood where you need to stay streetwise and keep a close eye on your bags.

AL *Hotel Ambassador*, C/del Pintor Fortuny 13, T93 412 05 30, F93 302 79 77. A graceful, modern hotel in a side street just off La Rambla, this offers excellent amenities including a piano bar and rooftop terrace with garden and swimming pool. The rooms are quietly elegant, although those on the upper floors are sunnier.

C *Gaudí*, 12 C/Nou de la Rambla, T93 317 90 32, F93 412 26 36, www.hotelgaudi.es Conveniently located, with comfortable rooms, the Gaudí has an undulating glass and wrought-iron entrance, and a multi-coloured fountain made of broken tiles just inside the door. None of it is genuine, but rooms on the top floors look over the real thing at the Palau Güell (see page 104) opposite. Service can be a little cool. **C** *Moderno*, C/de l'Hospital 11, T93 301 41 54, F93 302 78 70. There's a lot of fussy Spanish kitsch in the décor, but the Moderno is a well-priced, friendly hotel in the heart of Raval. **C** *Méson de Castilla*, C/de Valldonzella 5, T93 318 21 82, F93 412 40 20, www.husa.es The Méson de Castilla may be owned by the *Husa* chain, but there's little sense of it at this friendly hotel not far from the Museu d'Art Contemporani. Breakfast is served out on the pretty interior patio garden, and rooms are furnished in warm colourful fabrics and wicker. They also have some good-sized family rooms.

C *San Agustin*, Plaça Sant Agustí 3, T93 318 16 58, F93 317 29 28, www.hotelsa.com, hotelsa@hotelsa.com This is one of the city's oldest hotels, a graceful, apricot-coloured building overlooking Plaça Sant Agustí. The rooms on the top floor have wooden beams and wonderful views, and there are brand new bathrooms and all mod cons after the latest renovation. **C** *Turin*, C/Pintor Fortuny 9, T93 302 48 12, F93 302 10 05, hotelturin@teleline.es The Turin doesn't have much character, but it's reasonably priced and enjoys an excellent location just off the Rambla. The air-conditioned rooms are bland but comfortable.

Five of the best: hotels with swimming pools

- *Hotel Duques de Bergara* (see page 253)
- *Hotel Ambassador* (see page 256)
- *Hotel Regente* (see page 258)
- *Hotel Balmes* (see page 259)
- *Arts Barcelona* (see page 261)

D *España*, C/de Sant Pau 9-11, T93 318 17 58, F93 317 11 34.The España is marked on every tourist map thanks to Domènech i Montaner's stunning murals and swirling wooden fittings on the ground floor. Disappointingly, rooms are grimly functional although some at least open out onto a delightful interior terrace, and the service can be surly. **D** *Peninsular*, C/de Sant Pau 34-36, T93 302 31 38, F93 412 36 99. The Peninsular is a charming choice set in an old convent almost opposite the Hotel España. There's a charming interior patio filled with plants and greenery and the rooms are comfortable and good value. **D** *Principal*, C/Junta de Comerç 8, T93 318 89 70, F93 412 08 19, www.hotelprincipal.es There are several cheaper hostales and hotels along this street; this is one of the nicest – and perhaps the most eccentric, with florid rooms decorated with a mixture of antiques, junk and lots of nick-nacks. The owners are very friendly and also run the *Joventut* (on the same street at No12 with the same email and website), run by the same people. **D** *Hostería Grau*, C/Ramelleres 27, T93 301 81 35, F93 317 68 25, www.intercom.es/grau A spotless, friendly little hostal with a small café downstairs, and a pleasant sitting room upstairs. The owners are very happy to provide information on the city.

　D *Hostal Morató*, C/Sant Ramon 29, T93 442 36 69, F93 324 90 05, www.hostalmorato.com A basic, simple pension in the heart of the Raval; all rooms are light, reasonably equipped and offer small balconies. Those without bathrooms offer better value than those with. There's a pleasant little café downstairs and it's well located for the Raval's buzzing nightlife. **D** *Hostal Ramos*, C/Hospital 36, T93 302 07 23, F93 302 04 30. This is a very pleasant old hostal set in an attractive, rambling old building just off the Ramblas. Some rooms have balconies overlooking the peaceful Plaça Sant Agustí. **D** *La Terassa*, 11 C/Junta del Comerç, T93 302 51 74, F93 301 21 88. This is a very popular pension run by the same people as the Jardí; some of the nicer rooms have balconies overlooking the street, or the pretty interior patio where breakfast is served in summer.

E *Hostal Òpera*, C/Sant Pau 20, T93 318 82 01. This bright, clean hostal is just around the corner from the Liceu opera house. There is still some renovation going on, but many of the rooms are air-conditioned, and have spanking new bathrooms. **F** *Pension Venècia*, C/Junta del Comerç 13, T93 302 61 34. This is very nice little place, with a small sun terrace where you can sit out and sunbathe or get your laundry done. Rooms are basic – none have en suite facitilies – but the prices are very low and the staff very friendly.

Sleeping

Eixample

■ on maps, pages
120 and 122
The best of the city's hotels are located in this graceful grid. They are usually within easy walking distance of the sights of the old town and those of the **Quadrat d'Or** with its slew of creamy *modernista* buildings, and many have retained their old turn-of-the-century fittings. All this luxury comes at a price, of course, but there are also some charming reasonably priced hostals hidden away which are well worth seeking out.

AL *Alexandra*, C/Mallorca 251, T93 467 71 66, F93 488 02 58, www.hotel-alexandra.com Chic, modern hotel with lots of glass and ultra-modern design. Rooms are decorated with dark wood panelling and those at the back are the quietest. **AL** *Claris*, C/de Pau Claris 150, T93 487 62 62, F93 215 79 70, www.derbyhotels.es Set in an old palace, this is currently one of the most fashionable and stylish hotels in the city. It is filled with ancient art (the owner, Jordi Clos, has put the ancient Egyptian artefacts in his spanking new Egyptian Museum, see p119) and the rooms are decorated with the most luxurious understatement. There's a Japanese garden but best of all is the outdoor rooftop pool with wonderful views. **AL** *Condes de Barcelona*, Passeig de Gràcia 73, T93 467 47 80, F93 467 47 81, cbhotel@condesdebarcelona.com Converted from two 19th-century palaces, this is another charming and sumptuous hotel with large, elegant, light-filled rooms. Modern technology meets turn-of-the-century opulence and each room is equipped with fax and modem. There's a delightful piano bar and a small rooftop pool. **AL** *Gallery Hotel*, C/Rosselló 249, T93 415 99 11, F93 415 91 84, www.galleryhotel.com Large, sleek ultra-modern hotel with luxuriously appointed rooms. As well as extras like a sauna and gym, there's also an excellent restaurant overlooking the lovely garden terrace.

AL *Hotel Majestic*, Passeig de Gràcia 68, T93 488 17 17, F93 488 18 80, reservas@hotelmajestic.es Another grand old establishment, this was another of the city's most exclusive hotels and the favourite of Miró, Josephone Baker and a host of other celebrities. After decades of obscurity it has been thoroughly renovated to become a truly opulent address, with a very impressive entrance on the Passeig de Gràcia. There are sweeping stairways, luxurious, well-equipped rooms and an excellent restaurant, the *Drolma*, is very expensive but serves outstanding Catalan cuisine in very elegant surroundings. **AL** *Rey Juan Carlos I*, Avda Diagonal 661-671, T93 364 40 40, F93 364 43 64, www.hrjuancarlos.com Modern glassy ultra luxurious tower in the smartest part of town (a taxi ride from all the sights) which has all the amenities you could wish for; pool, bar, sauna, gym and very attentive service. **AL** *Ritz*, 668 Gran Vía des les Corts Catalanes, T93 318 52 00, F93 318 01 48, ritz@ritzbcn Classic luxury, with all the *Belle Epoque* trimmings. The Ritz opened in 1919 and has hosted everyone from Ava Gardner to Salvador Dali (who holed up in room 110). The bathrooms are magnificent; marble, Roman-style baths, and walls inlaid with Sevillano tiles. There's also a very fine restaurant, the Diana, which is open to non-residents.

AL *Diplomàtic*, C/Pau Claris 122, T93 272 38 10, F93 272 38 11, www.ac-hoteles.com, diplomatic@ac-hoteles.com A sleek, modern glassy hotel in a good central location, this offers superb amenities including sauna and gym and has fantastic views from its roof terrace. The airy rooms are crisply furnished, and the service is impeccable. **AL** *Gran Hotel Havana*, Gran Vía de les Corts Catalanes 647, T93 412 11 15, F93 412 26 11, www.hoteles-silken.com, hotelhavanasilken@retemail.es This *modernista* mansion was built in 1872 and has retained some of its swirling 19th-century fittings. The large, airy rooms have luxurious bathrooms decorated with Italian marble, and it's very well located for all the major sights. **AL** *Regente*, Rambla de Catalunya 76, T93 487 59 89, F93 487 32 27, www.hoteles-centro-ciudad.es Perfectly located on an elegant shopping street, this hotel is set in an old *modernista* building with some surviving original features. It offers traditional, very elegant rooms and those on the top floors have wonderful views. There's a small rooftop pool for sunning yourself and very polite, old-fashioned service. **AL** *Sant Moritz*, C/de la Diputació 264, T93 412 15 00, F93 412 12 36 This is a classically elegant hotel set in a 19th-century mansion, with a sweeping marble staircase and large, comfortable rooms which are unfortunately not as quiet as you might hope for the price. Still, it's conveniently located and has an excellent restaurant, the *San Galen*.

A *Avenida Palace*, Gran Vía de les Corts Catalanes 605, T93 301 96 00, F93 318 12 34, www.husa.es, avpalace@husa.es A smart, traditional hotel with lots of wood panelling, gilt and shimmering chandeliers. Rooms on the fourth floor upwards have the best views and have retained some original features. **A** *Balmes*, C/Mallorca 216, T93 451 19 14, F93 451 00 49, www.derbyhotels.es More unbridled luxury from Jordi Clos (of the *Hotel Claris*); the Balmes is an elegant, modern hotel with well-appointed, impeccably tasteful rooms. There's a lush interior garden with swimming pool and, if you are in the mood to splash out, the hotel even offers duplex apartments. **A** *Caledonian*, Gran Vía de les Corts Catalanes 574, T93 453 02 00, 93 451 77 03, www.hotel-caledonian.com This is a classic Eixample hotel which has recently been refurbished; the modern, airy rooms have all the amenities as well as generously proportioned bathrooms, and the public areas retain a turn-of-the-century grace. **A** *Gran Derby*, C/Loreto 28, T93 322 20 62, F93 419 68 20, www.derbyhotels.es A very swish business hotel owned by Jordi Clos, the Egyptologist behind the *Claris* Hotel, this is conveniently located in the main business district and offers top-class amenities. There's a sister hotel, the *Derby*, at C/Loreto 21.

C *Gran Via*, Gran Vía de les Corts Catalanes 642, T93 318 19 00, F93 318 99 97, hgranvia@nnhotels.es A very charming hotel, this converted 19th-century mansion retains many of its original fittings including a grand sweeping staircase and preserves an air of genteel luxury. The standard of the rooms varies considerably, but many of them are furnished with antiques. The service is very personal and friendly and there's a pretty, plant-filled courtyard.

D *Hotel Antibes*, C/Diputació 394, T93 232 62 11, F93 265 74 48. A modern, simple hotel with functional air-conditioned rooms at reasonable prices. It may not ooze charm, but it's good value for the area. **D** *Hotel Paseo de Gràcia*, Passeig de Gràcia 102, T93 215 58 24, F93 215 06 03. A simple, friendly very reasonably priced hotel in a superb location. The rooms are basic but all have phones and TVs and the staff are very helpful. Prices are at the bottom of this category. **D** *Hotel Ginebra*, Rambla de Catalunya 1, 3º, T93 317 10 63, F93 317 55 65. A friendly, cosy hotel in a graceful old building just off the Plaça de Catalunya: rooms are double-glazed and well-equipped and some have balconies with views across the square. **D** *Hostal Plaza*, C/Fontanella 18, T/F93 301 01 39, www.personal.redestb.es/plazahostal Run by a very friendly and welcoming family, the Plaza is a little home away from home – there is even a disco ball and pictures of Marilyn Monroe. All the simple rooms have showers and fans, and guests have use of a TV room, fridge and freezer, and there's even a laundry service.

E *Hostal Eden*, C/de Balmes 55, T93 454 73 63, F93 350 27 02, hostaleden@hotmail.com A charmingly eccentric little pension on the first and second floors of an old Eixample building. The rooms have all kinds of unexpected amenities – some have fridges, whirlpools and tiny terracotta patios. There is a coin-operated Internet machine, and the owners are very friendly and helpful. **E** *Hostal Neutral*, Rambla de Catalunya 42, T93 487 63 90. A good location and pretty interior terrace make up for the slightly dowdy décor of this pension. All 28 rooms have en suite showers or bathrooms. **E** *Hostal Oliva*, Passeig de Gràcia 32, T93 488 01 62 This pension has a fantastic location on the elegant Passeig de Gràcia in a ramshackle old building with a wonderful old lift. It offers spacious, simple rooms at very reasonable prices. **E** *Hostal Palacios*,

Gran Vía de les Corts Catalanes 629 bis, T93 301 30 79, F93 301 37 92. A simple, rather bland hostal which nonetheless offers good value for money thanks to its central location. **E** *Hostal Windsor*, Rambla de Catalunya 84, T93 215 11 98. An extremely popular pension, this has spotless, light and airy rooms, pleasant staff and a great location. Some rooms overlook the leafy Rambla de Catalunya, filled with smart shops and cafés.

F *Pensión Rondas*, C/Girona 4, T/F93 232 51 02. A charming little pensión run by a friendly brother and sister who speak excellent English. Rooms are simple but spotless, and there's a small sitting room with a TV. Best of all is the creaking, wooden lift which looks like a museum piece – remember to close all the doors or you won't get anywhere.

Gràcia, Tibidabo and outer districts

Gràcia
■ *on map, page 146*

Gràcia is a laid-back neighbourhood which still belongs to the locals, and is a good choice if you want to escape the tourist hordes. The nightlife is excellent, particularly around lively Plaça de Sol, but if you prefer a quiet life, there's a great old market, as well as several parks including the Park Güell on your doorstep.

B *Hotel Rubens*, Passeig de la Mare del Déu del Coll 10, T93 219 12 04, F93 219 12 69, www.hoteles-catalonia.es This is a well-equipped modern hotel set in a residential district near Park Güell and the Parc Creuta del Coll. The amenities are slanted towards business clientele, but it makes a peaceful retreat from the crowds of the old city – a short metro or bus ride away. Most rooms have balconies with great views across the city and there's also a terrace if you want to catch some sun. **C** *Guillem Hotel*, C/Guillem Tell 49, T93 415 40 00, F93 217 34 65. A new hotel, handily placed for the nightlife around Plaça Molina, this offers attractively furnished rooms. Those overlooking C/Guilem Tell are slightly larger than the others. **C** *Hotel Via Augusta*, Via Augusta 63, T93 217 92 50, F93 237 7714. A graceful old hotel on the edge of Gràcia, this has good amenities including a sun terrace and car parking. The rooms are well-equipped for the price, and the only downside is the noisy traffic on the Via Augusta. It's best to ask for a quiet room off the main road.

D *Pensión Abete*, C/Gran de Gràcia 67, T93 218 55 24. A simple, family-run pension with basic, pleasant rooms. This is no longer quite the bargain it used to be, but it's very friendly and well placed for the Gràcia nightlife. **E** *Pensión Norma*, C/Gran de Gràcia 87, T93 237 44 78 This doesn't look great from the outside; it's on the second floor of a shabby, rambling old building. Inside, it's an attractive, spotless pension with 18 well-kept basic rooms.

Tibidabo & outer districts
■ *on maps, pages 157 and 163*

A *Relais de Orsà*, C/Mont d'Orsà 35, T93 406 94 11, F93 406 94 71. With just a handful of rooms in an old modernista palace, this is a delightful hotel in the hilltop town of Vallvidriera. It's close to the attractions of Tibidabo, and is a perfect base if you want to do some walking in the Parc de Collserola. The views from the top of the village are astounding.

It's worth considering the options out here if you want a little peace from the hubbub

B *Hotel Alimara*, C/Berruguete 156, T93 427 00 00, F93 427 92 92, www.cett.es This is a very swish, modern hotel out in Horta, which was built in 1992 and is near the Olympic Velodrome and tennis courts. Nowadays it caters mainly to businesspeople, but offers excellent facilities for the price. The spacious rooms are elegant and airy and there's also an attractive terrace overlooking the gardens. **B** *Turó de Vilana*, C/Vilana 7, T93 434 03 63, F93 418 89 03, hotel@turodevilana.com A gleaming modern, attractive hotel with stylish décor, this is located in Tibidabo, not far from Norman Foster's telecommunications tower and the Parc de Collserola. There are only 20 rooms, all elegantly decorated and very well-equipped. (Prices are at the upper end of this category.)

B *Hotel Ònix*, C/Llançà 30, T93 426 00 87, F93 426 19 81, hotelonix@icyesa.es A pleasant, modern option near the Plaça d'Espanya and Sants station, this has a mini-pool on the rooftop, good views across the Miró Park and the Arenas bullring and each room has its own balcony. (Around €120 for a double room.) **B** *Hotel Roma*, Avda de Roma 31, T93 410 66 33, F93 410 13 52. Another good choice near Sants station, the Roma has elegant rooms decorated with antiques, a pleasant patio area, and friendly staff. Recent price hikes have made the tarifs a bit steep for the amenities on offer. (Around €1,503 for a double room.)

The hotels around Sants are handy for the airport or the main railway station

E *Barceló Sants*, Plaça Països Catalanes s/n, T93 490 95 95, F93 490 60 45. This large, bland modern hotel sits right on top of Sants station. It has all the amenities, packaged with faceless international efficiency, but at least you won't have far to drag your luggage. Around €1,803 for a double room. **E** *Pensión Sants*, C/Antoni de Campmany 82, T93 331 37 00, F93 421 68 64. A newly refubished large pensión with very reasonably priced rooms, handily close to the station. Most rooms have en suite facilites and some have balconies, but sometimes the traffic noise can be a bit overwhelming. Rooms on the upper floors are less noisy. (Around €33 for a double room with en suite facilities) **E** *Hostal Bèjar*, C/Bèjar 36-38, T93 325 59 53. This is a simple, but handily located hostal, offering basic rooms with or without bathrooms. (Around €39 for a double room.)

El Litoral

AL *Arts Barcelona*, C/Marina 19-21, T93 221 10 00, F93 221 10 70 Perhaps the most famous and, without doubt, the most glamorous hotel in the city, Hotel Arts is set in one of the enormous glassy towers at the entrance to the Port Olímpic. It was inaugurated in 1992, and offers 33 floors of unbridled luxury, including an indoor pool and an outdoor pool, a fine restaurant, a piano bar overlooking the hotel gardens and the sea, sauna, gym and beauty centre. The whole complex is decorated with original paintings and sculptures and very sleek design, and the rooms offer stupendous views. The top three floors have duplex apartments filled with all kinds of luxurious extras for those with a spare several thousand pesetas.

■ *on maps, pages 198 and 206*

B *Alfa Aeropuerto*, Zona Franca, Carrer K s/n, T93 336 25 64, F93 335 55 92, www.bestwestern.com A bland, featureless hotel in the *Best Western* chain, worth checking out only if you have a ridiculously early flight. Around €138 for a double room.

There are, perhaps surprisingly, just a couple of choices close to the seaside

D *Hotel Marina Folch*, C/del Mar 16, T93 310 53 27. This is a tiny, charming little hotel with just ten rooms hidden away in Barceloneta. It's extremely popular and gets booked up very quickly, so be sure to reserve weeks in advance.

Campsites

South of Barcelona *Cala-Gogo-Barcelona-El Prat* , Carretera de la Playa, El Prat de Llobregat, T93 379 46 00. Open mid-Mar until mid-Oct. Enormous campsite with good facilities including, an on-site supermarket, swimming pool, restaurant and bar. *El Toro Bravo*, Autovía de Castelldefels Km 11, Viladecans, T93 637 34 62. Open all year. *Albatros* Autovía de Castelldefels Km 15, Gavà, T93 633 06 42. Open May-Sep. **North of Barcelona** *Masnou*, El Masnou, Carretera N-II Km 656.8, T93 555 15 03. Open all year. A small campsite offering plenty of shade. The supermarket is open during the summer only, and there are diving and sailing facilities available at the nearby beach. Bungalows and rooms can also be rented.

There are no campsites close to town – the nearest is 7 km away. Contact, Asociació dels Campings, Gran Via 608, 3º, T93 412 59 55

Sleeping

Apartment hotels

Most are aimed at business travellers and are located in the business areas around Diagonal and Plaça Espanya

Apartaments Calàbria, C/Calàbria 129, T93 426 42 48, F93 426 76 40, metro Rocafort Functional and well-priced apartments in an old Eixample block. Rates are around €114 for two people. *Aparthotel Bertrán*, C/Bertrán 150, T93 212 75 50, F93 418 71 03, metro Vallcarca, FGC Tibidabo. This is a very popular hotel, up near Tibidabo. The excellent facilities include bike rental (the Parc de Collserola is fairly close), gym, rooftop terrace and a pool.

Atenea Aparthotel, C/Joan Guell 207-211, T93 490 66 40, F93 490 64 20, atenea@ city-hotels.es metro Les Corts. A sleek, bland apartment hotel very popular with business travellers. Facilities include bar, restaurant and meeting rooms. The rooms are all well-equipped with the business person in mind. *Citadines*, Rambla 122, T93 270 11 11, F93 412 74 21, www.citadines.com metro Liceu or Catalunya. The most central apartment hotel, this is right on La Rambla. Rates per night are a hefty €240, but they offer good facilities, and there are amazing views from the rooftop terrace. *Amílcar*, C/Amilcar 118, T93 455 30 42, F93 450 22 48, Cheap and cheerful option, the Amílcar has a terrace but few other facilities. Rates are about €39 per night.

Youth hostels

For more information, try the new IYHF website, www.hostalling international.com

If you don't have an international youth hostel (IYHF) card, you can buy one from the *Viatgeteca* student travel agency, C/Rocafort 116-122, 08015 Barcelona, T93 483 83 78, www.bcu.cesca.es which is part of the Catalan government's 'youth information point'. Not all the hostels below listed below require cards, but they quickly fill up in summer so you should call ahead to reserve a bed.

Hostal Hedy Holiday, C/Buenaventura Muñoz 4, T93 300 57 85, F93 300 94 44, metro Arc de Triomf. This is a brand new privately owned hostel close to the Parc de la Ciutadella. Large, airy rooms sleep between six and eight people and there's a bar-café offering light snacks and drinks, as well as an Internet room. *Hostel de Joves*, Passeig de Pujades 29, T93 300 31 04, metro Arc de Triomf. An attractive official IYHF hostal just next to the Parc de la Ciutadella, this will allow you to stay for one night without a card or five nights with one.

Albergue Kabul, 17 Plaça Reial, T93 318 51 90, F93 301 40 34, metro Liceu. Very centrally located on the Plaça Reial, this privately owned hostel has rooms sleeping from two to 12 people. It's noisy and some rooms are very run down, but you can't get any closer to the action. Facilities include TV and video and laundry. *Albergue Mare de Déu de Montserrat*, Passeig de la Mare de Déu del Coll 41-51, T93 210 51 51, metro Vallcarca. This is beautiful, well-equipped youth hostel set in an old mansion with its own grounds up in the hills near the Parc del Creuta del Coll. Rooms sleep from two to eight people and there are plenty of facilities, including Internet access and a laundry. There is a maximum stay of five nights, curfew is at midnight, and IYHF cards are required.

Albergue Pere Tarrés, C/Numancia 149, T93 410 23 09, F93 419 6268, metro Les Corts. This is a bit far out from the city centre but is handily placed for Sants station. Facilities include a laundry and parking area and there is also a pleasant roof terrace. There are strict rules including no smoking, eating or drinking in the dorms. IYHF cards are required, and curfew is at 11pm, although the doors open at hourly intervals through the night.

Background

11

Background

265 **History**

275 **Art**

279 Architecture

History

If you could ask the 450,000-year-old woman whose skull was found near Tautavel in 1971, where she lived, it's unlikely that she would say Catalunya. Primarily because she was a nomad but also because the area we now call Catalunya with a population of 6,000,000 people, its own language and cultural history, had around another 449,000 years to go before it could properly be said to exist. Despite the optimistic efforts of various Catalan historians to trace a line of collective identity stretching back through the mists of time, Catalunya was a long time in the making. But it's always been a popular destination.

Human remains found near Girona tell us that Middle Palaeolithic man (80,000-35,000 BC) dropped by. He was followed by representatives of the Upper Palaeolithic period, of whom there may have been as many as 8,000, who built dolmens, most of which are concentrated near Girona and Empordà in the north and Priorat and Baix Camp in the south. Artefacts such as collective burial mounds, vases and agricultural tools, especially from Collbato in the Llobregat Valley; tell us that they joined in the Neolithic and Bronze Age revolutions as enthusiastically as their counterparts elsewhere in Europe.

The Indo-European influx in the second millennium BC brought with it invasions of the Ter and Llobregat valleys and the first proper settlers in the form of Celts (from the north), Iberians (possibly from Libya) and Ligurians (provenance obscure). No one knows the exact nature of relations between these three peoples, but we can assume it involved a fair and paradoxical degree of mutual slaughter and peaceful co-habitation. Their economy was agrarian and when they weren't tilling the land, they were building things. Stone remains can still be seen at Ullastret in Costa Brava. The first people to settle in the area around where Barcelona now lies were the Laetani who traded in honey, grain and oysters.

Phoenician and Greek traders, who had already set up shop in Ibiza and Roses, arrived from the eighth century BC onwards and coastal towns, including Barcelona and far more importantly Empuries, became trading outposts. They introduced sculpture, coinage and perhaps just as important the olive and the vine.

The Roman conquest

The Carthaginians started to arrive from the south and the Romans from the north from the third century BC onwards. Being stuck in the middle of a war between two opposing forces was something the people of Catalunya were to get used to. One thing lead to another and when in 217 BC Hannibal assembled his horde of elephants, crossed the Pyrenees and headed for Rome, the Romans decided it was time to teach these upstart Carthaginians a lesson. This was known as the Second Punic War and there are no prizes for guessing who ended up on the winner's podium. The Carthaginians had to relinquish their Spanish territories and the Romans took Barcelona.

Whereas it took Caesar a mere 10 years to subdue the Gauls (Asterix excepted), the people of Hispania proved a harder nut to crack. And they didn't come any harder than the people of Catalunya, whom the Roman historian Livy described as *ferox genus* (a fierce people). Sporadic and at times concerted resistance continued for another 200 years, but by 197 BC most of the peninsula was under Roman control. It became known as the province of Hispania Citerior with Tarragona as its capital. The Romans soon showed that their appetite for killing was matched by their zest for construction. Roads, aqueducts, and baths were soon dotted across

Hispania. In Tarragona, they built a city covering an area of 70 ha and including a main street (the Via Augusta), shrines, an amphitheatre with seating for 11,000 and a circus for 27,000.

The astonishing remains of Barcino can be seen at the Museu d'Historia de la Ciutat, see page 70

Barcelona was still an infant by comparison and did not become a fully fledged Roman colony until about 15 BC, during the reign of the Emperor Augustus, when it was given the tongue-twister name of Colonia Julia Augusta Faventia Paterna Barcino.(supposedly named after Hamilcar Barca, Hannibal's father). Nestled neatly within the oval arc of the fortified walls, Barcino soon became a prosperous little city which made the most of the fertile plain which encircled it; the vineyards provided much of the empire's plonk and the sea provided the ingredients for the salted fish paste (*garum*) which no Roman household could do without.

The second wave

The Pax Romana stayed more or less intact for a while and commerce developed – until the next influx of uninvited guests arrived from about 409 AD. Again they came from the north, and this time they were Germanic tribes – the Suevi, Vandals and Alans. Although some of them made half-hearted efforts to settle and build, they had little time for the relative sophistication of Roman civilization. Their motto seems to have been 'destroy, steal, scarper'.

The only invaders who showed any interest in establishing durable settlements let alone some form of notional 'state' were the Visigoths who started arriving in the early part of the fifth century and eventually controlled the kingdoms of both France and Spain.

Barcelona was still a small and unimportant port, lying a distant third behind Tarragona and Empúries, but it was attractive enough and sufficiently well-fortified for the Visigoth chief Ataulf to make it the capital of his Kingdom. There are remnants of the episcopal buildings built by the Visigoths underneath the Palau Reial, which can also be visited as part of the tour of the Museu d'Historia de la Ciutat.

A period of relative calm ensued until the next invaders arrived – this time the Berber-Arabs from the Middle East and the Maghreb. Between 711 and 725, they swept all before them. Zaragossa was taken in 714, Tarragona was destroyed in 715, Levant was taken in 716, with Barcelona and Emporda overcome by Al-Hurr in 717-8. Despite resistance from the indigenous people, they soon took over the most of the peninsula. The new Muslim province was called al-Andalus. Many people fled into the Pyrenees and it is this trans-Pyrenean connection with the inhabitants of what is now southern France and Andorra which explains why Catalan as a language is much closer to Provencal than it is to Spanish.

In fact those Muslims who stayed and settled in Iberia were for the most part tolerant, cultured and peaceful. Local customs and religion (Christianity had spread through Iberia from the first century AD), were tolerated and collaboration between the indigenous inhabitants and Muslims was common. Even that epitome of Christian crusaders Rodrigo Diaz de Vivar (more commonly known as El Cid, a.k.a. Charlton Heston) transferred his allegiance from the Frankish king Alfonso VI to the Muslim King of Saragossa before setting himself up as king of an independent Valencia.

The Muslim invaders pushed north into France where they were repelled by Charles Martel at Poitiers in 732. Buoyed by their success, the Franks decided that attack was the best form of defence and started to move south. Their first efforts were disastrous, most notably Charlemagne's defeats at Zaragossa and Roncesvalles. However, Barcelona was recaptured by Charlemagne's son; Louis d'Aquitaine 'The Pious', in 801. They failed to get any further than the Llobregat however; and it would not be until 1492 and the recapture of Granada that the Muslims were genuinely could properly be said to have been evicted 'in the name of Christianity'. In the meantime, Catalunya became the outermost boundary of Frankish territory, known as the Marca Hispanica (the Spanish March) – in effect a buffer zone in the face of Muslim incursions, as well as a thoroughfare for trade and cultural exchange.

The birth of a nation

The Frankish kings headed home for a well-earned croissant, leaving behind nine hereditary earldoms, each under the control of a count loyal to the Frankish crown – the most famous of whom was Wilfred the Hairy (choosing a less self-satisfied appellation than many rulers of that time). Wilfred is credited with uniting the earldoms under the House of Barcelona, a dynasty which was to last 500 years, as well as restoring the Cathedral, establishing the Comte of Vic, and founding Abbeys at Rippoll and Sant Joan de les Abadesses. He is also the man behind the Catalan national flag, the Quatre Barres; consisting of four scarlet stripes on a golden background. The story goes that Wilfred was fighting alongside his Frankish emperor against the Saracen horde. Wilfred was wounded, fell to the ground and as he lay dying, the emperor dipped his fingers into Wilfred's blood and drew them across his golden shield.

With the lure of stability, people came back from the mountains and started to resettle. However, Barcelona continued to be the focal point of tensions between Muslim and Christian forces. The city was sacked by Al-Mansur in 985 and parts of it destroyed. The monastery of Sant Pere de Les Puelles was burned along with all its inhabitants. The hirsute King's grandson, Count Borrel, appealed to King Lothar of France (theoretically their lord) for help. The reply was not what he was hoping for, ties were severed and in 988 the county of Barcelona was declared autonomous.

As a sign of the fledgling state's constitutional boldness and innovation, the Usatjes were established in 1060 – effectively a bill of rights, applied according to traditional custom and law. The people of Barcelona were the first in Europe to do anything like it and this year is celebrated as the birth of the Catalan state. It was indeed a remarkable achievement. Two hundred years later, King Alfonso IV (a Catalan) encapsulated its essence when he said to his wife Leonor of Castile," … our people are not enslaved like the people of Castile – they see us as their lord and we look on them as vassals and good companions".

Easy for a monarch to say! This was basically a feudal system which provided a modicum of security but was founded ultimately on profound inequality. Rights didn't apply to or favour everyone – the peasantry and the poor, for instance. But it was a start.

Economic success and expansion

The 12th and 13th centuries saw massive development. Culturally this took the form of the building of monasteries and the flowering of Romanesque art and architecture, as well as the construction of new towns in Sant Pere and La Ribera. Buildings in Barcelona that remain from this era are the monastery of Sant Pau del Camp, the chapels of Santa Lucia, and of Sant Marcus, as well as the Carrer dels Banys Nous (new baths) built under Ramon Berenguer IV.

These developments were accompanied by an expansion of trade (in grain, wine and textiles) as well as more imperialistic ambitions. To the north, the Counts Ramon Berenguer, through marriage alliances and wads of cash, extended Catalan power into France as far as Carcassonne, Toulouse and Provence. And in 1137, Catalunya found itself bound to the rest of Iberia for the first time, when Ramon Berenguer IV married Petronella, heir to the throne of Aragon. Immediately afterwards he conquered Tortosa and Lleida, and signed treaties with Cazorla and Tudellen thus making himself sovereign over much of Castile.

It was during this period that the term Catalan came into existence, appearing for the first time in a historical (but highly romanticized) account of Ramon de Berenguer IV's expedition against Majorca in 1114.

But what does the word 'Catalan' mean? Ask any half-dozen historical linguists where the name comes from and you will get as many answers. There are those who nail their colours to the mast of ancestry, claiming that the name derives from early inhabitants such as the Gotholoni or Laketani; others claim that it refers to a place (Montcada, Taluniya); and for others it is a job title, derived from the word 'castla' (meaning castle keepers), which was often applied to the inhabitants of the area by visitors. There is no right difinitively answer, so take your pick.

When King Pere I (1196-1213) came to the throne, like all kings of that period worth their salt, he wanted to conquer and acquire, or in other words to colonize. The south of France took his fancy and he decided to head north and add the word 'occitan' to the Catalan state. Unfortunately for him the Franks put up stiff resistance and his bold enterprise ended in defeat and disaster in 1213 at the battle of Muret. His successor, Jaume I the Conqueror, was undeterred and looked elsewhere to extend the empire. Consequently the Balearics were conquered and colonized (1229-35), as were Valencia and Tarragona. Minorca was conquered in 1231 and Ibiza in 1235. And if you want to read a glamorized account of these conquests, then you can always leaf through Jaume's autobiography, the *Llibre dels Feits*, one of the first books written in Catalan. Sadly the more salacious aspects of his character and life are omitted: James was a notorious adulterer and fornicator, and is reputed, for reasons unknown, to have cut the Bishop of Girona's tongue out.

Closer to home, Jaume built a new enclosing wall around Barcelona, which roughly corresponds to the present area between La Rambla and the edge of the Parc de la Ciutadella. New buildings sprang up, and by 1300, Barca was the major city of northern Spain with a population of maybe 50,000. But troubles lay ahead.

The 14th century was punctuated by a suite of disasters: the plague, famine, and other natural catastrophes. Life for the poor and the peasantry became unbearable, enough to incite numerous popular revolts, grain riots and in 1391 a pogrom in which most of Barcelona's Jews were killed. But it was not enough to put the brakes on the juggernaut of imperial expansion and commercial exploitation. The nobility and traders were on a roll and the reign of Jaume II 'the Just' brought with it yet more success – namely a massive expansion into the Mediterranean and towards north Africa.

Within an astonishingly short period of time, Barcelona had become the centre of a virtual Mediterranean empire, rivalling and eventually overtaking their arch-rivals, the Italian maritime republics. Sicily was annexed in 1282, and the Pope handed over Sardinia and Corsica in 1295. Over 130 consulates were established across the Mediterranean, from Alep to Greece, whose purpose was to safeguard Catalan interests.

Realists will attribute this success to the fact the Catalans built the fastest ships in Europe, while romantics will attribute it to those who skippered them – the 'Almogàvars', of whom the most famous were those swashbuckling admirals, Roger de Llúria and Roger de Flor. They were in truth ruthless mercenaries (as one pope called them, 'sons of perdition, schooled in iniquity') whose skills lead them to be employed by the Byzantine Emperor Andronicus II in his fight against the Turks. They won but the feeling was that De Flor was getting too big for his boots and he was assassinated on his return. By way of response, the Catalans raided Macedonia, Thrace, Thebes and created a Catalan duchy in Athens. The real worth of these perceived successes would prove to be limited and the drain they came to place on the national coffers would soon come back to haunt the Catalans. But for the time being, they could justifiably claim to have an empire. A Catalan empire? Perhaps.

During this period, mediaeval Barcelona grew dramatically. Catalan Gothic reached its peak between 1336-387. For example, the cathedral, rebuilt on the ruins of a previous edifice demolished by the Moors, rose again, along with the churches of Santa Maria del Mar, Santa Maria del Pi as well as civic buildings such as the Salo de Tinell and the Llotja, the old market and stock exchange.

Not surprisingly perhaps, this era was accompanied by the development of Catalan language and poetry. The Catalan region was one of the first areas in Europe to use its vernacular language in written form, alongside Latin. Translations from the Bible, Dante and major Latin works were produced, and in 1450 a Joanot Martorell began writing his native Catalan chivalric epic the *Tirant lo Blanc*, considered by some to be the first proper European novel.

Seeds of revolt

Economic success and commercial expansion continued in the second half of the 14th century and the first half of the 15th century. Alfonso V 'the Magnanimous', regent of Castile, became King of Naples in 1443, courtesy of useful contacts in high places. The Crown of Aragon now ruled over an extensive empire: Albania, Slavia, Malta and several islands of the Aegean had been added, as well as several tribute-paying North African Kingdoms.

Behind the economic success and international renown, however, civil discontent (a regular ingredient of Catalan history) grew stronger and cracks in the edifice were beginning to appear. The fundamental incompatibility between the interests of the Counts and trades-people (who had all the money and power) and the rest of the population (who had nothing) remained. This was a period of economic and demographic regression for most of Catalunya. The population of both Barcelona, which had been 50,000 in 1340, and Catalunya as a whole had more than halved by 1477.

In the early part of the 13th century, the Church had set up assemblies to solve various internecine disputes and these evolved eventually into the *corts* (effectively a parliament). And (in 1274) Jaume I had given Barcelona a form of representative self-government, the *Consell de Cent*. But it was representative only in the loosest sense of the word: they represented only the patricians, the church and the traders, who made up less than 5% of the population. The first *corts* were summoned in Vilafranca (1218), Tortosa (1225) and Barcelona (1228) and the first municipal administrations were created in Barcelona between 1249-74. Although the King could in theory govern without their convocation he would have been dicing with disaster. By the end of the century the *corts* could (and did) demand that no law could be passed without their approval. In 1354, they created the Generalitat, the executive arm of the *corts*, comprising two members of the clergy, two nobles and three townspeople. This came into force in Barcelona in 1365.

And the peasants? Let's leave it to Eiximenis, a prominent Franciscan 'thinker' of the time, to give us his verdict: "These people – peasants who are servile, shameless and lacking in intelligence – should never be given any place of honour or respect, because all positions and dignities are descried by them ... their lives are bestial and demented".

These long-festering disputes and the economic consequences of trying to fund and maintain the 'empire', came to a head in the 1450s. In 1453, the Busca (the people's party) appealed to the King for some sort of political representation and a change in the economic policies being implemented by the Biga (the Corts and Generalitat). The King sided with the Busca in an effort to weaken the power of the Biga. The strategy worked insofar as the peasantry and lower trades-people gained more representation, but the economic policies failed and the Biga regained power. The uneasy love/hate relationship between the two political parties and the throne was a veritable soap opera and this was to be far from the final episode.

One thing lead to another, and, in this instance, to a civil war lasting between 1462 and 1472. The Generalitat lined up against King John II by offering the crown to various European regal luminaries. King John, meanwhile, had been joined by the serfs in return for a promise of an extension of their rights. The war went the King's way and Barcelona was besieged and finally capitulated in 1472. Furthermore, the King did not reward the serfs for their loyalty though they gained partial emancipation in 1486 in return for payment of a fixed levy.

Things could only get better for the bloodied and humiliated people of Catalunya. But they didn't. During the Civil War, in an effort to gain allies outside Catalunya, King John had married his heir Ferdinand to Isabella of the Castilian royal family. And it was this alliance which was to plunge Catalunya into one of the gloomiest periods in its history. Castile, which had lain long in the shadow of Catalunya as a commercial force, was ready to step out into the sunlight and announce itself. And just as Catalunya's empire had been grounded on colonization and trading, Castile was to do the same – not to countries in the Mediterranean, but across the Atlantic and the newly discovered Americas.

These events, coupled with the retaking of Granada, the last remaining Muslim stronghold, were celebrated by many historians as the first major act in the unification of Spain. For the people of Catalunya, it was anything but. The shift of political and juridical power from Barcelona to Madrid (in effect the creation of a centralist Catholic Spanish state), combined with the creation of a Madrid-based Inquisition (in 1484), could not have been more humiliating. Like naughty schoolchildren, they were despatched to the corner. Although they retained a modicum of independence in terms of institutions, currency and taxation and Catalan remained the principal language, nonetheless they found themselves drifting further and further out of the political and economic mainstream. The *corts* were summoned less and less frequently, Catalunya was officially barred from engaging in the lucrative development of trade in the Americas and, worse still, they were now ruled by viceroys imposed by Castile, who understood little and cared even less about Catalan tradition or interests. The 16th and 17th centuries were to be known as the Golden Age of Castilian Spain. For the people of Catalunya, they were known as the 'decadencia'.

The downside of having an empire

Like most builders of empires, the Habsburg rulers of the Spanish empire made more enemies than friends. Their heavyweight foes included Catholic France, Protestant England and Muslim Turkey. The Thirty Years' war (effectively a struggle for European hegemony between France and Spain), which began in 1635 during the reign of Philip IV, made the people of Catalunya hate them even more than any European rival. Philip needed money to fund the war and devised the plan of spreading the financial burden across the entire population. The plan backfired in 1640 on the streets of Barcelona. The oppression of taxation coupled with resentment at the billeting of troops (Castilian and prone to loutish behaviour) in the city, pushed them over the edge. A group of protesters, known as *Els Segadors* (the Reapers), gathered in La Rambla captured and murdered the Viceroy. The Generalitat promptly proclaimed a republic. It didn't last long, for he then named Louis XIII count of Barcelona in 1641, in effect declaring war against Spain. Louis installed himself in Roussillon and the War of the Reapers began. But when Louis lost his appetite for the fight and abandoned his Catalunyan friends to their fate, the game was up. The people of Barcelona tried valiantly to fight on alone, but siege and starvation (they ended up having to eat grass) brought them to their knees in 1652. The only positive relic of this disastrous war was the Catalan national anthem, *Els Segadors*.

War in Europe

Despite efforts to resuscitate the city of Barcelona after the war, much of it ironically at the instigation of the King's half-brother Don Juan Jose of Austria, further suffering was on the menu for years to come. War against France continued and Catalunya, and in particular Barcelona, suffered repeated assaults from French forces (in 1675, 1684 and1689). Barcelona was eventually captured in 1697 by Louis XIV.

When Charles II died without an heir, the Bourbon claimant, King Philip V, ascended to the Spanish throne. He promised to uphold Catalan law, but the Catalans had their doubts. Far from being discouraged by their previous failed attempts to wriggle free of what they saw as Castilian tyranny, and despite the natural reluctance of the mercantile class to engage in anything 'unprofitable', they threw themselves into the fight against Philip with fervour. And when the rest of Europe's major powers declared Charles, the son of the Emperor and Archduke of Austria, King of Spain, the Catalans could have been forgiven for believing that they were onto a winner.

They joined forces with England and the anti-Bourbon alliance in 1705. But once again the dice didn't fall their way. Charles was crowned King of Germany and pottered home to take up his throne, the allies lost interest in the war, and the people of Catalunya found themselves fighting a solitary battle against the Castilian army. After a year's siege, Barcelona fell on 11 September 1714. This is now Catalunya's National Day. Philip abolished all Catalan political institutions (the *corts*, the Generalitat, the *consell de cent*) and imposed Castilian law. Most of the universities were dissolved, the Catalan language was banned and Philip issued an edict that Castilian should be introduced into the villages. As the scholar Nebrija had remarked to Queen Isabella when handing over his handbook of Castilian grammar, "language is always the companion of empire". But was this the end of the Catalan nation? Far from it.

A nation of shippers

The people of Catalunya may have felt they had lost their independence, but they had certainly not the lost the art of enterprise. The opening up of the Americas to Catalan traders ushered in a new wave of commercial expansion and success. Mataró became a booming seaport and in 1784 a line of bank managers stood on the jetty of Barcelona's new harbour and waved an anxious goodbye to the 200 ships heading for the New World.

Ironically the loss of the war with Castile helped this new wave of growth. By the standards of most despots, King Carlos III (1759-88) was a liberal. Despite having no doubts as to his position at the top of the pile (he once said of his subjects, "they are like children: they cry when they are washed"), he encouraged cultural exchange and the liberalization of trade. The destruction of many of the old elitist structures of business and government allowed new industries to get their foot in the door. The professional guilds who had dominated Catalunya and especially Barcelona for centuries went into decline and other industries took over – vine-growing and above all the cotton industry. Catalunya became second only to England in its production of raw cotton.

People flooded into Barcelona and the city's population grew from 34,000 in 1718 to over 100,000 by the end of the century. The boom in population was matched by a boom in bricks and mortar; new streets and buildings included La Rambla, and the city's first industrial suburb Barceloneta, which was begun in 1753. The most emblematic building of the era was the hated fortress of La Ciutadella, built as part of the Bourbon backlash when the Catalans were defeated in 1714. During this period the city grew inwards, not outwards: restrictions on the expansion of the city perimeter were still in force and it would not be long before the disastrous consequences of overcrowding were to be felt by all.

Background

The end of the 18th and beginning of the 19th century brought more bickering and fighting between the Spanish, French and English. The nadir, as far as the Spanish were concerned, being the Battle of Trafalgar in 1805. But Napoleon was to make a mistake he would come to regret when, in a typical display of *force majeure,* he put his brother Joseph on the Spanish throne in place of Charles IV. This sparked off the War of Independence (also known as the Peninsular War). It was a case of all hands on deck and, unconvinced by Joseph's promise of autonomy, the Catalans threw their lot in with Madrid. Barcelona was looted, raided and finally fell to French forces in early 1808. Monasteries, including Montserrat, were sacked and pillaged and Girona withstood a seven-month siege. It was not until 1814 and with the help of the English that the Spanish got rid of the French and could breathe a collective sigh of relief.

Recovery was slow and not helped by outbreaks of cholera and yellow fever in 1821. Nonetheless, the first steamship hit the water in 1836 and Spain's first railway, from Barcelona to Mataro, was built in 1848. The traders and industrialists were nothing if not determined. However, it was now the turn of their employees to make themselves heard. The long-festering problems of overcrowding, poor working conditions, resentment at employers (including the Church) and the suppression of rights lead inevitably to a series of popular uprisings. In 1835, monasteries were sacked and factory machinery destroyed. This was followed in 1842 by the *Jamancia* – a full-scale uprising in which rebels took control of the city and destroyed over 400 buildings. The cannons from the Montjüic soon put a stop to them. In 1855, the first General Strike took place in protest at the increased automation of textile industry and in 1856 a workers' strike was held. Both uprisings were quelled ruthlessly. In the words of a conservative commentator of the time; "The rebels were massacred as they were captured the spectacle was magnificent".

As a placebo, Madrid had finally given the civic authorities in Barcelona permission to expand and develop the city. Plans for a new extension ('Eixample') to the city were submitted, and the local authorities chose Rovira I Trias' fan-shaped design. Madrid, for reasons which no one could ever make out, overruled their decision and insisted that the grid-like plan of Ildefons Cerdà be implemented. His socialist vision of a city in which everyone would live as equals side by side was quickly scuppered by architects and the wealthy bourgeoisie, who abhorred the idea of equality and commissioned ever grander mansions in the new extension in order to showcase their individual status, wealth and taste. Nonetheless, sanitation improved and the city quintrupled in size.

Since Isabella II's coronation in 1833, argument over the question of succession had been raging across Spain. In one corner (on the throne, to be precise) were the Bourbons, in the other the Carlists, who believed that Don Carlos was their legitimate monarch. The people of Catalunya were confirmed Carlists. This dispute (which had lead to outbreaks of civil war) came to a head in 1868, when a 'revolution' took place under General Prim. Unlike most military-lead revolutions, this one brought the promise of genuine democracy – not least universal suffrage, a free press and freedom of worship. The new government offered the crown to Amedeo of Savoire. But in 1873 Prim was assassinated, Amedeo abdicated and the First Spanish Republic was proclaimed.

By 1874 the Bourbons had returned to power under Alfonso XIII, but the people of Catalunya had got their breath back by now and were ready once again to launch themselves into a flurry of commercial activity. Picking up much faster than the rest of Spain on the industrial revolution and the benefits of steam power and mechanization, they traded in iron and above all textiles. It was not long before Barcelona was the fourth-largest textile producer in the world after England, France and the US.

Commercial success brought with it a spate of cultural development which reached its pinnacle in the Universal Exhibition of 1888 in the new Parc de la Ciutadella. These were the glory days of the Catalan *renaixença*, the enormous cultural revival which brought new life to Catalan arts and language. The Palau de Musica Catalana, the Liceu and La Boquería were all built, the first Catalan newspaper appeared in 1879, the medieval poetry games, the *Jocs Florals*, were reinstated, and people were reading the poems of Joan Maragall (1860-1911) and Jacint Verdaguer (1843-1902). This era also heralded the arrival of *modernisme*. Gaudí started work on the Sagrada Família in the 1880s and La Pedrera on the Passeig de Gràcia was completed in 1910.

Trouble on the horizon

However, the struggle for Catalan identity and independence is not the only war that the people of Catalunya have ever had to fight. While the drawing rooms of the *literati* were echoing to the poetry of Maragall, Aribau and Verdaguer, the impoverished workers on the streets were listening to something very different – the new political philosophy of Anarchism. Left-wing ideology had been taking root amongst the workers since 1840 and in 1891 the 'union catalanist' was born. The employers tried to suppress them by deploying gangs of well-trained thugs, but street battles and bombings were frequent. Both the Liceu and the religious procession of the Corpus Christi were bombed in 1896.

Exacerbated by the Spanish-American war of 1898 and the loss of Spain's last remaining colonies, the struggle both for regional autonomy and for workers' rights continued into the 20th century. The Catalans regained a modicum of political representation when the newly-formed Catalunya Solidarity Party won over 40 seats in the general election of 1907 and in 1914 with the creation of the Mancomunitat de Catalunya (a confederation of the four provinces). However, the battle for workers' rights was far from over. Following a series of major outbreaks of industrial action, tensions finally boiled over on the streets of Barcelona in 1909 in the Setmana Tràgica – a week of carnage and destruction which left 116 people dead and 80 buildings torched, with the most savage attacks saved for the churches and monasteries.

The First World War and Spain's neutrality brought a temporary alleviation of Catalunya's woes. The French army needed uniforms and the Catalans were more than happy to make them. The economy recovered and Barcelona became Spain's largest city. But as the economy waned at the end of the war, civil strife increased. There were over 800 strikes and the anarchist workers' union of Catalunya (the CNT, founded in 1911) became a political force and more importantly a threat to the government. With the approval of the King (Alfonso XIII) a military dictatorship was established in 1923 under the Captain General of Barcelona, Miguel Primo de Rivera. He was joined by the Catalan bourgeoisie and promised the 'abolition of the class struggle'. But his words were no match for his deeds: the CNT was banned, along with the Catalan language and national flag. The only item that can be entered into his credit column is his promotion of Barcelona's International Exhibition of 1929, staged principally on Montjüic. This brought with it the construction of the first metro line, as well as an influx of almost 200,000 immigrants, principally from Andalucia, Murcia and Galicia.

When Rivera made everyone's day by retiring in 1931, the left-wing parties immediately won a landslide victory in the municipal elections. Francesc Macià, a former army colonel and now head of the Esquerra Republicana (the Republican Left), stepped boldly forward and declared not just the Second Republic but also the Republic of Catalunya. The latter didn't last long, however. Three days later he agreed to its being an autonomous state under the direction of the Generalitat. Nonetheless, this victory brought together for the first time the forces of republicanism, Catalanism and democracy. It also gave King Alfonso a sufficiently firm nudge in the ribs to persuade him to slink down to Cartagena and board a ship for Marseilles.

Under the thumb

Partly because the relationship between the various left-wing parties and the republican movement was never fully settled, the political air remained clouded for years to come. The 1934 elections brought in a right-wing national government and a renewal of tensions between central and regional government. Flurries of insurrection lead to the jailing of leftist and Catalan leaders, amongst them Lluís Companys, the trade union lawyer who had succeeded Macià. The left wing regrouped as the Popular Front (comprising the CNT and the Worker's Party of Marxist Unification, or POUM) and won the elections of 1936. Companys became president of the Generalitat and declared an "independent Catalan state within the Federal Republic". Without the support of the anarchists, the coup was repressed by the army, the Statute of Catalan autonomy was revoked and Companys was arrested and executed in Montjüic Castle. Further uprisings across the country met the same fate.

And the man wielding the axe? None other than General Francisco Franco – whose popularity amongst the people of Catalunya can be judged by the quantities of cava consumed on in his death in 1975. Aided by Italy and Germany, he set about seeking to prove the dubious theory that coercion and slaughter are the only effective forms of government. In the years that followed the 1936 uprising, the whole country collapsed into a bloody and brutal civil war which ended only in 1939, with Franco the victor and over half a million dead. The 1940s, still known as the Years of Hunger, were miserable throughout the country. In Catalunya, all traces of Catalan nationalism were banned and throughout the 1940s even the speaking of Catalan was punishable with death.

Despite his friendship with Hitler, Franco kept Spain more or less neutral throughout the Second World War. 1945 brought hope to many of those who had fled during the Civil War and the exiled Generalitat elected a new government. But Franco was not to be knocked off his perch so easily. His obvious pro-fascist leanings had lead to a United Nations boycott, but his anti-communist credentials were enough to get him welcomed back into the fold in 1953.

A serious famine in 1947 and street protests in Barcelona in 1951 (caused by an increase in tram fares) persuaded Franco that if he wanted to avoid further civil conflict, he would need to be, or at any rate appear, more reasonable. The protests were not suppressed as brutally as before, various deals were made with the democrats and Catalan was decriminalized. By 1960, a new industrial boom was on the horizon, once again with Barcelona at the hub. Workers flooded in from Andalucia and Murcia and the population rose to almost 2,000,000. New housing developments arose, though without any concern for the inhabitants. Slowly but surely the aspirations to Catalan autonomy resurfaced. Well-organized communist labour groups, writers, poets and singers (most famously the Setze Jutges) started to be heard and make their presence felt. Even the press became more critical. The future Catalan President Jordi Pujol's decision to sing the Song of the Catalan flag at a concert attended by Franco's ministers in 1960 was perhaps not the smartest idea (he was arrested and imprisoned for two years) but it showed that there was life in the old Catalan dog yet.

Seeds of hope

Rarely can a death have been celebrated by so many or with so much joy as that of Franco on 20 September 1975. A constitutional monarchy under King Juan Carlos was set up by plebiscite and Catalan was recognized as an official language. When Adolfo Suarez became Prime Minister in 1977, to everyone's amazement he invited Josep Tarradellas, Catalunya's president-in-exile, to return and restore the Generalitat. In 1979, the Socialists won power in Catalunya, a position they have kept ever since. In 1980, the nationalist coalition Convergencia party under Pujol was elected to the Generalitat. After years of oppression, and thanks to a government in Madrid which seemed more sensitized to Catalan issues than its predecessors, the people of Catalunya suddenly found themselves with tax-raising powers and something approaching genuine autonomy. And just as importantly perhaps, they found themselves presented with the chance to show off not just in front of the rest of Spain, but in front of the rest of the world.

When Barcelona was announced as the stage for the Olympics Games in 1992, the city entered a period of frantic, enthusiastic and for the most part outstanding renovation and construction. Under Pujol and the popular socialist mayor Pasqual Maragall, this continued until well after the Olympics and included the whole harbour development around the new Port Olímpic and the dramatically refurbished Port Vell, the new buildings of the Olympic Ring on top of Montjüic, and a seemingly endless list of others.

Barcelona begins a new century with another grand scheme in which to flaunt its dynamism and flair; this is the 2004 Universal Forum of Cultures, which – like the Exhibitions of 1888 and 1929 and the 1992 Olympics – will encompass a massive building project. The area where Avinguda Diagonal meets the sea has been renamed Avinguda Diagonal Mar, and the former slum district is now the site of a brand new business park and entertainment zone. Barcelona is now Europe's most popular weekend destination, and the city is making the most of its new-found confidence and national pride.

A visitor to Barcelona today may know nothing of the glorious but bloody history of Catalunya that is inscribed on every stone of every museum, church, building and street – but just stop a Catalan in the street and they will be happy to tell you.

Art

Early period

Prior to the arrival of the Romans (from the third century onwards), signs of artistic endeavour in Catalunya are as fragmentary as they are in most parts of Europe. The most outstanding extant instances of prehistoric art are the cave paintings in Cogul and Tivissa, which date back to the late Palaeolithic period.

When the Romans entered what is now Catalunya, they brought with them the sophisticated construction techniques which are a prerequisite for building a lasting empire. These enabled them to build aqueducts, city walls, arches, vaults and columns. The most striking examples of their skills (and that of the Greeks who had got there first) are to be found in the Greco-Roman town of Empuriés. Many of the treasures found during excavation are now housed in the archaeology museums of Barcelona and Empuriés, but the site still has the remnants of noblemen's houses, an amphitheatre, and some stunning mosaics.

The Germanic tribes who swept across Spain in the first five centuries AD would today be mistaken for anarchists in their attitude to art. They created little and destroyed much. Not, as far as we know, out of any strongly-held aesthetic (or anti-aesthetic) convictions, but just for the hell of it. The Visigoths who followed them (also a Germanic tribe) were rather more genteel. Since most of their buildings were replaced or covered over by late generations, little evidence of their occupation of Catalunya remains, but what there is (mainly jewellery kept in the **Museu d'Arqueòlogía** in Barcelona) shows a refined and skilled workmanship.

It was with the arrival of the Berber-Arabs in the eighth century, that the first credible signs of an 'indigenous' artistic tradition could be seen. The new arrivals had only a tenuous hold on Catalunya compared to the south of the peninsula – the result being a fusion of local, Christian and Moorish styles, especially in architecture. Christians trained by Mudéjar craftsmen (the name given to the Moorish craftsmen) were heavily involved in the design and execution of many Catalan churches. The Moorish influence can be clearly seen in the horseshoe arch, pierced-stone tracery and intricate patters of the surface decoration. It is also worth mentioning the popular illustrated biblical narrative, the *Beato de Verona* (kept in Gerona Cathedral), an interesting mixture of Visigothic, Islamic and Christian styles, which is accompanied by drawings by Spain's first recorded woman artist, a nun by the name of Ende.

Romanesque

The slow reconquest of Iberia by Christian forces from the 10th century onwards and the opening up of trade routes brought with it exposure to the wonders of Roman and Byzantine architecture and a zest for construction.

Catalunya has more than its fair share of Romanesque churches (over 2,000), many of them dotted among the valleys or perched on the hilltops of the Pyrenees. The most extraordinary collection of churches can be found in the Vall de Boí, which was declared a World Heritage Site in 2000. Built between the 11th and 13th centuries, they boast bell towers, barrel-vaulted naves, rounded arches, fantastic sculptures and, above all, splendid wall paintings. Their character depended to some extent on the materials available – stone, brick or marble as well as materials pinched from existing Roman buildings. The paintings themselves, particularly the stylization of the hands and faces, bear a remarkable resemblance to the Romanesque/Byzantine murals in Constantinople and Ravenna. It seems likely that some of these murals were painted by peripatetic artists who, like the troubadours, travelled across Europe hiring their skills out to whoever would pay them.

While many of the paintings from these churches have now been transferred to the **Museu Nacional d'Art de Catalunya** in Barcelona (the largest Romanesque collection in the world) and the Museu Episcopal de Vic, there are still a few *in situ*. One of the most extraordinary mural groups in the MNAC comes from the church of Sant Climent de Taull in the Boí valley, which has a magnificent six-storey bell tower; the outstanding, luminous, almost expressionist frescoes have been copied onto the church walls. Other outstanding murals are still intact at the Sant Pere de Galligants, a former Benedictine Monastery with an octagonal bell tower, now housing Girona's archaeology museum. Most striking of all is the monastery of Santa Maria de Ripoll, with its extraordinary portal, built in about 1150 and depicting over 100 mini-narrative scenes. And not just biblical: alongside the characters of Moses, Daniel and the Messiah, are depicted none other than the then Counts of Barcelona, early devotees of 'product placement' and clearly in no doubt as to their own place in global history.

There are also excellent examples of Romanesque architecture in Barcelona itself, notably the exquisitely simple 12th-century church and cloister of San Pau del Camp, built as part of a larger monastery, and the ninth-century church of Sants Just i Pastor.

Gothic

From the 12th to 16th centuries, the commercial growth and prosperity which came with the development of Barcelona as the hub of Mediterranean trade, provided the background and funding for massive ecclesiastic and civic construction. The style which evolved came to be known as Catalan Gothic. And everyone wanted a piece of the action – despite the crisis and chaos caused by plague, famine and epidemics, most of the population of Barcelona worked on these edifices and many of the city's finest buildings were started and completed at this time.

The chief characteristic of Catalan Gothic which distinguishes it from French Gothic lies in the visible influence of the Mudéjar craftsmen, who stayed behind long after their fellow countrymen had been chivvied home, and worked happily with Christian artisans. Catalan Gothic is simple, keeping the number of columns to a minimum, and attaching more importance to the solid plain walls between columns as opposed to the open spaces we see between the complex flying buttresses of French Gothic. It is quite common for churches to have only a single nave without aisles. Frills are avoided at all costs and the few decorative devices permitted are reserved for windows, arches and portals.

Fine examples can be seen on some of Barcelona's most important church buildings, most notably the new Cathedral which was began in1298 (replacing the 11th-century building). One of the first churches to be completed, the sublimely beautiful **Santa Maria del Mar**, was designed by architects Ramon Desping and Berenguer de Montegut. Displaying extraordinary flair and daring, the masons stretched the early pointed-lancet Gothic arch to its limit, creating a single-span arch which no architect today would dare to try without steel reinforcement (or a watertight insurance policy).

Catalan Gothic is visible in civic and domestic buildings too. In the late-14th century, work commenced on the **Ajuntament** and the **Palau de la Generalitat**, and major additions were made to the **Palau Reial** of the Count-kings of Barcelona and Aragon. Work also began on the **Llotja**, the trading exchange which later was to become the School of Fine Arts, which was finished in 1392. The **Saló de Tinell**, designed by the Court Architect Carbonell, has probably the largest arch spans in Europe (over 40 ft). The line of palaces of the rich merchants and noblemen of this period can still be seen along the **Carrer Montcada**. Like chocolates wrapped in brown paper, they present a rather plain exterior, behind which you will find enchanting loggias, galleries, patios, courtyards with staircases and often gardens with fountains. Many of these buildings now house some of the cultural institutions of Barcelona, in particular the Picasso Museum.

Almost all the painting of this time was religious. Those adventurous artists who set foot outside Spain brought back with them the influences of the Sienese School, French Gothic and later on, Flemish naturalism. Perhaps as a reaction to the Islamic ban on human representation, their portrayal of the human figure displayed a meticulous attention to detail and 'realism'. They used tempera gesso, gold leaf, glass (for eyes and tears) and some painters and sculptors even used real human hair and clothing. The best example of Spain's new hybrid, 'international' style from the 14th century is the work of **Ferrer Bassa**, who painted the Giotto-esque mural in the **Monastery of Pedralbes** in Barcelona in 1346.

In the 15th century, the work of three major artists – **Bernat Martorell**, **Luis Dalmau** and **Jaume Huguet** – shows the increasing influence of Flemish naturalism. Bernat Martorell's retablos (altarpieces) depicting Saint Vincent (circa 1435-40) and the Saints John (1434-35), as well as Luis Dalmau's *The Madonna of Councillors* (painted for the Barcelona Town Hall, 1443-1445) and Jaume Huguet's *The Episcopal Coronation of St Augustine* (commissioned by the Barcelona Tanners' Guild, 1463-85) are fine examples of the Flemish influence. (All are exhibited at the Museu National d'Art de Catalunya, see page 178) While the expressions and postures of some of the faces and figures are clearly naturalistic, the geometric patterns and stiff rigidity of some of the other figures, and the backdrop, show that the formalism of the Mudéjar style had not been entirely forgotten.

Background

Decadencia

The Golden Age of Castilian Spain, stretching from the 16th to19th century, was known as the 'decadencia' for the people of Catalunya. While Madrid, Valencia, Seville and Toledo became centres of artistic invention and could boast the out-standing talents of El Greco, Zurbaran, Velasquez, Murillo and Goya (who was in fact born in Zaragoza), Catalunya became an artistic backwater. The only painter of note was the Romantic **Maria Fortuny** (1838-74) who set a precedent for all future Cata-lan artists by seeking the bright lights of Paris, and whose works, including his enor-mous (although unfinished) painting of *The Battle of Tetuán* (1863), are well represented in the Museu d'Art Modern. In the late 1880s, **Joaquim Vayreda** (1843-94) founded the **Olot School** of landscape art, which, although derided by critics, was very popular. Most art of the period was realistic and narrative, but Vayreda's landscapes were soft, hazy celebrations of the Catalan countryside.

From the 16th century onwards, building continued in a desultory fashion, with fewer patrons and little that was noticeably Catalan or for that matter remarkable. Around 1550 the **Palau del Lloctinent** was built for the Royal Viceroys in one side of the Placa del Rei, and 1596 saw the addition of the main façade to the Generalitat, built in the Italian Renaissance manner. The Church, however (whose coffers remained overflowing), continued to build lavishly – in particular the Baroque convents and churches along Las Ramblas such as the church of **Betlem** on the Rambla which was finished in 1729. The architect Francesco Molina (a fan of the English Regency architect John Nash) built the **Plaça Sant Josep** in Nash's Neo-Classical style. It is now buried beneath the 10th-century market building **Mercat de la Boquerería**, but its Doric colonnade, reminiscent of the Mall in Lon-don, can still be seen.

By the 1850's Barcelona showed signs of coming out of its 300-year coma and the great rediscovery and celebration of Catalanya's cultural identity, the Renaixença (Renaissance) was beginning.

When the Bourbon walls were finally torn down in 1854, the city council held a competition for a new extension (Eixample) to the city. A fan-shaped design by Antoni Rovira i Trias (you can see a model of it at the foot of his statue in Gràcia, see page 145) was selected by the city council, but their decision was over-ruled by Madrid six months later. Ildefons Cerdà, inspired by the socialist, egalitarian theories of Étienne Cabet (see page 118) and the boldness of Haussman's new boulevards and buildings in Paris, dreamt up a grid-shaped city formed of modular apartment blocks surrounding leafy central gardens, in which families from different walks of life would live side by side in harmony. His Utopian vision was condemned on all sides: the property speculators saw the gardens as a wasted opportunity to build more apartment blocks; the architects were resentful of the 'dull monotony' of the grid-shape; and the bourgeoisie, who were leaving the cramped old city for the space of the new district, were appalled at the idea of living on 'equal' terms with tradesmen and other riff-raff. Inevitably, the original plan was distorted as the spec-ulators swallowed up the interior gardens, the architects dreamt up fantastical ways to escape the blandness of modular housing, and the wealthy commissioned the most celebrated architects and designers to create mansions which would defy Cerdà's notions of equality by demonstrating that some of the Eixample's new resi-dents were infinitely more equal than others.

By the end of the 19th century, thanks to the massive influx of wealth generated during the industrial revolution, the wallets of the traders of Barcelona were bulging again. There was a boom in the art world, as the newly rich eagerly sought artworks to decorate their fancy homes, and the first art gallery in Barcelona, the Sala Parés, opened in 1877. Pretty, if usually rather nondescript paintings of street scenes, dances or country scenes became enormously popular – works by painters like Frances Miralles (1848-1901), and sculptors like Manuel Fuxà (1850-1926) adorned the salons of the newly rich. This prosperity engendered a new spirit of endeavour and innovation. The time was ripe for something bold, something different – something Catalan.

Modernisme

The rekindling of interest in the Catalan cultural identity which came to be known as the Renaixença was characterized by a new spirit of cultural and political optimism and a determined interest in the formation of a regional art movement. Architecture, painting, sculpture, illustration, furniture, jewellery, weaving, crafts and the making and design of everyday objects were all affected and began to flourish. This movement across the arts came to be known as Modernisme, and was partly influenced by the international Art Nouveau and Jugenstil movements. Those who espoused and practised Modernisme (the Modernistas) came from various levels of society, more often than not the bourgeoisie.

Like most collective art terms, Modernisme is a confusing word. And not to be confused with Modernism, which, for British people for example, could mean anything from Sickert to Damien Hirst and all movements in between. In Catalunya, Modernisme meant effectively the local branch of Art Nouveau, with the stress on 'local'. It embraced many different activities and styles, all linked by a common search for something modern in the face of tradition. In the words of one of its most well-known exponents, the charismatic painter Santiago Rusiñol (1861-1931), it was necessary "to live by the abnormal and the strange, to arrive at the tragic by frequenting the mysterious, to divine the unknown, to foretell destiny, such is the aesthetic of this art of our time, splendid and nebulous, mystic and sensual, medieval and modern."

If only life were that simple. In fact, Modernisme was something of a paradox. While its main thrust was directed forward and away from the past, it was also committed to exploring and epitomizing Catalan identity. This meant including elements of the past and it was this peculiar fusion of new and old which was to produce some of Modernisme's most exciting and distinctive achievements.

Architecture

One of the buildings that stood out at the Universal Exhibition of 1888 was known as the 'Castell dels Tres Dragons' (now the **Museu de Zoologia**), built by the architect **Lluis Domenech i Montaner**, considered by many to be the father of Modernista architecture. It was characterized by the fusion of sculpture and architecture, curved lines and a repertory of naturalist ornamentation, influenced by the theories of William Morris and Ruskin which he had absorbed on a trip to England. His aim was to put these revised techniques to use in new forms of architecture. In order to achieve this aim, Muntaner had pulled together craftsmen and artisans who still practised the old techniques of iron-work, ceramic tiling, metallic glazing, glasswork, woodwork and stone carving.

Montaner was also responsible for the astounding **Palau de la Música Catalana** and the delightful **Hospital de la Santa Creu i Sant Pau** – both typical examples of Modernisme in the importance attached to decoration, the use of sculptural figures within the structure, and the use of balustrades which incorporated coloured glass, tiles, mosaics and wrought iron. Another of the leading Modernista architects was **Josep Puig i Cadafalch**, surely one of the most eclectic artists in history. The exuberant neo-Gothic **Palau Baró de Quadras**, now the music museum (see page 128), is one of his finest works, and the **Casa Terrades** (better known as the Casa de las Punxes, 'the house of spikes') on the Avinguda Diagonal is another excellent example of his very original medley of styles; everything went into the pot for this brew, including elements of medieval, Gothic and Renaissance architecture. But the stone ornamentation and curved brickwork are pure Modernisme.

The **Mansana de la Discòrdia** (the 'Block of Discord') in the Passeig de Gràcia, is so called because this stretch of the Eixample's most elegant street contains examples of the works of the greatest exponents of *modernista* architecture: Domènech's Casa Lleó Morera, Puig's Casa Amattler and Gaudí's Casa Batlló, three mesmerizing and entirely distinctive mansions built for the most important families of the day (see page 124 for descriptions of the buildings). Of the three, it was **Antoni Gaudí i Cornet** who was to become the most famous, if not infamous.

Gaudí

Gaudí, perhaps more than any anyone else, typifies the Modernisme movement in spirit, achievement and Catalan sentiment. In his private life he was a misanthropic loner, fanatically religious, and contemptuous of those younger bohemian contemporaries whose version of Modernisme stood, in his opinion, for moral decay. As a student in Barcelona, he showed his strong-minded temperament and there was no doubt in the mind of the Chairman of the Faculty that the student who had been allowed to pass the examination was either a genius or a madman – an opinion Gaudí was to encounter frequently throughout his career.

His earliest commission for the city were the lamp posts which adorn the Plaça Reial (see page 65), and he was also part of the team which helped create the new Parc de la Ciutadella (see page 96) in La Ribera. One of his earliest major commissions was the new-Moorish **Casa Vicens** in Gràcia (see page 147), built for a wealthy ceramics manufacturer and encrusted with green and white tiling. Under the patronage of the Eusebi Güell, who shared his fervent Catalanism and religious devotion, Gaudí created a series of extraordinary buildings: the first of these was the **Palau Güell** (see page 104), followed by the highly original **Park Güell** (see page 148), both of which have been declared World Heritage Sites. One of his most important collaborators was the the architect **Josep Jujol**, who was responsible for the remarkable array of mosaics which shimmer on the immense undulating bench which snakes around the Park Güell (perhaps the first 'collage' in art history) which was to have a great influence on the thinking and work of Picasso, Dalí and Miró. These years also saw the construction of the **Casa Milà**, better known as La Pedrera (see page 126), a good example of Gaudí's use of the applied arts – wrought iron, mosaics, spiral chimneys and the warped surfaces of the mansard roof. This combination of forms, styles and materials (beautiful, quirky and just plain wacky) help give the building its unique character as an inspired and authentic work of art.

In 1884, Gaudí was commissioned to complete the expiatory temple of the **Sagrada Família**. The work became an obsession; he spent the last years of his life living in a shack on-site, selling his few possessions in order to help finance the construction and importuning strangers on the street for contributions. Several decades after the Gaudí's death (in 1926), the vast temple remains unfinished; construction has begun again after years of neglect but the project has caused huge controversy. The original plans and models for the temple were destroyed during the Civil War when the anarchists torched the crypt and the site workshops – but Gaudí famously made changes to his initial plans almost daily, rendering it virtually impossible to guess what his original intentions might have been. The suspicion has often been expressed that it looked as though he was making it up as he went along. Perhaps this is true, perhaps he was anticipating Picasso's maxim – "if you know exactly what you are going to do, why do it?" Work, under the architect Jordi Bonet and the sculptor Josep Subirachs, continues nonetheless, although the recently completed Passion façade has caused uproar.

Whatever the future holds for the Sagrada Família, one can be sure that it will remain, in the words of Evelyn Waugh, an "astonishing curiosity". The initial hostility toward it from the locals has long evaporated, and it is one of the city's most visited (if not loved) sights.

Els Quatre Gats

In 1897, the painters Ramon Casas and Santiago Rusiñol, along with Miquel Utrillo and Pere Romeu opened the tavern of Els Quatre Gats (The Four Cats, see page 78). It rapidly became the meeting place for like-minded *modernista* artists, musicians, poets and writers. The name was inspired by the famous bohemian 'Chat Noir' café in Paris and it advertised itself as a 'Gothic beer hall for the Amorous of the North' and a 'House of Healing'. The foursome had spent time in Montmartre, where they had become friends with Toulouse Lautrec, Eric Satie and older French artists such as Puvis de Chavannes and Eugene Carriere. They had even exhibited at the 'Salon des Independents' and remained in constant touch with the Fin de Siècle artistic currents of Paris.

When they returned from France, Rusiñol and Casas exhibited the work they had recently completed in Paris at the Sala Parés gallery in 1890, ushering in a new era of painting. Their paintings broke with tradition by eschewing the popular notion of a 'theme' which was the hallmark of the simpering paintings then in vogue, and the critics hated them. Their bold paintings concentrated on capturing a brief moment, like a snapshot, in a highly naturalistic manner, with unusual compositions which seemed to bleed off the page. The outraged critics didn't take long to see which way the wind was blowing and soon the pair were two of the most fêted artists in the city.

Santiago Rusiñol was a wealthy dandy with an addiction to morphine (his early painting of the *Morphine Addict* caused uproar); he held the flamboyant *festes Modernistes* at his Sitges home, Cau Ferrat (now a museum, see page 228), and created a series of shimmering seascapes which flirted with Symbolism. His friend **Ramon Casas** was an overtly political painter, whose work (in the tradition of Goya), offered a sombre and ruthless depiction of the world. His most outstanding and representative works are *The Vile Garrotting* showing the public execution of the Liceu bomber (see page 64) with the penitents in their sinister black conical hats, and *La Carga* (The Charge) showing the mounted Guardia Civil attacking striking workers with drawn sabers – not for the fainthearted. His early promise petered out, and he became little more than an accomplished painter of society portraits. Rusiñol, too, found purchasers rather than critical success for the gentle landscapes and bucolic scenes which were the subjects of his later painting.

Els Quatre Gats lasted only six years but during its life earned a great reputation not only for the artists who were attracted by its atmosphere but also as a the venue for many *avant garde* artistic and cultural events, including exhibitions, poetry readings, theatrical performances and concerts given by distinguished young musicians such as Albeniz, Granados and Morera. It was into this tavern one day that a young poet by the name of Jaume Sabartes set foot. And accompanying him was a friend – a promising young artist called Pablo Picasso.

Pablo Picasso

The name of Picasso, along with that of Gaudí, is the name which will always be linked with Barcelona. Although Picasso was not in fact Catalan at all (he was born in Malaga) that has never stopped the people of Barcelona adopting him as one of their own.

Born in 1881, the son of an art professor, Picasso moved to Barcelona at the age of 14, when his father was appointed Professor of Art at the School of Fine Arts in the Casa Llotja. He was allowed to sit the entrance test for the School immediately (despite officially being four years too young) and took just three days to complete the exams which were supposed to take a month. The drawings for this exam on paper bearing the official stamp are now exhibited in the **Museu Picasso**. The jury were at once convinced that they were faced with a prodigy. And they were right.

Despite frequent sorties to France and especially Paris throughout his life, Catalunya and Barcelona always had a special place in Picasso's heart. And while he continued throughout his career to embrace and explore a multitude of influences and styles, the impact of the city and indeed Spain in general can be seen throughout his work, most notably in *Les Demoiselles D'Avinyò* (1907), said to have been based on the prostitutes of the Carrer d'Avinyò (see page 81), his anguished anti-war painting *Guernica* (1937), and the melancholy works of his Blue Period (1901-19) which can be seen at the Museu Picasso (see page 92). Picasso used the desperate figures from the streets as models from these paintings – beggars, blind men, unhappy women – and was partly influenced by Isidre Nonell, who made countless moving and expressive studies of gypsies and the dispossessed. When he died aged just 35, he was given a gypsy burial. Picasso retained a sentimental attachment to his memories of the *fin de siècle* bohemia of those formative years and left almost all his works from that period to the Museu Picasso in Barcelona.

Noucentisme

By the end of the first decade of the new century, people had tired of Modernisme. A new movement, called Noucentisme, came into being. It was promoted by the Mancomunitat de Catalunya (the Catalan government of the day) rather than the bourgeoisie, and eschewed the influences of northern Europe which had under-pinned the *Modernista* ideology in favour of a return to the classical style. In the words of the painter Torres Garcia, their ambition was to "return to the tradition of art belonging to the Mediterranean lands and abandon French Impressionism, English Pre-Raphaelitesm and German symbolism which are alien to us here." The leading light of the movement was the painter Joaquim Sunyer, whose paintings depict idealized versions of Mediterranean landscapes and people.

Noucentisme architecture was sadly derivative and disappointing. The International Exhibition on Montjüic in 1929 (supposedly the celebration of Noucentisme) was a flop (see page 174). Among the pompous, flamboyant buildings erected for the Exhibition were the Palau Nacional (now home to the Museu National d'Art de Catalunya, see page 178), the Post Office on the Via Laietana, the Noucentista Stadium decorated by the gifted sculptor Pau Gargallo, the Estació de Francá and the Graphic Arts Palace. It is, however, worth noting the exceptional work of the muralist Josep Maria Sert, artist of the Saló de les Cróniques in the Ajuntament (see page 80), whose work defies any attempt at categorization. Noucentiste sculptors include the prolific Josep Clarà, who was deeply influenced by Rodin, and Enric Casanovas who produced classically inspired figures and busts.

Although Noucentisme was in essence conservative and reactionary, it came to be associated with the *avant garde*, thanks to a new wave of artists known as the Generation of 1917. They were profoundly influenced by the new theories of art which arrived with exiles who fled the horrors of the First World War and settled in neutral Barcelona. The Generation of 1917 – which included painters like Francesc Domingo and Josep Tagores, and sculptors like Josep Granyer and Josep Viladomat – idealized Cézanne and moved away from subject painting, popular imagery and the idealistic tendencies associated with the return to classicism. They preferred instead to depict realistic landscapes, often suburban scenes, and developed a figurative style which came close to Avant Garde attitudes.

The creation of the Second Republic in 1931 brought a shared determination to 'do something' about the appalling state of the city. This gave rise to the formation of the 'Group of Catalan Artists and Technicians for the progress of Contemporary Architecture' or GATPAC. With Josep Lluis Sert and Josep Torres Clavè at their head and the rationalist ideas of Le Corbusier in their heads, they set to work. Although they managed to complete the Dispensarí Antituberculós in El Raval and the extraordinary Casa Bloc on the Passeig de Torras i Bages, the advent of Civil War in July 1936 soon gave them other priorities.

Surrealism

When Andre Breton's Surrealist manifestoes landed on the streets of Barcelona in the late 1920s, two young artists, eager to slip through the net of the Noucentisme, were quick to sign up. The first was **Salvador Dalí**, whose museum in Figueres (see page 220), home in Cadaqués, and castle in Púbol offer illuminating insights into his bizarre Surrealist vision of the world. He soaked up a variety of artistic and political/religious influences (Miniaturist realism, Cubism, Anarchism, Marxism and finally Catholicism), but is perhaps best known for his brilliant self-publicity stunts. His art may have been diminished by his tireless self-aggrandizing, but, along with Picasso, he can be thanked for reminding the world at large that Spanish art was a force to be reckoned with.

The second and perhaps the only artist of this era who could be said to have remained genuinely faithful to the ambitions and principles of the *avant garde* was the third of Barcelona's great artists – **Joan Miró**. Although born and bred in Barcelona, Miró spent most of his life elsewhere, firstly in Paris, before finally choosing to settle in Majorca. But he remained deeply Catalanist, and often returned to carry out commissions. His public works can be seen everywhere in Barcelona: the huge ceramic murals at Barcelona's airport, the mosaic pavement in the middle of La Rambla (see page 60), the towering sculpture in the Parc Joan Miró (see page 134) and of course the colourful logo for La Caixa Bank.

Miro's work has all too often been dumped unceremoniously into the Surrealist pigeon-hole. And while it's true that he was championed as the father of 'organic Surrealism', he saw himself also very much as an 'artisan and folk artist'. The diversity and ingenuity of his work cannot be overstated and he was to become a strong influence on the Abstract Expressionists. His drawings and paintings are characterized by deceptively simple shapes, colour and symbols, and a lightness of touch and attitude. He worked in ceramics and tapestry, printmaking and theatre design as well as producing a wealth of playful sculptures. The **Fundacio Miró** (see page 186) building on Montjüic designed by his friend Josep Sert is a delightful, luminous space which contains an excellent selection of his works.

Whether Miro would have been able to work in such a prolific and joyful way within the barren and grey period of Franco's fascism is questionable.

From Franco to the present day

In 1939, an official edict was issued by the Franco Government stating unequivocally that "Architecture expresses the power and mission of the State". This was probably enough to make most artists of the time wary about poking their heads too far above the parapet, especially those in Catalunya, who were always going to come under closer scrutiny than their colleagues in elsewhere in Spain.

Background

Consequently, very little art of interest or importance was produced in Barcelona while Franco had his finger on the trigger. The outstanding exception was **Antoni Tàpies**, perhaps Spain's best-known living artist. Tàpies was a member of a clandestine group of artists known as the **Dau al Set** (the Seven-spot die), who formed in 1949 and were strongly influenced by the French Surrealists, Klee, Ernst and, in particular, Joan Miró. Other members of the group included **Joan Ponç**, **Joan Brossa** and **Modest Cuixart**. He is best known for his striking 'material paintings', which he began after the dissolution of the short-lived Dau al Set group, adopting radically innovative techniques and media, particularly the use of found objects. While remaining very much a Barcelonan (he lives in the Catalan hills and has a studio in Gràcia), his work has long been acclaimed outside Spain. His paintings were submitted at the Venice Biennale and later exhibited at the Guggenheim Museum, the Kunsthaus in Zurich, as well as retrospective shows in Paris and Vienna. In 1984 the **Fundacio Tàpies** (set in an early Modernista building by Domènech i Muntaner) was created and contains one of the largest collections of his work in the world. (It's worth noting that MACBA also contains several of his works, along with some of the delicious 'Poem-Objects' of his fellow Dau al Set member, Joan Brossa.)

Franco's death and the staging of the Olympics in 1992 brought not only a degree of autonomy to Catalunya and the people of Barcelona, but also an artistic impetus, principally in architecture and urban design. Design became the watchword of the newly energized city – everything was given the 'design' treatment, from bars and restaurants to ashtrays and pencils. Fancy designer bars like the Torres de Avila (see page 241) and Nick Havannah (see page 246) were erected, and designers like **Javier Mariscal** (who designed the blobby Olympic mascot 'Cobi' on view at the Galeria Olímpica, see page 185) were fêted and lauded. The extensive, relentless, joyous spate of construction which has taken place over the past 30 years has made Barcelona a role model for all other major cities. There have been some failures – the woeful Vila Olímpica being the most obvious example – but the new harbour development of the Port Vell, and the massive regeneration of the Raval and other areas have breathed new life into previously cramped and seedy neighbourhoods. Public art projects were initiated, resulting in a huge number of sculptures and parks.

In 1999, The Royal Institute of British Architects made the unprecedented gesture of awarding their annual Gold Medal to the City of Barcelona, an honour usually bestowed on individual architects. Yet it was a fitting tribute.

Barcelona today is suffused with numerous galleries, which offer a fantastic panorama of the entire history of Catalan art. These include the Museu Nacional d'Art de Catalunya, filled with treasures from Catalunya's glorious Gothic and Romanesque periods, and the Thyssen-Bornemisza Collection, which contains many outstanding mediaeval, Renaissance and baroque paintings. And if you visit the Museu d'Art Contemporani, you will see not only some of the work of Tàpies and other members of the Dau al Set group but works by Conceptualists and the latest wave of Catalan artists – among the best known are Miguel Barceló, Pere Jaume (whose work adorns the ceiling of the Liceu opera house) and Susana Solano.

Footnotes

12

Footnotes

287   Spanish and Catalan words and phrases

290   Index

294   Barcelona by cuisine

Spanish and Catalan words and phrases

English	Castilian	Catalan	
Hello	hola (diga on phone)	hola	**Greetings**
goodbye	adios	adéu	**& basic**
please	por favor	si us plau	**expressions**
thank you	gracias	gràcies	
you're welcome	de nada	de res	
good morning	buenos días	bon dia	
good afternoon	buenos tardes	bona tarda	
good night	buenos noches	bona nit	
How are you?	Cómo está?/Qué tal?	Com està?/Què tal?	
Fine, thank you	Muy bien, gracias	Molt bè, gracies	
My name is…	Me llamo…	Em dic…	
Do you speak English?	¿Habla inglès?	Parla anglés?	
I don't speak Spanish/Catalan	No hablo Castellano/Catalàn	No parlo Castellano/ Català	
I don't understand	No entiendo	No l'entenc	
Speak more slowly, please	hable más despacio, por favor	Pot parlar més poc a poc, si us plau?	
I am English/ American	Soy inglés(a)/ americano/a	Soc anglès/ americà	
excuse me/sorry	perdón	perdoni/disculpi	
excuse me (for attention)	oiga!	escolti	
Do you have a room	¿Tiene una habitación?	Té alguna habitació?	**Accommo-**
…for one person?	…para una persona?	…per a una persona?	**dation**
…with twin beds	…con dos camas	…amb dos llits	
…with double bed	…con una cama matrimonial	…amb llit per dues persones	
…with shower/bath	…con ducha/baño	…amb dutxa/bany	
…for one night/one week	…para una noche/ una semana	…per una nit/ una setmana	
Is breakfast included?	¿Incluido el desayuno?	Inclòs el desdejuni?	
I have a reservation	Tengo reserva	Tinc una habitació reservada	
How much is it for one night?	¿Cuál es el precio por una noche?	Quin és el preu por una nit?	
I would like…	Quisiera…	Vull…	**Sightseeing**
Where is…?	¿Dónde está…?	On és…?'	**& shopping**
How much is it?	¿Cuánto cuesta/vale?	Quant es/val?	
I like/I don't like	Me gusta…/No me gusta...	m'agrada/no m'agrada	
open/closed	abierto/cerrado	obert/tancat	
cheap/expensive	barato/caro	barat(a)/car(a)	
more/less	mas/menos	més/menys	
with/without	con/sin	amb/sense	
price	precio	preu	
change/exchange	cambio	canvi	
free (no charge)	gratuito	gratuit	
free (unoccuppied)	libre	lliure	

Numbers	English	Castilian	Catalan
	1	uno	un (a)
	2	dos	dos/dues
	3	tres	tres
	4	cuatro	quatre
	5	cinco	cinc
	6	seis	sis
	7	siete	set
	8	ocho	vuit
	9	nueve	nou
	10	diez	deu
	11	once	onze
	12	doce	dotze
	13	trece	tretze
	14	catorce	catorze
	15	quince	quinze
	16	dieciseis	setze
	17	diecisiete	disset
	18	dieciocho	divuit
	19	diecinueve	dinou
	20	veinte	vint
	21	veintiuno	vint-i-un
	30	treinta	trenta
	40	cuarenta	quaranta
	50	cincuenta	cinquanta
	60	sesenta	seixanta
	70	setenta	setanta
	80	ochenta	vuitanta
	90	noventa	novanta
	100	cien	cent
	101	cento uno	cent un
	200	cinco	cinc
	500	quinientos	cinc cents
	1000	mil	mil

Time	English	Castilian	Catalan
	What time is it?	¿Qué hora es?	Quina hora és?
	At what time..?	¿A qué hora ..?	A quina hora...?
	At 3 o'clock	A las tres	A les tres
	… a quarter past 3	…las tres y cuarto	…a un quart de quatre
	… half past 3	…las tres y media	…a dos quarts de quatre/a les tres i mitja
	… a quarter to 4	…las cuatro menos cuarto	…a tres quarts de quatre
	week	semana	la setmana
	month	mes	el mes
	morning	mañana	el mati
	afternoon	tarde	la tarda
	evening	noche	la nit
	at noon	a mediodía	al migdia
	at midnight	a mitjanit	a medianoche
	today	hoy	avui
	yesterday	ayer	ahir
	tomorrow	mañana	demà

English	Castilian	Catalan	
English	**Castilian**	**Catalan**	Travel
Where is…?	¿Dónde está…?	On és…?	
I'm lost	Me he perdido	M'he perdut	
How can I get to…?	¿Por donde se va a…?	Per anar a…?	
What time does it leave (arrive)?	a qué hora? ¿Sale (llega)	A quina hora surt (arriba)?	
From where does it leave?	¿De dónde sale?	De on surt?	
I'd like a (return) ticket to…	Quisiera un billete (de ida y vuelta) para…	Voldria un bitlete (d'anar i tornar) a…	
The next stop..	la pròxima parada		
here/there	aquí/allí	aquí/allí	
near/far	cerca/lejos	a prop/lluny	
left	izquierda	esquerra	
right	derecha	dreta	
straight on	todo recto	tot recte	
towards	hacia	cap a	
corner	esquina	cantonada	
Breakfast	desayuna	esmorzar	Eating out
Lunch	almuerzo	dinar	
Dinner	cena	sopar	
Snack	merendar	berenar	
A table for two	una mesa para dos persones	una taula per a dues persones	
Menu	carta (de platos)	carta (de plats)	
Fixed price menu	menú del día	menú del dia	
bill/check	la cuenta	el compte	
Enjoy your meal	¡Buen provecho!	Bon profit!	
fish	pescados	peix	
clams	almejas	cloïsses	
anchovies	anchoas/boquerones	anxoves/seitons	
eels	anguilas	anguiles	
salt cod	bacalao	bacallà	
crab	cangrejo	cranc	
prawns	gambas	gambes	
sole	lenguado	llenguado	
sea bass	lubina	llobarro	
shellfish	mariscos	mariscos	
mussels	Mejillones	musclos	
hake	merluza	lluç	
swordfish	pez espada	peix espasa	
trout	trucha	truita	
scallops	vieiras	vieires	
meat	carne	carn	
pork	cerdo	porc	
chops	chuletas	llonza/costella	
suckling pig	cochinillo	garrí/porcell	
rabbit	conejo	conill	
lamb	cordero	be/xai/corder	
duck	pato	ànec	
turkey	pavo	fall dindi	
chicken	pollo	pollastre	

Index

A

accommodation 32
Aigua-xel-lida 214
air travel 23
airlines 25
airport 29
Anella Olímpica 184
Antic Hospital de la
  Santa Creu 103, 107
Antic Mercat del Born 89
Antigua Casa Figueres 63
Apartment hotels 262
Architecture 279
Arenes 175
Art 275
Auditori de Barcelona 166
Avinguda Gaudí 132
Avinguda Miramar 188

B

Banyoles 218
Banys Àrabs 218
Baquèira-Beret 222
Bar Marsella 106
Barri Gòtic 69
Barri Xinès 104
Bars 242
Base Nàutica de Mar
  Bella 208
Basilica de La Mercé 82
basketball 48
Begur 214
Besalú 219
bike 39
Blanes 214
Bogatell 207
books 53
bullfighting 48
Bureaux de change 22

C

cable cars 36
Cadaques 215
Cambrils 229
Camp Nou 155
Campsites 261
Can Manco 104
Can Serra 128
Cap de Creus 215
Capella
  de Saint Agatha 71
  de Sant Feliu 81
  de Sant Miquel 160
  de Santa Llucia 76
  de Santa Maria d'en
    Marcus 94
Capuchin Cemetery 217

car 28, 37
car hire 38
Carrer
  Carme 107
  d'Avinyó 81
  de Hospital 107
  de Sant Pau 105
  França Xica 191
  Gran de Gràcia 146
  Maquinista 204
  Montcada 90
  Sant Pere més Baix 95
  Sardenya 131
  Sicília 130
Casa
  Amatller 124
  Batlló 125
  Bonaventura Ferrer 127
  Bonet 125
  Comalat 128
  Companys 135
  de l'Ardiaca 76
  de la Lactància 134
  de la Papallona 175
  de les Punxes 129
  Dolors Calm 128
  Fargas 128
  Fuster 127
  Golferichs 134
  Lleó Morera 124
  Milà 126
  Museu Gaudí 150
  Planells 130
  Ramon Mulleras 125
  Rubinat 145
  Sayrach 135
  Vicens 126, 147
Casaramona 175
Casas Ramos 148
casas rurales 34
Casc Antic 228
Cases Pascual i Pons 119
Cases Rocamora 119
Castell Montjüic 188
Castellde Púbol 221
Castelldefels 227
Càtedra Gaudí 158
Catedral de la Seu 74
Cau Ferrat 228
Cementiri de l'Est 209
Cementiri de Santa
  Elena 188
Centra Bonastruc Ça
  Porta 217
Centre d'Art Santa
  Mònica 66
children 18, 19
Churches
  Santa Maria del Pi 79
Cinema 248

Ciutat de la
  Teatre 190, 233
Classical 234
climate 14
Clubs 238
coach 25
Col.lecio Thyssen-
  Bornemisza 160
Collegi d'Arquitectes 77
community resident's
  card 20
consulates 21
Contemporary music 237
Convento de Els
  Àngels 107
Costa Brava 214
Credit cards 22
cuisine 45
customs 20

D

Dance 249
Delta de L'Ebre 229
Diagonal 127
disabled facilities 17
Drassanes Reials 196
drink 45
driving 37
Duana Vella 90

E

Eixample 61
El Born 89
El Mercat de Sarrià 161
El Pis de La Pedrera 126
El Prat de Llobregat 29
El Priorat 225
El Raval 103
El Sagrat Cor 164
electricity 29
Els Encants Vells 166
Els Quatre Gats 281
embassies 21
Empordà 215
Empúries 215
entertainment 39
entry 20
Escola Industrial 135
Escola Ramon Llull 130
Església
  Esglesia de Betlem 61
  de Sant Joan 145
  de Sant Llàtzer 107
  de Sant Miquel 203
  de Sant Pau
    de Camp 103
  de Sant Vicenç 161

de St Augustí 106
dels Josepets 148
Santa Maria del Mar 89
Esquerra de l'Eixample 134
essentials 11
Estació de França 90
Estadi Olímpic 185

F

Falset 225
Farmacia Bolós 128
ferry 28
festivals 40
Figueres 220
flights 23
Foment de les Arts
  Decoratives 109
Font de las Canaletes 60
Font Màgica 175
food 45
football 48
Fossar de les Morares 89
Francesc Berenguer 145
Fundació Antoni
  Tàpies 118, 122
Fundació Francisco
  Godia 121
Fundació Miró 186
funiculars 36

G

Galeria Olímpica 185
Gallery Maeght 91
Gaudí 280
gay travel 18
Girona 217
Glòries 166
golf 49
Gràcia 144
Gran Via 134

H

health 52
History 265
Hivernacle 97
hockey 49
holidays 40
Horta 165
Hospital de la Santa Creu
  i Sant Pau 133
Hospital del Mar 204
Hostafrancs 154
Hotel Cuatro Naciones 66
Hotel de Arts
  Barcelona 207
Hotel Espanya 106

Hotel Internacional 200
Hotel Oriente 66
hotels 32
Hotels 253

I

ice skating 50
Ictíneo 129
Illes Medes 215
IMAX 199
Institut Nacional
d'Educazió Fisica de
Catalunya 184
Institute of Catalan
Studies 107
insurance 20
International Exhibition
of 1929 174
internet 51, 53
itineraries 13

J

Jardins Costa I
Llobrera 188
Jardins de Laberint
d'Horta 165
Jardins de Miramar 188
Jardins de Mossén
Cinto 189
Jardins Mestre Balcells 146
Jardins Princep de
Girona 133
Jean Forestier 174
Josep Maria Jujol 149

L

L' Escala 215
L'Aquàrium 199
L'Espai Gaudí 126
L'Estartit 215
L'Observatori Fabra 164
La Boqueria 63
La Bordeta 154
La Colmena 70
La Garrotxa 219
La Mercé 81
La Rambla 60
La Rambla de las
Canaletes 61
La Rambla de los
Caputxins 64
La Rambla de Sant
Josep 63
La Rambla dels Estudis 61
La Ribera 87
La Terrrazza 184
language 17
Les Corts 154
Liceu 64
Llafranc 214
Llotja 90
Luz de Gas 201

M

magazines 52
Mansana de la
Discòrdia 124
Mansana de La
Discòrdia 118
Mapfre 207
Mar Bella 204
Maremàgnum 198
Mercat de Libertat 147
Mercat de Santa
Caterina 94
Mercat di Sant Antoni 107
Méson del Café 70
metro 36
Mirador del Rei Martí 72
Modernisme 279
Moll de Barcelona 197
Moll de la Fusta 200
Monestir
de Pedralbes 159
de Sant Pere de
Galligants 218
de Sant Pere de
les Puelles 95
de Sant Pere
de Rodes 216
Santa Maria
de Pedralbes 158
de Santa María de
Poblet 225
Sant Pere de
les Puelles 94
money 21
Montblanc 225
Montserrat 223
Monument a Colom 196
Monument a Dr
Bartolorneu Robert 129
motor racing 48
motorbike hire 38
Museo
de los Judeos en
Catalunya 217
Barbier-Mueller d'Art
Precolumbí 92
d'Arqueològia de
Catalunya 190, 218
d'Art Contemporani
103
d'Art Modern 97
d'Autòmates del
Tibidabo 163
d'Història de
Catalunya 200
d'Història de
la Ciutat 217
d'Art Modern 96
de Calçat 76
de Carosses
Funebres166
de Cera 66
de Ceràmica 157
de Geologia 97
de l'Eròtica 64

de la Ciència 164
de la Romanitat 229
de Xocolata 89
Museu de Zoologia 97
del Clavegueram 129
del Còmic i la
Il.lustració133
de la Música 128
de les Artes
Decoratives157
Diocesà 77
Egípci 118, 119
Etnològic 189
Frederic Marés 73
Centre d'Estudis de
l'Esport 135
i Necròpolis
Paleocristians 229
Maricel 228
Marítim 197
Militar 188
Nacional
Arqueològic 229
Nacional d'Art de
Catalunya 178
Picasso 92
Tèxtil 91
Verdaguer 161
museums
(information)19
Montjüic 171
music scene 234

N

Narcís Monturiol 200
newspapers 52
nightlife 39
Noguera Palleresa
Valley 221
Noucentisme 282

O

Olot 219
opera 234
Orfeó Català 95

P

Pabeliones Finca
Güell 158
Pablo Picasso 281
Palafrugell 214
Palau
Baró de Quadras 128
Dalmases 91
de Comunicaions i
Transports 175
de la Música
Catalana 94
de la Virreina 63
del Lloctinet 70
del Mar 200
Güell 103
Moixó 81

Nacional 178
Macaya 130
Reial Major 71
Reial 155
Robert 127
Sant Jordi 185
Sessa Larrard 82
Pals 214
paradores 34
Paral.lel 106
Parc
Aigües 132
d' Attraccions 163
de Carles I 207
de Collserola 161
de la Barceloneta 204
de la Ciutadella 96
de les Tres
Xemenies 191
de l'Espanya
Industrial 154
de Torre de les
Aigües 127
del Castell de
l'Oreneta 160
Joan Miró 134
les Heures 165
Nacional d'Aigüestortes
i Estany de Maurici 222
Natural Cap de
Creus 216
Natural de la Zona
Volcanical de la
Garrotxa 219
Turó 155
Güell 148
Parks (information) 50
Passatge Permanyer 127
Passeig
Arqueològic 218
de Colom 200
de Gràcia 119
de Lluis Companys 97
de Sant Joan 129
Joan de Borbó 200
Santa Madrona 189
passports 20
Pati dels Tarrongers 80
Pavelló Mies van der
Rohe 175
Pere Falqués 132
Pia Almoina 77
Piscines Bernat
Martoll 185
Pla del Palau 90
Plaça
Àngels 107
Armada 188
de Catalunya 60
d'Antonio Lopez 200
d'Espanya 174
de Barceloneta 203
de la Llana 94
de la Virreina 145
de Sant Agustí Vel 94
de Sant Felip Neri 76
de Sant Vincenç 161

de Toros 134
del Diamant 145
del Duc de
  Medicaneli 82
del Font 203
del Mar 201
del Nord 146
del Pi 79
del Poble Romani 145
del Relotge 144
del Sol 145
del Teatre 65
dels Països
  Catalans 154
des Armes 97
Dr Andreu 163
Frances Maçia 155
Francesc Macià 135
George Orwell 81
Jacinct Verdaguer 129
John F. Kennedy 162
John Lennon 145
Lesseps 147
Nova 77
Portal de la Pau 196
Prim 209
Reial 65
Rius i Taulet 144
Rovira i Trias 145
Sant Jaume 79
Sant Jaume 69
Sant Josep Oriol 79
Sant Just 81
Sortidor 191
Tetuan 129
Tirant lo Blanc 207
Plaçeta del Pi 79
Platja Nova Icària 207
Platja Nova Mar Bella 204
Platja Sant Sebastià 204
Poble Espanyol 184
Poble Sec 190
Port Authority 196
Port de la Bonanaigua 222
Port de la Selva 216
Port Lligat 215
Port Olímpic 207
Port Vell 196
Port-Ainé 222
Porxos de Xifre 90
post 51
Puerta de Europa 197

Q

Quadrat d'Or 118

R

radio 52
Rambla de Catalunya 128
Rambla de Prat 147
Rambla de Raval 105
Rambla de Santa
  Monica 65
Rambla Poble Nou 209

reading 53
Rovira i Trias 144

S

Sa Riera 214
Sa Tuna 214
safety 31, 34
Sagrada Família 118, 131
sailing 50
Sala Antoni Tàpies 80
Sala Femenina 74
Sala Montcada 92
Sala Paré 79
Saló de Tinell 71
Sant Pere 94
Sant Salvadera de
  Verdera 216
Santa Ana 69, 78
Sants 154
Sarrià 160
serpentine bench 149
shopping 47
Sitges 227
sleeping 32
Somorrostro 204
Sort 222
sport 48
St Sebastià 201
Super Espot 222
Surrealism 283
swimming 49

T

Tamariu 214
tapas 46
Tarragona 228
tax 20
taxi 37
Teatre
  del Bosc 147
  Grec 190
  Nacional de
    Catalunya 166
  Principal 66
  Romeu 107
Teatre-Museu Dalí 220
telefèric 36
telephones 51
television 52
temperatures 14
tennis 49, 50
Theatre 233
Tibidabo 162
time zone 29
tipping 23
Torre
  Bellesguard 165
  Colón 104
  de Calatrava 185
  de Collserola 164
  de Jaume I 197
  de les Aigües 204
  de Sant Sebastià 201
  Rosa 150

Tossa de Mar 214
tour operators 16
tourist offices 31
tours 16
train 26
tram 36
transport 23
travellers' cheques 22
Travessera de Dalt 148

U

Union y el Fénix
  Español 119
Universal Studios Port
  Aventura 229

V

Vall d'Aran 222
Vall d'Hebron 165
Vallvidrera 161
Vapor Nou 154
Vèlodrom d'Horta 165
Verdera watchtower 215
Vielha 222
Villafranca de Penedès 224
visas 20

W

watersports 50
websites 55
Western Diagonal 155
World music 236
World Trade Center 197

Y

yoga 50
youth hostels 35
Youth hostels 262

Z

Zona Franca 197
Zoo 98

Map index

77	Around La Seu	**88**	La Ribera & Sant Pere
72	Barri Gòtic	**176**	Montjüic
91	Carrer Montcada and around	**162**	Parc de Collserola
75	Catedral de la Seu	**120**	Passeig de Gràcia
122	Eixample	**198**	Port Vell and Barceloneta
108	El Raval	**206**	Vila Olímpica and Poble Nou
146	Gràcia	**156**	Western District
62	La Rambla		

Shorts

93	A walk in Picasso's footsteps	**42**	Giants, dragons and castles in the air
210	Barcelona presents…		
189	Castell de Montjüic	**130**	History of the Sagrada família: a never-ending story
221	Dalí, Diary of a Genius		
133	Gaudí – opinions of the Sagrada Família	**107**	It's just an illusion
		179	Romanesque art
150	Gaudí and God's favoured nation	**159**	Visca el Barça – Up with Barça!

Five of the best

100	cafés with terraces	**241**	places to eat and dance
85	cheap eats	**104**	sights in El Raval
254	cheap sleeps	**145**	sights in Gràcia
168	drinks with a view	**89**	sights in La Ribera
119	Eixample sights	**178**	sights in Montjüic
164	highest viewpoints	**158**	sights in Zona Alta
257	hotels with swimming pools	**137**	top restaurants
239	hottest clubs and bars	**101**	veggie restaurants

Barcelona by cuisine

A quick reference guide to help you locate a restaurant to suit your taste and budget near to you. Further details can be found by turning to the page ▸▸

Codes are: € under €20; €€ €20-35; €€€ over €35.

Basque

Eixample	Beltxenea	€€€
	T93 215 30 24	▸▸ 135
	Gorria	€€€
	T93 245 11 64	▸▸ 135
Gràcia	Txistulari	€
	T93 237 13 26	▸▸ 152
La Rambla	Amaya	€€
	T93 302 10 37	▸▸ 66

Desserts

| La Ribera | Espai Sucre | €€€ |
| | T93 268 16 30 | ▸▸ 98 |

Castilian

| Outer districts | El Asador de Aranda | €€€ |
| | T93 417 01 15 | ▸▸ 166 |

Catalan

Barceloneta	Antigua Casa Solé	€€€
	T93 221 51 12	▸▸ 204
	Set Portes	€€
	T93 319 30 33	▸▸ 205
Barri Gòtic	Agut	€€
	T93 315 17 09	▸▸ 82
	La Bona Cuina	€€€
	T93 268 23 94	▸▸ 82
	Café de l'Acadèmia	€€
	T93 319 82 53	▸▸ 82
	El Gran Café	€€
	T93 318 79 86	▸▸ 83
	La Fonda	€€
	T93 301 75 15	▸▸ 83
	Hostal El Pintor	€€
	T93 301 40 65	▸▸ 83
	Pitarra	€€
	T93 301 16 47	▸▸ 83
Eixample	L'Hostal de Rita	€€
	T93 487 23 76	▸▸ 136
	Madrid-Barcelona	€€
	T93 215 70 6	▸▸ 136
	Mandalay Café	€€
	T93 458 60 17	▸▸ 136
	L'Olive	€€
	T93 430 90 27	▸▸ 136

Catalan cont.

	Semproniana	€€
	T93 453 18 20	▸▸ 136
Gràcia	Jaume de Provença	€€€
	T93 430 00 29	▸▸ 151
	Ot	€€€
	T93 284 77 52	▸▸ 151
	Roig Robi	€€€
	T93 218 92 22	▸▸ 151
Montjüic	Ca L'Isidre	€€€
	T93 441 11 39	▸▸ 191
	Cuixart	€€
	T93 441 30 78	▸▸ 191
Outer districts	Can Cortada	€€
	T93 427 23 15	▸▸ 167
	El Vell Sarrià	€€
	T93 205 45 41	▸▸ 167
	Gaig	€€€
	T93 429 10 17	▸▸ 166
	Pipper's	€
	T93 430 51 54	▸▸ 167
	Tram Tram	€€€
	T93 204 85 18	▸▸ 167
	Vinya Rosa-Magi	€€
	T93 430 00 03	▸▸ 167
	Via Veneto	€€€
	T93 200 70 24	▸▸ 167
	Vivanda	€€
	T93 203 19 18	▸▸ 167
Port Vell	La Llotja	€€
	T93 302 64 02	▸▸ 202
	Marítim de Barcelona	€€
	T93 221 62 56	▸▸ 202
La Rambla	Egipte	€
	T93 317 95 45	▸▸ 66
	Les Quinze Nits	€
	T93 317 30 75	▸▸ 66
El Raval	Can Lluís	€€
	T93 441 11 87	▸▸ 111
	Casa Leopoldo	€€€
	T93 441 30 14	▸▸ 111
	El Convent	€€
	T93 317 10 52	▸▸ 111
	Elisabets	€
	T93 317 58 26	▸▸ 112

Catalan cont.

	La Gardunya	€€	
	T93 302 43 23	▸ 111	
	La Llotja	€€	
	T93 302 64 02	▸ 111	
La Ribera	*Bar-Restaurante Rodrigo*	€	
	T93 310 78 14	▸ 100	
	Future	€	
	T93 319 92 99	▸ 100	
	Nou Celler	€	
	T93 310 47 73	▸ 100	
	Pla de la Garsa	€	
	T93 315 24 13	▸ 100	
	Senyor Parellada	€€	
	T93 310 50 94	▸ 99	

Catalan/Mediterranean

Eixample	*Jean-Luc Figueras*	€€€	
	T93 415 28 77	▸ 135	
Outer districts	*La Balsa*	€€€	
	T93 211 50 48	▸ 166	
	La Vaquería	€€	
	T93 439 35 56	▸ 167	

Chinese

Barceloneta	*Dzi*	€€	
	T93 221 21 82	▸ 204	

French

La Ribera	*Hofmann*	€€€	
	T93 319 58 89	▸ 98	

French/Catalan

Barri Gótic	*La Dentellière*	€€	
	T93 319 68 21	▸ 83	
Eixample	*Casa Calvet*	€€€	
	T93 413 40 12	▸ 135	
Gràcia	*Octubre*	€€	
	T93 218 25 18	▸ 151	
El Raval	*Quo Vadis*	€€€	
	T93 302 40 72	▸ 111	
La Ribera	*Brassería Flo*	€€	
	T93 319 31 02	▸ 99	

French/Japanese

Outer districts	*Satoru Miyano*	€€	
	T93 414 31 04	▸ 167	

French/Mediterranean

Outer districts	*Neichel*	€€€	
	T93 203 84 08	▸ 166	

Fusion

Barceloneta	*Agua*	€€	
	T93 225 12 72	▸ 208	
	Can Ganassa	€	
	T93 221 67 39	▸ 205	
Barri Gòtic	*Agut d'Avignon*	€€€	
	T93 302 60 34	▸ 82	
	Can Culleretes	€€	
	T93 317 31 22	▸ 83	
	El Salón	€€	
	T93 315 21 59	▸ 83	
	Oolong	€€	
	T93 315 12 59	▸ 84	
	Restaurante Pakistani	€	
	T93 302 60 25	▸ 84	
	Slokai	€€	
	T93 317 90 94	▸ 83	
	Zoo	€	
	T93 302 77 28	▸ 84	
Eixample	*L'Atzavara*	€	
	T93 454 59 25	▸ 137	
	Domèstic	€€	
	T93 453 16 61	▸ 136	
	La Tramoia	€€	
	T93 412 36 34	▸ 136	
Gràcia	*La Barbacoade*	€€	
	T93 210 22 53	▸ 151	
	Bilboa	€€€	
	T93 458 96 24	▸ 151	
	El Galliner	€€	
	T93 218 53 27	▸ 151	
	Flash Flash	€	
	T93 237 09 90	▸ 152	
	La Singular	€	
	T93 237 50 98	▸ 152	
	Tábata	€€	
	T93 237 89 46	▸ 152	
Port Vell	*Ruccola*	€€€	
	T93 508 82 68	▸ 201	
El Raval	*Carles Restaurant*	€	
	T93 302 25 01	▸ 112	
	Imprevist	€	
	T93 342 58 59	▸ 112	
	Iposa Bar	€	
	T93 318 60 86	▸ 112	
	Mamacafé	€€	
	T93 302 26 80	▸ 111	
	Pla dels Angels	€	
	T93 443 31 03	▸ 112	
	Restaurante Romesco	€	
	T93 318 93 81	▸ 112	
La Ribera	*El Foro*	€€	
	T93 310 10 20	▸ 99	

Fusion cont.

	El Pebre Blau	€€
	T93 319 13 08	▶▶ 99
	L'Ou Com Balla	€€
	T93 310 53 78	▶▶ 99
Vila Olímpica	Catamaran	€
		▶▶ 208
	La Taverna de Cel Ros	€
	T93 221 00 33	▶▶ 208

Indian

| El Raval | Govinda | € |
| | T93 318 77 29 | ▶▶ 67 |

International

| La Ribera | Sikkim | €€ |
| | T93 268 43 13 | ▶▶ 99 |

International/Catalan

| El Raval | Silenus | €€ |
| | T93 302 26 80 | ▶▶ 111 |

Iraqi

| Gràcia | Mesopotamia | €€ |
| | T93 237 15 63 | ▶▶ 151 |

Italian

Barri Gòtic	La Veronica	€
	T93 412 11 22	▶▶ 83
Outer districts	Bene Asai	€
	T93 434 06 77	▶▶ 168
	Cuatro	€
	T93 330 68 60	▶▶ 167
Vila Olímpica	Lungomare	€€
	T93 221 04 28	▶▶ 208

Japanese

Eixample	El Japonés	€€
	T93 487 25 92	▶▶ 135
	Ginza	€€
	T93 451 71 93	▶▶ 135
El Raval	Sushi & News	€
	T93 318 58 57	▶▶ 112

Lebanese

| Gràcia | Equinox Sol | € |
| | | ▶▶ 152 |

Mediterranean

Barri Gótic	Ateneu Gastronòmic	€€
	T93 302 11 98	▶▶ 82
	Cometacinc	€€
	T93 310 15 58	▶▶ 83

Mediterranean cont.

	Plà	€€
	T93 412 65 52	▶▶ 83
Eixample	Cava di Donna Fugata	€€
	T93 231 77 29	▶▶ 135
Outer districts	A Contraluz	€€
	T93 203 06 58	▶▶ 167
	Tragaluz	€€
	T93 487 06 21	▶▶ 136
La Ribera	Little Italy	€€
	T93 319 79 73	▶▶ 99

Mediterranean/Japanese

| La Ribera | Salero | €€ |
| | T93 319 80 22 | ▶▶ 99 |

Sandwiches

| La Ribera | Sandwich & Friends | € |
| | T93 310 07 86 | ▶▶ 100 |

Seafood

Barceloneta	Can Costa	€€
	T93 221 59 03	▶▶ 204
	Can Majó	€€
	T93 221 58 18	▶▶ 205
	El Rey de la Gamba	€€
	T93 222 56 401	▶▶ 205
	Merendero de la Mari	€€
	T93 221 31 41	▶▶ 204
Eixample	La Musclería	€
		▶▶ 136
	Rosalert	€€
	T93 207 19 48	▶▶ 136
Gràcia	Botafumeiro	€€€
	T93 218 42 30	▶▶ 151
Poble Nou	Els Pescadors	€€€
	T93 225 20 18	▶▶ 210
El Raval	Méson David	€
	T93 441 59 34	▶▶ 112
La Ribera	Hofmann	€€€
	T93 319 58 89	▶▶ 98
	Passadís d'en Pep	€€€
	T93 310 10 21	▶▶ 98
	Vascelum	€€
	T93 319 01 67	▶▶ 99
Vila Olímpica	El Cangrejo Loco	€€
	T93 221 05 33	▶▶ 208

Tapas

Barri Gòtic	La Vinateria del Call	€
	T93 302 60 92	▶▶ 83
La Ribera	Arcano	€
	T93 310 21 79	▶▶ 99

To see, experience, and enjoy the most charming capital of the Mediterranean.

The Bus Turístic gives you two routes – with 26 stops – for the price of one, to visit the most emblematic sights of Barcelona. You can do the whole journey passing from one route to the other as often as you like, as both coincide at three points: Plaça de Catalunya, Passeig de Gràcia – La Pedrera, and Plaça de Francesc Macià

Route
North
Red

Route
South
Blue

The ticket allows you to get on and off the bus as many times as you like. You will also receive a fantastic pass with considerable discounts, valid for a whole year, that you can make use of in the city's most interesting places.

  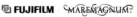

FRANCE

Puigcerdà
lans
Parc Natural
adí-Moixeró
Serra de Montgrony
Toses
Serra Cavallera
Ribes de Freser
C-151
Selcases
Mollo
Sant Jaume de Frontanyà
St Joan de les Abbesses
Sant Salvador de Bianya
Sardenes
Albanyà
Panta de Boadella
Maçanet de Cabrenys
Paratge Natural d'Int Nac de l'Albera
Espolla
Porbou
Porta da la Selva
cebre
gols
Ripoll
C-149
Olot
Parc Natural de la Zona Volcànica de la Garrotxa
Serinyà
Besalú
Llers
Figueres
Peralada
Castelló d'Empúries
N260
A7
Cadaqués
Parc Natural del Cap de Creus
Vilada
Berga
Perafita
Sant Feliu de Pallerols
Banyoles
Bascara
Fortià
Parc Natural dels Aiguamolls de l'Empordà
Golf de Roses
onella
Prats de Lluçanes
Torelló
Manlleu
C-152
Panta de Susqueda
la Cellera de Ter
Salt
Camallera
Garrigoles
l'Estartit
Cap d'Oltrera
Area protegida de les Illes Medes
Olost
Onsta
Vic
Vilanova de Sau
Girona-Costa Brava
Girona
Verges
Corçà
la Bisbal d'Empordà
Toroella de Montgri
Begur
Cap da Sal
Cap da Begur
Palafrugell
Cap de Sant Sebastià
Navàs
Santa Maria d'Olo
Riudeperes
N-152
Calonge
C-255
Costa Brava
Sallent
Artés
Molà
N-141
Tona
Centelles
C-253
Maçanet de la Selva
Vidreres
Llagostera
Palamós
Manresa
la Garriga
Sant Celoni
Lloret de Mar
Sant Feliu de Guixols
Tossa de Mar
Castellar de Vallès
Caldes de Montbui
Granollers
Arenys de Mun
Blanes
Malgrat de Mar
Terrassa
Sabadell
Argentona
Canet de Mar
Arenys de Mar
ellades
Santa Perpetua de Mogoda
Mollet del Valles
Mataró
Martorell
A-7
Rubí
Ripollet
Santa Coloma de Gramenet
Badelona
Cornella de Llobregat
BARCELONA
llafranca l Penedès
Gava
Hospitalet de Llobregat
el Prat de Llobregat
C-246
Castelldefels
Sitges
ilanova i la Geltrú

Mediterranean Sea

N

0 km   10
0 miles   10

Altitude in metres
2000
1000
500
200
100
0

Neighbouring Country

———— Motorway
———— Main road
———— Minor road
———— Other road
- - - - International border

A
B
C
4
5
6

Map 2 Barcelona

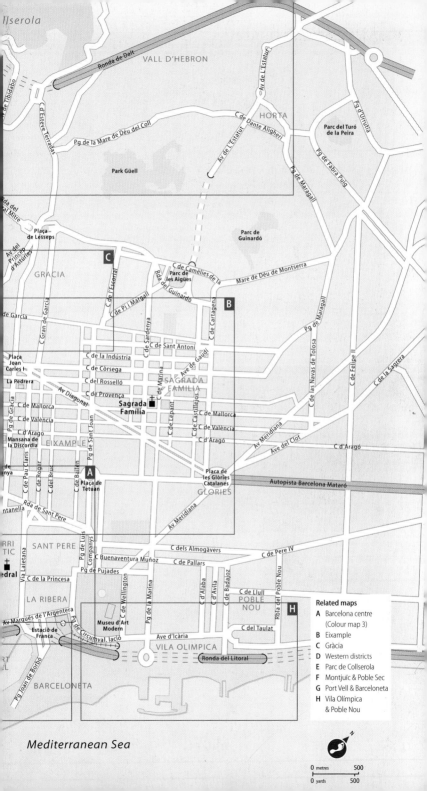

ll]serola

VALL D'HEBRON

Ronda de Dalt

Av de l'Estatut

HORTA

C de Dante Alighieri

Parc del Turó
de la Peira

Pg d'Urrutia

Pg de la Mare de Déu del Coll

Av de l'Estatut

Pg de Fabra i Puig

Pg de Maragall

C d'Esteve Terradas

C de Thidabo

Park Güell

Parc de
Guinardó

Plaça
de Lesseps

GRACIA

Parc de
les Aigües

C de Camèlies de la

Mare de Déu de Montserra

Rda. del Guinardó

Av del
Princep
d'Asturies

C de l'Escorial

C de Pi i Margall

C de Camèlies de la

Pg de Maragall

C de Garcia

C de García

C Gran de Gràcia

C de Sardenya

C de Sant Antoni

C de Cartagena

C de las Navas de Tolosa

C de Felipe II

C de la Sagrera

C de la Indústria

Av de Gaudí

C de Còrsega

Plaça
Joan
Carles I

C del Rosselló

C de Marina

SAGRADA
FAMÍLIA

La Pedrera

C de Provença

Av Diagonal

Sagrada
Família

C de Lepant

C de Castillejos

C de Mallorca

C de Gràcia

C de Mallorca

C de València

C de València

C d'Aragó

Pg de Sant Joan

C d'Aragó

Mansana
de la Discordia

EIXAMPLE

C de Pau Claris

C de Roger

C del Bruc

C de Bailèn

Av Meridiana

Ave del Clot

C d'Aragó

Plaça de
Tetuan

Plaça de
les Glòries
Catalanes

GLORIES

Rda. de Sant Pere

Av Meridiana

Autopista Barcelona Mataró

antanella

RRI
TIC

SANT PERE

Pg de Lluís
Companys

Buenaventura Muñoz

C dels Almogàvers

C de Pere IV

edral

Pg de Pujades

C de Pallars

Via Laietana

C de la Princesa

LA RIBERA

Pg de Circumval.lació

C d'Àlaba

C d'Àvila

C de Badajoz

C de Llull

Rbla. del Poble Nou

POBLE
NOU

H

Av Marquès de l'Argentera

Estació de
França

Museu d'Art
Modern

Pg de la Marina

Pg de Wellington

Ave d'Icària

C del Taulat

Pg Joan de Borbó

BARCELONETA

VILA OLÍMPICA

Ronda del Litoral

RT
L

Related maps

A Barcelona centre
   (Colour map 3)
B Eixample
C Gràcia
D Western districts
E Parc de Collserola
F Montjuïc & Poble Sec
G Port Vell & Barceloneta
H Vila Olímpica
   & Poble Nou

Mediterranean Sea

0 metres   500
0 yards   500

N

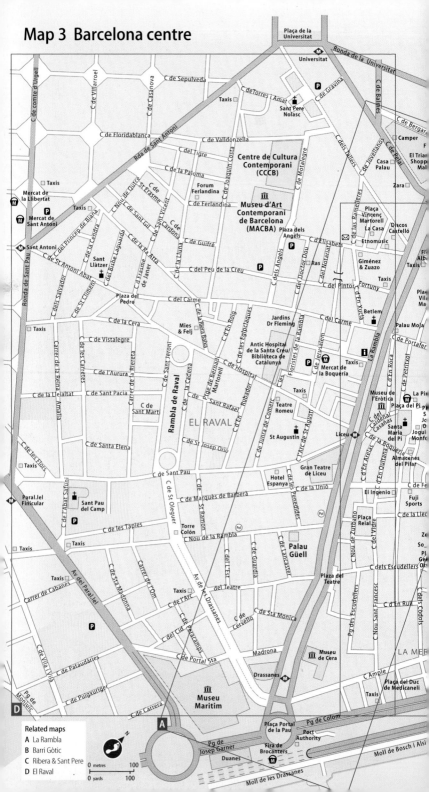

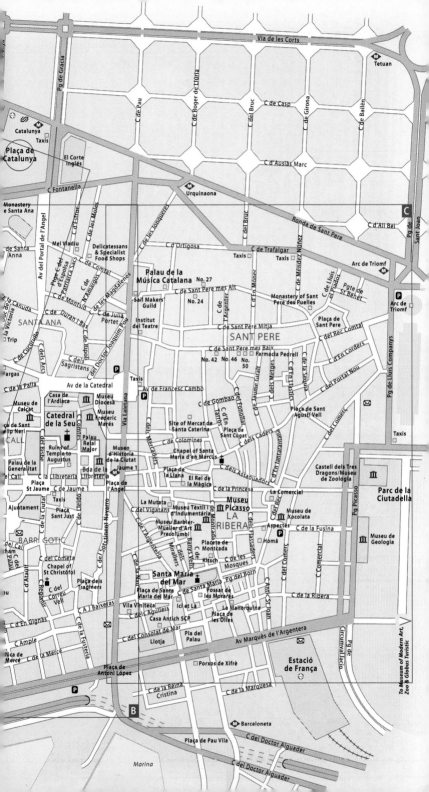

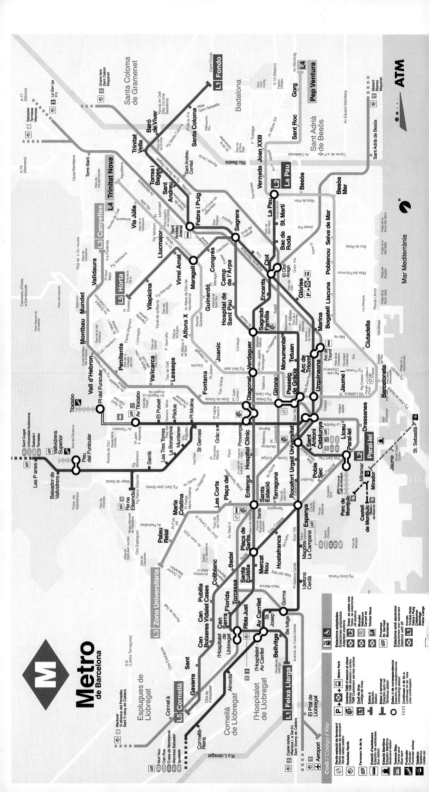

Acknowledgements

Huge thanks to Ajo, Raquel and Andrea for being such good friends and taking me to every bar in the city; to Adolfo for the road trips (never, ever again); to Lucy, Kate and Pedro for keeping me company and helping me out; to Susannah for the beautiful pictures and the fun; to Patrick for the nights I wish I could remember; to Marina for all her kindness; and to everyone especially Juan and Claire who gave me their recommendations. Thanks to my favourite travel writer in the world, Dana, for being an inspiration, and to Linda, Catherine, Kate, Claudia and Christine for all their much-needed support. Extra-special thanks to my family, especially my dad for being researcher, chauffeur and general factotum, to mum for all that help with cafés, to my brother for the website help, to Aunt Margaret for the industrious research, to Oscar for being my lucky mascot, and to Andrew for constant support and encouragement (and terrible gags).

At the Catalunya Tourist Information Centre, I'd like to thank Gloria Illas and especially Carmen Acosta who was absolutely brilliant.

At Footprint, I'd like to thank the indefatigable Caroline who has tied herself in knots to get this finished and to Rachel for commissioning me.

Finally, I'd like to thank the contributors for their wonderful contributions: Robert Gallagher, for the description of Catalan wine; Andrew Bampfield, for the history section; and to Krystina Fouyia for the art and architecture section.

About the author

Mary-Ann Gallagher graduated in modern languages from St Andrew's university and (having failed to catch a prince) went around the world instead. She has contributed to numerous guidebooks, mainly dealing with Spain, and writes regular travel articles for websites and magazines. She lives in London but is happiest with a glass of cava at a terrace café in the Born.